# A Critical Companion to Sofia Coppola

# CRITICAL COMPANIONS TO CONTEMPORARY DIRECTORS

Series Editors: Adam Barkman and Antonio Sanna

**Critical Companions to Contemporary Directors** covers many directors who have not been studied previously in academic publications and whose works nonetheless are highly renowned nowadays. The intent of the series is to offer interesting and illuminating interpretations of the various directors' films that will be accessible to both scholars of the academic community and critically-minded fans of the directors' works. Each volume combines discussions of a director's oeuvre from a broad range of disciplines and methodologies, thus offering the reader a variegated and compelling picture of the directors' works. In this sense, the volumes will be of interest (and will be instructive) for students and scholars engaged in subjects as different as film studies, literature, philosophy, popular culture studies, religion and others. We welcome proposals for both monographs and edited collections that offer interdisciplinary analyses, focusing on the complete oeuvre of one contemporary director per volume.

## Titles in the Series

*A Critical Companion to Robert Zemeckis*
Edited by Adam Barkman and Antonio Sanna
*A Critical Companion to Stanley Kubrick*
Edited by Elsa Colombani
*A Critical Companion to Terrence Malick*
Edited by Joshua Sikora
*A Critical Companion to Steven Spielberg*
Edited by Adam Barkman and Antonio Sanna
*A Critical Companion to Sofia Coppola*
By Naaman Wood and Christopher Booth

# A Critical Companion to Sofia Coppola

Naaman Wood and Christopher Booth

LEXINGTON BOOKS
*Lanham • Boulder • New York • London*

Published by Lexington Books
An imprint of The Rowman & Littlefield Publishing Group, Inc.
4501 Forbes Boulevard, Suite 200, Lanham, Maryland 20706
www.rowman.com

86-90 Paul Street, London EC2A 4NE

Copyright © 2022 The Rowman & Littlefield Publishing Group, Inc.

*All rights reserved.* No part of this book may be reproduced in any form or by any electronic or mechanical means, including information storage and retrieval systems, without written permission from the publisher, except by a reviewer who may quote passages in a review.

British Library Cataloguing in Publication Information Available

**Library of Congress Cataloging-in-Publication Data**

Names: Wood, Naaman, author. | Booth, Christopher, author.
Title: A critical companion to Sofia Coppola / Naaman Wood and Christopher Booth.
Description: Lanham : Lexington Books, [2022] | Series: Critical companions to contemporary directors | Includes bibliographical references and index. | Summary: "This volume offers eight interdisciplinary readings to the films of Sofia Coppola, analyzing her oeuvre with a focus on her treatment of masculinity, sexual politics, bodies, and love"— Provided by publisher.
Identifiers: LCCN 2022026079 (print) | LCCN 2022026080 (ebook) | ISBN 9781793636799 (cloth) | ISBN 9781793636812 (paper) | ISBN 9781793636805 (ebook)
Subjects: LCSH: Coppola, Sofia, 1971- —Criticism and interpretation. | Motion pictures—United States—History—21st century. | Women motion picture producers and directors—United States—Biography.
Classification: LCC PN1998.3.C672 W66 2022  (print) | LCC PN1998.3.C672  (ebook) | DDC 791.4302/3092—dc23/eng/20220714
LC record available at https://lccn.loc.gov/2022026079
LC ebook record available at https://lccn.loc.gov/2022026080

# Contents

| | |
|---|---:|
| Introduction | 1 |
| **PART I: MASCULINITY** | 32 |
| Chapter One: An Alternative Masculinity: The Habitus of Vulnerability, Presence, and Mundane Delight in *Somewhere* | 35 |
| Chapter Two: Limits of Masculinity: Excess, Mimicry, and Ambivalence in *The Virgin Suicides* | 65 |
| **PART II: SEXUAL POLITICS** | |
| Chapter Three: A Limited Liberation: Film Music, Suture, Feminism, and Anachronism in *Marie Antoinette* | 95 |
| Chapter Four: Tables Turned: Hospitality, Phallogocentrism, and Virginity in *The Beguiled* (2017) | 119 |
| **PART III: BODIES** | |
| Chapter Five: A Bodily Desire: (Micro)celebrity, Celebrity Culture as Parareligion, and the Erotic in *The Bling Ring* | 149 |
| Chapter Six: An Embodied Joy: Carnivalesque Subversions and Grotesque Bodies in *A Very Murray Christmas* (2015) | 177 |
| **PART IV: LOVE** | |
| Chapter Seven: A Liminal Love: Charles Taylor's Malaise and Chela Sandoval's Decolonial Love in *Lost in Translation* | 209 |
| Chapter Eight: A Managed Love: Emotional Labor, Exhaustion, and Unhappiness in *On the Rocks* (2020) | 239 |

| | |
|---|---|
| Conclusion | 265 |
| Index | 289 |
| About the Authors | 293 |

*Naaman: For my teachers, Kim, Jo, Claire, Kiara, Sheri, Ilana, and Amber*

*Christopher: For my daughters, Cadence and Cameron*

## INTRODUCTION

The term "excess" describes the wide range of reactions writers and audiences have had to the films of writer/director Sofia Coppola. By the time her third film, *Marie Antoinette* (2006), was released, *Vanity Fair* writer Evgenia Peretz expressed the split some audiences made: "It might be tempting to dismiss Coppola as a ditz who has successfully parlayed her famous name, the right clothes, and the right friends into an overblown image, if it weren't for the enormous, deserved success she has had as a director, whose three films seem to be extensions of herself: ethereal, stylish, child-like, yet powerful."[1] Peretz captures the reality that many have dismissed Coppola for her temperament and demeanor, her family connections, and, perhaps most importantly, her femininity. Others have also dismissed particular films. Audiences at the Cannes Film Festival booed *Marie Antoinette*,[2] and it was panned by some critics. Her 2010 film *Somewhere* earned a quip on the hit television show *30 Rock* (2006–2013), "You wouldn't expect a movie called *Somewhere* to go absolutely nowhere."[3] Scholars also critique her films as susceptible to postfeminism, or the deployment of femininity and empowerment in ways that "undermine feminist commitments to gender justice."[4] Yet, at the opposite end of excess, she has been highly praised. Her second feature film, *Lost in Translation* (2003), received almost universal critical praise, successful box-office numbers, and an Academy Award for Best Screenplay. She was the first women to be awarded the Golden Lion, the top prize at the Venice Film Festival. Some scholars defend her films as radically feminist. Others describe her as a "pioneer"[5] and an "icon."[6] And, as feminist critic Jessa Crispin once wrote, "She's the auteur of girlhood, she's the pretty princess of Hollywood, she's the female gaze, she's our female [François] Truffaut."[7]

These responses are important to foreground, because, as we note above, she has built success and longevity in a male-dominated field. Perhaps no other director in American film history has portrayed such femininity throughout her career, and it is precisely her interest in the experience of women and girls that often prompts some to dismiss her. For example, filmmaker Kathryn Bigalow is certainly one of the most successful Hollywood filmmakers in film history. However, she tends to work in the male-centric action film. Coppola's success is, by contrast, an important accomplishment. Film studies scholar Belinda Smaill suggests that "Coppola is arguably the most successful American female director of her generation,"[8] which includes, on either side of her debut in 1999, directors such as Quentin Tarantino, David Fincher, Richard Linklater, Alexander Payne, the Wachowskis, Paul Thomas Anderson, Wes Anderson, and former husband Spike Jonze. Put in broader perspective, her stature among other women filmmakers, especially, cannot be underplayed. On the BBC's poll of the "100 greatest films directed by women," Coppola has four films on the list, only to be outdone by Agnès Varda (six films) and Kathryn Bigelow (five). *Lost in Translation* appears in the number 5 spot, behind masterpieces like Claire Denis' *Beau Travail* (1999), Chantal Akerman's *Jeanne Dielman, 23 Quai du Commerce, 1080 Bruxelles* (1975), Agnès Varda's *Cléo from 5 to 7* (1962), and Jane Campion's *The Piano* (1993). Journalist and film critic Anthony Carew states Coppola's status simply and plainly, "Sofia Coppola is one of the most acclaimed female filmmakers in the world."[9]

Unlike the other women, such as the Wakowskis or Kathryn Bigelow, Coppola works across a variety of film genres, but she returns to a handful of themes and often emphasizes more ephemeral qualities of cinema. Carew points out that Coppola's themes emphasize the ennui of wealth and celebrity, especially in her early works.[10] While she has written several films with male protagonists, the theme to which Coppola returns most often is the existential experience of heterosexual women and girls, either in characters coming of age (*The Virgin Suicides* [1999], *Lost in Translation* [2003], *Marie Antoinette*, *The Bling Ring* [2013]), navigating relationships with other women (*The Beguiled* [2017]) or men in their lives (*On the Rocks* [2020], *Somewhere*). In capturing these experiences and navigations, Coppola will often employ minimalism. Her films have been compared to the famous minimalist filmmakers in the art cinema tradition, particularly Italian director Michelangelo Antonioni (see, for example, *L'Eclisse* [1962]) and Belgian director Chantal Akerman (see, for example, *Jeanne Dielman, 23 Quai du Commerce, 1080 Bruxelles*). Using long takes, minimal and sometimes awkward dialogue, and location shooting, Coppola emphasizes mood or atmosphere, or the "microclimates of feeling and longing."[11] Perhaps the most evocative element of her work is her use of music.[12] While she draws most often on post-punk and indie music sensibilities, the director has employed ambient atmospheres, period music sources, and has worked with the French synth pop band Phoenix, a group fronted by her spouse Thomas Mars. Fashion and sensuality also play an important part in bringing beauty to her work. Film scholar Anna Backman Rogers observes that "aesthetically pleasing fashion, photography and art" drive the "sensuality . . . of the viewing process,"[13] perhaps most notably in *Marie Antoinette* and *The Bling Ring*.

Coppola was born on May 14, 1971 in New York City, to an Italian American family deeply invested in arts and entertainment. Her grandfather Carmine Coppola was first a musician and composer on Broadway before turning to Hollywood films, where he won an Academy Award for the score to *The Godfather Part II* (1974).[14] Sofia's father is the famed filmmaker Francis Ford Coppola, who has directed some of the most important films of American cinema, including *The Godfather* (1972), *The Godfather Part*

*II* (1974), and *Apocalypse Now* (1979). Eleanor Coppola, her mother, is also a filmmaker, most notably co-directing *Hearts of Darkness: A Filmmaker's Apocalypse* (1991), a documentary about the making of Francis' *Apocalypse Now*. Her aunt, Talia Shire, is an actress, whose most enduring performance is "Adrian" in Silvester Stallone's *Rocky* (1976) and the rest of the Rocky franchise. Her cousin, actor Nicholas Cage, has starred in a wide range of films, from independent films like the Coen brothers's *Raising Arizona* (1987) to large Hollywood productions such as *National Treasure* (2004). Jason Schwartzman, also Coppola's cousin, is known for his comedic roles, like "Max Fisher" in Wes Anderson's *Rushmore* (1998). And her brother, Roman Coppola, runs the day-to-day operations at the family production company, American Zoetrope. He has also produced several of Sofia's films, has collaborated with Wes Anderson, and is executive producer and creator of the television series *Mozart in the Jungle* (2014–2018). Perhaps because of these connections, Coppola was involved at an early age in films. She appeared, first, as an infant in *The Godfather*, was on set for several of Francis' films including *Apocalypse Now*,[15] co-wrote the script for Francis' short film *Life Without Zoe* (on *New York Stories* [1989]), performed small parts on films throughout the 1980s, and played "Mary Corleone" in *The Godfather: Part III* (1990). Despite her proximity to the film industry, Sofia showed little initial interest in filmmaking.

During her teens and twenties, she pursued interests in art, popular culture, and the fashion industry. At the age of 16, she interned with Karl Lagerfeld, the famed creative director for the luxury brand Chanel.[16] Later, Coppola attended the California School of Art and Design and then the ArtCenter College of Design, where she wanted to study painting. After a painting teacher discouraged her, she turned to photography, where she credits her teacher, Paul Jasmine,[17] as having encouraged her point of view with the camera.[18] She eventually worked as a commercial photographer and had some of her work published in fashion magazines including *Paris Vogue* and *Allure*.[19] Additionally, Coppola met fashion designer Marc Jacobs[20] in the early 1990s and became his friend, muse,[21] and eventual collaborator.[22] In 1994, she started Milk Fed, a fashion company that sold t-shirts, mainly in Japan. While the company is still in business,[23] Coppola is no longer affiliated with the organization.[24] Also in 1994, she produced four episodes of a Comedy Central show called, *Hi Octane*.[25] It was only a few years later that she finally turned to film in a substantial way, writing and directing her short film, *Lick the Star* (1998), about a group of teenage girls who plan to poison boys in their school. Film, Coppola realized, brought together in one medium many of her interests, like photography, music, design, and clothing.[26] And, in retrospect, Coppola recounts one of the key benefits of having a filmmaker father, "I had a 20-year tutorial on film in my own home . . . Now when I am on film sets it's really comfortable because it's so familiar."[27]

Around the time of *Lick the Star*, Coppola learned that a film studio purchased the rights to the Jeffrey Eugenides novel, *The Virgin Suicides* (1993). Coppola loved the novel, recounts her reaction to the news in this way, saying to herself, "I hope they don't do this, and I hope they do this. I just felt so protective that I kept thinking about how I would make it as a movie. And I started working on a screenplay just as an exercise."[28] On the basis of her script, Coppola convinced the studio to let her direct the film. Her first feature film, *The Virgin Suicides* (1999), recounts memories of a group of boys in suburbs of Detroit, Michigan, who, as men looking back on the events of their youth, are still obsessed with the five sisters of the Lisbon family. As the title indicates, the sisters all commit suicide, and the film documents the boys' failed attempt to try to make sense of the sisters' deaths. While not as minimalistic as some of her later work, *The Virgin Suicides* has many of the director's stylistic traits: music that captures the moody atmosphere of youth, girls coming of age, ennui, and displays of girly femininity. The distribution company, Paramount Pictures, provided the film with a limited release in the United States. Even though the film did not find an American audience, *The Virgin Suicides* developed a cult following in the 2010s, which Coppola credits to writer Tavi Gevinson's reflections on the film in her popular fashion blog *Rookie*.[29] The film received favorable critical reception and made her a "breakout" director.[30] But it was her second film that catapulted Coppola to international recognition.

Her most successful film to date is indeed her second feature film, *Lost in Translation* (2003), which follows two characters adrift in Tokyo, Japan. Charlotte (Scarlett Johansson) is a recent graduate in philosophy who is having trouble finding herself and her future career. Bob (Bill Murray) is an action star past his prime and is having a mid-life crisis. Alienated from their marital relationships, from Japanese culture, and from their work, the two find solace in each other's company. Coppola's cinematic signatures are present here. She uses minimal, awkward dialogue and long takes. Most pronounced, perhaps, is her sense of atmosphere and mood. Music captures the ennui, aimlessness, and eventual hope the characters experience. In addition to post-punk selections, like the dreamy "Just Like Honey," from the Scottish indie rock band The Jesus and Mary Chain, the director uses melancholy, ambient soundscapes by Kevin Shields, the former front man for the indie band My Bloody Valentine.

The film was an overwhelming critical and commercial success. With a reported $4 million budget, it grossed over $119 million worldwide.[31] Additionally, the film garnered a host of major awards and nominations. It received four Academy Award nominations: Best Picture, Best Screenplay,

Best Director, and Best Actor. Although Coppola's screenplay was the only winner, her nomination for Best Director was notable for several reasons. She was the first American woman and only the third woman to be nominated in the category. Lina Wertmüller for *Seven Beauties* (1976) and Jane Campion for *The Piano* (1993) were the only two women nominated previously. These three nominees paved the way for two women who would later win in the category: Kathryn Bigelow for *The Hurt Locker* (2009) and Chloé Zhao for *Nomadland* (2020). While the film was awarded three Golden Globes (Best Motion Picture–Musical or Comedy, Best Actor–Motion Picture Musical or Comedy, and Best Screenplay),[32] one of its important legacies is the revitalization of Bill Murray's career. With Wes Anderson's *Rushmore* (1998) the previous year, "*Lost in Translation* marked a key moment of reinvention for Murray."[33] The actor would, over the next twenty years, appear in many films and television shows and draw a fandom for his off-camera antics with strangers, like crashing a couple's engagement photos,[34] crashing a kickball game,[35] being invited to a house party where he helped the host wash dishes, or the time he crashed a bachelor party and gave a toast.[36] But perhaps the legacy of *Lost in Translation* is that it became "one of the defining films of the early 21st century," "solidified Coppola's success," and "is held close to many a film fan's heart."[37]

While her first two films established Coppola's success, her third feature film, *Marie Antoinette* (2006), gave way to the first significant critique or backlash to her work, a pattern that would continue through many of her works. Continuing with her practice of shooting on location, Coppola shot *Marie Antoinette* in Versailles, France, the places where the real Marie Antoinette lived. In explaining how she persuaded the caretakers of Versailles to let her shoot there, Coppola simply says, "I guess they liked *Lost in Translation*."[38] And, unlike her previous film, the budget for *Marie Antionette* was much larger than any of her films to date, a reported $40 million.[39] Like her other films, the plot of *Marie Antoinette* is quite simple. Antoinette (Kirsten Dunst) travels to Versailles to become the wife of Louis XVI (Jason Schwartzman). She has trouble finding her place in courtly life but eventually finds slivers of happiness, sometimes through consumption, fashion, children, her house, and a love affair. Stylistically, the film diverges somewhat from her previous films. Not only is the film a costume drama, but Coppola also uses quick, music video montage-like editing, which diverges from the moody and slow pace of her previous films. She still focuses on the themes of ennui, femininity, the isolation of wealth (or characters trapped in gilded cages),[40] and she engages in some realistic cinematic techniques, like handheld camerawork. Certainly, the moments in the film that drew the most negative attention were Coppola's use of anachronism, bringing 20th popular culture into the 18th century French aristocracy. For example, she opens the film with the post-punk band Gang of Four's "Natural's Not in It" and includes contemporary fashion pieces, like Converse All-Star and Manolo Blahnik shoes. The film upset the Cannes film festival audience, and many critics panned it for its apparent lack of historical rigor and investment in surfaces. A few critics, like Roger Ebert[41] and A.O. Scott,[42] tentatively defended the film.

In response to the massive scope of *Marie Antoinette*, Coppola, working with director of photography Harris Savides, produced her fourth feature film, *Somewhere* (2010), in a minimalist way, "simple" and "intimate."[43] The film follows Johnny Marco (Stephen Dorff), an action movie star in his prime, who is not happy with his celebrity life. As a way to cope, Johnny attends parties, takes drugs, and drinks heavily. However, he slowly begins to alter his way of life once his ex-wife leaves their daughter, Cleo (Elle Fanning), with him. Her presence in his life alters the way he moves through the world. While Coppola compared their process on *Somewhere* to how she had "worked before on *Lost in Translation*,"[44] this film has an intensified minimalism, often relying on actors' performances to convey what dialogue might usually do. Likewise, there is nothing like the brash, anachronistic music of *Marie Antoinette*, or the moody, dreamy soundscapes of *Lost in Translation*. This film attracted some of her highest praise, particularly at the Venice Film Festival. Recognized as the "oldest and one of the most prestigious in the world," the festival highlights what it considers to be "innovative, independent cinema."[45] The Jury for the Main Competition awarded Coppola the festival's top prize, the Golden Lion.[46] Quentin Tarantino, who served as the jury's president, was so moved emotionally, that he "seemed to fight back tears when he was about to announce that Coppola had won the Golden Lion."[47] Despite this international recognition, *Somewhere* remains her lowest grossing movie to date.[48] However, the film solidified Coppola as an established filmmaker with work that might be considered part of European art cinema tradition.[49]

In the same way that *Somewhere* shifted away from some features of *Marie Antoinette*, her fifth production, *The Bling Ring* (2013) marked a similar tonal shift. "After *Somewhere* was so slow and minimal," Coppola recounted, "I was looking to do something fast paced."[50] The film explored the way in which celebrity culture exploits materiality to gain "status and attention."[51] Based on the real life events that Nancy Jo Sales reported in her 2010 *Vanity Fair* piece, "The Suspects Wore Louboutins," the film follows a group of Los Angeles area teenagers who enter celebrity homes and steal clothes, money, and jewelry. After their series of serial robberies garners the attention of the police, the press gives the group the moniker "The Bling Ring." While not as minimalist as her previous film, *The Bling Ring* incorporates many realist elements that appear in her previous films. Coppola shoots on location, most notably in a home of one of the real-life victims, reality-TV star Paris Hilton. The director also incorporates naturalistic and realistic dialogue, some of which was taken directly from the article or from Nancy Jo Sales' interview transcripts. Perhaps the most realist moment and most discussed shot in the film is Harry Savides' long, uninterrupted single zoom shot of the Bling Ring's burglary of reality-TV star Audrina Patridge's home. The music also returns to the bombastic energy of *Marie Antoinette*, this time emphasizing the hip-hop sensibility of the Bling Ring's own musical tastes.

Like Coppola's two previous films, *The Bling Ring* garnered polarized responses, but responses that begin to capture what some consider singular about Coppola's voice. A representative disagreement appears clearly on an episode of the web series "The Guardian Film Show" (2013–2016). Film critic Catharine Shoard castigates the film by claiming that Coppola's "exoneration of these kids actually acts as a positive brand reinforcement for the very celebrities she [Coppola] is apparently attacking . . . It [the film] doesn't say anything at the end."[52] Likewise, film critic Alex Chafey summarizes his take on the film, saying that it is "a film about shallow people that becomes . . . a shallow film."[53] However, film critic Peter Bradshaw defends it: "[A] conventional ironist or satirist would have distanced you from these ridiculous people [the Bling Ring]," Bradshaw claims, and would have "perpetually signaled that these people are crazy . . . but Sofia Coppola, with this weird unjudging tone that she takes, really puts you next to them."[54] The intimacy Bradshaw experiences with these "ridiculous," "crazy," "shallow" people produces some effect upon him that he cannot quite describe or justify to his interlocutors. Like Bradshaw, former director of the New York Film Festival, Kent Jones, touches on this effect Coppola's films have on some viewers. In an interview with the director, Jones suggests that she is often "in pursuit of something that's almost so delicate that it's unnameable . . . [which becomes] very difficult to write about or talk about."[55] Coppola responds in an affirmative manner, saying that writing and directing a film is not unlike "trying to remember a dream," and the film becomes "an impression of what it [the dream] feels like."[56] Bradshaw and Jones suggest that Coppola's cinematic technique emphasizes the intangibility of feeling, the ephemera of the body, or the morphology of feeling. Such an effect, it appears, proves both too subtle and too off-putting for some audiences.

In her 2015 television special, *A Very Murray Christmas*, Coppola takes yet another turn. In conversations with film producer Mitch Glazer, he observed that old, traditional television Christmas specials—a variety style show, with stars singing Christmas songs on sound stages—do not exist anymore. Perhaps nostalgic for those programs, Coppola and Glazer produced *A Very Murray Christmas*, albeit modified in some significant ways. The special follows Bill Murray (playing himself), as he and Paul Shaffer (playing himself) attempt and fail to perform a traditional Christmas special to an audience of A-list Hollywood celebrities. Once the special is canceled, Murray and Shaffer retire to the bar. The former sings Christmas songs, reunites an estranged bride and groom, feasts and drinks with other folks in the bar, and, eventually, passes out drunk on the floor. In his drunken fantasy, he performs Christmas numbers reminiscent of old television specials, with singer Miley Cyrus (playing herself) and actor George Clooney (playing himself). Murray wakes on Christmas morning, thankful for the day. In terms of style, the project is a departure from her previous work, primarily because it uses multiple cameras and fourteen musical numbers, most of which were performed live. Most critics responded positively to the harmless and playful tone of the piece, offering little if any criticism on the scale of her previous three films.[57] However, her next film would return Coppola to critical scrutiny, this time over race.

Her 2017 Civil War-era costume drama, *The Beguiled*, is often described as a remake of Don Seigel's 1971 hyper-masculine film of the same name. Coppola claims to have had no interest in remakes, but her production designer, Anne Ross, encouraged her consider it.[58] After screening the film, Coppola decided to produce a version much more interested in femininity and female interactions. Returning to the 1966 Thomas Cullinan novel, *The Beguiled*, the director tells the same story from the perspective of the women. In the waning years of the American Civil War, a small school for girls, located near the front in Virginia, has survived the ravages of the war virtually unscathed. While foraging for mushrooms, one of the girls, Amy (Oona Laurence) stumbles across a wounded Union soldier, McBurney (Colin Farrell). The teachers and girls decide to let McBurney recuperate at the school. However charming he appears at first, he eventually reveals himself to be a violent threat to everyone, and they murder him, poisoning one of his favorite dishes. Less minimalist than her previous work, Coppola explores again the lives of girls and women who are trapped from the outside world. Like *The Virgin Suicides*, an older woman, Miss Martha (Nicole Kidman) attempts to control Kirsten Dunst's (playing Edwina) body and desires. Although the film enters the realm of melodrama within a Southern Gothic setting, *The Beguiled* plays out scenes with looks and gazes, much like *Somewhere*. It premiered at the Cannes Film Festival, where Coppola became only the second woman in the festival's history to win Best Director (Jane Campion is the other).[59] Despite this success, *The Beguiled* proved to attract what is perhaps the most intense criticism of her films.

Before turning to the substance of those criticism, a bit of context is required, particularly concerning the important cultural shifts about race and whiteness in the United States. The most direct way to describe such shifts is with the emergence of the Black Lives Matter (BLM) movement and the rhetoric of race that has emerged in its wake. In 2013, a neighborhood watch volunteer in Sanford, Florida, George Zimmerman, called police to report a suspicious person. Against police instruction, Zimmerman approached and killed what turned out to be a 17-year-old Black boy, Trayvon Martin. When a Florida jury acquitted Zimmerman of murder, three Black women activists— Alicia Garza, Patrisse Cullors, and Opal Tometi—began a #blacklivesmatter hashtag on social media. In the wake of the deaths of many other unarmed men and women, dying mostly at the hands of police (see for example, Eric Garner, Michael Brown, Tamir Rice Freddie Gray, Alton Sterling, Philandro Castile, Terence Crutcher, Sandra Bland, Breonna Taylor, Ahmaud Arbery, and George Floyd), the hashtag developed into a global movement. This and other activist movements around racial justice have popularized anti-racist aims and rhetoric. Although terms like "whiteness," "white supremacy," and "white privilege" (or, simply, "privilege") have existed for many years, these movements have pushed such rhetoric into mainstream culture and provide ways for people of all racial groups to name and describe more clearly both their existential and historical experiences of inequality. In many social, political, and educational circles, anti-racist rhetoric has permitted many white folks a greater awareness of the unearned advantages they receive simply by virtue of the color of their skin. One of the basic insights of anti-racism is to differentiate "intent" from "impact." A white person, for example, may not "intend" to say or do racist things, but that intent does not necessarily reduce the negative impact of their words or actions. There is a deep sense, within anti-racist conversations, that because white people created racialized systems, they have an obligation to dismantle them.

Within this anti-racist context, *The Beguiled* received considerable backlash, because Coppola removed the only Black character from the film, a slave named Mattie in the book and Hallie (Mae Mercer) in Siegal's film. The backlash proved so intense that Coppola defended her choice in a piece for *IndieWire*, making appeals to historicity, gender, and respect for the Black experience. First, she claims that, at the end of the Civil War, slaves often fled their masters, leaving white, Southern women isolated from the outside world. The omission of Hallie is, therefore, "[a]ccording to historians and several women's journals from the time," historically accurate.[60] Second, the filmmaker wants to tell the story of how women and girls "deal with repression and desire" when a man enters and disrupts their isolation, and "the high cost of [that] denial and repression."[61] She believed "there were universal themes, about desire and male and female power dynamics that could relate to all women."[62] Here, Coppola suggests that Hallie was not necessary to deal with the politics of white, female desire. Third, the director did not want to portray a Black slave and, in so doing, "perpetuate an objectionable stereotype" and "treat slavery as a side-plot," which "would be insulting" to

Black audience members.[63] Therefore, removing the slave character was, for Coppola, a sign of "respect."[64] She concludes her statement saying how disheartened she was "to hear my artistic choices, grounded in historical facts, being characterized as insensitive when my intention was the opposite."[65]

Given the cultural shifts around race, her response garnered a range of criticism. Some critics simply wonder about the omission. For example, film critic Anthony Lane notes that, in Siegel's film, the dynamic between McBurney (Clint Eastwood) and Hallie "is as fraught and as fruitful as anything in the story, so why has Coppola got rid of her? Might any racial friction abrade the smoothness of the style?"[66] Other critics note that the omission implicitly if unintentionally denies the racialized reality of the Civil War. Film critic Dana Stevens admits that not "every film set in the Civil War–era South" must "focus exclusively on the power dynamics between masters and enslaved people. But to eliminate this element from the story—to effectively run plantation life in 1864 through the bleach cycle—not only places *The Beguiled* in a space outside history; it drains the plot of much of its potential stakes."[67] Journalist Joanne Lauer thinks that the removal of Hallie was an attempt on the director's part to avoid the "racial insensitivity" of a white filmmaker "daring to portray black suffering . . . the exclusive jurisdiction of African American filmmakers."[68] As a result, however, Coppola's avoidance of "difficult" racial issues removes the "compelling and important life out of her version of *The Beguiled*."[69]

Other critics note the problems with Coppola's other films, particularly around issues like race and class. Journalist Steve Macfarlane writes that since *Lost in Translation*, "Coppola has alternated between accusations of flaunting her privilege and hosannas for being honest about it. But if *The Virgin Suicides*, *Marie Antoinette*, and (perhaps more debatably) *Somewhere* girded themselves against these considerations by putting their own haute-bourgeois blinkeredness front and center, the terrain is far murkier in Coppola's *The Beguiled*."[70] Journalist Kendra James contrasts the film to pop singer Beyonce's visual album, *Lemonade* (2016), both of which were shot on the same location. She writes:

> The actors in *The Beguiled* look entirely different than the women in Beyoncé's visual album. Their whiteness is jarring—not only because of *Lemonade*'s recent use of the plantation house, but because of the type of whiteness we're asked to root for. The women in this film are Confederates. They're former slave owners. And to paint them as heroic victims erases race, racism, and the entire Black experience.[71]

The erasure of Blackness from *The Beguiled* also reminded journalist Corey Atad of the erasure of a Latina character from *The Bling Ring*. Although he characterizes it as "a sort of tale of class struggle," Coppola removed "one member of the real life bling ring, a young undocumented immigrant from Mexico named Diana Tamayo."[72] But perhaps the most helpful critique comes from journalist Jenna Wortham. To the extent that Coppola explores gender without reference to race, she commits one of the key mistakes of white feminism. "White feminism," Wortham argues, "prioritizes white stories at the expense of everyone else."[73] In trying not to harm black viewers through stereotyping, Coppola not only harms Black viewers through erasure, she also fails to understand the most basic anti-racist insight. She does not realize that her intent to respect Black experiences produced the impact of harm.

Perhaps as a response to the racial criticisms of *The Beguiled*, Coppola cast Rashida Jones as her first non-white lead in her 2020 film, *On the Rocks*. The film is part of a multi-project deal between the independent distributor A24 and streaming service Apple+, and Coppola is, reportedly, developing a television series for Apple+ based on Edith Wharton's novel *The Custom of the Country* (1913).[74] Inspired by classic screwball comedies like *The Thin Man* (1934),[75] *On the Rocks* is a father-daughter buddy film, where Laura (Rashida Jones) and her father Felix (Bill Murray) try to figure out whether her husband is having an affair. If *The Beguiled* drew on the melodramatic Southern Gothic genre, *On the Rocks* also leaves behind the minimalism of *Somewhere* and *The Bling Ring* in favor of a more classical Hollywood style. Shot in New York and Mexico before the COVID-19 pandemic, the film relies, like her others, on location shooting and naturalism.

While *On the Rocks* received generally positive critical ratings, reviews of the film suggest that wealth, privilege, and whiteness are all topics much more open for debate, topics that critics might not have discussed earlier in her career. Some critics see Laura's wealth as an implicit form of critique. Stephanie Zacharek for example suggests that the film serves as "a reminder that having money never protects you from loneliness and confusion."[76] Likewise, journalist David Sims notes that the film "plays out against a backdrop of unattainable wealth," but he concludes that the director portrays wealth "as alluring as it is deadening, lending every scene a fancy sheen but offering no solution to Laura's existential woes."[77] Other writers are less sympathetic and reflect the impact anti-racist rhetoric has had on wider culture. For example, film critic Lindsey Bahr takes an almost mocking tone, focusing her description on the protagonist's wealth and privilege. Laura's "Chanel purse is almost never carried without a stroller and a canvas Strand bookstore tote bag," and she now only cooks "instant mac and cheese" in a beautiful and expensive ceramic Dutch oven.[78] Making reference to the seersucker suit Felix wears early in the film, film critic Ann Hornaday quips that *On the Rocks* "wears its privilege like a spanking new seersucker jacket."[79] David Ehrlich observes that Laura does not fit the typical protagonist of a Coppola film. Most notably, there are "Black people in it."[80] Nevertheless, Laura still retains many of the privileges that Coppola does, like the "casual ability to throw on a Radarte sweatshirt like it's from the Gap."[81] He rightly argues, however, that even though the film has a biracial protagonist and Black family members, "Race itself is only an ambient concept in the film," and has seemingly little impact on the way Laura moves through her world.[82]

Although Coppola has had a successful career, authors have written relatively few books on her or her work. As of 2021, there are five scholarly books offering various approaches to the director's films. One of the strongest is film scholar Anna Backman Rogers' wonderful text *Sofia Coppola: The Politics of Visual Pleasure* (2019). Working primarily through feminist film theory, Rogers notes that most scholarship on Coppola situates her work within, primarily, a postfeminist context. Some scholars have had a tendency to critique the director as perhaps unwittingly caught in the harm postfeminism engages. However, Rogers reads Coppola as one who responds not within postfeminism but from the outside, offering "an outspoken and at times radical form of feminism."[83] Offering close readings on every Coppola film to date (except *A Very Murray Christmas*), her readings focus on topics like female abjection, subjectivities, and bodies. Preceding Rogers' book is film studies scholar Fiona Handyside's *Sofia Coppola: A Cinema of Girlhood* (2017). Like Rogers, Handyside takes a feminist approach; however, instead of offering close readings of each film, she focuses on themes across Coppola's work, including postfeminism, girlhood, the home, and fashion. Handyside comes to a more ambivalent conclusion than Rogers, arguing that Coppola's work is caught between feminism and postfeminism. Structured in a similar way to Handyside's text, literature scholar Suzanne Ferriss' *The Cinema of Sofia Coppola: Fashion, Culture, Celebrity* (2021) explores a range of themes throughout Coppola's work. Taking "fashioning" or the work of creation, as her central metaphor, Ferriss explores themes like identity, film style, the film-fashion industry, and world making.

The two other books that explore one of Coppola's films in depth are: film and television studies scholar Geoff King's *Lost in Translation* (2010) and film and media scholar Justin Wyatt's *The Virgin Suicides: Reverie, Sorrow and Young Love* (2018). King's text explains how the film, which is ostensibly a piece of art cinema, gained the kind of commercial success usually expected of mainstream Hollywood films. The author explores the context of the film industry, stardom, and authorship, as well as the film's style and themes. King concludes that the film is situated in a liminal space, between Hollywood and independent filmmaking and between a capitulation to Western ideologies (race, gender, class) and a critique of them.[84] Wyatt's book proceeds similarly. He first attends to the context of female independent filmmaking in the 1990s and the history of American Zoetrope, the Coppola family's production company. Then Wyatt turns to textual analysis, attending to narrative, music, advertising, themes, and style. He argues that identity formation is the centralizing tenet of not only *Lost in Translation* but of Coppola's entire body of work,[85] concluding that the director is more of a "humanist" storyteller rather than a feminist or postfeminist one.[86]

*A Critical Companion to Sofia Coppola* responds to the feminist background of much of Coppola studies and expand upon it in three ways. First, this monograph will offer the most updated, comprehensive, and complete study of Coppola's cinematic oeuvre to date. We offer, to our knowledge, the first scholarly works on *A Very Murray Christmas* and *On the Rocks* to appear in print. Second, this volume continues the practice of the "Critical Companion to Popular Directors" series by offering an interdisciplinary approach. As opposed to other works that tend to focus on a single disciplinary perspective (feminism, fashion, media studies, etc.), each chapter in this volume offers a close reading of one of Coppola's films described above from a unique disciplinary perspective, including approaches like masculinity studies, musicology, Chicana studies, literary studies, celebrity studies, religious studies, and sociology. Third, we expand upon feminist concerns with four themes: masculinity, sexual politics, bodies, and love. It is certainly not the case that Coppola studies have not discussed some of these themes before (sexual politics and bodies in particular). Rather, we bring Coppola studies more deeply into conversation with fourth-wave feminist concerns, which we will engage in our concluding paragraph.

We open the book discussing "Masculinity." While men have long been a topic of concern to feminism, cultural critic and Black feminist scholar bell hooks observes that no "body of writing by women about men" has been written.[87] The same is true for feminist reflection on Coppola's work. No sustained treatment about men or masculinity exists. Yet, for a filmmaker of such expansive femininity, she not only incorporates men into her work, but she sometimes makes them central to her plots. Because we, the authors of this book, identify as white, straight, cis-gendered, middle-aged and middle-class men, we are particularly moved by hooks' insistence that we all "need to live in a world where women and men can belong together."[88] For that belonging to take place men—like us—must change. "Men cannot change," hooks insists, "if there are no blueprints for change."[89] We think that *Somewhere* and *The Virgin Suicides* have particularly helpful reflections about what changes might look like.

In chapter one, we draw on anthropologist Saba Mahmood's account of *habitus* and sociologist Tracy Karner's notion of toxic masculinity to argue that *Somewhere* represents an alternative *habitus*, or way of life, to toxic masculinity. The film traces the everyday life of action film star Johnny Marco. Through his Ferrari, risky behaviors, and seeing women's bodies as sexual surfaces, Johnny inhabits toxic cycles of masculinity. The presence of his daughter Cleo, however, disrupts those cycles. When Johnny's ex-wife forces him to take Cleo to Italy for a film opening, Johnny and Cleo's life together outlines an alternative *habitus* for Johnny. Upon their return home, their alternative expands to include shared memory, shared delights, and humor. During this period, Johnny sees women's bodies differently. Then, on one day together, Johnny and Cleo live out a fuller possibility of an alternative *habitus*, through play, sensuousness, time, and joy. When Johnny drops Cleo off at her summer camp, he returns to his normal life. However, Johnny's *habitus* has changed. The film ends with Johnny on the threshold of an alternative masculinity.

Because the protagonists of *The Virgin Suicides*, the neighborhood boys, experience trauma when they find the dead bodies of the Lisbon sisters at the end of the film, chapter two devotes attention to the link between the boys' trauma and the masculinity they are trying so desperately to emulate. It is their masculinity and their failure to live up to those standards that keep them from seeing the significance of the sisters' suicides. Using insights on mimicry, trauma studies, and sociologist R. W. Connell's notion of hegemonic masculinity, we argue that their failure to know the girls illuminates the limits of masculinity's ways of knowing and loving. The boys are caught within a system of hegemonic masculinity that oppresses the Lisbon sisters and orients themselves to Trip Fontaine (Josh Hartnett), who sits at the top of the hegemonic system. Within this system, the protagonists perform symbolic violence against the girls, through objectification, fantasy, voyeurism, and love. Nevertheless, the Lisbon sisters exceed the boys' understanding of them. The film uses juxtapositions, Cecilia's apparitions, authorial intrusions, and the girls' conversation to register their agency. The protagonists' failure to make sense of their deaths could have been a point of discovery, revealing to them the damaging hegemonic masculinity in which they live. However, they seem unwilling or unable to exit that form of masculinity and, therefore, they cannot accept the Lisbon sisters' invitation to be witnesses of the meaning of their deaths. If *Somewhere* shows a man on the brink of an alternative to toxic masculinity (i.e., a blueprint for change), *The Virgin Suicides* shows men unable or unwilling to leave a damaging form of hegemonic masculinity (i.e., men without a blueprint for change).

In the next section of the book, we turn to the "Sexual Politics" of *Marie Antoinette* and *The Beguiled*. From first-wave feminism to its current incarnations, feminists have always been concerned with unequal power distributions. If first-wave feminism sought the right to vote for women[90] and the second wave aimed for women's social, political, and economic liberation and freedom,[91] then the third wave was the first to engage in compensations for past failures.[92] In the 1980s and 1990s, women of color drew attention, for example, to white feminism's lack of racial diversity. Some writers describe a fourth-wave of feminism, revolving around the use of technology and an increased call to take diversities of race, sexuality, and gender even more seriously. "While intersectionality, critical race theory, queer theory, transgender theory, and more, came into being during third wave feminism," notes film and television scholar Hilary Neroni, "they have had only a limited impact on the third wave."[93] The fourth wave aims to undo that limited impact.

When writing about Coppola's work, scholars typically view it from third-wave sensibilities. Reading the director as a radical feminist, Anna Backman Rogers describes her films as bearing with them second-wave sensibilities. "[I]f white, rich, privileged, Western women are not free (as is the case with nearly all Coppola's characters), then who precisely is? . . . I think Coppola's question—in fact, the central tenet that determines her thinking on film—is the question of freedom."[94] From a different feminist vantagepoint, Fiona Handyside uses Coppola's status as a female auteur to grapple, more broadly, with the agency of women. Handyside notes that her very name "Coppola" already places her agency "under erasure" as the "daughter of a famous filmmaker."[95] Through her films, the scholar notes that Coppola "acts out, exposes, [and] glamorizes the role of girl/daughter . . . allow[ing] us to map a complex constellation of girlhood, understood as a political . . . and aesthetic state."[96] Our chapters expand on these feminist concerns that Backman and Handyside see as central to Coppola's work—the sexual politics of anachronism, liberation, and hospitality.

Chapter three focuses on Coppola's use of anachronisms in *Marie Antoinette*, and our reading points to ways white scholars might grapple more deeply with a racialized and limited understanding of liberation. Grounded in the concept of *suture*, the film's use of an eighteenth-century composition, Antonio Vivaldi's Concerto alla Rustica, provides a contrast to the way in which the director uses anachronistic music, especially the sequence that features the Bow Wow Wow's "I Want Candy." Expanding on Backman Rogers's reading of such a scene, we attend more closely to the anachronisms of music and fashion, which complicates, we think, feminist notions of masquerade and mimicry. These complications lead us to the work of Chicana scholar Gloria Anzaldúa, through whom we conclude that what white scholars might take for liberation should, more rightfully, be understood as a limited liberation.

Chapter four uses *The Beguiled* to grapple with the sexual politics (or lack thereof) of philosopher Jacques Derrida's (1930–2004) understanding of hospitality. Drawing on the ancient notions of the term, Derrida offers a radical notion of hospitality, in which hosts should accept any and all guests. *The Beguiled* portrays Miss Martha as a giver of hospitality, not unlike the ancient character Dido in Virgil's *Aeneid*, a woman leader who created a haven of safety amid uneasy and problematic wartime gendered relationships. As misogynist propaganda and practice of the Civil War South exemplifies, the ubiquity of patriarchal domination is precisely that power from which Miss Martha and the rest of the characters built a community against. Like Dido's hospitable acceptance of the wounded soldier Aeneas, Miss Martha's hospitality to the wounded Corporal McBurney risks the safety of her community. And like the story of Shechem and Dinah in the Hebrew Bible, the soldier's intrusion into the school's feminine refuge has indelible effects upon everyone, but especially the future of Edwina. Given the way gender impacts the giving of hospitality in the film (and in the ancient world), we suggest that Derrida's radical hospitality can only be hospitality if directed to those who hold power, to men like us.

Next, we turn to the theme of "Bodies." Within feminist reflection, there is a long record of reflection on bodies. As philosopher Gail Weiss (1959–) points out, the Western tradition, beginning with Plato and through to the Enlightenment, has often seen the body as a problem to be transcended with the mind. While the West produced mind/body dualism from this outlook, the dichotomy was always already gendered along the binaries of the impermeable and rational male body over and against the so-called weak and irrational female body. As Weiss observes, "Vulnerability, in short, is historically associated with women's allegedly deficient bodies, invulnerability with men's allegedly divine faculty of reason."[97] Hence, the Western tradition bears with it a masculine imaginary, one that has degraded the body in gendered terms. Weiss traces such an assumption even into writers associated with feminism and decolonialism, like Simone de Beauvoir and Franz Fanon, respectively. Weiss' arguments do not downplay their insights or significance, but they simply register how powerful and enduring the masculine imaginary is in the Western tradition.

In the twentieth century, however, scholars have turned affirmatively to the body, in general, and the female body, in particular. Philosopher Maurice Merleau-Ponty (1908–1961) argued, against the Western tradition, that we can know the world through our bodies, rather than our minds.[98] In his wake, feminist philosophers have turned to the body in a host of ways. Elizabeth Grosz (1952–) takes the body as the center point of investigation and, in recounting the history of philosophy of the body, traces the contradictions and gaps the masculine imaginary has left. Abjection, she argues, is how the Western tradition has imagined the female body, a body that cannot control itself and therefore is an inferior body.[99] Where much of Western contemporary theory, like the work of psychologist Jacques Lacan (1901–81), works from an implicit phenomenology of the male body (centered as it were around concepts like the "phallus,") Luce Irigaray (1930–) uses the phenomenology of the female body as her point of departure.[100] When she uses vaginal and/

or oral images like "the two lips touching" or "mucous,"[101] she aims to craft a new imaginary by which women can exist within philosophical discourse without the constraints of a masculine imagination.[102] Philosopher Judith Butler (1956–) has also argued that part of what connects all human beings is the bodily reality of vulnerability. "[W]hen we say that every infant is surely vulnerable,"[103] part of what that entails is that humanity has "a 'common' corporeal vulnerability."[104] The most recent thinker to impact reflection of the body is legal scholar Kimberlé Crenshaw. Her concept of intersectionality suggests that "patriarchy interacts with other systems of power—namely, racism—to uniquely disadvantage some groups of women more than others."[105] The racialized body a woman lives in impacts the various forms of oppression she will likely face. While not an exhaustive list, these scholars establish that the body as a site of reflection is not only a lively one but also one that is at the heart of feminist reflection. Our work here contributes to that conversation through the religious, erotic nature of celebrity culture and through so-called weak, deficient, vulnerable, or grotesque bodies.

In chapter five, we read the *The Bling Ring* as a meditation on religious aspects of celebrity culture, centering the relationship between relics and bodily desire. Although the Bling Ring behave in ways consistent with a form of celebrity called microcelebrity, the concept does not explain why the group both reveres and harms celebrities. Christian theologian Pete Ward's parareligious account of celebrity helps explain their behavior. The teenagers use relics that have been near to celebrities as a means of possessing their extraordinariness and freedom, engaging in rites of ascent and decent. The Bling Ring sees the celebrities they target as possessing an extraordinary capacity for fashion and a freedom to behave badly. To take possession of that power, the Bling Ring elevates themselves through a rite of ascent: they take relics from celebrity's homes. But that rite demands a sacrifice or a scapegoat, the celebrities themselves. Like many who aspire to celebrity status, the Bling Ring eventually facilitate their own rite of descent. Although the parareligious language of rites and relics helps explain how Bling Ring transfer power onto themselves, a Christian account of *eros*, or the erotic, sheds further light on the embodied nature of their veneration. The Bling Ring displays a range of erotic responses though their reaction to celebrity relics. Members of the group attach sexual desire to their break-ins to Paris Hilton's home or to a gun from Megan Fox's house. The leader, Rebecca (Katie Chang), reaches the apex of eroticism during the break-in of her fashion icon, Lindsay Lohan. Our reading suggests that there are echoes of religious embodiment and desire present in secular society, social media, and contemporary experiences of boredom.

Chapter six explores how *A Very Murray Christmas* subverts the television Christmas special, especially specials like the 1970s Carpenters, in such a way that points to the related realities of embodiment and joy. Taking *The Carpenters at Christmas* as a fulfillment of the Christmas television special, *A Very Murray Christmas* both affirms and subverts the genre. However, the methodology of genre analysis fails to fully name the ways Coppola deploys her subversions. Russian literary theorist Mikhail Bakhtin's notion of the carnivalesque offers better ways of describing how the film engages in acts of subversion. Bahktin's notions of food, drink, and sex subvert the disembodiment of Christmas specials more broadly. And Coppola's use of hybridized, grotesque bodies of so-called "bad" singers subverts the professionalism of Christmas specials. Despite the centrality of the body and the inclusion of many different types of bodies, the film leaves whiteness as its uninterrogated center.

Finally, we explore the theme of "Love." African American studies scholar Jennifer C. Nash argues that love is central to Black feminist reflection, especially the political foundation of self-love.[106] Love, she claims, "is a labor of actively reorienting the self, pushing the self to be configured in new ways that might be challenging or difficult."[107] One of most well-known treatments of love is by bell hooks, in her trilogy on love. Arguing that the world is now cynical about love, *All About Love: New Visions* (1999) places love at the center of what it means for people to have hope, joy, and be transformed.[108] In *Salvation: Black People and Love* (2001), hooks argues that love is what will enable Black people to survive and "triumph over the forces of evil and destruction."[109] *Communion: The Female Search for Love* (2002) addresses how women approaching middle age struggle, search out, and find communion in a wide variety of relationships and tasks.[110] In the wake of such reflections, the topic of love has proliferated. In 2017, a newly developed area of "feminist love studies" emerged, one that not only traced the role of love in feminist reflection from Mary Wollstonecraft to current thinkers, but also in philosophical sources like Søren Kierkegaard and Immanuel Kant.[111] Our readings of *Lost in Translation* and *On the Rocks* draw from these conversations, particularly in decolonial love and emotional or affective labor of love.

In chapter seven, we argue that *Lost in Translation* represents the love Bob and Charlotte experience as liminal, a love that has moved past Western love but has not arrived at what Chicana scholar Chela Sandoval names as "decolonial love." Where dichotomies undergird Western notions of love, decolonial love resists those dichotomies to create affiliations across lines of difference, affiliations that can lead to social transformation. Decolonial love can move in three stages: disruption, attachment, and a return to drifting, albeit with a sense of ease and wholeness. If disruption is a puncture in ordinary life, Bob and Charlotte experience each other as a puncture to their alienation. Attachment is a non-dualistic way of being in the world, and Bob and

Charlotte experience attachment through an intimacy that binaries like father/daughter or lover/beloved cannot contain. And finally, since drifting involves a state of wholeness and being at ease in the world, then Bob and Charlotte return to their lives in a different state—relieved and centered. There are also limitations to the love Bob and Charlotte experience. They fail to engage in social transformation and remain unaware of how colonial, global capital structures the love they share. In a colonial context, both personal and social transformation are necessary for settlers, like Bob and Charlotte, to imagine and live a form of life different from their colonial ones.

In chapter eight, *On the Rocks* points to both a critical and constructive account of love primarily through Laura and Felix's experiences of emotional labor, exhaustion, and unhappiness. If emotional labor is the task of managing the emotions of the self and others, then Laura and Felix are constantly engaged in such tasks. Dean (Marlon Wayans), Laura's husband, generates emotional labor for her through his odd behavior and his lack of appreciation. And her emotional labor occurs within the context of an unrelenting and emotionally monotonous daily routine. Where Laura is simply trying to survive, Felix's emotional labor is productive, primarily producing in others the experiences of recognition and affirmation. Emotional labor is, however, not without hidden costs, such as the inability to process the impacts of exhaustion on the body. Laura's relationship with her extended family and Vanessa (Jenny Slate) exhausts her. By contrast, however, Laura experiences Felix as both exhausting and energizing. She also experiences unhappiness. Drawing from feminist Sara Ahmed, the image of a happy housewife appears in eighteen-century philosopher Jean-Jacques Rousseau. He claims that a housewife must align her happiness to the happiness of others, and the philosopher substantiates his claims from a self-justifying appeal to nature. Like Rousseau, Felix's misogyny uses self-justifying appeals to nature, through which he expresses his desire for control and his denigration of marriage. At first, Laura experiences only ephemeral flashes of unhappiness, but with Felix, she explores her unhappiness in moments of vulnerability and anger. Because Laura and Felix's vulnerability suggests a more expansive definition of emotional labor, the film offers both a critical and constructive account of the relationship between love and emotional labor.

Through our treatment of masculinity, sexual politics, bodies, and love, we hope that the diversity and range of the approaches we use suggest that Coppola's films are, at a structural level, incredibly complex and rich texts for scholarly reflection. While her work is often minimal and spare on the surface, there are depths that those surfaces betray, depths that can animate a wide variety of conversations. And, as we will demonstrate in the conclusion, we hope our reflection here broadens the scope of feminist reflection on Coppola's work, pressing more deeply into fourth-wave feminist reflection, particularly with regard to race. We begin not only with a reflection on masculinity, but on what might be a blueprint for imagining what entering a different form of masculinity might look like in what might be our favorite of Coppola's film, *Somewhere*.

## REFERENCES

"A Short History of Bill Murray's Offscreen Antics." *Rolling Stone*, June 12, 2014. www.rollingstone.com/culture/culture-lists/a-short-history-of-bill-murrays-offscreen-antics-10501/bill-murray-mcs-eric-claptons-crossroads-guitar-festival-220504/.

*A Very Murray Christmas*. Sofia Coppola, director. 2015; Netflix: Los Gatos, CA, 2015. Streaming. www.netflix.com/title/80042368.

Alcoff, Linda Martín. *Visible Identities: Race, Gender, and the Self*. New York: Oxford University Press, 2006.

Atad, Corey. "Lost in Adaptation." *Slate*, June 20, 2017. slate.com/culture/2017/06/sofia-coppolas-whitewashed-new-movie-the-beguiled.html.

Aylward, Christine. "Sit Down with Sofia Coppola in this Exclusive Interview." *MakingOf*, May 31, 2011. www.youtube.com/watch?v=iH4vaTKTgXw.

Bahr, Lindsey. "Review: Sofia Coppola's 'On the Rocks' Is a Modest Delight." *AP News*, October 1, 2020. apnews.com/article/film-reviews-sofia-coppola-marlon-wayans-archive-rashida-jones-04faf1c620d32b15272923c694cfb2a9.

Bartky, Sandra Lee. *Femininity and Domination: Studies in the Phenomenology of Oppression*. New York: Routledge, 1990.

Bell, Keaton. "Sofia Coppola on the 20th Anniversary of *The Virgin Suicides*: 'It Means a Lot to Me That It Has a Life Now.'" *Vogue*, April 21, 2020. www.vogue.com/article/sofia-coppola-interview-the-virgin-suicides-20th-anniversary.

Bland, Simon. "'I Never Expected People to Connect with it So Much'–Sofia Coppola on *Lost in Translation* at 15." *Little White Lies*, August 26, 2018. lwlies.com/articles/sofia-coppola-lost-in-translation-interview/.

Blasberg, Derek. "Marc and Sofia: The Dreamy Team." *Harper's Bazaar*, August 13, 2014. www.harpersbazaar.com/fashion/designers/a3169/marc-jacobs-sofia-coppola-0914/.

Busis, Hillary. "Bill Murray Crashes NYC Kickball Game." *Entertainment Weekly*, October 15, 2012. ew.com/article/2012/10/15/bill-murray-kickball-game/.

Butler, Judith P. *Precarious Life: The Powers of Mourning and Violence*. London: Verso, 2004.

Cannon, Kay and Matt Hubbard. *30 Rock*. Season 5, episode 22, "Everything Sunny All the Time Always." Directed by John Riggi. Aired April 28, 2011, NBC. www.netflix.com/title/70136124.

Carew, Anthony. "Sofia Coppola." *Screen Education* 81 (April 2016): 93–105.

Chafey, Alex. "Rachel Bilson Speaks Out Against Sofia Coppola's *The Bling Ring*." *The Guardian*, July 5, 2013. www.theguardian.com/film/2013/jul/05/rachel-bilson-sofia-coppola-bling-ring.

Chang, Justin. "Review: Bill Murray and Sofia Coppola Reunite in 'On the Rocks,' with Mixed Results." *Los Angeles Times*, September 22, 2020. www.latimes.com/entertainment-arts/movies/story/2020-09-22/on-the-rocks-review-apple-bill-murray.

Cooper, Brittney. "Intersectionality." In *The Oxford Handbook of Feminist Theory*, edited by Lisa Disch and Mary Hawkesworth, 385–406. Oxford: Oxford UP, 2016.

Coppola, Sofia. "Sofia Coppola Responds to 'The Beguiled' Backlash—Exclusive." *IndieWire*, July 15, 2017. www.indiewire.com/2017/07/sofia-coppola-the-beguiled-backlash-response-1201855684/.

Crenshaw, Kimberlé. *On Intersectionality: Selected Writings*. New York: The New Press, 2019.

Crispin, Jessa. "Six Theories About Sofia Coppola." *Caesura*, May 27, 2021. caesuramag.org/posts/jessa-crispin-six-theories-sofia-coppola.

Donaldson, Kayleigh. "Joker's Insane Venice Film Festival Win Explained." *ScreenRant*, September 11, 2019. screenrant.com/joker-film-festival-win-venice-golden-lion-explained/.

"DP/30: *Somewhere*, Writer/director Sofia Coppola." *DP/30: The Oral History Of Hollywood*, August 28, 2011. www.youtube.com/watch?v=0Wmbm5f50OA&t=36s.

Ebert, Roger. "Pretty in Pink." *RogerEbert.com*, October 19, 2006. www.rogerebert.com/reviews/marie-antoinette-2006.

Ehrlich, David. "'On the Rocks' Review: Sofia Coppola Reunites with Bill Murray for a Fizzy Comedy About the Cost of Being Cool." *IndieWire*, September 22, 2020. www.indiewire.com/2020/09/on-the-rocks-review-sofia-coppola-1234588107/.

Erbland, Kate. "Why Sofia Coppola Should Not Make a Studio Movie." *IndieWire*, July 7, 2017. www.indiewire.com/2017/07/sofia-coppola-studio-movie-1201851385/.

Ferguson, Ann and Margaret E. Toye. "Feminist Love Studies—Editors' Introduction." *Hypatia* 32, no. 1 (2017): 1–14.

Fienberg, Daniel. "'A Very Murray Christmas': TV Review." *The Hollywood Reporter*, December 1, 2015. www.hollywoodreporter.com/tv/tv-reviews/a-very-murray-christmas-tv-844898/.

Fixmer-Oraiz, Natalie and Julia T. Wood. *Gendered Lives: Communication, Gender, and Culture*. Boston: Cengage, 2019.

Garcia, Patricia. "Mutual Appreciation: Marc Jacobs and Sofia Coppola's Long-Term Fashion Love Affair." *Vogue*, June 6, 2011. www.vogue.com/article/mutual-appreciation-marc-jacobs-and-sofia-coppolas-long-term-fashion-love-affair.

Gefter, Philip. "Sofia Coppola on Pictures." *Aperture*, May 30, 2018. aperture.org/editorial/sofia-coppola-pictures/.

Gevinson, Tavi. "Editor's Letter." *Rookie Magazine*, June 3, 2013. www.rookiemag.com/2013/06/editors-letter-20/.

Grosz, Elizabeth. *Volatile Bodies: Toward a Corporeal Feminism*. Bloomington: Indiana University Press, 1994.

Handyside, Fiona. *Sofia Coppola: A Cinema of Girlhood*. London: I.B. Tauris, 2017.
hooks, bell. *All About Love: New Visions*. New York: William Morrow and Company, 2000.
———. *Communion: The Female Search for Love*. New York: William Morrow and Company, 2002.
———. *Salvation: Black People and Love*. New York: William Morrow and Company, 2001.
———. *The Will to Change: Men, Masculinity, and Love*. New York: Atria Books, 2004. iBooks.
Hornaday, Ann. "'On the Rocks' Has All the Right Ingredients: Bill Murray, Rashida Jones, Sofia Coppola. But It's a Flavorless Dish." *The Washington Post*, October 6, 2020. www.washingtonpost.com/goingoutguide/movies/on-the-rocks-movie-review/2020/10/06/65c68980-01b3-11eb-b7ed-141dd88560ea_story.html.
James, Kendra. "'The Beguiled' Sanitizes Racism by Masking It with the Pretty Faces of Nicole Kidman and Elle Fanning." *Marie Claire*, June 23, 2017. www.marieclaire.com/celebrity/news/a27844/beguiled-racism-black-erasure/.
Jennifer C. Nash, "Practicing Love: Black Feminism, Love-Politics, and Post-Intersectionality," *Meridians* 11, no. 2 (2011): 1–24.
Jennings, Sheri. "Sofia Coppola's 'Somewhere' Wins Top Venice Prize." *The Washington Times*, September 11, 2010. www.washingtontimes.com/news/2010/sep/11/sofia-coppolas-somewhere-wins-top-venice-prize/utm_source=RSS_Feed&utm_medium=RSS.
King, Geoff. *Lost in Translation*. Edinburgh: Edinburgh University Press, 2010.
KrolØkke, Charlotte and Anne Scott. *Gender Communication Theories and Analyses: From Silence to Performance*. London: Sage Publications, 2006.
Lane, Anthony. "'The Beguiled' and 'The Big Sick.'" *The New Yorker*, June 19, 2017. www.newyorker.com/magazine/2017/06/26/the-beguiled-and-the-big-sick.
Laurier, Joanne. "Sofia Coppola's *The Beguiled*: Historical Drama with Hardly Any History." *WSWS.org*, July 7, 2017. www.wsws.org/en/articles/2017/07/07/begu-j07.html.
*Lost in Translation*. Sofia Coppola, director. 2003; Los Angeles CA: Universal Pictures Home Entertainment, 2003. DVD.
"Lost in Translation." *The Golden Globes*. www.goldenglobes.com/film/lost-translation.
Lyman, Eric J. "Sofia Coppola wins Venice's Golden Lion." *The Hollywood Reporter*, September 11, 2010. www.hollywoodreporter.com/business/business-news/sofia-coppola-wins-venices-golden-27685/.
Macfarlane, Steve. "Review: *The Beguiled*." *Slant Magazine*, June 22, 2017. www.slantmagazine.com/film/the-beguiled/.
*Marie Antoinette*. Sofia Coppola, director. 2006; San Francisco, CA: American Zoetrope, 2007. DVD.
"MILKFED." *Milkfed Official Site*. milkfed.jp/en/.
Miller, Julie. "Bill Murray Took Engagement Photos with a Couple He Had Never Met." *Vanity Fair*, June 11, 2014. www.vanityfair.com/hollywood/2014/06/bill-murray-crash-engagement-photo.

Morris, Wesley and Jenna Wortham. "History's Crucial Role in the Films 'All Eyez on Me' and 'The Beguiled.'" *Still Processing*, June 29, 2017. www.nytimes.com/2017/06/29/podcasts/historys-crucial-role-in-the-films-all-eyez-on-me-and-the-beguiled.html.

Moylan, Brian. "*A Very Murray Christmas*: Bill and Friends' Happy Hipster Holiday." *The Guardian*, December 4, 2015. www.theguardian.com/tv-and-radio/2015/dec/04/a-very-murray-christmas-george-clooney-netflix-special.

"Music Winners: 1975 Oscars." *Oscars*, February 4, 2016. www.youtube.com/watch?v=WMZjdqD2CTg.

N.B. "Sofia Coppola on Being a Pioneer for Women Directors." *The Economist*, June 30, 2017. www.economist.com/prospero/2017/06/30/sofia-coppola-on-being-a-pioneer-for-women-directors.

Neroni, Hilary. *Feminist Film Theory and Cléo from 5 to 7*. New York: Bloomsbury, 2016.

*On the Rocks*. Sofia Coppola, director. 2020; New York City: A24, 2020. Streaming. tv.apple.com/us/movie/on-the-rocks/umc.cmc.1mydlea6wicrm013138speg6m.

Peretz, Evegina. "Something About Sofia." *Vanity Fair*, September 2006. archive.vanityfair.com/article/2006/9/something-about-sofia.

Porter, Rick. "Sofia Coppola Developing Edith Wharton Drama at Apple." *The Hollywood Reporter*, May 12, 2020. www.hollywoodreporter.com/tv/tv-news/sofia-coppola-developing-edith-wharton-drama-at-apple-1294356/.

Reilly, Phoebe. "'The Beguiled': How Sofia Coppola Reimagined a Macho Seventies War Film," *Rolling Stone*, June 22, 2017. www.rollingstone.com/movies/movie-features/the-beguiled-how-sofia-coppola-reimagined-a-macho-seventies-war-film-200432/.

Rickey, Carrie. "Lost and Found." *DGA Quarterly*, Spring 2013. http://www.dga.org/Craft/DGAQ/All-Articles/1302-Spring-2013/Sofia-Coppola.aspx.

Righetti, Jamie and Eric Kohn. "Cannes Film Festival: 40 Movies That Got Booed." *IndieWire*, May 26, 2017. www.indiewire.com/2017/05/movies-booed-cannes-film-festival-1201831444/.

Rogers, Anna Backman. *Sofia Coppola: The Politics of Visual Pleasure*. New York: Berghahn, 2019.

Rogers, Anna. "Sofia Coppola." *Senses of Cinema* 45 (November 2007). http://www.sensesofcinema.com/2007/great-directors/sofia-coppola/.

Ryan, Maureen. "TV Review: 'A Very Murray Christmas.'" *Variety*, December 1, 2015. variety.com/2015/tv/reviews/bill-murray-a-very-murray-christmas-netflix-review-1201639889/.

Satenstein, Liana. "Sofia Coppola and Zoe Cassavetes Look Back on Their Cult '90s It Girl Show." *Vogue*, May 29, 2020. www.vogue.com/article/sofia-coppola-zoe-cassavetes-hi-octane-90s-show-interview.

Scott, A. O. "A Lonely Petit Four a Queen." *New York Times*, September 13, 2006. www.nytimes.com/2006/10/13/movies/13mari.html?ref=movies.

Sharf, Zack. "'Lost in Translation,' 15 Years Later: Sofia Coppola on Ending the Film on Her Terms and the Year It Took to Cast Bill Murray." *IndieWire*, August

27, 2018. www.indiewire.com/2018/08/lost-in-translation-15th-anniversary-sofia-coppola-interview-ending-whisper-meaning-1201998010/.

———. "Cannes 2017: Sofia Coppola Makes History as the Second Female Filmmaker to Win Best Director." *IndieWire*, May 28, 2017. www.indiewire.com/2017/05/cannes-sofia-coppola-best-director-beguiled-1201833491/.

Sims, David. "Let Sofia Coppola's New Film Transport You." *The Atlantic*, October 21, 2020. www.theatlantic.com/culture/archive/2020/10/sofia-coppolas-on-the-rocks-movie/616802/.

Smaill, Belinda. "Sofia Coppola." *Feminist Media Studies* 13, no. 1 (2013): 148–162.

"Sofia Coppola: Career in Four Minutes." *Total Film*, July 3, 2013. www.youtube.com/watch?v=Xszf3TvSnaA&t=45s.

"Sofia Coppola." *Charlie Rose*, September 18, 2003. charlierose.com/videos/13710.

*Somewhere*. Sofia Coppola, director. 2010; Universal City, CA: Focus Features, 2011. DVD.

"*Somewhere*: About the Production." *Focus Features*, August 16, 2010. www.focusfeatures.com/article/somewhere__about__the_production.

Stern, Marlow. "Sofia Coppola Discusses 'Lost in Translation' on its 10th Anniversary." *Daily Beast*, September 12, 2013. www.thedailybeast.com/sofia-coppola-discusses-lost-in-translation-on-its-10th-anniversary.

Stevens, Dana. "Queen Bees Sofia Coppola and Marie Antoinette Have a Lot in Common." *Slate*, October 19, 2006. slate.com/culture/2006/10/marie-antoinette-reviewed.html.

Stevens, Dana. "*The Beguiled*." *The Slate*, June 21, 2017. slate.com/culture/2017/06/the-beguiled-sofia-coppolas-new-movie-reviewed.html.

"Summer Talks | Sofia Coppola, 'The Bling Ring.'" *Film at Lincoln Center*, June 17, 2013. www.youtube.com/watch?v=DjUOgiwlk2w.

Tallerico, Brian. "Netflix's 'A Very Murray Christmas' Nails Its Target Audience." *RogerEbert.com*, December 2, 2015. www.rogerebert.com/streaming/netflixs-a-very-murray-christmas-nails-its-target-audience.

Tay, Sharon Lin. *Women on the Edge: Twelve Political Film Practices*. New York: Palgrave, 2009.

*The Bling Ring*. Sofia Coppola, director. 2013; New York City: A24, 2013. DVD.

"THE BLING RING—Behind the Scenes Part 1—Interview with Sofia Coppola." *StudiocanalUK*, June 14, 2013. www.youtube.com/watch?v=6bwH9dngayI.

*The Beguiled*. Sofia Coppola, director. 2017; Universal City, CA: Focus Features, 2017. DVD.

"The History of Venice Film Festival's Golden Lion." *Reuters*, September 12, 2020. www.youtube.com/watch?v=K-y6bIWbm9E.

*The Virgin Suicides*. Sofia Coppola, director. 1999; New York: The Criterion Collection, 2018. DVD.

Travers, Ben. "Review: 'A Very Murray Christmas' Deconstructs the Myth of Bill Murray to Magical Effect." *IndieWire*, November 18, 2015. www.indiewire.com/2015/11/review-a-very-murray-christmas-deconstructs-the-myth-of-bill-murray-to-magical-effect-53503/.

Underdown, Annabelle. "The Orientalist Implications of Sofia Coppola's 'Lost in Translation.'" *Screen Queens*, November 24, 2020.

screen-queens.com/2020/11/24/the-orientalist-implications-of-sofia-coppolas-lost-in-translation/.

Weiss, Gail. "A Genealogy of Women's (Un)Ethical Bodies." In *New Feminist Perspectives on Embodiment*, edited by Clara Fischer and Luna Dolezal, 17–35. London: Palgrave Macmillan, 2018.

White, Peter. "Apple & Sofia Coppola Developing Adaptation of Edith Wharton's Novel 'The Custom of The Country' for TV." *Deadline*, May 12, 2020. deadline.com/2020/05/apple-sofia-coppola-edith-whartons-novel-the-custom-of-the-country-1202932700/.

Wischover, Cheryl. "Sofia Coppola Goes from Muse to Full-On Collaborator for Vuitton Cruise Collection." *Fashionista*, June 9, 2011. fashionista.com/2011/06/sofia-coppola-role-as-muse-morphs-into-full-on-collaborator-for-vuitton-cruise-collection.

"WTF Podcast—Sofia Coppola." *WTF with Marc Maron Podcast*, May 2, 2021. www.youtube.com/watch?v=XbsWUugeOJE.

Wyatt, Justin. *The Virgin Suicides: Reverie, Sorrow and Young Love*. New York: Routledge, 2019.

Young, Iris Marion. *On Female Body Experience: "Throwing Like a Girl" and Other Essays*. Oxford: Oxford UP, 2005.

Zacherek, Stephanie. "Bill Murray and Rashida Jones Match Each Other Beat for Beat in Sofia Coppola's Wistful On the Rocks." *Time*, October 23, 2020. time.com/5903143/on-the-rocks-review-sofia-coppola/.

## NOTES

1. Evegina Peretz, "Something About Sofia," *Vanity Fair*, September 2006, accessed October 18, 2021, archive.vanityfair.com/article/2006/9/something-about-sofia.

2. Jamie Righetti and Eric Kohn, "Cannes Film Festival: 40 Movies That Got Booed," *IndieWire*, May 26, 2017, www.indiewire.com/2017/05/movies-booed-cannes-film-festival-1201831444/.

3. *30 Rock*, season 5, episode 22, "Everything Sunny All the Time Always," *30 Rock*, directed by John Riggi, written by Kay Cannon Matt Hubbard, aired April 28, 2011, NBC, www.netflix.com/title/70136124.

4. Natalie Fixmer-Oraiz and Julia T. Wood, *Gendered Lives: Communication, Gender, and Culture* (Boston: Cengage, 2019), 72.

5. N.B., "Sofia Coppola on Being a Pioneer for Women Directors," *The Economist*, June 30, 2017, www.economist.com/prospero/2017/06/30/sofia-coppola-on-being-a-pioneer-for-women-directors.

6. Ibid.

7. Jessa Crispin, "Six Theories About Sofia Coppola," *Caesura*, May 27, 2021, caesuramag.org/posts/jessa-crispin-six-theories-sofia-coppola.

8. Belinda Smaill, "Sofia Coppola," *Feminist Media Studies* 13, no. 1 (2013): 149.

9. Anthony Carew, "Sofia Coppola," *Screen Education* 81 (April 2016): 93.

10. Ibid., 103.

11. Carrie Rickey, "Lost and Found," *DGA Quarterly*, Spring 2013, www.dga.org/Craft/DGAQ/All-Articles/1302-Spring-2013/Sofia-Coppola.aspx.

12. Smaill, "Sofia Coppola," 155.

13. Anna Rogers, "Sofia Coppola," *Senses of Cinema* 45 (November 2007), www.sensesofcinema.com/2007/great-directors/sofia-coppola/.

14. "Music Winners: 1975 Oscars," *Oscars*, February 4, 2016, www.youtube.com/watch?v=WMZjdqD2CTg.

15. "WTF Podcast—Sofia Coppola," *WTF with Marc Maron Podcast*, May 2, 2021, www.youtube.com/watch?v=XbsWUugeOJE.

16. Rickey, "Lost and Found."

17. "WTF Podcast—Sofia Coppola."

18. Philip Gefter, "Sofia Coppola on Pictures," *Aperture*, May 30, 2018, aperture.org/editorial/sofia-coppola-pictures/.

19. Rickey, "Lost and Found."

20. Derek Blasberg, "Marc and Sofia: The Dreamy Team," *Harper's Bazaar*, August 13, 2014, www.harpersbazaar.com/fashion/designers/a3169/marc-jacobs-sofia-coppola-0914/.

21. Patricia Garcia, "Mutual Appreciation: Marc Jacobs and Sofia Coppola's Long-Term Fashion Love Affair," *Vogue*, June 6, 2011, www.vogue.com/article/mutual-appreciation-marc-jacobs-and-sofia-coppolas-long-term-fashion-love-affair.

22. Cheryl Wischover, "Sofia Coppola Goes from Muse To Full-On Collaborator for Vuitton Cruise Collection," *Fashionista*, June 9, 2011, fashionista.com/2011/06/sofia-coppola-role-as-muse-morphs-into-full-on-collaborator-for-vuitton-cruise-collection.

23. "MILKFED," *Milkfed Official Site*, accessed July 16, 2021, milkfed.jp/en/.

24. Coppola somewhat diminished the success of Milkfed in 2021, saying "It was an early 90s moment," and "It did well in Japan." "WTF Podcast—Sofia Coppola." However, Milk Fed was successful enough that, at the time she was promoting *Lost in Translation*, she claims to have made enough money from her fashion work to not need to make a living from her film's success. "Sofia Coppola," *Charlie Rose*, September 18, 2003, charlierose.com/videos/13710.

25. Liana Satenstein, "Sofia Coppola and Zoe Cassavetes Look Back on Their Cult '90s It Girl Show," *Vogue*, May 29, 2020, www.vogue.com/article/sofia-coppola-zoe-cassavetes-hi-octane-90s-show-interview.

26. Christine Aylward, "Sit Down with Sofia Coppola in this Exclusive Interview," *MakingOf*, May 31, 2011, www.youtube.com/watch?v=iH4vaTKTgXw.

27. Carew, "Sofia Coppola," 93.

28. "Sofia Coppola: Career in Four Minutes," *Total Film*, July 3, 2013, www.youtube.com/watch?v=Xszf3TvSnaA&t=45s.

29. Keaton Bell, "Sofia Coppola on the 20th Anniversary of *The Virgin Suicides*: 'It Means a Lot to Me That It Has a Life Now,'" *Vogue*, April 21, 2020, www.vogue.com/article/sofia-coppola-interview-the-virgin-suicides-20th-anniversary. See also Tavi Gevinson, "Editor's Letter," *Rookie Magazine*, June 03, 2013, www.rookiemag.com/2013/06/editors-letter-20/.

30. Zack Sharf, "'Lost In Translation,' 15 Years Later: Sofia Coppola on Ending the Film on Her Terms and the Year It Took to Cast Bill Murray," *IndieWire*, August 27, 2018, www.indiewire.com/2018/08/lost-in-translation-15th-anniversary-sofia-coppola-interview-ending-whisper-meaning-1201998010/.

31. Marlow Stern, "Sofia Coppola Discusses 'Lost in Translation' on its 10th Anniversary," *Daily Beast*, September 12, 2013, www.thedailybeast.com/sofia-coppola-discusses-lost-in-translation-on-its-10th-anniversary.

32. "Lost in Translation," *The Golden Globes*, accessed October 10, 2021, www.goldenglobes.com/film/lost-translation.

33. Simon Bland, "'I Never Expected People to Connect with it So Much'—Sofia Coppola on *Lost in Translation* at 15," *Little White Lies*, August 26, 2018, lwlies.com/articles/sofia-coppola-lost-in-translation-interview/.

34. Julie Miller, "Bill Murray Took Engagement Photos with a Couple He Had Never Met," *Vanity Fair*, June 11, 2014, www.vanityfair.com/hollywood/2014/06/bill-murray-crash-engagement-photo.

35. Hillary Busis, "Bill Murray Crashes NYC Kickball Game," *Entertainment Weekly*, October 15, 2012, ew.com/article/2012/10/15/bill-murray-kickball-game/.

36. "A Short History of Bill Murray's Offscreen Antics," *Rolling Stone*, June 12, 2014, www.rollingstone.com/culture/culture-lists/a-short-history-of-bill-murrays-offscreen-antics-10501/bill-murray-mcs-eric-claptons-crossroads-guitar-festival-220504/.

37. While writer Annabelle Underdown affirms the place of the film in wider film culture, she rightly notes the film's uninterrogated colonialism, a theme we explore in our chapter. Annabelle Underdown, "The Orientalist Implications of Sofia Coppola's 'Lost in Translation,'" *Screen Queens*, November 24, 2020, screen-queens.com/2020/11/24/the-orientalist-implications-of-sofia-coppolas-lost-in-translation/.

38. "WTF Podcast—Sofia Coppola."

39. Dana Stevens, "Queen Bees Sofia Coppola and Marie Antoinette Have a Lot in Common," *Slate*, October 19, 2006, slate.com/culture/2006/10/marie-antoinette-reviewed.html.

40. Sharon Lin Tay, *Women on the Edge: Twelve Political Film Practices* (New York: Palgrave, 2009), 134.

41. Roger Ebert, "Pretty in Pink," *RogerEbert.com*, October 19, 2006, www.rogerebert.com/reviews/marie-antoinette-2006.

42. A.O. Scott, "A Lonely Petit Four a Queen," *New York Times*, September 13, 2006, www.nytimes.com/2006/10/13/movies/13mari.html?ref=movies.

43. "DP/30: *Somewhere*, Writer/director Sofia Coppola," *DP/30: The Oral History Of Hollywood*, August 28, 2011, www.youtube.com/watch?v=0Wmbm5f50OA&t=36s.

44. Ibid.

45. "The History of Venice Film Festival's Golden Lion," *Reuters*, September 12, 2020, www.youtube.com/watch?v=K-y6blWbm9E. Recently, several films that have won the Golden Lion have also won the Academy Award for Best Picture. See Kayleigh Donaldson, "Joker's Insane Venice Film Festival Win Explained," *ScreenRant*, September 11, 2019, screenrant.com/joker-film-festival-win-venice-golden-lion-explained/.

46. Eric J. Lyman, "Sofia Coppola wins Venice's Golden Lion," *The Hollywood Reporter*, September 11, 2010, www.hollywoodreporter.com/business/business-news/sofia-coppola-wins-venices-golden-27685/.

47. Sheri Jennings, "Sofia Coppola's 'Somewhere' Wins Top Venice Prize," *The Washington Times*, September 11, 2010, www.washingtontimes.com/news/2010/sep/11/sofia-coppolas-somewhere-wins-top-venice-prize/?utm_source=RSS_Feed&utm_medium=RSS.

48. Kate Erbland, "Why Sofia Coppola Should Not Make a Studio Movie," *IndieWire*, July 7, 2017, www.indiewire.com/2017/07/sofia-coppola-studio-movie-1201851385/.

49. "*Somewhere*: About the Production," *Focus Features*, August 16, 2010, www.focusfeatures.com/article/somewhere__about__the_production.

50. "Summer Talks | Sofia Coppola, 'The Bling Ring,'" *Film at Lincoln Center*, June 17, 2013, www.youtube.com/watch?v=DjUOgiwlk2w.

51. "THE BLING RING—Behind the Scenes Part 1—Interview with Sofia Coppola," *StudiocanalUK*, June 14, 2013, www.youtube.com/watch?v=6bwH9dngayI.

52. Alex Chafey, "Rachel Bilson Speaks Out Against Sofia Coppola's *The Bling Ring*," *The Guardian*, July 5, 2013, www.theguardian.com/film/2013/jul/05/rachel-bilson-sofia-coppola-bling-ring.

53. Ibid.

54. Ibid.

55. "Summer Talks | Sofia Coppola, 'The Bling Ring,'" *Film at Lincoln Center*.

56. Ibid.

57. See for example, Maureen Ryan, "TV Review: 'A Very Murray Christmas,'" *Variety*, December 1, 2015, variety.com/2015/tv/reviews/bill-murray-a-very-murray-christmas-netflix-review-1201639889/. See also Brian Tallerico, "Netflix's 'A Very Murray Christmas' Nails Its Target Audience," *RogerEbert.com*, December 2, 2015, www.rogerebert.com/streaming/netflixs-a-very-murray-christmas-nails-its-target-audience. See also Brian Moylan, "*A Very Murray Christmas*: Bill and Friends' Happy Hipster Holiday," *The Guardian*, December 4, 2015, www.theguardian.com/tv-and-radio/2015/dec/04/a-very-murray-christmas-george-clooney-netflix-special. See also Ben Travers, "Review: 'A Very Murray Christmas' Deconstructs the Myth of Bill Murray to Magical Effect," *IndieWire*, November 18, 2015, www.indiewire.com/2015/11/review-a-very-murray-christmas-deconstructs-the-myth-of-bill-murray-to-magical-effect-53503/. See also Daniel Fienberg, "'A Very Murray Christmas': TV Review," *The Hollywood Reporter*, December 1, 2015, www.hollywoodreporter.com/tv/tv-reviews/a-very-murray-christmas-tv-844898/.

58. Phoebe Reilly, "'The Beguiled': How Sofia Coppola Reimagined a Macho Seventies War Film," *Rolling Stone*, June 22, 2017, www.rollingstone.com/movies/movie-features/the-beguiled-how-sofia-coppola-reimagined-a-macho-seventies-war-film-200432/.

59. Zack Sharf, "Cannes 2017: Sofia Coppola Makes History as the Second Female Filmmaker to Win Best Director," *IndieWire*, May 28, 2017, www.indiewire.com/2017/05/cannes-sofia-coppola-best-director-beguiled-1201833491/.

60. Sofia Coppola, "Sofia Coppola Responds to 'The Beguiled' Backlash—Exclusive," *IndieWire*, July 15, 2017, www.indiewire.com/2017/07/sofia-coppola-the-beguiled-backlash-response-1201855684/.
61. Ibid.
62. Ibid.
63. Ibid.
64. Ibid.
65. Ibid.
66. Anthony Lane, "'The Beguiled' and 'The Big Sick,'" *The New Yorker*, June 19, 2017, www.newyorker.com/magazine/2017/06/26/the-beguiled-and-the-big-sick.
67. Dana Stevens, "*The Beguiled*," *The Slate*, June 21, 2017, slate.com/culture/2017/06/the-beguiled-sofia-coppolas-new-movie-reviewed.html.
68. Joanne Laurier, "Sofia Coppola's *The Beguiled*: Historical Drama with Hardly Any History," *WSWS.org*, July 7, 2017, www.wsws.org/en/articles/2017/07/07/begu-j07.html.
69. Ibid.
70. Steve Macfarlane, "Review: *The Beguiled*," *Slant Magazine*, June 22, 2017, www.slantmagazine.com/film/the-beguiled/.
71. Kendra James, "'The Beguiled' Sanitizes Racism by Masking It with the Pretty Faces of Nicole Kidman and Elle Fanning," *Marie Claire*, June 23, 2017, www.marieclaire.com/celebrity/news/a27844/beguiled-racism-black-erasure/.
72. Corey Atad, "Lost in Adaptation," *Slate*, June 20, 2017, slate.com/culture/2017/06/sofia-coppolas-whitewashed-new-movie-the-beguiled.html.
73. Wesley Morris and Jenna Wortham, "History's Crucial Role in the Films 'All Eyez on Me' and 'The Beguiled,'" *Still Processing*, June 29, 2017, www.nytimes.com/2017/06/29/podcasts/historys-crucial-role-in-the-films-all-eyez-on-me-and-the-beguiled.html.
74. Rick Porter, "Sofia Coppola Developing Edith Wharton Drama at Apple," *The Hollywood Reporter*, May 12, 2020, www.hollywoodreporter.com/tv/tv-news/sofia-coppola-developing-edith-wharton-drama-at-apple-1294356/. See also Peter White, "Apple & Sofia Coppola Developing Adaptation of Edith Wharton's Novel 'The Custom of The Country' For TV," *Deadline*, May 12, 2020, deadline.com/2020/05/apple-sofia-coppola-edith-whartons-novel-the-custom-of-the-country-1202932700/.
75. Justin Chang, "Review: Bill Murray and Sofia Coppola Reunite in 'On the Rocks,' with Mixed Results," *Los Angeles Times*, September 22, 2020, www.latimes.com/entertainment-arts/movies/story/2020-09-22/on-the-rocks-review-apple-bill-murray.
76. Stephanie Zacherek, "Bill Murray and Rashida Jones Match Each Other Beat for Beat in Sofia Coppola's Wistful *On the Rocks*," *Time*, October 23, 2020, time.com/5903143/on-the-rocks-review-sofia-coppola/.
77. David Sims, "Let Sofia Coppola's New Film Transport You," *The Atlantic*, October 21, 2020, www.theatlantic.com/culture/archive/2020/10/sofia-coppolas-on-the-rocks-movie/616802/.
78. Lindsey Bahr, "Review: Sofia Coppola's 'On the Rocks' Is a Modest Delight," *AP News*, October 1, 2020, apnews.com/

article/film-reviews-sofia-coppola-marlon-wayans-archive-rashida-jones
04faf1c620d32b15272923c694cfb2a9.

79. Ann Hornaday, "'On the Rocks' Has All the Right Ingredients: Bill Murray, Rashida Jones, Sofia Coppola. But It's a Flavorless Dish," *The Washington Post*, October 6, 2020, www.washingtonpost.com/goingoutguide/movies/on-the-rocks-movie-review/2020/10/06/65c68980-01b3-11eb-b7ed-141dd88560ea_story.html.

80. David Ehrlich, "'On the Rocks' Review: Sofia Coppola Reunites with Bill Murray for a Fizzy Comedy About the Cost of Being Cool," *IndieWire*, September 22, 2020, www.indiewire.com/2020/09/on-the-rocks-review-sofia-coppola-1234588107/.

81. Ibid.

82. Ibid.

83. Anna Backman Rogers, *Sofia Coppola: The Politics of Visual Pleasure* (New York: Berghahn, 2019), 5.

84. Geoff King, *Lost in Translation* (Edinburgh: Edinburgh University Press, 2010), 134–140.

85. Ibid., 85.

86. Ibid., 99.

87. bell hooks, *The Will to Change: Men, Masculinity, and Love* (New York: Atria Books, 2004), iBooks.

88. Ibid.

89. Ibid.

90. Charlotte Kroløkke and Anne Scott, *Gender Communication Theories and Analyses: From Silence to Performance* (London: Sage Publications, Inc., 2006), 2–3.

91. Ibid., 7–8.

92. Hilary Neroni, *Feminist Film Theory and Cléo from 5 to 7* (New York: Bloomsbury, 2016), 5.

93. Ibid., 53.

94. Rogers, *Sofia Coppola*, 163.

95. Handyside, *Sofia Coppola*, 162.

96. Ibid.

97. Gail Weiss, "A Genealogy of Women's (Un)Ethical Bodies," in *New Feminist Perspectives on Embodiment*, eds. Clara Fischer and Luna Dolezal (London: Palgrave Macmillan, 2018), 29.

98. Ibid., 25.

99. Elizabeth Grosz, *Volatile Bodies: Toward a Corporeal Feminism* (Bloomington: Indiana UP, 1994), 192–3 and 206–8.

100. Margaret Whitford, "Irigaray's Body Symbolic," *Hypatia* 6, no. 3 (Autumn 1991): 104.

101. Ibid., 98.

102. For other phenomenologies of the female body, see Iris Marion Young, *On Female Body Experience: "Throwing Like a Girl" and Other Essays* (Oxford: Oxford UP, 2005). Sandra Lee Bartky, *Femininity and Domination: Studies in the Phenomenology of Oppression* (New York: Routledge, 1990). Linda Martín Alcoff, *Visible Identities: Race, Gender, and the Self* (New York: Oxford University Press, 2006).

103. Judith P. Butler, *Precarious Life: The Powers of Mourning and Violence*, (London: Verso, 2004), 43.

104. Ibid., 42.

105. Brittney Cooper, "Intersectionality," in *The Oxford Handbook of Feminist Theory*, eds. Lisa Disch and Mary Hawkesworth (Oxford: Oxford UP, 2016), 387. See also Kimberlé Crenshaw, *On Intersectionality: Selected Writings* (New York: The New Press 2019).

106. Jennifer C. Nash, "Practicing Love: Black Feminism, Love-Politics, and Post-Intersectionality," *Meridians* 11, no. 2 (2011): 8–9.

107. Ibid., 11.

108. bell hooks, *All About Love: New Visions* (New York: William Morrow and Company, 2000), xxviii-xxvii.

109. bell hooks, *Salvation: Black People and Love* (New York: William Morrow and Company, 2001), xxiv.

110. bell hooks, *Communion: The Female Search for Love* (New York: William Morrow and Company, 2002), xix.

111. Ann Ferguson and Margaret E. Toye, "Feminist Love Studies—Editors' Introduction," *Hypatia* 32, no. 1 (2017): 1–2.

# PART I
*MASCULINITY*

*Chapter One*

# An Alternative Masculinity

## *The Habitus of Vulnerability, Presence, and Mundane Delight in* Somewhere

In her reading of Coppola's fourth feature film, *Somewhere*, scholar of feminist philosophy and visual culture, Anna Backman Rogers, argues that many films present male subjects as imperfect examples of masculine ideas, unable to fully realize the unattainable standard of masculine power and authority. As feminist scholars have argued, such representations establish these failures or "cycles of crisis and fracture" only to inevitably "re-establish," masculinity's "central convictions more strongly."[1] Male characters, however, often recover from their failure and conform to the ideal image of power and authority. Rogers argues that *Somewhere* portrays its central character, Johnny Marco (Stephen Dorff), as inhabiting a similar cycle of crisis and disruption. However, the film challenges the pattern of re-establishment. Unlike the *Die Hard* and *Lethal Weapon* franchises, in which images of hard masculinity are reinstated at the end of the film, "*Somewhere* . . . tears asunder this image . . . replacing strength with vulnerability."[2] This chapter extends Rogers' insights, particularly regarding masculinity, cycles, and vulnerability. We submit that *Somewhere*, through its depiction of Johnny's *habitus,* or his formation, offers a way of imagining an alternative to toxic forms of masculinity.

Our chapter unfolds in six main sections. First, we open with anthropologist Saba Mahmood's account of *habitus*. In her work with Muslim women, she offers an alternative understanding of the way the veil functions in the lives of women. Beyond a mere symbol of oppression, the veil becomes a way of cultivating an interior life, through bodily acts, materiality, and imagining alternative ways of being in the world. Then, we turn to the connections between Federico Fellini's art-house classic *La Dolce Vita* (1960) and *Somewhere* and the role of the *inetto* figure in *La Dolce Vita*. These connections help establish the need for toxic masculinity as a way of looking at Johnny's behavior in the film. Coined by sociologist Tracy Karner, toxic masculinity describes the harmful cycles of behaviors men perform on others and themselves. Based on Mahmood and Karner, we begin an analysis of *Somewhere*, third, tracing the everyday life of action film star Johnny Marco. Through the materiality of his Ferrari, bodily acts of risky behaviors, and seeing women's bodies as sexual surfaces, Johnny inhabits toxic cycles of masculinity. The bodily presence of his daughter Cleo (Elle Fanning), however, disrupts those cycles, namely through various forms of juxtapositions and mundane delights. Next, when Johnny's ex-wife forces him to take Cleo to Italy for a film opening, Johnny and Cleo create an outline of an alternative *habitus*. Taken with their return home to Los Angeles, the outline of their alternative includes bodily acts of shared memory, shared delights and humor. During this period, Johnny resists the temptation to see women's bodies as sexual surfaces. Fifth, during one day together, the possibility of an alternative *habitus* comes into clearer view. They inhabit play, sensuousness, making up for lost time, and joy. Finally, when Johnny drops Cleo off at her summer camp, he returns to his normal life. His behavior, however, indicates that Cleo's bodily presence and the vulnerability and delight they share together has changed him. The film ends with Johnny on the threshold of an alternative masculinity. By way of conclusion, we offer four implications our reading of the film has for masculinity more broadly.

## MAHMOOD'S ACCOUNT OF *HABITUS*

In her article "Feminist Theory, Embodiment, and the Docile Agent: Some Reflections on the Egyptian Islamic Revival" (2001), anthropologist Saba Mahmood suggests that the concept of *habitus* offers an alternative to feminist philosopher Judith Butler's account of agency. Butler claims, on Mahmood's reading, that gender is not innate in humans. Rather, we learn and perform gender. Because, historically, patriarchal forces perform harm to women through these learned performances, the harmful norms of gender can and should be resisted, precisely at the site of bodily practices. However, Mahmood notes that "what remains intact," in Butler's analysis, "is the natural status accorded to the desire for resistance to social norms, and the incarceration of the notion of agency to the space of emancipatory politics."[3] Because Mahmood performs anthropological work in contexts outside of the West, she points out that Butler's account of resistance and liberation might not apply to every situation. Her work with Egyptian Muslim women demonstrates that agency and notions of the self can take other, non-Western forms.

Working with women who wear veils as a means of cultivating virtue, Mahmood suggests the word *habitus* offers one alternative to resistance and liberation. Rooted in the Aristotelean tradition, "*habitus* . . . refers to a specific pedagogical process by which moral virtues are acquired through a coordination of outward behavior (e.g. bodily acts, social demeanor) with inward dispositions (e.g. emotional states, thoughts, intentions)."[4] By this account of outward bodily practice and inward desire, "innate human desires" do not always produce outward conduct; rather, like a musician or an athlete, "it is the sequence of practices and actions one is engaged in that determines one's desires and emotions . . . it is through repeated bodily acts that one trains one's memory, desire and intellect."[5] As feminist reflection demonstrates, social forces and bodily acts have produced and continue to produce harm upon women's bodies and lives. Mahmood demonstrates that bodily acts can also cultivate virtue in human beings. Her analysis "necessitates a much deeper engagement with the architecture of the self that undergirds a particular mode of living."[6] Her work also suggests that "the desire for freedom and liberation is a historically situated desire whose motivational force cannot be assumed *a priori*."[7] While agency as resistance and liberation are vital, they need not be the only means by which agency and bodily acts might be thought.

As a case study of *habitus* at work, Mahmood's interviews with four Muslim women demonstrate how the veil, as a material object, functions in their lives to cultivate virtue. The women Mahmood interviewed were part of Egypt's Mosque Movement, in which large numbers of women responded to the perception that religious knowledge had become increasingly marginalized in daily life.[8] These women "mobilized to hold public meetings in mosques to teach each other Islamic doctrine, thereby altering the historically male-centered character of mosques as well as Islamic pedagogy."[9] Within that context, Mahmood's fieldwork centered on four middle-class women, in their late 30s, whom she describes as "virtuosos of piety."[10] One virtue that Muslims in general, but women in particular, are expected to cultivate is the virtue of shyness. In discussion with these women, Mahmood learned that candidness, self-confidence, and being outspoken could, indeed, be embodied in such a "way that was in keeping with Islamic standards of reserve, restraint and modesty required of pious Muslim women," even if reserve, restraint, and modesty were not qualities these women naturally inhabit.[11] These characteristics must be learned. One participant made explicit connection between the virtue and the bodily act of wearing a veil. "It's just like the veil (*hijab*)," she says, "In the beginning when you wear it, you're embarrassed (*maksufa*) . . . But . . . with time, your inside learns to feel shy without the veil, and if you were to take it off your entire being feels uncomfortable."[12] Mahmood concludes that the veil is not merely a symbol. Rather, "while wearing the veil at first serves as a means to tutor oneself," she suggests that "one cannot simply discard wearing the veil once a modest deportment has been acquired."[13] This way of interpreting a woman's use of a veil offers an alternative to typical understandings of the veil as a "symbolic . . . marker of women's subordination."[14] While Mahmood signals that the existence of the veil is, indeed, grounded in the logic of gender inequality, "there is more at stake in this [habitual] conception of veiling as a disciplinary practice."[15] In short, the symbolic import of the veil should not overshadow the veil's habitual status in the life of these women.

Mahmood's work suggests three important insights. First, as stated above, *habitus* demonstrates that inward desires and virtues can be cultivated through outward bodily acts. Second, the materiality (i.e., the veil) of those practices are internal to the cultivation of those virtues. The veil, for these women, cannot simply be discarded once internalization of virtue takes place. Therefore, to see the veil symbolically in terms of identity is to miss the deeper function of the veil. Materiality is internal to the process of becoming a more virtuous human. Third, and perhaps most important, *habitus* suggests that alternative modes of being in the world can be learned. Her language of "living" and "attachment" point to this reality.[16] If, for example, one of the women in Mahmood's study removed her veil, she would, in effect, likely be embarking on an alternative way of life with an alternative set of attachments.

Because *Somewhere* focuses on the experience of its male protagonist, Johnny Marco, Mahmood's account of *habitus* provides ways of explaining how bodily acts, materiality, and change are possible. However, Mahmood's description of virtue formation does not account for the particular dysfunctional masculinity Johnny inhabits. As a way of establishing the need to understand toxic masculinity, we begin with the relationship *Somewhere* has to *La Dolce Vita* and the *inetto* figure.

## *LA DOLCE VITA*, THE *INETTO* FIGURE, AND TOXIC MASCULINITY

The connections between Federico Fellini's *La Dolce Vita* and *Somewhere* and the role of the *inetto* figure in *La Dolce Vita* help establish the need for toxic masculinity as a way of looking at Johnny's behavior in the film. Film scholar Fiona Handyside outlines the important connections between *La Dolce Vita* and *Somewhere*. *Somewhere* "offers a series of refractions," she submits, which permit Coppola to "reframe" *La Dolce Vita*.[17] Handyside focuses on *Somewhere*'s use of Fellini's opening sequence. *La Dolce Vita* begins with a helicopter transporting a large statue of Jesus over Rome's city-scape. The main character—tabloid journalist Marcello Rubini (Marcello Mastroianni) and his photographer Paparazzo (Walter Santesso)—follow the statue in another helicopter. They eventually pass over a building with four women sunbathing, and they hover over the building. Marcello tries to talk with them, but the roar of the helicopter drowns out their voices. Fellini returns to this auditory device in the closing moments of the film. After a raucous party where Marcello publicly humiliates a woman, Marcello sits on a beach, away from his fellow partygoers. He sees Paola (Valeria Ciangottini), a waitress whom he met earlier in the film. She is trying to communicate with him, but Marcello cannot hear her over the sound of the ocean. Eventually, he gives up and walks away. In *Somewhere*, the film opens on a race track in the desert. In a single long take, the protagonist, Johnny Marco, drives his Ferrari sports car in circles around the track. After three laps, he gets out of the car and stands beside it, alone and isolated.

Handyside reads *Somewhere* in "a sustained comparison" to *La Dolce Vita*.[18] For example, both opening sequences establish setting and character, "through a particularly ostentatious mode of transport that speaks of masculinity, wealth, and individualism."[19] *Somewhere* also echoes *La Dolce Vita*'s opening in two other moments. In one scene, Johnny steps onto his balcony and sees a woman sunbathing on the balcony below. "She leans back against the railing and smiles up at Johnny, shot from his point-of-view, echoing Marcello's aerial perspective on sunbathing women" in *La Dolce Vita* opening sequence.[20] Coppola also uses Fellini's sonic motif of a helicopter sound drowning out human communication. Toward the end of *Somewhere*, Johnny and Cleo ride in a helicopter. After they got out of the helicopter, Johnny tries to apologize to Cleo, but she cannot hear him over the sound of the helicopter. "This scene," Handyside points out, "reprises both Marcello's helicopter noise and the image of the girl unable to communicate with a man, bringing together the beginning and the end" of Fellini's film.[21] But perhaps the more pronounced relationship between the films is between their protagonists. The films depict "the pampered world of wealthy individuals and suggest a moment of spiritual crisis, either through the figure of a film star Johnny Marco, or celebrity journalist, Marcello Rubini."[22] This link between Johnny and Marcello can be drawn more tightly together through the figure of *inetto*.

Comparative literature scholar Jacqueline Reich analyzes Marcello Mastroianni's career, particularly the films in which he played the figure of the *inetto*, or the passive, impotent man. The literary roots of the *inetto* reach back "to the mid-to-late-sixteenth-century theater, in particular the *commedia dell'arte*, whose characters and scenarios formed the foundation for much of Italian humor."[23] However, in the wake of the changing gendered landscape of the post-World War II era, Reich argues that the *inetto* figure registered a crisis of Italian masculinity. Far from a potent lover or a Hollywood hero, *inettos* "are defined not by action but, rather, by passivity . . . they are failures rather than successes, mired in bourgeois mediocrity."[24] In *La Dolce Vita*,

Marcello is an *inetto*, unable to choose between the life of a true journalist and a literary intellectual. As a result, "he semi-prostitutes himself" to tabloid publications, and "he succumbs to the temptations of bourgeois and aristocratic decadence."[25] As such, he "fails to accomplish anything," and his passivity is most acute "in his relationships with women."[26] As the film progresses, Marcello also descends into "moral emptiness," spiritual darkness, and social alienation.[27] Reich concludes her reading of *La Dolce Vita* saying, "Passive rather than active, conquered rather than conqueror," Mastroianni's portrayal of the tabloid journalist "reflects the crisis of masculinity in an Italy dominated by materialism and spiritual decadence," and his ultimate choice in dealing with this crisis are acts of "physical masochism."[28] We think this passing reference to masochism is vital, and we will return to it below.

While Johnny does bear similarities to Marcello's passivity, the figure of the *inetto* bears with it some limitations, particularly in reference to Johnny's toxic masculinity. Both Handyside and Reich's work helps explain features of Johnny's character. As we will discuss further below, he is a failure, especially in his relationships with women. He also succumbs to many of the trappings of a celebrity, bourgeois life, which leads a similar state of relational, moral, and social emptiness, alienation, and isolation. However, Reich's rendering of the *inetto* in *La Dolce Vita* does not adequately account for the toxic masculinity which characterizes features of Johnny's behavior. In the early twenty-first century popular culture, the term "toxic masculinity" has come to serve as "a catchall explanation for male violence and sexism . . . such as aggression and self-entitlement,"[29] which also can include "acts like bullying and catcalling."[30] But like many such terms that come from scholarship and enter the popular lexicon (like emotional labor, which we will discuss in our reading of *On the Rocks* [2020]), the origin of toxic masculinity is far more interesting and helpful.

In her study of Vietnam veterans suffering from post-traumatic stress disorder (PTSD), sociologist Tracy Karner implicitly describes the cycles or patterns of destructive behavior that these veterans performed. Her term, "toxic masculinity," describes the abusive behaviors, the implicit scripts that set them up for failure, and the harmful behaviors these men performed on themselves. Such toxicity is on full display during the concluding party sequence in *La Dolce Vita*. When asked to entertain the guests of the party, Marcello eventually erupts in what Reich rightfully describes as "physical masochism." Although she only mentions this violent behavior in passing, Marcello clearly engages in not only physically abusive behavior, he also engages in emotionally humiliating a female party goer. Toxic masculinity is important to name at this moment, because passivity is not the only feature of the *inetto*. Marcello's passivity culminates and finds its full expression in violence against women, in toxic behaviors. Even though Johnny (and Marcello) did not fight in Vietnam and likely have not experienced PTSD, Karner's insights suggest that many men can engage in cycles of behaviors that harm themselves and others. More than the mere powerless, or the passivity of the *inetto*, toxicity describes one set of outcomes that ineptitude or powerlessness can produce in the lives of men. And it is to Karner's account we now turn.

Veterans, during their childhood, internalized a script based on their fathers' masculinity and a more widespread cultural script boys and men were expected to inhabit. Many of the veterans' fathers proudly served in World War II and returned home to widespread praise, to nuclear families, and to steady jobs. However, "[m]any of these fathers," Karner writes, "were violent, strict, authoritarian men with alcohol problems."[31] It is also likely that, as boys, these sons encountered what sociologist Deborah S. David and psychiatrist Robert Brannon describe as the four key elements of a script men and boys are expected to inhabit: "1. No Sissy Stuff: The stigma of all stereotyped feminine characteristics and qualities, including openness and vulnerability. 2. The Big Wheel: Success, status, and the need to be looked up to. 3. The Sturdy Oak: A manly air of toughness, confidence, and self-reliance. 4. Give 'Em Hell!: The aura of aggression, violence, and daring."[32] Psychologist William Pollack elaborates on this script, noting that boys are expected to "bury those feelings" of "dependence, warmth, empathy"; they must also "repress feelings of failure or unhappiness."[33] The script also calls them to embrace "the misconception that somehow boys are biologically wired to act . . . macho [and] engage in risky behaviors."[34] Sociologist Michael Kimmel also notes that as these boys reach late adolescence, they often develop a strong sense of homophobia.[35]

Upon their return from Vietnam, these veterans engaged in patterns of toxic behavior, and they did so as a means of dealing with the shame of failing to live up to the scripts they inherited. What Karner calls "toxic masculinity" includes a wide range of self-destructive and violent behaviors, all of which reveal a desire for control. She includes risky behaviors like "excessive drinking,"[36] "self-medication" and "substance abuse."[37] They were also "prone to resort to physical violence against others or themselves to regain control" over those whom these men perceived to be disruptive to their immediate surroundings, like their wives.[38] Control was also a theme connected to their time in the military. Hierarchical structure minimized from some soldiers a "sense of control" that was experienced as "emasculating."[39] Taken together, their perceived failures and lack of control over their own reaction and those of others is part of what drove these men to assert control over themselves and others, through toxic behaviors of drinking, drugs, and violence.

From Karner, we discern at least one distinct toxic pattern of dysfunction that arises from the intersection of *habitus* and toxic masculinity. When society produces subjects, it cultivates desires, virtues, and vices through both bodily acts and scripts. However, failures to produce that subject occur in two ways, either through the failure of that script itself and/or the failure of individuals to live up to the script. The individual will likely experience failure in negative ways and attempt to control that negativity. Those attempts at control will likely take the form of bodily acts that harm one's own body and the bodies of others. The individual, however, can exit the script and the destructive practices used to maintain the script through, as Mahmood implies, an alternative *habitus*, or an alternative set of bodily acts that facilitate the taking on of alternative scripts, and alternative virtues. It is precisely this pattern, or what we call a "toxic cycle," that we see at play in *Somewhere*. This cycle, however, does not have the final word. Through disruption of that cycle, the film posits that an alternative *habitus* of masculinity is possible.

## ESTABLISHING AND DISRUPTING A TOXIC CYCLE

Coppola opens the film with Johnny's car, a symbol of his toxic *habitus*. Johnny drives an early 2000s era Ferrari 360 Modena. He takes laps on a racetrack, literally driving in circles. After completing three loops, Johnny stops the car, gets out, and stands next to it. He looks into the distance. This opening image functions as, perhaps, the fullest embodiment of Johnny's *habitus*, his toxic way of moving through the world. The Ferrari company describes its brand as "An icon of style, luxury, speed," and its "Prancing Horse" logo as a symbol of "luxury, exclusivity, performance, design and quality."[40] These claims are fueled, in part, by the company's long-held tradition of success in car races, especially Formula 1.[41] Drawing perhaps unintentionally on traits of masculinity, motoring journalist and former *Top Gear* host, Quentin Willson, describes the experience of driving high end sports cars, like a Ferrari, as "a very, very special sensation of courting death. It's as simple as that."[42] In addition to such risk-taking behavior, Ray Maranges, owner of one of the few 349 Ferrari Enzos ever made, describes driving a Ferrari this way: "Can I say it's better than sex?"[43] Drawing implicitly on these features, *Somewhere*'s producer Roman Coppola interprets the significance of his Ferrari in this way, "He has this incredible car, he has wealth and fame and opportunity, but he's stifled. The fact that you would have a car that goes 200 mph that you can only drive at 35 mph seems to relate to that character trait."[44]

Not merely a symbol of his toxic masculinity, the car is the materiality of Johnny's toxic habituation, which the opening image critiques. If, as

Mahmood says, the veil offers a means by which pious women can inhabit the virtue of shyness, then the car functions for Johnny like a dysfunctional veil. While the Ferrari is not merely a symbol of risk taking (i.e., "courting death") and powerful masculine sexuality (i.e., "better than sex), Coppola's opening image takes precisely Johnny's habitation with it as a dysfunctional form of masculinity. However, to exercise the full power, risk-taking, and eroticism of the car, Johnny drives the car in an auto-erotic gesture. He races alone, full-throttle, at a remote track in the desert, seemingly miles away from others. Rather than going "somewhere," Johnny's inhabitation of success, wealth, power, and sexuality brings him into a space of loneliness. Isolated from the world, he moves in circles, going "nowhere." This seed of loneliness, risk-taking, andsexuality is what Coppola unpacks in the opening section of the film.

Back at the Chateau Marmont, where many movie stars like Johnny have lived, the protagonist parties with friends when he suddenly falls down the stairs. In the next image, he lies in bed with a cast on his left arm. Twin sisters, Bambi (Kristina Shannon) and Cindy (Karissa Shannon), pole dance for him in his room. Johnny is falling asleep, as latter scenes will confirm, from mixing the pain medication and alcohol, both of which are on his lamp table. Perhaps in response to his inebriation, the women offer an obviously lackluster performance. With a flat emotional affect, they simply go through the motions. Once Johnny falls asleep, they gather their things and leave. These scenes present Johnny as both participating in masculine expectations and failing to meet those expectations. Johnny engages in risky behavior, partying with his friends, that leads to a bodily vulnerability, his broken arm. As a way of compensating for his vulnerability, he engages in sexual behavior that does not demand emotional vulnerability from him. However, having engaged again in the risky behavior of mixing pain medication and alcohol, he falls asleep during their performance, and is, thus, unable to engage in any sexual behavior with the girls. The first toxic cycle ends with Johnny unable to compensate for his bodily vulnerability. Rather, he ends the scene in a double state of vulnerability—passed out and with a broken arm.

This pattern continues in the next set of scenes. The following day, he enters his bathroom, touches his receding hairline, and takes two pills from a Propecia box on his sink, a treatment for his hair loss. He steps out on his balcony, smokes, and then takes a meal at a restaurant. Even though two women at the restaurant smile at him with sexual interest, he drinks alcohol and dines alone. During his meal, he receives the first in a series of anonymous texts, "Why are you such an asshole?" He raises an eyebrow in response, suggesting that, to some extent, this demeaning message affects him. Later, as he drives his Ferrari, a woman in another car smiles at him. Taking her smile as sexual interest, he follows her, until she disappears behind a gated driveway.

Disappointed, he returns to his room, and three models (Maryna Linchuk, Meghan Collison, and Jessica Miller) dressed like high-fashion vampires pass him. One of the models notices him, and he looks back at her, with apparent sexual interest. That night, he sits in his room and drinks alone. Out of that loneliness and risk taking, he invites Cindy and Bambi over to dance. As he lies on his bed, but awake this time, the women perform for him. With more life in their performance, they smile and make eye contact with him, but they still perform with a perfunctory, matter-of-fact-ness. After they finish, he smiles, applauds lightly, and says, "That was great," before turning to his drink. As one of the twins walks near him, he reaches out to her, attempting to bring her into bed with him, and calls her by the wrong name, Bambi. She pushes him away, "I'm Cindy, you moron." Bambi crawls on the bed with him. "I'm the other one." She kisses him and pops her bubble gum. On the pop, the screen cuts to black. Given the kiss and the manner in which he assumed to have access to Cindy's body (thinking it was Bambi's), the pop connotes an orgasmic overtone and the cut to black suggests that Johnny passed out again.

Like in the previous sequence, these events suggest two realities in the film: they confirm Johnny's cycle of toxic responses to failures, and they also establish a world in which women's bodies function as sexualized surfaces. Even though Johnny receives sexual attention, including a sexual encounter with Bambi, Johnny uses these so-called successes as compensation for his failures or vulnerabilities, which include his anxiety about hair loss, the anonymous texts, the woman in the car, and his loneliness. This sequence also highlights the reality that Johnny lives in a world where women's bodies constitute sexual surfaces, upon which he can assert his own desire. Whether it is the models who pass him, the women in the restaurant, the woman in the car, or Bambi, the film does not present these women as characters. These women rarely speak and tend to see Johnny as a locus of their own sexual desire. They are, rather, surfaces with no depth. The film presents most of these interactions as benign and consensual. However, with the woman in the car, Johnny's behavior brings him to the threshold of criminality, especially if the woman interpreted his toxic behavior as stalking. When Johnny compensate for failures, his primary responses include substances (like drinking, Propecia, and drugs) and the use of women's bodies as sexual surfaces.

The next morning, Johnny wakes in bed; however, he finds his daughter Cleo in his bed, signing her name on his cast. His ex-wife Layla is dropping Cleo off with Johnny for his day's visit. After lying to Layla about how he broke his harm, he drives Cleo to her ice-skating lesson. On the way, Johnny expresses an emotional vulnerability with her: he is paranoid that the paparazzo is following him. At her lesson, Cleo begins her routine. At first, Johnny's phone distracts him, but soon, Cleo's performance transfixes his attention. As he watches her, a range of reactions registers on his face. He seems impressed, touched, and concerned. As Johnny and Cleo will both state later in the film, Johnny has not been present in Cleo's life. At this moment, he appears concerned about the reality that there is a side of Cleo he knows nothing about, as if a world he had not imagined is now opening up to him for the first time. Once Cleo completes her routine, Johnny smiles and applauds loud enough for Cleo to hear it across the ice. Back in the car, he praises her, "You're really good." "Thanks," she replies. "When did you learn how to ice skate?" "I've been going for three years." "Really?" Johnny then looks in his rearview mirror and wonders out loud if the car behind them is the same one as before. Instead of dismissing his paranoia, Cleo pulls out her phone and types down the license plate number of the car. Johnny seems impressed in her clever solution to his paranoia.

Throughout this day, Cleo disrupts his toxic cycle, which the film presents through juxtapositions. In the shot previous to Cleo's introduction, Johnny was in bed with Bambi. Johnny wakes, however, to a different bodily presence, the presence of his daughter. Against the pop of Bambi's gum, which brings darkness to the screen, Cleo's marker writing on Johnny's cast wakes him. Her signature is the first signature on his cast, a sign that he has few friends who care enough about his body to attend to his bodily vulnerability with affection. She demonstrates her affection precisely at the site of his woundedness. During Bambi and Cindy's routine, Johnny gazes on their bodies and then distracts himself with alcohol once they are finished. In reverse order, Cleo begins her routine with Johnny in a state of distraction, this time by his phone. However, he looks on her body with a different form of attention. When he gazes at the twins, he sees them as surfaces which serve his toxic cycle. During their performance, the camera remains static. At different points during their dance, the camera cuts off portions of the women's bodies as they move off screen. Johnny's gaze, in effect, dismembers them. With Cleo, the camera remains in a fixed location but pans and tilts, following her every move, usually in wide shots of her whole body. Unlike his gaze upon the twins, his gaze upon Cleo elicits from him a wide range of reactions, drawing forth from him more of his humanity. While both performances elicit from Johnny smiles, applause, and compliments, his response to Cleo involves a more fulsome bodily act. He claps more loudly, responds more intensely, praises her more deeply. His praise also, unlike his interactions with the twins, exposes a relational vulnerability. Johnny does not know that she has been taking lessons for years. On the other hand, when Johnny mistakes Cindy for Bambi, she rightfully judges his error. However, Cleo does not judge Johnny's ignorance of her life or his paranoia. These disruptions and juxtapositions hint at an alternative *habitus* that Johnny might inhabit, a *habitus* that Cleo's bodily presence makes possible for him.

Over the next few days, however, the film returns Johnny to his toxic cycles, this time without interruption. Through these days, he encounters a series of failures or vulnerabilities for which he compensates, rarely with success and never escaping his loneliness. His toxic cycle begins as he drives home from Cleo's house. Alone in his car, Johnny receives another anonymous text, "You think you're such hot shit, don't you?" As with the previous message, he reacts with only a raised eyebrow. The reaction suggests that the insult affects him, although the impact is not clear. Returning home, he finds that his friend Sammy (Chris Pontius) is throwing a party, and his room is filled with people, many of whom he does not know. At the party, Johnny experiences loneliness, and Coppola registers his experience in a single long take of Johnny in a medium shot. Although the sound of the room is filled with life, no one else but him appears on screen. Within this single, long take, Johnny compensates for his loneliness with risky behavior, mixing alcohol and pills. Coppola's mise-en-scène traps Johnny visually as he is trapped inside of his toxic cycle and his loneliness.

During the party, he encounters another inadequacy or vulnerability in his life, his acting, and he compensates for that vulnerability through treating a woman as a sexual surface. A man he does not know, a young male actor (uncredited), stops Johnny and asks him about his acting craft, whether he uses an acting method or not. He tells the young man that he simply acquired an agent and began auditioning. Even though Johnny is a movie star, his reaction to the actor reveals that he does not know or understand, in any significant intellectual or embodied way, the craft of acting. The interaction clearly bothers him, and he excuses himself to engage in an act of compensation: seeing a woman (Lauren Hastings) across the room, he walks over to her, leans into her personal space, and introduces herself. Like many of the women he encounters, she smiles and makes sustained eye contact with him, inviting his sexual attention. Coppola cuts abruptly from the party to his dark bedroom. With only a sliver of light on their bodies, they kiss on his bed, and he removes her underwear. The sounds they make suggest sexual pleasure and anticipation, but Johnny's drinking and drug use causes him to pass out, this time with his face in her lap. The party, then, presents Johnny's cycles of failure (text message, loneliness, acting) and compensation (drinking, drugs, and sex). His compensations, however, do not alleviate his vulnerabilities but instead exacerbate them.

The following day presents Johnny in a new set of vulnerabilities, but, like the party, his compensations do not alleviate his failures, especially his loneliness. As Johnny wakes alone, the film introduces another bodily vulnerability. He loses time. A woman named Marge (Amanda Anka) calls to remind him about a junket for his upcoming film, which he forgot about. At the junket, he poses for publicity photos with his co-star, Rebecca (Michelle

Monaghan). Although she smiles at the camera, she insults Johnny between shots and looks at him with scorn when the photographer is not taking photos. Once the shoot is complete, she turns to Johnny, says, "It wasn't even that good," and leaves. In addition to lost time, Rebecca's reaction to him suggests that Johnny's life is likely filled with relational and sexual failures. His ex-wife, the text messages, and Rebecca's reaction then suggest a pattern in Johnny's life. He fails at relationships, and, presumably, at sex. Rebecca's demeaning behavior clearly affects Johnny, which he carries into his next failure. His publicist (Ellie Kemper) leads him into a room filled with reporters. They ask him questions to which he does not have any substantial answer. He can only offer banal responses. During the scene, the camera embodies his vulnerability with a long zoom. As the questions pile up and Johnny repeatedly does not know how to respond, the image grows tighter and tighter around him. The scene ends with a question that clearly troubles him: "Who is Johnny Marco?" Like the previous question about acting, Johnny does not know how to answer. He sits in silence and humiliation. In response to his relational and sexual vulnerabilities with Rebecca and his failure to know the right answers, he compensates. He has the driver take him to Bambi's, where he has sex with her. As successful as this compensation is, he returns home and is alone. He stands on his balcony and gazes at yet another sexual surface, a large ad of a young woman. The ad stares back at him from across the street. Even Johnny's so-called successful attempts at compensation do not alleviate his loneliness and reassert his loneliness in a world of sexual surfaces.

The next day presents Johnny's toxic cycle but adds the vulnerabilities of old age and homophobia. Again, Johnny wakes up alone and has lost time. Marge calls again, this time to remind him about a special effects session. The special effects artists cover his entire head in plaster, and they instruct him to sit still while it sets. Alone, Johnny sits motionless. Echoing the previous zoom, Coppola zooms in on him again, except this shot is significantly longer than the previous one. The zoom is so slow as to be almost imperceptible at first. The only sound is Johnny's breath, inhaling and exhaling. Like the previous zoom, this shot emphasizes Johnny's feelings of vulnerability, this time his sense of loneliness and lack of bodily agency. In the next shot, the special effect artists have used the plaster cast to age Johnny significantly. He looks in the mirror and laughs at first, but then his gaze narrows. In the mirror, he no longer sees a movie star in his prime. Rather, he encounters another bodily vulnerability, his eventual old age and death. As a way of compensating, when he gets home he invites his massage therapist to his room. He expects a woman named Lori, but instead, a man named Ron (Paul Greene) arrives. He begins Johnny's message, but before too long, Ron removes his own clothes. Johnny sees Ron's pants on the floor and recoils. Ron tries to explain his technique and that his website lays out his approach to nudity. Johnny's reaction is not dissimilar from the homophobic reaction of the boy and guy codes. He thanks Ron, dismisses him, and spends the night alone watching television. Like his previous nights, his compensations do not function to alleviate his vulnerabilities. They only leave him alone.

Johnny begins his next day entering into cycles he has previously inhabited, but Cleo's bodily presence disrupts them, through both juxtapositions and mundane delights. After taking a shower, Johnny goes to his front door dressed only in a towel and picks up his newspaper. He sees his neighbor across the hall, a beautiful blonde woman (Eliza Coupe). Likely as a way to compensate for his loneliness, he enters her room, where they have sex. Like his interaction with the twins, he calls her, a mere sexual surface, by the wrong name. When he walks out of her room in his towel, he finds Cleo sitting on the floor outside his room. Cleo quickly asks him why he took a shower in another room and if his bathroom is broken. He lies to her and then changes the subject, "What a nice surprise . . . Shouldn't you be in school today?" She responds, "It's Sunday." Johnny has lost track of time, likely because the cycles that form his life render time as relatively insignificant. And losing time has brought Cleo in proximity to his sexual practices. His lie suggests that he wants to avoid the juxtaposition. They spend the rest of the day engaged in mundane bodily acts which brings to Johnny delights his other practices fail to do. While Sammy sits on the couch, Johnny and Cleo play the popular video game, "Guitar Hero." Johnny moves his body in ways he has not up until now, almost dancing along with Cleo while they play music. After their game, Johnny gives both Cleo and Sammy enthusiastic high fives. Because of Cleo's presence, Johnny moves, behaves, and reacts in ways different from his normal life. It suggests that Johnny is, in fact, capable of moving through the world in an alternative way.

Cleo's presence also disturbs Johnny's treatment of women's bodies as sexual surfaces. While he takes a phone call from Marge, Johnny stands on his balcony. Below him, he encounters a sexual surface, a beautiful woman in a red bikini (Nicole Trunfio). Like nearly every woman he encounters, she smiles at him. She then invites his sexual attention by removing her top. Unlike his response to his neighbor or the woman in the car, Johnny does not reciprocate her invitation. He turns his back, walks away from her, and finishes his phone call. Given his previous lie to Cleo, it is not surprising that Johnny would refuse the woman's sexual invitation. What is surprising is that he barely acknowledges it. He does not reciprocate her smile, which he has done in every previous encounter. This moment suggests that Johnny can, of his own volition, embody an alternative *habitus*, an alternative way of encountering women's bodies.

The next scenes both establish Cleo's maturity and Johnny's motivation to spend more time with Cleo. Over the phone, Cleo orders the ingredients to make macaroni and cheese from scratch (like she does with eggs benedict in another scene) and later makes the meal. This moment establishes several realities. First, as later scenes will confirm, Johnny and Cleo do not have to cook. Johnny regularly orders food from the hotel. Therefore, she does not cook out of necessity but out of affection. Second, in making meals from scratch, as she will do later, it establishes that although Cleo is young, she is not an immature child. She inhabits a level of maturity that is unusual for her age. The minimalist manner in which Coppola and director of photography Harris Savides covers her cooking may provide overtones of her maturity. Taking inspiration from filmmaker Chantal Akerman's feminist and minimalist classic, *Jeanne Dielman, 23, Quai du Commerce, 1080 Bruxelles* (1975), *Somewhere* uses long, uninterrupted takes, similar to the way Akerman shoots Jeanne Dielman (Delphine Seyrig) engaged in mundane tasks, like cooking. Savides notes that Akerman's film serves as "precursor for *Somewhere*'s gradual unfolding of tasks from daily life such as cooking."[45] The comparison may imply that Cleo behaves more like a woman than a girl. In his bedroom, Johnny takes another phone call, this time from his ex-wife Layla. She tells Johnny that she is going away and that he will need to take Cleo to camp in the next few weeks. He asks her when she will return, and she claims to not know. In response, Johnny protests, because he has a movie premier in Italy. Layla ignores his protest and reminds him to take Cleo to camp. Johnny takes Cleo with him to Italy. If Cleo's presence has disrupted his cycles of toxicity and suggests that he is capable of an alternative *habitus*, then her presence with him full time will begin to outline that alternative.

## OUTLINING AN ALTERNATIVE HABITUS

When Johnny and Cleo arrive in Italy and go to their hotel, a concierge shows them their massive hotel suite, which has multiple bedrooms and a swimming pool. Johnny's handler, Pupi (Nunzio Alfredo 'Pupi' D'Angieri), and his entourage, greet him in the living room of the suite. Down in the lobby, however, Johnny's past failures follow him. There, a woman named Sylvia (Laura Chiatti) pulls him aside. Cleo sees them speak and observes her negativity, which is reminiscent of Rebecca's. Sylvia says, "What the fuck Johnny? Did you think you'd never fucking see me again?" Later, a member of the Italian press surprises Johnny with an interview, and like his previous interactions with the press, this interview goes poorly. When the journalist asks him to speak in Italian, he offers only two phrases, "Buongiorno" (Good morning) and "Buona sera" (Good evening).

Where, in the past, Johnny might have responded to these vulnerabilities with sex, drinking, or drug use, Cleo's presence offers an alternative set of possibilities. Johnny hangs out with Cleo as she swims in the pool. His cast relegates him to the jacuzzi adjoining the pool where he drinks a beer, but he still interacts with Cleo in mundane but delightful ways. He challenges her to hold her breath for a lap in the pool and encourages her to perform a handstand. Johnny smiles at Cleo during this time of play, watches her intently, and praises her. Later that night, both Johnny and Cleo cannot fall asleep, so Johnny orders six gelatos from room service. When he receives another anonymous text, "What's your fucking problem?" Johnny raises his eyebrows and puts the phone away. Once the gelatos arrive, they taste them all, while watching the television show *Friends*, dubbed in Italian. They share a seemingly banal conversation, which circulates around mundane delight. Johnny says, "I like strawberry the best." Cleo responds, "I like chocolate." "I know you do," says Johnny and smiles at her.

Even though these mundane delights seem to serve as alternative to his previous cycles of drinking and sex, the film brings women's bodies as sexual surfaces into contact with Cleo. After Cleo falls asleep, Johnny hears a knock. He makes sure she is asleep and goes to the front door, where he invites Sylvia in. He takes her by the hand and brings her into the hotel suite. The next day at the breakfast table, Cleo sits alone while Sylvia walks into frame, dressed in a bathrobe, and speaks loudly on her phone in Italian. Eventually, she sits with Cleo for breakfast and tries to make small talk. Cleo expresses her displeasure in Sylvia's presence through angry glances and short, minimal responses to Sylvia. When Johnny eventually sits at the table, Cleo expresses her negative feelings about Sylvia through her lowered head and intense stare. Johnny responds with a look, which not only communicates an acknowledgement of Cleo's feelings but also an implicit apology. The previous night, when Johnny checked to see if Cleo was asleep before letting Sylvia in, his behavior suggested he knew Cleo would find Sylvia's presence objectionable. Having brought sexual surfaces into contact with Cleo, her negative reaction brings the toxicity of his compensations out into the open.

Later that day, the film brings Cleo a third time into contact with women's bodies as sexual surfaces, and in response, both father and daughter flee the country. In their hotel suite, Pupi, his entourage, and Johnny are each dressed in formal attire, when Pupi explains to Johnny that they are going to an awards show. While Pupi speaks, Cleo enters the room, wearing a pale, peach dress. She stops and smiles at her father, who says, "Wow. You look beautiful, Cleo." "Thanks," she replies. He puts out his arm, and she takes it. Johnny smiles widely at Cleo's presence, clearly delighted. At the awards show, Johnny and Cleo sit in the front row. They exchange glances. Johnny seems nervous, and Cleo is excited for him. The awards show host invites Johnny on stage where they give him an award and a microphone. He turns to the audience and begins a speech in Italian that he has clearly prepared, likely in response to his previous failure with the language. But before he can finish his speech, music plays over the sound system and a group of five scantily clad female dancers enter the stage. One of women dances near Johnny, moving her body against his in sexually suggestive gestures. Johnny and Cleo exchange knowing glances about the bizarre nature of the event. In response, Johnny appears frozen, not knowing how to process the proximity of his daughter and the sexual surfaces that he stands among. He stands awkwardly as the women finish their routine. The next morning, Johnny and Cleo march down the hallway of the hotel, looking around as if they are trying to escape the hotel unnoticed. They slip into a black car and convince the driver to take them to the airport. In the back of the car, Johnny looks at Cleo apologetically. Cleo responds with a look suggestive of annoyance. Their interaction is not an interaction about Italy. Rather, it is an interaction about how sexual surfaces function in the alternative they are outlining together. Their time together in Italy clarifies for Johnny the boundaries of an alternative *habitus* that Cleo's presence demands of him.

If Italy has clarified that sexual surfaces are antithetical to their alternative *habitus*, their few days back at the Chateau Marmont bring both of them more fully into bodily vulnerabilities, shared memory, shared delights, and praise. After returning home, Johnny and Cleo sit in the lobby of the Chateau. Cleo says that she is tired and leans against her father. A hotel employee, an older man named Romulo, approaches them and asks if they want to hear a song. Johnny responds affirmatively. He turns to his daughter, smiles, and praises Romulo's voice. On an out of tune guitar, Romulo plunks out terrible sounding chords that slip in and out of time. His voice is old, weak, and nasally, and he sings the 1957 Bernie Low and Kal Mann composition, "Teddy Bear," first recorded by Elvis Presley. However technically poor Romulo's performance might be, Johnny and Cleo find it charming and calming. At first Johnny and Cleo exchange glances and affirming smiles. Soon, Cleo responds to the song like a lullaby. She lays her head on her father's shoulder and nearly falls asleep. After the song, Johnny applauds quietly so as not to disturb Cleo and whispers thanks to Romulo. Cleo tucks her head more deeply into her father's shoulder and closes her eyes. The song, the presence of her father, and her tired state have created an environment where she feels safe enough to fall asleep in public.

Bodily vulnerability is emblematic here, as it differs from sexual surfaces and toxic cycles. Romulo sings and plays not as a professional musician but as an older, vulnerable man. He does not attempt to hide his embodied state, and it is precisely his vulnerability that Johnny and Cleo find charming and reassuring. If Johnny's *habitus* has been one of toxic masculinity, one where he responds negatively to the image of an aged face, Romulo's presence signals that the vulnerability of his age is precisely what creates a space of safety for both Cleo and Johnny. This moment differs from the twins' dancing, because Bambi and Cindy perform without an embodiment of vulnerability. They perform with a flat affect. They do not smile or make eye contact with Johnny, and they perform with low energy. Romulo's singing is more like Cleo's ice skating: the tension between her proficiency and lack of it is, in part, what Johnny finds captivating about her performance (and it is this feature that we will explore more fully in our chapter on *A Very Murray Christmas* [2015]). Vulnerability, here in the form of imperfection, is vital to their alternative way of life.

However, Romulo's song is not without problems. As Johnny will also demonstrate later in the film, Romulo does not appear to have the tools to connect to her appropriately. When Elvis performed the song, it was a love song with sexual overtones. The opening verse places the singer in a subordinate, sexual relationship to the person hearing the song. "Put a chain around my neck / And lead me anywhere," implying a form of sadomasochistic sexual practice. The second verse continues this implication. The singer does not want to be a tiger, because "tigers play too rough." When Romulo sings the song, it functions as either an inappropriate sexualization of Cleo or, what is more likely, a condescending song about a stuffed animal, an object that is appropriate to a girl much younger than Cleo. Either reading signals that Romulo might not be equipped to connect with a girl Cleo's age and maturity. However, the film, through Cleo's affirmative reaction to the song, does not judge him for his choice. She accepts his intent to connect with father and daughter, and, more importantly, his bodily vulnerability.

If vulnerability creates a relational space of safety, then Cleo and Johnny's bodily delight, memory, and praise bring them more fully into an alternative. The next day begins with Cleo cooking eggs benedict for her father and his friend Sammy. Cleo plates the food with serious care, as though she delights in the act of cooking. Johnny and Sammy sleep while she works. Johnny's nightstand is empty of alcohol bottles. She prances joyfully to the door where a waiter has brought a carafe of orange juice. At the breakfast table, Johnny and Sammy praise her cooking, not out of obligation but as a sincere response. "You got the sauce perfect," says Johnny, "It's, like, not too heavy." Unlike Johnny's engagement with women as sexual surfaces, this delight brings forth from Johnny more of his personhood. His delight in the meal is rooted in his previous memories of the dish, and it is out of this past embodied experience and memories that he praises her. Cleo's delight in making the dish produces for Johnny his own bodily experience of delight. In this way, their horizons of delight intersect in their embodied experience of the meal.

Furthermore, this scene establishes Cleo's maturity and, later in the scene, connects father and daughter in a shared memory from Italy. When Cleo makes hollandaise sauce and poached eggs as well as she does, it signals a discipline unusual for a girl of Cleo's age. She has clearly spent time refining her craft. Furthermore, the affection with which she plates the food signals her delight in the process. Cleo's maturity contrasts to Romulo's song choice. She is too mature for childish things like teddy bears. However, her maturity does not make her immune to Johnny and Sammy's compliments. Rather, they affect her in a sincere way. She smiles so widely her eyes squint. While the men eat, Cleo makes a list of items she needs for camp. Johnny suggests, in reference to their late-night gelato snack in Italy, "Maybe some snacks. You might get hungry." She says that such snacks are not allowed, but Johnny jokes that perhaps she could sneak them in, just in case she gets hungry at night. The two, reminiscing about the gelatos in Italy, exchange smiles. Like their bodily delight and memory of the meal, Johnny and Cleo share not only a horizon of delight but a memory.

The outlines of their alternative *habitus* continue to develop, including humor, jokes, and the breakdown of Johnny's car. Later, while Johnny removes his cast, Cleo dances in the living room. Because Johnny is distracted by his cast, her dance move catches him by surprise, and he says, "Oh, I like that spin move. What is that?" She says that the move is a chaine turn. She smiles widely, delighting not only in the move but in sharing it with her father. The three of them continue to joke and tell stories, until Johnny removes his cast. They all laugh at its terrible smell. Then Johnny and Cleo leave a sporting goods store where they purchased items for camp. In the car, they return to a previous conversation. Johnny asks with a lightness that was not present earlier "Alright. Anybody following us?" She turns and looks behind the car. "No," she says, "The coast is clear." Johnny's source of paranoia has now become a point of relational contact, about which he can now joke with self-awareness. While they drive, however, Johnny's Ferrari breaks down on the side of the road. Johnny calls for a tow, and the two stand on the side of a busy road. Beyond the irony that a $300,000 car would break down, the scene suggests the failure of the key materiality of his toxic *habitus*. Throughout much of the film, Johnny attempts to reduce the visibility of his vulnerabilities. But here, while both visible and vulnerable, he does not respond with toxic behaviors.

Taken together, these scenes outline an alternative *habitus* for Johnny, composed of mundane delights and vulnerabilities and boundaries against engaging women's bodies as sexual surfaces and risky behavior. Both in Italy and in Los Angeles, Johnny and Cleo share bodily experiences of mundane delights. Whether in the pool, eating gelato, Cleo's dress, eggs benedict, jokes and humor, or praise, Cleo and Johnny's shared practices produce pleasure and praise. Furthermore, this sequence establishes bodily vulnerability as internal to their *habitus*. Romulo's song establishes this alternative as creating space for safety and rest. The breakdown of Johnny's Ferrari also leaves

Johnny in a position of visibility and vulnerability, but he does not respond with toxic compensations. The sequence also establishes boundaries necessary for this alternative *habitus*. Not only does Cleo's presence demand that Johnny avoids risky behavior like drinking and drugs (which he virtually stops), it also demands that Johnny stop seeing women's bodies as sexual surfaces. When Cleo does come into contact with sexual surfaces, her reaction clarifies for Johnny that such toxicity is not appropriate for their relationship. It violates the alternative *habitus* they are outlining together.

However, Johnny's toxicity follows him, with one final juxtaposition between Cleo and sexual surfaces. Upon returning home, Johnny walks into his bedroom where he sees a naked woman, wearing only a sailor's cap (Laura Ramsey). "It is not a good time," he says. She responds in a sexually suggestive manner, "Are you sure?" Insistent, Johnny says, "Yeah," and walks out of the room, closing the door behind him. He then suggests that he and Cleo can get food in the hotel's restaurant, presumably to keep Cleo from seeing the woman. Over food, the two play cards, Cleo wins multiple hands, and they both smile over her winning streak. Johnny tries to garner Cleo's attention by throwing a french fry in the air and catching it in his mouth; the woman who was in his room interrupts their mundane delights. Now dressed and without a sailor's hat, she walks up to Johnny and flirts with him. Cleo looks suspicious, but Johnny protests, "I don't know her that well." With these outlines of their alternative established, father and daughter then enter the possibility of inhabiting that alternative.

## THE POSSIBILITY OF AN ALTERNATIVE *HABITUS*

The possibility of an alternative *habitus* brings Johnny and Cleo into more mundane bodily delights, this time in the form of play, sensuousness, and making up for lost time. On their way back to his room, Johnny picks Cleo up, puts her over his shoulder, and runs down the hallway. She squeals with delight. At the end of the hall, before they enter the room, Johnny asks if Cleo wants to stay another day before she leaves, and she agrees. Coppola compresses their day in a montage, which begins with Johnny and Cleo playing a game of ping pong. While the song "I'll Try Anything Once" by the Strokes plays on the soundtrack, the sound of the ping pong ball on the table is the focal, sensuous sound of the scene. It is so focal, the players comment on it. "It's that sound it [the ball] makes when we are doing good," says Johnny, and Cleo, too, "I like that sound." As the volume of the song rises slightly, Coppola cuts to an underwater shot of a pool. Johnny falls in frame from above and looks up. In a reverse shot, Cleo falls into the pool, too, and the two of them find their way to the bottom. Under the sensuous pressure of the water and the pressure of holding their breath, the two pretend to have a tea party. Johnny gestures, raising an imaginary cup to his lips with his pinky extended. He pretends to sip tea and looks around the imaginary room as if to say, "What a swanky place this tea shop is." He glances at Cleo, smiling as widely as he has in the entire film. In a reverse shot, Cleo laughs several times as she pretends to sip tea. Embracing a faux elegance makes her laugh. Unable to hold her breath any longer, she swims to the surface. Playing "tea" is an activity usually reserved for much younger girls, certainly not girls of Cleo's age or maturity. However, Cleo plays tea with her father, implying that, as both Johnny and Cleo will say later in the film, that he was not present for much of her life. Their game also suggests that Cleo is letting her father make up for lost time.

The remainder of the montage introduces more mundane delights and vulnerableness, evoking a sense of rest. In the next shot, the two lie in reclined chair, resting in the sun. Sunglasses cover their faces. Johnny leans his head toward her and asks, "How are you doing?" "I'm good," she smiles. While the shot begins in a two-shot, it zooms out slowly. Other people surround them or walk across frame, but the two sit, unmolested, unworried, in a seeming sense of safety and rest. Later in the hotel lobby, Cleo lies in a chair, slumped over as if she is about to fall asleep. Johnny sits at the piano and plays the "Aria" from J.S. Bach's "Goldberg Variations." He plays as if he has not played the Aria in years.[46] He takes long pauses between phrases, presumably thinking about the next phrase in the silence between them.

This montage represents the possibility that Johnny can inhabit an alternative *habitus*, where the two experience joy, rest, and vulnerability. Coppola embodies Johnny and Cleo's joy in the delight of their shared and sensual embodied experience. Emphasizing the sense of hearing, the ping pong game highlights the sound of the ball. The rhythm evokes joy, because it signifies that they are sharing play together, which occurs in the chain of connections they make through the medium of the ball. In the next shot, their joy takes place in the disparity between the sensuousness of water, the bodily pressure of holding their breath, and the faux sophistication of a high tea. As philosopher Søren Kierkegaard notes, comedy, at its root, occurs in a disparity between two things or situations.[47] As their performance suggests, it is impossible to have a high tea at the bottom of a pool. They both find joy and comedy inside of that disparity. Furthermore, their inability to breathe gives their game the pressure of time. Cleo especially must engage in a hyperbolic performance, overdoing her sophistication, before she has to return to the surface for air. Likewise, Coppola presents rest in a long, zoom-out shot. Previously, the two zoom-in shots present Johnny in states of isolation, loneliness, and vulnerability. In this shot, he is not alone. He is with his daughter. If the zoom-in evokes a sense of confinement, the zoom-out presents Johnny in a cinematic moment of expansiveness. For Johnny, he is surrounded by other people, but he is not faced with his inadequacy from what those people want from him. He can, in this moment, rest with Cleo. Finally, the sequence ends with Johnny's performance of Bach's "Aria." Like Romulo's performance of "Teddy Bear," Johnny offers a technically deficient performance. However, his vulnerability—his lack of capacity—does not carry a negative connotation, like it had previously with his failed interviews. Rather, Cleo experiences rest while Johnny is vulnerable with her. Johnny does not need toxic patterns to compensate for his vulnerability. Now, vulnerability is his context for rest.

As Johnny takes Cleo to camp, Johnny confronts his limitations, especially in his inability to console Cleo. The next day, Johnny and Cleo get in his Ferrari to take Cleo to camp. While in the car, Cleo begins to cry. Johnny asks, "Cleo what's wrong? Why are you crying?" She responds, "I don't know when Mom's coming back. She said she had to go away for a while. But she didn't say when she was coming back. And you're always gone." She looks at him with an emotional vulnerability Johnny has not witnessed in the film. However, Johnny seems incapable of fully embracing or acknowledging it. He looks pained at her pain, but he attempts to diffuse the negative feelings. "Come here," he says, encouraging her to lean on him, "Don't cry honey." Back inside of his Ferrari, his dysfunctional veil, this moment reveals that Johnny has not fully entered into an alternative *habitus*. He does not appear to have the tools to deal productively with her emotional vulnerability. He can only minimize it or attempt to usher it away.

Johnny can only partially face his inability to take responsibility for his failures as a parent. Johnny drives her to Las Vegas, where the two take a helicopter to a location closer to the camp. There, Johnny ushers Cleo into a cab that will take her to camp. As the helicopter revs its engine, Johnny steps away from the cab and turns to look at Cleo. She sticks her head out of the cab's window and looks back at him. Johnny yells, "Cleo! I'm sorry I haven't been around," but the sound of the engine drowns out his words. Cleo changes her face from serious to a smile, waves goodbye, and the cab pulls away. This moment, like the previous moment with Cleo's tears, implies that Johnny's formation inside the cycles of toxic masculinity still exerts pressure on the way he moves through the world. While he is, at this moment, his most vulnerable with Cleo—admitting that he has not been a good father to her, that he has failed her—he says it out loud but not in a space where she can receive it. Like his inability to console Cleo, this moment reveals that Johnny cannot bring himself to take responsibly for the manner in which his toxic *habitus* impacted Cleo. He cannot admit to her that his loneliness has contributed to her loneliness.

## AT THE THRESHOLD OF AN ALTERNATIVE MASCULINITY

In the final moments, the film returns Johnny to his loneliness, changed by Cleo's presence in his life. Having been changed, he, first, responds differently to situations in which he finds himself; second, he makes himself willingly vulnerable with his ex-wife; and, finally, he abandons the materiality that funds his toxic cycles of behavior. First, back at the Chateau Marmont, Johnny finds himself returned to situations he experienced previous to Cleo's disruptions. However, he responds to those moments as if Cleo might have been present. When he returns to his room, Johnny sees a model (C.C. Sheffield) at the end of his hallway, sitting outside. While a man cuts her hair, she sits topless and smokes a cigarette. Like his response to the woman who removes her bikini top in response to Johnny's presence, he does not show any interest in her. Without Cleo's presence, Johnny willingly participated in seeing women as surfaces for sexual desire. Cleo's presence has facilitated an internal change. He does not look at the woman as though she exists for his sexual gratification. Inside his room, Johnny sits on his couch alone, not unlike he did earlier in the film. However, he does not attempt to compensate for his isolation with sex or drinking. The next day, like the beginning of the film, Johnny goes into his bathroom and looks at himself in the mirror. However, he does not touch his hairline or take Propecia. He simply looks at himself. In both of these moments, it is as if Johnny carries Cleo's presence with him, though she is bodily absent.

Second, in the wake of Cleo's absence and without turning to toxic behaviors, Johnny willingly reaches out in emotional vulnerability to his ex-wife and does not compensate when she rejects him. Later than night, Johnny sits in his bedroom floor emotionally distraught. He calls Layla, his ex-wife, on the phone. He says to her, "I'm fucking nothing. I'm not even a person." Layla responds, "Why don't you try volunteering or something?" Johnny immediate rejects the notion. While her suggestion seems, on its surface, to function as an easy answer to his emotional distress, "volunteering" would likely only serve to exacerbate Johnny's toxicity. Part of what pushes Johnny into toxic cycles is his inability to function in public. He does not have the emotional equipment to be visible. Because celebrity charitable work is often highly visible, it is likely that such "volunteering" would exacerbate his self-loathing rather than diminish it. Changing the subject, Johnny says, "Can you come over?" Layla does not engage with his situation and draws clear boundaries with him, "No I can't." After hanging up the phone, he performs an act he has never performed in the film: he weeps. Furthermore, in the wake of her rejection, Johnny does not respond in any of the toxic ways he has previously.

He does not drink heavily or engage women as surfaces for his sexual desire. Rather, he returns to a space where he experienced joy, the pool, and floats there alone. Later, he performs an act he witnessed Cleo perform. Johnny makes his own dinner. He fixes himself a plate of pasta and tomato sauce. In these scenes, Johnny has engaged in emotional vulnerability with another person, accepted her rejection, and responded in non-toxic ways. Like the previous scenes, it is as though Johnny behaves as if Cleo is with him.

Finally, Johnny vacates the materiality that facilitated his toxic cycles, his room and his car, both of which suggest that he might have arrived at the threshold of an alternative *habitus*, an alternative masculinity. The next day, Johnny calls the lobby of the hotel and informs the attendant that he will be moving out. She offers to put his things in storage, presumably for his return to the hotel. However, Johnny tells her that he will leave a forwarding address. This phrase signals that he will be moving out of the Chateau Marmont in a potentially permanent way. Then Johnny gets in his Ferrari and drives. In a long driving sequence, the camera follows his car. At first, he appears to simply drive on the freeway, but soon he is outside of Los Angeles. He drives far outside the city, on a rural, two-lane road. Brown grassy fields surround him. The camera reveals mountains in the distance. In this rural space, he pulls his car to the side of the road, turns it off, leaves the keys in the ignition, and walks away from his car. In a medium close-up, the camera shows him walking away from his car. He smiles briefly, and the film cuts to black.

If, as Mahmood suggests, the material of the veil is instrumental in cultivating virtue, then Johnny's experience in the film also demonstrates that materiality is instrumental in cultivating vice, which must be abandoned if he is to inhabit an alternative *habitus*. Mahmood points out that the women in her study find that, once the veil becomes part of their *habitus*, it cannot simply be abandoned. It is, in a real sense, substantive of the way they move through the world. Johnny's veils, however, are dysfunctional ones. The Chateau Marmont is a veil that encourages Johnny to see women as sexual surfaces and inhabit toxic cycles of substance use. His car is that veil that encourages risk-taking, success, power, and isolation. If Johnny can successfully inhabit an alternative to the toxic cycles he has previously inhabited, he needs alternative veils, alternative infrastructures of materiality if he is to inhabit an alternative masculinity. Coppola does not reveal if he is successful or not. She does, however, present Johnny at the threshold of this alternative. But it is precisely this threshold that he must cross if his life is to become, as he says to Layla, "a person" other than "nothing," and if he, as the film's title suggest, is to go somewhere.

By way of conclusion, we suggest four implications that our reading of *Somewhere* has for scholarly discussions of toxic masculinity and *habitus*. First, our analysis implies an effort to think of dysfunctional ways of being a man, like toxic masculinity (or hegemonic masculinity in *The Virgin Suicides* chapter), as *habitus*, which provides a way to think productively about how large-scale social forces impact the everyday life of individuals. Certainly, large-scale governmental polices are vital if our contemporary society is to be just and equitable for women. What *Somewhere* reiterates, in a powerful way, is that gender inequality is lived inside the quotidian, mundane realities of our collective formation. *Habitus* is an especially vital locus in which masculinity needs to be analyzed, because it is the locus at which men imagine and live out masculinities. Toxic masculinity is, as Karner rightly points out, composed of harmful behaviors. It is also comproed of habitual practices, materials, and scripts that have formed and continue to form the interior lives of men (and women). One need only perform a simple internet search for the ways male students sexually assault women on college campuses for the evidence of such damaging *habitus* at work. While attending to systemic oppression is vital, disrupting toxic masculinity needs also to occur through an alternative *habitus*, an alternative set of materials, bodily acts, and scripts by which we imagine what it is to be a man. Mahmood's work suggests that men can becoming differing kinds of people, whose interiors, as Coppola suggests in the film, are attuned to realities like vulnerability, bodily presence, joy, and rest. As colonial historian Catharine Hall implies about colonialism, masculinity studies needs to account for the manner in which large scale social forces (like the Vietnam War or the Boy Code) intersect in everyday life.[48] Coppola's *Somewhere* suggests that *habitus* is one mechanism for giving that account.

Furthermore, our reading of *Somewhere* suggests that scholarly analysis of toxic masculinities should attend not only to the content of harmful behaviors, but it should also give an account of the pattern or cycles that fund it. For example, as our chapter on Coppola's *Marie Antoinette* (2006) argues, communication scholar Susan Douglas notes how the postfemininist movement, which wrongly encourages women and girls to appropriate traditional forms of female beauty as a form of power, in real ways repackages old patterns of patriarchal oppression in the guise of empowerment.[49] Similarly, legal scholar Michelle Alexander's analysis of mass incarceration suggests that racist structures of the past, like slavery and Jim Crow segregation, do not disappear.[50] They simply change. While the contents of patriarchy and racism change, patterns often retain their basic shape. In *Somewhere*, the content of toxic masculinity, for example, drops its excessive features. Johnny does not exhibit overt acts of violence against women's bodies. Rather, he harms women through his engagement with their bodies as sexual surfaces, in which many of the women he encounters participate. The content has changed, but Johnny still engages in analogous patterns of behavior that produce harm, as the anonymous texts suggest. The analysis of patterns and the mobilization of new ones, precisely as a form of *habitus*, is vital if men's reflection on masculinity is going to produce meaningful change to the lives of both women and men.

Third, without losing focus on the harm toxic masculinity causes to women, it will be necessary for men to attend more seriously and substantially to the harm toxic forms of masculinity performs on themselves. Here, taking a cue from indigenous activist Mark Charles and Christian theologian Soong-Chan Rah, when settler colonialists colonized and occupied indigenous lands and performed violence against indigenous peoples, those harmful bodily acts produce trauma upon those who have colonized and upon those who benefit from and perpetuate harm against indigenous peoples.[51] Patriarchal realities, like toxic masculinity, likewise produce asymmetrical forms of suffering. Throughout the film, Coppola presents Johnny as one who suffers these kinds of asymmetrical harm. He lives in a toxic pattern of self-destruction, especially through his risk-taking behaviors. However, his loneliness appears also to be a form of self-destruction. Cut off from meaningful relationships to others, he has become "nothing . . . not even a person." He has, in effect, participated in the eradication of his own humanity. Men must never lose sight of how toxic forms of masculinity harm women. Men must also see, as clearly as we can, how those systems both benefit and harm us. We must see how our *habitus* eradicates the humanity of women and our own humanity in the process.

Fourth and finally, if toxic *habituses* of masculinity have the potential to eradicate the humanity of cis-men like Johnny, then collaboration between cis-men and women, trans, and non-binary persons will be necessary to imagine and inhabit alternatives to hegemonic and toxic masculinities, and the language of *habitus* can provide a powerful way of doing that work. In the next chapter on *The Virgin Suicides*, we argue that love and violence can exist entangled with one another. What *Somewhere* suggests is that part of the work of untangling love from violence is through *habitus*, through disrupting toxic cycles, engaging in disrupting harmful bodily acts, adopting alternative materials, and developing alternative ways of seeing others. What that alternative masculinity is is an open question. *Somewhere* leaves Johnny on the threshold of that alternative. Coppola's film suggests that realities like vulnerability, bodily presence, rest, and joy might be vital to whatever that alternative might is. In our next chapter, *The Virgin Suicides* serves as almost an antithesis to Johnny, portraying boys who cannot escape the limits their masculinity puts on them and their way of knowing.

## REFERENCES

Alexander, Michelle. *The New Jim Crow: Mass Incarceration in the Age of Colorblindness*. Revised Edition. New York: The New Press, 2012.
Charles, Mark and Soong-Chan Rah. *Unsetlling Truth: The Ongoing, Dehumanizing Legacy of the Doctrine of Discovery*. Grand Rapids, MI: Inter Varsity Press, 2020.
David, Deborah S. and Robert Brannon. "The Male Sex Role: Our Culture's Blueprint of Manhood, and What It's Done For Us Lately." In *The Forty-Nine Percent Majority: The Male Sex Role*. Edited by Deborah S. David and Robert Brannon, 1–48. Reading, MA: Addison-Wesley, 1976.
Douglas, Susan J. *The Rise of Enlightened Sexism: How Pop Culture Took Us from Girl Power to Girls Gone Wild*. New York: St. Martin's, 2010.
Ferrari Corporate. "Brand." About Us. corporate.ferrari.com/en/about-us/brand.
———. "Racing." About Us. corporate.ferrari.com/en/about-us/racing.
Hall, Catherine. *Civilizing Subjects: Metropole and Colony in the English Imagination 1830–1867*. Chicago: University of Chicago Press, 2002.
Handyside, Fiona. "Postfeminist (D)au(gh)teurs: Sofia Coppola and the Girl's Voyage to Italy in *Somewhere* (2010)." In *New Visions of the Child in Italian Cinema*. Edited by Danielle Hipkins and Roger Pitt, 129–148. Oxford: Peter Lang, 2014.
———. *Sofia Coppola: A Cinema of Girlhood*. London: I.B. Tauris, 2017.
Karner, Tracy. "Fathers, Sons, and Vietnam: Masculinity and Betrayal in the Life Narratives of Vietnam Veterans with Post Traumatic Stress Disorder." *American Studies* 37 no. 1 (Spring, 1996): 63–94. www.jstor.org/stable/40642783.
Kierkegaard, Søren. *Concluding Unscientific Postscript*, edited and translated by Alastair Hannayd. Cambridge: Cambridge University Press, 2009.
Kreindler, Derek. "Ferrari Used In 'Somewhere' Re-Painted, Sold to Lucky Buyer," *AutoGuide.com*, February 17, 2011. www.autoguide.com/auto-news/2011/02/ferrari-used-in-somewhere-re-painted-sold-to-lucky-buyer.html.
Mahmood, Saba. "Feminist Theory, Embodiment, and the Docile Agent: Some Reflections on the Egyptian Islamic Revival." *Cultural Anthropology* 16, no. 2 (May 2001), 202–36.
Pollack, William. *Real Boys: Rescuing our Sons from the Myths of Boyhood*. New York: Owl Books, 1998.
O'Rawe, Catherine. *Stars and Masculinity in Contemporary Italian Cinema*. New York: Palgrave MacMillan, 2014.
Reich, Jacqueline. *Beyond the Latin Lover: Marcello Mastroianni, Masculinity, and Italian Cinema*. Bloomington: University Indiana Press, 2004.
Rogers, Anna Backman. *Sofia Coppola: The Politics of Visual Pleasure*. New York: Berghahn Book, 2019.
Salam, Maya. "What Is Toxic Masculinity?" *The New York Times* (January 22, 2019), www.nytimes.com/2019/01/22/us/toxic-masculinity.html.
Salter, Michael. "The Problem With a Fight Against Toxic Masculinity." *The Atlantic* (February 27, 2019), www.theatlantic.com/health/archive/2019/02/toxic-masculinity-history/583411/.

Tyree, J. M. "Searching for *Somewhere*." *Film Quarterly* 64 no. 4 (Summer 2011): 12–16.

*The Greatest Ever,* episode 2, "Sports Cars," featuring Quentin Willson and Ray Maranges, Cineflix International Media Limited Series, 2005, fod-infobase-com.proxy.lib.duke.edu/p_ViewVideo.aspx?xtid=203051.

## NOTES

1. Anna Backman Rogers, *Sofia Coppola: The Politics of Visual Pleasure* (New York: Berghahn Book, 2019), 92.
2. Ibid.
3. Saba Mahmood, "Feminist Theory, Embodiment, and the Docile Agent: Some Reflections on the Egyptian Islamic Revival," *Cultural Anthropology* 16 no. 2 (May 2001), 211.
4. Ibid., 215.
5. Ibid., 214.
6. Ibid., 217.
7. Ibid., 223.
8. Ibid., 204.
9. Ibid., 203.
10. Ibid., 212.
11. Ibid., 213.
12. Ibid., 213.
13. Ibid., 214.
14. Ibid.
15. Ibid.
16. Ibid., 217.
17. Fiona Handyside, "Postfeminist (D)au(gh)teurs: Sofia Coppola and the Girl's Voyage to Italy in *Somewhere*," in *New Visions of the Child in Italian Cinema*, eds. Danielle Hipkins and Roger Pitt (Oxford: Peter Lang, 2014), 141, 144.
18. Fiona Handyside, *Sofia Coppola: A Cinema of Girlhood* (London: I.B. Tauris, 2017), 29.
19. Handyside, "Postfeminist (D)au(gh)teurs," 142.
20. Ibid., 144.
21. Ibid., 146.
22. Ibid., 141.
23. Jacqueline Reich, *Beyond the Latin Lover: Marcello Mastroianni, Masculinity, and Italian Cinema* (Bloomington: University Indiana Press, 2004), 7.
24. Ibid. See also Catherine O'Rawe, *Stars and Masculinity in Contemporary Italian Cinema* (New York: Palgrave MacMillan, 2014), 11.
25. Reich, *Beyond the Latin Lover*, 40.
26. Ibid., 43.
27. Ibid., 44, 45.
28. Ibid., 48.

29. Michael Salter, "The Problem With a Fight Against Toxic Masculinity," *The Atlantic* (February 27, 2019), www.theatlantic.com/health/archive/2019/02/toxic-masculinity-history/583411/.

30. Maya Salam, "What Is Toxic Masculinity?," *The New York Times* (January 22, 2019), www.nytimes.com/2019/01/22/us/toxic-masculinity.html.

31. Tracy Karner, "Fathers, Sons, and Vietnam: Masculinity and Betrayal in the Life Narratives of Vietnam Veterans with Post Traumatic Stress Disorder," *American Studies* 37 no. 1 (Spring 1996), 68, www.jstor.org/stable/40642783.

32. Deborah S. David and Robert Brannon, "The Male Sex Role: Our Culture's Blueprint of Manhood, and What It's Done For Us Lately," in *The Forty-Nine Percent Majority: The Male Sex Role*, eds. Deborah S. David and Robert Brannon (Reading, MA: Addison-Wesley, 1976), 12.

33. William Pollack, *Real Boys: Rescuing our Sons from the Myths of Boyhood* (New York: Owl Books, 1998), iBooks.

34. Ibid.

35. Michael Kimmel, *Guyland: The Perilous World Where Boys Become Men* (New York: Harper, 2008), 48–9, 50–1, and 58.

36. Ibid., 77.

37. Ibid., 85.

38. Ibid.

39. Ibid., 89.

40. "Brand," About Us, Ferrari Corporate, accessed October 12, 2020, corporate.ferrari.com/en/about-us/brand.

41. "Racing," About Us, Ferrari Corporate, accessed October 12, 2020, corporate.ferrari.com/en/about-us/racing.

42. *The Greatest Ever,* episode 2, "Sports Cars," featuring Quentin Willson, Cineflix International Media Limited Series, 2005, fod-infobase-com.proxy.lib.duke.edu/p_ViewVideo.aspx?xtid=203051.

43. Ibid., featuring Ray Maranges.

44. Derek Kreindler, "Ferrari Used In 'Somewhere' Re-Painted, Sold to Lucky Buyer," *AutoGuide.com*, February 17, 2011, accessed October 12, 2020, www.autoguide.com/auto-news/2011/02/ferrari-used-in-somewhere-re-painted-sold-to-lucky-buyer.html.

45. J. M. Tyree, "Searching for *Somewhere*," *Film Quarterly* 64 no. 4 (Summer 2011): 16.

46. The selection of this particular music work suggests an alternative trajectory of Johnny's pre-acting life. Bach's "Goldberg Variations" is an ambitious piece, usually reserved for professional musicians. Typically, the "Goldberg Variations" appears on piano performance programs in its entirety, which can take an hour and a half to play. If musicians do not perform the entire suite of variations, then they will often perform large selections of the piece. Rarely does the "Aria," the first movement, appear on its own. This common practice suggests that, perhaps, Johnny was, at one time in his past, studying to be a professional musician. And then, for whatever reason, he, as he says in the film, got an agent and started auditioning. It is interesting to meditate on

the possibility that Johnny might have enjoyed the introversion of a life as a classical pianist more than his life as a movie star.

47. Søren Kierkegaard, *Concluding Unscientific Postscript*, ed. and tr. by Alastair Hannayd (Cambridge: Cambridge University Press, 2009), 431.

48. Catherine Hall, *Civilizing Subjects: Metropole and Colony in the English Imagination 1830–1867* (Chicago: University of Chicago Press, 2002), 9–13.

49. Susan J. Douglas, *The Rise of Enlightened Sexism: How Pop Culture Took Us from Girl Power to Girls Gone Wild* (New York: St. Martin's, 2010), 10.

50. Michelle Alexander, *The New Jim Crow: Mass Incarceration in the Age of Colorblindness*, revised edition (New York: The New Press, 2012), 2.

51. Mark Charles and Soong-Chan Rah, *Unsetlling Truth: The Ongoing, Dehumanizing Legacy of the Doctrine of Discovery* (Grand Rapids, MI: InterVarsity Press, 2020), 185.

*Chapter Two*

# Limits of Masculinity

## *Excess, Mimicry, and Ambivalence in* The Virgin Suicides

In the late 1970s, psychiatrist Dori Laub began what would later be named the Holocaust Survivors Film Project, which he would later discuss in the book, *Testimony: Crises of Witnessing in Literature* (1992). In one passage, he describes one of his videotaped survivor's stories. A woman in her sixties recounted an uprising of prisoners at Auschwitz. "'All of sudden,' she said, 'we saw four chimneys going up in flames, exploding. The flames shot into the sky, people were running. It was unbelievable.'"[1] Later at a conference, Laub presented the video to a group of historians, psychoanalysts, and artists, which caused a lively debate.[2] The historians in the group rejected her account, because they documented that the prisoners destroyed only one chimney. Laub writes about the historians, "Since the memory of the testifying woman turned out to be, in this way, fallible, one could not accept—nor give credence to—her whole account of the events."[3] Laub, however, listened with an attitude that differed from the historians. The event of the four chimneys is, according to Laub, an inconceivable event. "[S]he came to testify to the unbelievability, precisely, of what she had eyewitnessed—this bursting open of the very frame of Auschwitz."[4] Laub did not hear the survivor's story as empirical history. He heard her story as testimony, as revealing a reality that exceeded the facts of the event.

The distinction between history and testimony grounds precisely what we see at play in *The Virgin Suicides*. As we stated in the introduction, we—the cis-gendered, middle-aged, white men who are writing this book—agree with feminist reflection that men like us have significant work to do in abolishing the misogyny that subordinates and harms women. Part of that work is learning, naming, and fighting against the harmful mechanisms that fund the masculinity we have inherited. Therefore, in this first part of the book, we read

Coppola's male protagonists as representative of masculinity more broadly, and we see in the lives of some of these characters those harmful mechanisms at work. Part of what we find so helpful about *The Virgin Suicides* is the manner in which Coppola represents masculinity and its harmful mechanisms. The protagonists of the film, the neighborhood boys, investigate the lives and suicides of the Lisbon sisters with the posture of Laub's historian, trying desperately yet failing to make empirical, historical sense of the girls' suicides. Like Laub's historian, the boys do not attend to the Lisbon girls' lives and deaths as testimony, as a way of communicating a reality that exceeds empirical knowledge. The boys' refusal to hear the sisters' testimony reflects the broader limitations of masculine ways of knowing and loving; furthermore, we not only trace the harmful mechanisms that the boys deploy in response to the Lisbon sisters, but we also outline the manner in which the girls' testimony exceeds masculine limitations.

Our argument unfolds in three sections. After a summary of the film, we first draw on postcolonial scholar Homi Bhabha's insights on mimicry and ambivalence, particularly the way colonized persons do not fully mimic colonizers. We acknowledge that scholars who write about feminism and masculinity have pointed out, not unlike Bhabha, that men regularly fail to live up to the standards of being a man. We also acknowledge that the concept of mimicry appears in feminist reflection, which we will engage more deeply in our reading of *Marie Antoinette* (2006). In this chapter, we draw on Bhabha, because he sees in one's failure to meet a standard a potential for resistance. We think his insights are especially helpful in understanding the neighborhood boys' failure to meet standards of masculinity, and we return to this notion in the conclusion, where we tease out some implications on how those in positions of power and privilege might deal more productively with their own failures.

Second, we draw on trauma studies to unpack the role of a witness, the listening a witness needs to perform, the dangers of listening, and the haunting of the world testimonies demand. As other writers on *The Virgin Suicides* have mentioned, the neighborhood boys certainly experience trauma when they unexpectedly find the dead bodies of the Lisbon sisters at the end of the film.[5] However, no writer that we know of has devoted sustained attention to the link between trauma, witnessing, and testimony in the film, nor seen in these dynamics the outworking of masculinity. In order to link these concepts together, we, third, turn to sociologist R.W. Connell's notion of hegemonic masculinity, which focuses on the practices and legitimation of unequal, gendered relationship. Alongside Connell, we highlight the ways Enlightenment epistemology functions as part of the practices of hegemonic masculinity. Highlighting the gendering of epistemology is vital, because Coppola has structured the film as an investigation. The very structure of the film, therefore, demands an account of epistemology. The neighborhood boys try and fail to answer the central question: Why did the Lisbon sisters commit suicide? Like witnessing, the boys' epistemology is a gendered problem.

In our reading of the film, the boys, caught within a system of hegemonic masculinity, resist the role of witness through their acts of fact-finding and awe. The boys, along with Mrs. Lisbon, subordinate the girls, and the boys orient themselves to Trip Fontaine (Josh Hartnett), who sits at the top of the hegemonic system. Within this system, the boys perform symbolic violence through objectification, fantasy, voyeurism, and love. We also describe the means by which the Lisbon sisters exceed the boys' understanding of them. The film uses juxtapositions, Cecilia's apparitions, authorial intrusions, and the girls' conversation to register their agency. By way of conclusion, we suggest three ways Coppola's film contributes to the concepts of mimicry, testimony, and hegemonic masculinity.

*The Virgin Suicides* opens in the sleepy Detroit suburb of Gross Pointe, Michigan. In dreamy shots of the late afternoon, sun shines through green leaves of neighborhood trees. But the camera suddenly cuts to the interior of the Lisbon household, to a shelf filled with candles, makeup, perfume, and other personal items. In recounting the first Lisbon sister's suicide attempt, a male narrator (Giovanni Ribisi) says, "Cecilia was the first to go." The camera then reveals Cecilia (Hanna Hall) lying in a tub of water, the site of her suicide attempt. This single narrator speaks from the perspective of the adult men, who, decades later recount the events leading up to the suicide pact the Lisbon sisters made. The narrator speaks for four neighborhood boys—Chase (Anthony DeSimone), David (Lee Kagan), Parkie (Noah Shebib), and Tim (Jonathan Tucker)—who try and fail to "understand" the Lisbon girls: Cecilia, Lux (Kirsten Dunst), Bonnie (Chelse Swain), Mary (A.J. Cook), and Therese (Leslie Hayman).

Cecilia's therapist (Danny Devito) tells Mr. Lisbon (James Woods) and Mrs. Lisbon (Kathleen Turner) that Cecilia's suicide attempt was a cry for help and suggests they allow the girls social exchanges with boys their own age. Such a suggestion is especially difficult for Mrs. Lisbon, who wants to protect the girls. At first they invite Peter (Chris Hale) over for dinner, but eventually, the family has a party in their basement. They invite several boys, including the four neighborhood boys. Cecilia excuses herself from the party, and while everyone is downstairs, she jumps from her second-floor bedroom window and impales herself on a fence. In the wake of Cecilia's suicide, the neighborhood boys collect items the girls owned, including Cecilia's diary. The boys' failed attempt to understand her diary yields to their fantasy of the girls. It is a montage, influenced by 1970s pop culture. Following Cecilia's funeral, Mr. Lisbon, Parkie, and Chase all see apparitions of Cecilia.

As the neighborhood boys and the Lisbon sisters return to school, the boys continue to try to learn more about the girls, and they rely primarily on Trip Fontaine's reports, mainly about Lux. The film present Trip as the epitome of masculinity. He smokes marijuana, cuts class, plays football, and attracts the sexual attention of most girls, except Lux. While Trip falls for Lux the first time he meets her, he must work to gain Lux's attention. Eventually, Trip persuades Mr. and Mrs. Lisbon to let him and some other boys take all the sisters to the homecoming dance. At the dance, everyone has a good time. Lux and Trip, along with Bonnie and Parkie, sneak under the bleachers to kiss and drink alcohol. Afterwards, everyone returns home, except for Trip and Lux. Trip takes Lux to the football field, has sex with her, and leaves her there. Abandoned, Lux returns home the next morning, and, in response, their parents disenroll the girls from school and do not let them leave the home, presumably to keep them safe.

In order to connect with the Lisbon girls, the boys construct elaborate travel fantasies, based on the travel catalogues the girls have sent to their house. Eventually, the girls reach out to the neighborhood boys through handwritten notes, Morse code delivered from lamps, Catholic saint trading cards, and eventually through phone calls. Ultimately, the girls send a message the boys interpret as a cry for deliverance from the house, "Tomorrow Midnight wait for our signal" [sic]. Upon receiving the signal, the boys sneak over and meet Lux, who tells them to wait in the house while their parents fall asleep. However, the boys discover that all the Lisbon sisters have committed suicide. Frightened, the boys flee. Life eventually moves on for the neighborhood. The boys, however, remain emotionally trapped within the trauma of the Lisbon sisters' suicide. At the end of the film, the neighborhood boys stand in front of the Lisbon house and hold up lighters in memorial.

## TRAUMA AND WITNESS

Nursing scholar Debra Jackson outlines the relationship between the survivor (or victim), testimony, and the listening witness in the aftermath of traumatic experience. When an individual experiences trauma (Jackson focuses on women survivors of sexual assault), the event shatters the survivor's self.[6] In order to assist in integrating the shattered self, the survivor can "master the trauma" through her testimony.[7] Through telling and retelling her story—often through pain, fits and starts, and the failure of language—the survivor can heal. But the survivor cannot heal alone. She needs a witness.[8] The witness helps "her get outside the event rather than being lost in it."[9] To get outside of the traumatic event, the witness must listen in an empathetic and non-judgmental manner. By empathy, Jackson means that the witness might not have experienced the same traumatic event as the survivor, but she has likely experienced similar emotions, which the witness brings to the listening moment.[10] In the empathetic response, the witness brackets judgments of the testimony or the victim's choices.[11] Not all witnesses, however, listen well.

The example of the "four chimneys" story illustrates the distinction between a witness listening to testimony and listening to history. The historians listened to the woman's memory as a source for empirical, historical fact.[12] When her memory proved empirically inaccurate, the historian disregarded her. In this way, the historians listened with "their own agenda, carrying what they know into the listening enterprise, searching for consistency or inconsistency," and ultimately silencing the survivor.[13] Laub, however, did not view her utterance as an account of empirical fact. Rather, he engaged her words as testimony.[14] Her testimony demonstrates the imaginative limits of the historian. In his writing on this moment, Laub's rhetoric is revealing. He shifts abruptly from the past to the present tense, implicating that the work of testimony, somehow, occurs in the present rather than the past. "The woman's testimony," Laub insists, "is breaking the frame of the concentration camp by and through her very testimony: she is breaking out of Auschwitz even by her very talking. She had come, indeed, to testify, not to the empirical number of the chimneys, but to resistance, to the affirmation of survival, to the breakage of the frame of death."[15] In focusing on the facts of the case—one chimney, not four—the historian cannot break the frame of Auschwitz. Testimony, Laub implies, has the potential to break the very (im)moral infrastructure that make atrocities like Auschwitz possible. Her testimony refuses to give it the final word.

Given the emotional weight of the survivor's trauma, listening to a testimony can pose dangers or hazards to the witness, from which the witness might try to protect herself. In reflecting on her work as a suicide prevention volunteer and a rape survivor advocate, Jackson rightfully claims: "Witnessing trauma is anything but easy . . . To be open and connect with a victim's experience is terrifying. The witness enters a world filled with fear, shame, and guilt."[16] To maintain safety, the witness might engage in defensive reactions. Laub documents that the witness might experience a "sense of total paralysis," a "sense of outrage and of anger," or a "sense of total withdrawal and numbness."[17] The witness might also experience a "flood of awe and fear; we endow the survivor with a kind of sanctity, both to pay our tribute to him and to keep him at a distance, to avoid the intimacy entailed in knowing."[18] Likewise, the witness might "foreclose" the significance of the testimony "through an obsession with fact finding; an absorbing interest in the factual details of the account which serve to circumvent the human experience."[19] Such defensive procedures make it difficult, if not impossible, for the witness to listen well to the survivor's testimony.

Philosopher Giorgio Agamben (1942–) submits that a proper understanding of testimony should reorient the witness to events in the present, such that the testimony haunts the witness. In making the claim, the philosopher meditates on the work of Holocaust survivor Primo Levi, who wrote extensively about his experience in Auschwitz. Levi recounts a work break at the camp, in which members of the SS and the prisoners played a soccer match. Levi underscores how normal the game was. Spectators arrived, the players took "sides, bet, [and] applaud[ed] . . . as if, rather than at the gates of hell, the game were taking place on the village green."[20] Agamben comments that, rather than understand the game as an incarnation of human dignity, he sees the game as "the true horror of the camp."[21] He claims,

> we can perhaps think that the massacres are over—even if here and there they are repeated, not so far away from us. But that match is never over; it continues as if uninterrupted. But also hence our shame, the shame of those who did not know the camps and yet, without knowing how are spectators of that match, which repeats itself in every match in our stadiums, in every television broadcast, in the normalcy of everyday life. If we do not succeed in understanding that match, in stopping it, there will never be hope.[22]

Agamben's account suggests at least two relevant insights. First, the true horror of Auschwitz is indifference. Indifference exists at the very site of Auschwitz itself, transforming the gates of hell into a village green. Second, in witnessing Levi's testimony, witnesses carry the testimony wherever they go. Or perhaps more directly, testimonies, rightly heard, haunt the witness's daily life, in which every soccer match functions as a memorial to Auschwitz. As a memorial, everyday life is a site of shame, because the testimony exposes the witness's own indifference and willful ignorance. Unless the witness can understand and stop the forces of indifference that made that game possible, shame will persist.

Rooted in the notions of trauma and witness, the film documents the unresolved trauma the boys experienced as unwitting witnesses to the Lisbon girls' suicide. After the homecoming dance, Mr. and Mrs. Lisbon refuse to let their daughters out of their house. Toward the end of the film, the sisters send a message to the boys, "Tomorrow Midnight wait for our signal" [sic]. Because the Lisbon girls previously asked for help through their morse code message (the likely misinterpreted message "Send help Bobo"), the boys assume the message is a request for rescue. However, what the boys come to realize is that the girls chose them to be the people to find their bodies, to bear witness to their final act of agency. The boys respond in two ways.

First, witnessing the girls' suicide traumatizes them. As film and media scholar Justin Wyatt points out, "the boys have experienced trauma directly through being witnesses to the Lisbon girls."[23] Likewise, film studies scholar Michelle Aaron observes that the neighborhood boys are a focal point of trauma in the film.[24] In addition to scholarly reflection, the evidence of trauma emerges through details that, as Jackson claims, present the adult men as being trapped and lost in the event after all these years.[25] For example, the narrator describes their inability have functional heterosexual relationships. In their travel fantasy sequence, the boys imagine taking impossible trips with girls. Collaging photographs of the sisters, the boys, and images from travel catalogs and vacation brochures, Coppola represents their fantasies in the form of a slide show. The boys place themselves with the sisters at famous locations throughout the world and imagine that Cecelia had not died. Their fantasies take sensual, erotic contact with the sisters. The narrator recalls that in these fantasies they would stop and help one of the sisters with their backpacks and place their "hands on their [the sisters'] warm moist shoulders." With images of the fantasy slide show on the screen, the narrator concludes that these impossible and sensuous fantasies "scarred us forever, making us happier with dreams than wives . . . the Lisbon girls wouldn't leave our minds." He delivers the line as he delivers all of the lines, with flat, emotionless affect. However, their second response dooms them to remain trapped inside of their trauma.

The boys resist their role as witnesses in two ways: they engage in obsessive fact-finding, and they revere the girls in awe and fear. For example, as the boys flee from the girls' dead bodies, the narrator meditates on facts. "We would never be sure about the sequence of events. We argue about it still." The sequence of events the narrator ponders is the order of the girls' death: he describes how Bonnie died while the boys were in in the living room. After that, Mary placed her head in the oven. Therese took sleeping pills and was likely dead when the boys arrived. "Lux," however, "was the last to go." In addition to fact-finding, their fear takes place in mundane ways, like when Chase tries to talk to Mary. "Hi, I'm Chase," he says. Mary responds dismissively, "I know who you are. I've only been going to this school my whole life. You don't have to talk to me." She walks away and Chase never tries to talk to her again. At other times, the awe takes a more melodramatic tone. During their fantasy responding to Cecelia's diary, the narrator seems to worship the girls: "We knew the girls were really women in disguise, that they understood love, and even death, and that our job was merely to create the noise that seemed to fascinate them. We knew that they knew everything about us and that we couldn't fathom them at all." In these cases, as Laub points out, fact-finding and awe both serve to keep the girls at a distance, rendering the boys unable to hear their testimony. But it was not only their trauma that kept them from hearing the sisters. Hegemonic masculinity becomes another means by which they refuse to bear witness.

## HEGEMONIC MASCULINITY

R.W. Connell argues that hegemonic masculinity is a pattern of social and bodily practices that legitimates unequal, hierarchical gender relations between men and women and among men, through normative, historical, hegemonic practices.[26] Hegemonic masculinity does not describe a fixed set of "male" traits for all times and places. Hegemonic masculinity is not normal in any statistical sense. While "only a minority of men might enact it,"[27] hegemonic masculinity is for Connell "certainly normative," because it embodies a "most honored way of being a man."[28] This honored way of being demands "all other men . . . position themselves in relation to it."[29] Connell claims that a culture might have many honored ways of being a man that bring all other forms of masculinity and femininity in relationship to them. Hegemonic masculinities also change over time. Connell encourages scholars to discern the historically shifting social practices that legitimate the subordination of women and (most) men to historically shifting ways of being a man. In relationship to the concept of hegemony, toxic social practices, like physical violence, need not be the only means of legitimization or of policing the hierarchical relationship between men and women. In fact, much of the policing is discursive or embodied in language, media, and other social practices, persuading or encouraging both men and women "to consent to, unite around, and embody such unequal gender relations."[30]

Many pieces of scholarship using hegemonic masculinity are life-history studies, which explore how men and women negotiate with ideal ways of being a men.[31] For example, sociologist Chad Broughton conducted life histories of sixteen low-income men from southern Mexico, all of whom contemplated migrating north for work. Broughton notes that research has shattered the generalization that Mexico has a single *machismo* way of being man. Rather, contemporary Mexican culture reveals "complexity, ambiguity and contradiction" in the way men inhabit masculinities.[32] As such, Broughton's research reveals that his subjects encountered three, local and fluid hegemonic masculinities: the "traditionalist," "adventurer," and "breadwinner."[33] Because the traditionalist viewed the U.S.-Mexico border as a "minefield of moral hazards,"[34] this type of man decided to "endure destitution in the south and refrain from migrating in order to protect his family from such dangers up north."[35] The adventurer saw the border as a way to embody "his masculinity in new ways, such as through seeking thrills and breaking free from the inflexibility of rural life."[36] For the breadwinner, migration to the north was something he did reluctantly, in order to "provide for his wife and children."[37] Broughton argues that these "three stances are ideal types that do not necessarily neatly map onto individuals at the exclusion of other stances;

they are negotiated, gendered approaches for meeting instrumental and identity goals related to work, family and place."[38] While Broughton does not explore the role of women, Connell claims that *emphasized femininity*—or a social practice of a complementary, compliant female practice—is necessary for hegemony to work. The system needs women to facilitate their own subordination.[39] Like Connell's original insights, honored ways of being men had the power to orient men and women in the daily lives.

Related to hegemonic masculinity, masculine Enlightenment epistemology is also relevant to the film, particularly a Cartesian epistemology which embodies control, coercion, and violence. In his reading of Enlightenment philosopher Rene Descartes, philosopher Charles Taylor claims that Cartesian epistemology demands that the knower disengage from his embodied experience of the world. One must "objectify the world" and approach such a phenomenon "mechanistically and functionally, in the same way that an uninvolved external observer would."[40] Philosopher Lorraine Code describes the binary thinking at work in these epistemologies as a "S-knows-that-$p$" epistemology, in which the knower (the S) seeks to "control the behavior of the objects known" (the $p$).[41] Lifting the knower out of his embodied experience of the world, Enlightenment epistemologies confer upon the knower a false sense that he can know the world from the ideal position of "nowhere," "anywhere," and "everywhere."[42] Because this mode of knowing is an honored way of being a man in the Western world, it functions as an aspect of hegemonic masculinity, subordinating others to the role of object or "the $p$." Similarly, philosopher Anupam Yadav argues that not only does this mode of knowing place a "tremendous faith in the cognitive abilities of men to know and master everything," but it also proves to be a "coercive rationality."[43] Feminist Donna Haraway characterizes the coercion of masculine, Enlightenment epistemology in the language of violence and rape. Such knowledge is a "perverse vision"[44] of the world in which the god-like eye of the knower "fucks the world" or devours the world with a "cannibal eye" of masculine knowing.[45] As a result, the hegemonic masculinity of Enlightenment epistemology impacts social ways of being in the world. If the "S" is traditionally male, "the $p$" involves not only the natural world but also all other things, including a woman's body. Violence constitutes the relationship of knower to others, as the neighborhood boys' knowledge and love demonstrates.

The boys' strategies of fact-finding and awe take place against the backdrop of hegemonic masculinity, first by way of the boys subordinating Lux and the Lisbon girls to their sexual desire. Before the boys find the girls' dead bodies, Chase finally reveals his interest in the girls, "These girls make me crazy. If I could just feel one of 'em up just once." Chase is not alone. In the first interview of the film, the boys hear Paul Baldino (Robert Schwartzman) tell his fictitious story about finding Cecilia after her suicide attempt, entering the Lisbon house through the sewers. In explaining his motive, he tells the neighborhood boys, "So I went up, thinking I could see the Lisbon girls taking a shower." Most of the boys focus their fantasies on Lux. For example, the neighborhood boys interview two other boys who claim to have had sexual contact with Lux: "Squeezebox is all right," says one boy, "Let me tell you, she's the hottest girl in this school, for sure." Another says, "If you wanna know what happened, smell my fingers, man." A third says, "Nah, she didn't talk about Cecilia. We weren't exactly talking if you know what I mean." Taken together, nearly all of the boys in the film subordinate the Lisbon girls through sexual desire.

However, as Connell insists, the subjugation of women demands that women work to perform or facilitate oppression through *emphasized femininity*, and Mrs. Lisbon plays that role, subordinating the girls to her fear. When Peter has dinner at the Lisbon house and Trip comes over to the house to watch TV with the Lisbon family, Mrs. Lisbon controls Lux's bodily flirtations. She tells Lux to put her "shirt on" and take her "feet down" from the coffee table. Both, Mrs. Lisbon implies, draw the gaze of young boys. Mrs. Lisbon is also responsible for not letting the girls travel in cars, "We almost never allow the girls to go out in cars unless it's necessary. There are so many accidents nowadays." Mr. Lisbon supports his wife's restrictions. He says to Trip, "You cannot take Lux out, especially not in a car." When Lux comes home late from the homecoming dance, Mrs. Lisbon takes the girls out of school, closing the girls off from the outside world, and forces Lux to burn her record collection. When Lux protests their subordination, her mother insists, "You're safe here." Whether motivated by sexual desire or safety, the effect of subordination is the same. The cumulative effect of these bodily subordinations is part of what motivates their suicides.

In addition to the subordination of the Lisbon girls' bodies, hegemonic masculinity also arranges the boys in a hierarchical relationship to Trip. The film singles out Trip as the most honored way the neighborhood boys know to be a man. In introducing Trip, the narrator links his epistemological power—his reliability as a source of knowledge—with his physicality, sexuality, and drug use. The narrator says, "the only reliable boy who actually got to know Lux was Trip Fontaine, who only eight months before the suicides, had emerged from baby fat to the delight of girls and mothers alike." To comic effect, Coppola accompanies his introduction with Heart's song "Magic Man." Trip is magic, because he garners the attention of nearly every girl in school and regularly smokes marijuana in his car between classes. Trip is also a football player. He even brags about his capacity for physical violence to Lux when they are on the football field. "Hey, you see that divot there?" he says. "That's where I reamed this guy today." He then enacts violence, tackling Lux and bringing her to the ground. Additionally, in persuading Mr. and Mrs. Lisbon to let Trip take Lux and her sisters to homecoming, Trip becomes the gatekeeper to the sisters' bodies, choosing the boys who will be their dates. Trip's choices function as enactment of his hegemonic power. The narrator recounts that Trip chose Parkie, one of the neighborhood boys who does not conform to Trip's masculinity, because he has access to one aspect of being a man. He has access to a Cadillac, a car big enough to transport everyone. Trip chose Kevin Head (Joe Roncetti) because of his access to marijuana. However, Trip breaks with honored ways of being a man as a strategic appeal to Mr. and Mrs. Lisbon. He chose Jake Hill Conley (Hayden Christensen) because he was an excellent student, "which Trip thought would impress Mr. and Mrs. Lisbon." The rest of the neighborhood boys—Chase, Tim, and David—exist in such a subordinate social relationship to Trip that he never acknowledges their existence, except in their interview with him as an adult.

## MIMICRY AND AMBIVALENCE

Postcolonial scholar Homi Bhabha uses the term mimicry to describe an act of imitation that can be used to destabilize colonial powers. Mimicry occurs when a colonized person imitates aspects of colonizer culture, be it dress, manners, patterns of thought, music, food, and the like.[46] Mimicry is a result of the colonizer's "desire for a reformed, recognizable Other"; however, the colonized person will never completely imitate the colonizer.[47] Mimicry is always *"almost the same, but not quite,"*[48] or a "blurred copy" of the original.[49] Bhabha describes mimicry as farcical, ironic, and mocking, all of which has the potential to destabilize colonial power.[50] Literary scholar Amardeep Singh offers two examples of destabilization. In E. M. Forster's novel, *A Passage to India* (1924), the author includes a minor character named Mr. Amritrao, an Indian lawyer whom the British dread. The British dread him, because "he has learned enough of the principles of British law to realize that those principles should, in all fairness, apply to Indians as much as to the British."[51] Singh also cites Mohandas K. Gandhi. He "took symbols of Indian asceticism and simplicity (such as traditional Indian dress and fabric) along with progressive western concepts of socialism," through which he sought justice from the British for the colonized Indian people.[52] Such destabilizations are a result of the ambivalence embedded within mimicry.

Drawing on the work of French psychologist Jacques Lacan, ambivalence is a result of a repression, or an excess or disavowal, of a "simultaneous attraction and repulsion."[53] Mimicry becomes ambivalent because, in the case of India, the British colonizer wants the colonized subject to be Anglicized but not fully British. If an Indian could become entirely British, then colonizers would lose their sense of cultural superiority. Therefore, colonizers both want and do not want the colonized to become identical to themselves. Bhabha offers two illustrations. The Enlightenment philosopher John Stuart Mill admits, perhaps without embarrassment, that he understood himself to be "a democrat in my own country . . . and a despot in someone else's country, as a member of a colonial power."[54] In this case, Mill is ambivalent about democracy, which allows him equality with others in one setting but permits behavior that contradicts democracy in another. Bhabha also notes a similar moment in Enlightenment philosopher John Locke's *Second Treatise of Civil Government* (1689), revolving around the term "slave." Locke first uses "slave . . . as the locus of a legitimate form of ownership, then as the trope for an intolerable, illegitimate exercise of power."[55] Locke refuses to be a slave and yet sees no problem enslaving others. The seeming lack of awareness of Mill's and Locke's inconsistency is, for Bhabha, the moment of ambivalence (or repression) that upholds the injustices of the colonizing West.

Drawing from this account of mimicry and ambivalence, we apply Bhabha's insights to the neighborhood boys of *The Virgin Suicides*. Bhabha uses mimicry and ambivalence to describe modes of resistance against colonizers. Taking India as a prime location, Bhabha asks implicitly: "How are the colonized taught to embrace colonization? And how do colonized subjects use what they have learned to resist the colonizer?" Such implicit questions are present in passages such as this: "mimicry . . . produces a subversive strategy of subaltern agency that negotiates its own authority through a process of iterative 'unpicking' and incommensurable, insurgent relinking."[56] Because mimicry is palimpsestuous, the colonized can use that blurriness to deconstruct colonial power and reconstruct a more just way of living. In shifting the context of Bhabha's insights, we also shift the implicit questions that undergird mimicry and ambivalence. Instead of asking about the colonized, we want to focus on the colonizer. "What are aspects of the colonizer's (mal)formation? And how does that (mal)formation impact the colonizer?" Mutating the questions once again, we apply them to the neighborhood boys: "What are aspects of the neighborhood boys' masculine formation? How does their (mal)formation impact them?" Because masculine formation is a cultural practice, Bhabha's language of mimicry and ambivalence yields insight to these questions, albeit in a different register and with differing effects.

Drawing on both masculinity and mimicry outlined above, the neighborhood boys mimic epistemological masculinity, and their mimicries are acts of symbolic violence, which they perform through fact-finding objectification. Their objectification takes the form of a "S-knows-that-$p$" stance, or an unrelenting belief that the boys can know the girls as objects from their position as knowers. The narrator reveals their objectifying gaze through the metaphor of a puzzle. The girls' lives and deaths are pieces that must have a knowable, final form. The film opens with this commitment, "Even then, as teenagers, we tried to put the pieces together. We still can't." Likewise, at the end of the film, the narrator claims, "In the end, we had pieces of the puzzle, but no matter how we put them together, gaps remained." Their objectification fails to deliver a knowable answer as to why the girls committed suicide. This failure, however, does not produce a resistance to hegemonic masculinity or a form of self-criticism, as Bhabha's "blurred copy" might suggest. Rather, their epistemological form of knowing, as Yadav and Haraway suggest, constitutes a form of violence, because it closes off the possibility that the objects of their knowledge—the Lisbon sisters—are, in fact, agents.

They also enact symbolic violence through their fantasies. Film scholar Anna Backman Rogers describes the neighborhood boys' fantasies in terms of 1970s advertising and pornography.[57] She takes special attention to the fantasy montage that occurs when the neighborhood boys read Cecilia's diary. The boys imagine Cecilia reading a passage from her diary. The passage launches the boys' fantasy of the sisters with images unrelated to the words. Their fantasy places the girls in an open field, surrounded by trees and tall grass. The boys imagine the girls dressed in white sun dresses, Lux in a bikini top, and all of them bathed in warm light of a setting sun. They also imagine 1970s cinematic tropes, namely superimposed images of the girls and themselves. The girls sit in quiet reflection or leap into the air. On the soundtrack, 1970s synthetic string sounds give way to a solo flugelhorn, perhaps reminiscent of flugelhorn player Chuck Mangione 1977 hit, "Feels So Good." Coppola confirms the pornographic origin of the sequence. In the special features to the film, Coppola claims that she used the "*Playboy*" trope of the "nature-fantasy-70s girl" to model the sequence.[58] Therefore, the boys' fantasy is made possible by the pornographic media of the time. The montage suggests their formation into a hegemonic masculinity that objectifies women's bodies for masculine sexual desire.[59]

With their puzzle-solving, "S-knows-that-$p$" epistemology, their fantasy also holds objectification together with awe. Their fantasy continues with the narrator's extended reflection on Cecilia's diary. Based on her writing, the boys bear witness to the "imprisonment of being a girl," but they seem unable to resist the temptation to objectify the girls through their Playboy, nature-girl fantasies. Since the boys are committed to solving the puzzle of the girls with their objectifying epistemology, their fantasy distances themselves from the girls through awe. The girls possessed powers that ranged from the mundane ("knowing what colors went together") to the philosophical ("they understood love, and even death"). In elevating the girls, they also diminish themselves. The boys are merely "noise" that served to "fascinate" the girls. Furthermore, the girls "knew everything about us," and the boys "couldn't fathom them at all." Their fantasy exacerbates their objectification of the girls with the distance of awe.

The neighborhood boys objectify the girls through voyeurism. Immediately after the opening credits, the neighborhood boys sit on the curb outside of the Lisbon house. The boys sit in a wide shot, watching as the Lisbons return home in a station wagon. The camera then shows each boy in close-up, watching the girls get out of their car one by one. In a reciprocal close-up and freeze frame on the girls, the film superimposes each girl's name on their close-ups with a personalized, handwritten font. With this myopic view, the boys describe each girl with the most mundane fact them: their age. Once school starts, the boys sit in class, and Parkie looks out a window at Lux and a boy. The boy whispers something to Lux, and she laughs. In a flirtatious gesture, the boy throws grass on Lux's shirt. From Parkie's point of view, the camera shows a close-up on the grass and on her shirt, and then it follows with an extreme close-up on her smile and neck. The distance from Lux's body and the close-ups emphasize Parkie's lustful gaze. After Mr. and Mrs. Lisbon imprison the girls, the narrator notes that Lux began having sex on her roof. In the following sequence, the boys watch Lux through a telescope and argue among themselves. "What else? Come on, is she naked?" asks Tim, followed by Chase's, "What's she doing?" In these scenes, the boys' voyeurism betrays a desire to be in proximity to the girls, especially Lux. Whether it is other boys at school or the those on the roof, the neighborhood boys use voyeurism as an extension of their fantasy, projecting themselves vicariously into sexual relationship with Lux, keeping themselves at a distant, and subordinating her body to their sexual desire.

Given both the boys' and Mrs. Lisbon's objectification of the sisters, it should be little surprise that their conception of love, which the film tethers to their epistemology, is similarly problematic. The first character who expresses his so-called love is Dominic (Joe Dinicol). Having fallen in love with Diana Porter, Dominic denounced God when she left for vacation. To demonstrate his love, he jumped off the roof of his relative's house. However, when Dominic jumps, he does not jump off the roof. He jumps out of a second story window. The disjunction between the narrator's statement and the image underscores the boys' epistemological unreliability, which occurs at the site of Dominic's so-called love. Furthermore, as Mrs. Lisbon reflects on the suicide of her daughters, she says, "None of my daughters lacked for any love. There was plenty of love in our house. I never understood why." Like Dominic, Mrs. Lisbon misunderstands that her love is entangled with unreliable epistemology.

The film develops the linkage with Trip's similar epistemologically problematic love. Quoting T.S. Eliot's "Burnt Norton," an adult Trip (Michael Paré) describes his affection for Lux as heartfelt and intelligent, "She was the still point of the turning world, man," says an adult Trip, "I never got over that girl . . . I loved a lot of ladies, but not like that. That was real." However, after Trip abandoned her on the football field, his so-called love takes the form of indifference and consumption. At once, he claims that he did not care how Lux returned home that night, and also says, "You know, most people will never taste that kind of love. But at least I tasted it once, right?" In describing knowledge of Lux's body as a love that can be "tasted," he objectifies her, subordinating her to the status of food. After Trip delivers the line, a nurse approaches him and informs him that he needs to attend his next group session. With only this detail, Coppola reveals that the neighborhood boys, now adults, are interviewing Trip in a rehab facility. His status as a drug addict subtly (and perhaps unfairly) calls into question the reliability of his claims. Where Trip was, as a teenager, the only reliable epistemological source, the film presents adult Trip as epistemologically dubious.

Finally, the narrator ends the film with a reflection on their love for the Lisbon girls, "It didn't matter in the end how old they had been or that they were girls, but only that we had loved them and that they hadn't heard us calling." The film concludes with the trivializing gesture of the boys holding up lighters, presumably in memoriam for the girls. If the boys' engagement with the girls has, throughout the film, taken the form of symbolic violence of objectification, fantasy, and voyeurism, then their entrapment inside of a system of hegemonic masculinity has resulted in a confusion of symbolic violence with, what the ultimately describe here as, love. The boys, therefore, cannot truly love the girls any more than Dominic, Trip, or Mrs. Lisbon do. In a system of hegemonic masculinity, love of this kind is part of what drives the girls to suicide.

Based on this analysis, we return to the two questions we asked in relations to Bhabha, the first of which concerns the boys as masculine subjects. The boys mimic a rationally and sexually honored way of being a man, that bears a strong similarity to Enlightenment philosophers and Trip. Like their Enlightenment predecessors, the boys' binary, "S-knows-that-$p$" epistemology expresses an unwavering faith in their ability to master the girls' testimony into a completed puzzle that makes sense to them. Like Trip, the boys treat the girls as sexual objects, and Trip, mirroring the feminist understanding of Western epistemology as violent, describes his own sexual contact with Lux as a devouring encounter.[60] With the Lisbon girls functioning as subordinate sexual objects, the neighborhood boys reproduce the contours of hegemonic masculinity, arranging the other boys they encounter honoring Trip's epistemological reliability and sexual proximity to Lux. Even though the neighborhood boys occupy a non-hegemonic masculinity in relation to Trip, they desire to emulate his reliability and proximity to Lux. While many other boys claim to have access to Lux's body, the boys tend to only trust

Trip's account, despite his ultimate epistemological unreliability. Within the hegemonic system, Trip also functions as a masculine gatekeeper, excluding most of the neighborhood boys from dates with the girls. While they inhabit a non-hegemonic status, they still desire to benefit from the violence of the system.

Like Bhabha's description of mimicry, the boys cannot fully mimic this ideal form of being a man. They boys are blurred copies of the ideal form of masculinity. Epistemologically, the boys cannot solve the puzzle of the girls' lives and deaths. The concluding narration admits their failure: "we will never find the pieces to put them back together." Furthermore, the boys never inhabit a a sexually potent form of masculinity, like Trip does. Parkie highlights this reality. While Parkie accompanies Bonnie to homecoming, kisses her, and drinks Peach Schnapps with her, the boys never bestow on him a masculine status relative to Trip.

Their inability to mimic their ideal masculinity, secondly, affects the boys in negative ways, especially through the damaging linkage of masculine knowing and love. As men, the boys are trapped inside of their obsession with the girls and trapped inside of the trauma of finding their girls' dead bodies. As adults. they seem unable to move on from this trauma. The narrator recounts, we "find ourselves in the corner going over the evidence one more time," whether at "business lunches or cocktail parties." And their travel fantasies of the girls made them "happier with dreams than wives." Their failed attempt to heal their trauma through hegemonic masculinity's fact-finding and awe outlines the limitations of masculine ways of knowing and love. Like the historians who could not hear the woman's testimony of the four chimneys, the neighborhood boys cannot hear, in the Lisbon girls' suicides, the desire to break the frame of death that surrounds their lives. However, Coppola presents the girls as not bound to the boys' limitations.

## THE LISBON SISTERS

Both critics and the novel's author, Jeffrey Eugenides, point to the power of the Lisbon sisters to exceed the boys' limited understanding and love. In reference to the novel, Eugenides claims, "I think of the book as extremely male. It's written from the point of view of males. I'm always surprised to find that most of the readers of the book are teenaged girls who feel their life is being addressed and described."[61] Other readers of the novel assert something similar. Novelist and journalist Emma Cline notes that the novel "allows the Lisbon girls the dignity of existing beyond the boys' conceptions of them," and "gives us [readers] glimpses of their real, breathing selves."[62] In reflecting on Coppola's adaptation of his novel, Eugenides recalls that the director pointed out to him that the boys' limited point of view "opens a kind of vacuum or emptiness in which . . . a female reader, especially a young female reader, can fill it with her own experience."[63] He goes on to say that, in Coppola's film, "the point of view . . . had shifted toward the girls," because, "the girls are presented as real characters, as physical characters in the film, so that you take their experiences as real."[64] Journalist and film critic Hannah Woodhead notes a similar point. "In Eugenides' novel, we know everything we know about the Lisbons through the voice of the neighborhood boys trying to unpack the mystery of their deaths. But Coppola's film reveals the secret lives of these girls in a less voyeuristic manner—we don't spy on the girls, as the boys do. We become them."[65] Writer Tavi Gevinson claims that the significance of the girls' secret lives occurs through their material culture: "The point made to focus in on seemingly minor details—a yearbook photo, an eyelash curler—when the larger story is so tragic, gives those same meaningless signifiers of a normal teenage life . . . some kind of poignancy."[66] This evidence from both authors and readers points to the reality that even though the film is, narratively speaking, confined to the point of view of the neighborhood boys, somehow, the Lisbon sisters exceed their limitations.

Such liminal breaches takes the form of juxtapositions, apparitions, authorial intrusions, and conversation. First, the film uses juxtapositions to highlight the excess of the girls' material culture and experience, as the opening of the film establishes. After an opening shot of Lux eating a red popsicle, the camera shows the suburban neighborhood in which the film takes place. In the warm glow of afternoon light, a man waters his lawn. Two women walk a dog and chat. Workers dressed in orange jump suits post a "Notice for Removal" on a tree. A man grills in his driveway while his son plays basketball. The sun dapples through bright green leaves, all the while a dreamy instrumental version of Air's "Playground Love" plays on the soundtrack. However, on a cut from the exterior shot of leaves to the interior of the Lisbon girls' house, the music cuts abruptly, mid-phrase. Instead of warm sunlight, blue light covers a window ledge with many of the girls' mundane material possessions: perfume, fingernail polish, candles, crucifixes, makeup accessories, and a fan. The girls have covered the shelf with stickers. The juxtaposition between the warm exterior to the cold interior, between the dreamy sounds of Air and the relative silence of Cecilia's suicide is the first signal that the Lisbon girls exist outside of, in excess of, the world they inhabit.

A similar juxtaposition occurs when Cecilia is in the hospital. Likely using green filters on the camera, Coppola saturates images of the hospital in a sickly green tint. This place of healing, for Cecilia, represent its opposite. And the doctor utters words that trivialize Ceclia's experience, "What are you doing here, honey? You're not even old enough to know how bad life gets." In a wide shot, Cecilia says, "Obviously, Doctor," then, mid-phrase, Coppola cuts to an abrupt close up, emphasizing her sentiment, "you've never been a thirteen-year-old girl." These are the first words that any of the sisters speak in the film. Like the cold, girlie world the sisters inhabit, Cecilia's experience exceeds the sickly space and condescending knowledge of men, like the doctor. This moment, like the sisters' shelf, establishes—through word, color, and mid-phrase editing—the distance between the girls and the world they inhabit.

The film also juxtaposes the neighborhood boys' fantasies and expectations with the girls' bodies and their suicides. When Peter has dinner with the Lisbon family, early in the film, Mrs. Lisbon directs him to the bathroom in Cecilia's room. Once he enters the bathroom, he investigates. He sprays a perfume bottle, touches a glass unicorn bottle, and opens a cupboard full of tampons. He then finds and opens a lipstick, brings it to his nose, and inhales. Peter then lapses into a fantasy of Lux. She appears in close-up, backlit by the sun. She tosses her hair, looks into the camera seductively, and throws her head back in ecstasy. Lux's knock at the door interrupts his fantasy, and she says, "You done hogging the bathroom? I need something." He opens the door and stands in the bathroom as she walks to the cupboard with tampons in it. She moves as though she is going to take a one. She stops, however, puts her hand on one hip, and says to Peter, "Do you mind?" Embarrassed, Peter flees from the house. In film scholar Fiona Handyside's reading of this scene, she observes that "this replacement of his [Peter's] vision of feminine sexuality compared to its (literally) bloody reality," is precisely what produces Peter's embarrassment.[67] If the red lipstick represents the fantasy of his sexual desire, then the scene juxtaposes his attraction to the red lipstick with his repulsion to the red blood of Lux's menstruating body.[68] Her body exceeds his fantasy.

The most profound juxtapositions, however, are the girls' choices to commit suicide, which juxtaposes the expectations, fantasies, and sexual desires of the neighborhood boys with the reality of the girls' choices. The first suicide, Cecilia's, comes during the party in the Lisbons' basement. The neighborhood boys expect social fun with the Lisbon girls during the party in their basement. However, Cecilia chooses to end her life. Similarly, at the end of the film, Coppola fills with the scene with a series of juxtapositions. At night, having received the signal from the sister, the boys approach the house in secret. When they knock on the back door, Lux answers. The boys appear tense, trying not to wake Mr. and Mrs. Lisbon. But Lux carries herself with a flirtatious, relaxed swagger. As she smokes a cigarette, Parkie explains that they have a car and a full tank of gas and can travel with the girls anywhere they want to go. With disinterest in escaping, Lux flirts with the boys. She asks if she can sit in the front seat, asks which of the boys will sit upfront with her, and asks if she can steer the car while Chase drives. She invites the boys into the house to wait for her parents to fall asleep and informs the boys that she will wait in the car. As boys stand in living room, the boys fantasize about being on the open road with the sisters. Within the tight space the house, the boys stand in darkness, with their backs to the camera. They move slowly and silently. The reality of the house differs from their fantasy. They fantasize themselves, not alone, but with all the Lisbon sisters, in the daytime, on the wide space of the open road. Instead of silence, the sound of wind fills the soundtrack. Lux laughs. A female voice hums a simple melody. Instead of Lux's tense and serious flirtation, the girls smile. Lux hangs out of the window, with her hair blowing in the wind. Bonnie and Mary lean on Parkie's shoulders. Back in the house, the boys hear a sound in the basement. Downstairs and likely in response to Lux's flirtations, Chase finally exclaims, "These girls make me crazy. If I could just feel one of 'em up just once." The girls do not conform to the boys' expectations, fantasies, or sexual desires. They exceed them.

Second, Cecilia's apparitions exceed masculine epistemology, appearing to her father, Parkie, Chase, and possibly later in the film, watering her lawn. After Cecilia dies, her father walks into her bedroom and sees a vision of her in a lace dress. She does not look at him. Rather, she looks out the open window as the wind blows her dress and a mobile hanging behind her head. Her father does not seem shocked at her appearance. He, instead, looks out the same open window Cecilia had jumped out of. He closes the window and hears a voice from behind him saying, "Don't worry." He turns around to see Bonnie speaking, "They took the fence out." In the following scene, Parkie wakes from a night's sleep to find Cecilia sitting at the foot of his bed. Unlike her father, Cecilia, dressed in the same lace dress, looks at Parkie, smiles, and says, "God, you snore loud." His alarm goes off, and he turns from her to shut it off. When he looks back at the foot of her bed, she is gone. In the following scene, Chase sits in the back of his mother's car. He looks up into a tree and sees Cecilia lounging in a branch, dressed in her lace dress, with bangles around her wrist. Cecilia looks directly at Chase before turning her gaze to the horizon. Literary scholar Debra Shostak notes a potential fourth appearance of Cecilia. As workers arrive at the house to cut down their elm tree, the girls attempt to stop the workers, until journalist Lydia Perl (Suki Kaiser) appears on the scene. As audio of Perl's reporting plays on the soundtrack, the workers remove branches from a yard, Shostak says, "the camera lingers on a figure in the distance who looks very much like Cecilia, watering bushes with a hose. Because she is turned away from the camera, we cannot confirm whether the image is Cecilia."[69] Taken together, the male characters who see Cecilia's apparition never discuss the apparitions, as if such a reality would even further demonstrate the limitations of the masculine ways of knowing what the characters inhabit. Nevertheless, her appearances demonstrate the inadequacy of the boys' "S-knows-that-p" epistemology.

Third, Coppola uses authorial intrusions of girlie culture to express the sisters' agency. In film scholar David Bordwell's discussion of art cinema, he notes how art film directors incorporate, "stylistic signatures in the narration: technical touches (Truffaut's freeze frames, Antonioni's pans) and obsessive motifs (Buñuel's anticlericalism, Fellini's shows, Bergman's character names)."[70] These intrusions, in effect, come into the film, not necessarily from within the film's narrative. Rather, the author intrudes into the narrative in real and substantial ways. Coppola's opening authorial intrusions occur in the film's title sequence. After Cecilia's visit to the hospital, in which she informs the doctor that he "obviously" knows nothing about the experience of being the thirteen-year-old girl, the camera tracks down the street of the suburban neighborhood. The image fades to a blue sky and clouds. In handwritten girlie script, the title "The Virgin Suicides" appears, with hearts instead of dots for the "i's." Slowly, the screen films with handwritten scripts of the title, including childlike drawings of roses, hearts, crosses, unicorns, crying eyes, and a caterpillar, all reminiscent of the kinds of drawing that might appear in a school notebook. As the titles fade, a close-up of Lux appears. She looks directly into the camera, at the audience, perhaps in a gaze of confrontation. However, her gaze softens to a knowing, self-aware smile and a wink, directly into camera. The sound of a high-pitched chime accompanies her wink, communicating a sense of knowing, self-awareness.

A similar moment appears when Trip meets Lux for the first time. When she looks over her shoulder at Trip, a small, hand-drawn star flashes at the center of her eye. Instead of winking at Trip (like she did in the film's opening), it is as if her eye twinkles at Trip, and the same high-pitched chime accompanies the flash. The final intrusion occurs when the boys arrive to pick the girls up from the homecoming dance. As Trip pins a corsage on Lux's dress, the camera tilts down from her shoulder to her waist. Beneath her dress, the camera reveals that Lux has written Trip's name on her underwear, with a heart instead of the dot on the "i."

Finally, Coppola uses the sisters' conversations and suicides to register their agency. For example, during the basement party, the girls, especially Theresa, interact with the boys in a way that seems to humor their failed attempts at socialization. Therese asks Tim, "Do you know where you're applying yet?" Tim replies, "Well, no, but my parents are pushing towards Yale . . . You've heard of Yale?" Therese replies, "Oh, yeah," with a smile that appears at once knowing, amused, and insulted. When Mr. Lisbon describes the boys who are taking the girls to the homecoming dance, Mary asks, "Who's taking who?" Therese responds matter-of-factly, "They're just gonna raffle us off." In addition to Therese's amused, knowing, and matter-of-fact responses, mundane conversations portray the girls as critical of the world around them. While on their way to the dance, the camera observes a house with a car in the driveway. Bonnie says, "Oh, my gosh, look, you guys. Her car is there late again. I'm sure Mr. Leo's having an affair with the maid. I saw him follow her into the laundry room." Therese response, "He's so sad, that red nose. Totally an alcoholic." Bonnie continues, "Yeah, what about the Hessens? You know they're Nazis." "They're Nazi sympathizers, Bonnie," Mary offers in correction. Therese notes, "They had a fit when the Schwartzmans tried to join the tennis club." The girls' suicides, in fact, serve as the clearest demonstration of their agency. As Rogers notes, "If the girls embody a lost past, they also represent a refusal to take up their place within a patriarchal society that confines them precisely to a form of living death."[71] Through these moments, the girls display agency. They carry an awareness of themselves and the world that exceeds the boys' epistemological framework.

By way of conclusion, we suggest three implications The Virgin Suicides has for the theoretical frameworks we explored above. First, our reading of the film suggests that the Lisbon sisters expressed their agency, in part, through the testimony of their lives and deaths. And testimony, as Laub points out, has the potential to break the frame of death. Throughout the film, the boys' mimicry of masculinity—that is their failure to know and love the girls—demonstrates that the frame of death that surrounds them does not have the final word on the girls' lives. For those of us who witness patriarchal violence, the breakage of patriarchy's framework of living death may only occur for witnesses to the extent that they listen well, as both Laub and Jackson suggest. But witnesses must also let a testimony haunt them in the appropriate way. For Agamben, the haunting takes place through the mundane resonance between the site of trauma (Auchwitzch) and so-called ordinary life (any soccer match). As adult men, the neighborhood boys appear on the verge of such connections. At the beginning of the film, for example, the narrator links the death of the elm trees and the death of the automotive industry to the girls's\ death. The boys, as men, also cannot stop talking about an event that happened decades in their past. However, the boys seem unable or unwilling to see that the violence performed upon the Lisbon sisters exists in the lives of women and girls they know. Whether it is five suicides or one, the girls bear witness to a world that makes them the living dead.[72] Rather than let the testimony of the Lisbon sisters shed new light on that world in their present life, the men have let the Lisbon sisters eclipse nearly any reference to women or girls in their present. In fact, the men cannot engage in healthy relationships with their spouses. While not every woman makes the choices that the Lisbon sisters made, every woman lives in the same world that confined the Lisbon sisters to living death.[73] If we, like Agamben claims, are unable to see in all women the faces of Therese, Mary, Lux, Bonnie, and

Cecilia, then we have not borne witness to their testimony, to the testimony of the women who came before them, and to the testimonies who will come after them.

Second, Coppola's rendering of the Lisbon sisters' testimony offers a contribution to the task of being haunted properly, particularly on love and violence. The work of scholars like Connell and Haraway rightly link hegemonic masculinity and masculine epistemology to violence, like sexual assault and the objectification of women's bodies. To those insights, Coppola's film suggests that it is not merely our social order or epistemology that masculinity has imbued with sexual violence. Love is also, potentially, a domain of violence. For some, like Trip, the boys, and Mrs. Lisbon, individuals imagine love as a domain of pure goodness. Love is not immune to violence. *The Virgin Suicides* suggests that the same vigilance that Haraway urges us to apply to epistemology, we should also apply to love.

Finally, Coppola's film illustrates the necessity for those in social locations of power and privilege, like the neighborhood boys in the film, to take more seriously the conditions in which their ambivalence takes place. Bhabha's insights regarding ambivalence and mimicry's blurred copy suggest that mimicry holds within it a potential for critical engagement with colonial power. However, when transposed onto the formation of those people who have traditionally oppressed others, mimicry's potential to resist systems of oppression demand a more robust contextual attention. Like Laub's and Agamben's insights regarding a witness, oppressors, like the neighborhood boys, engage in failed attempts at mimicry, but the experience of being a blurred copy is a necessary but insufficient means of destabilizing the oppressive powers that formed them. The oppressor must listen to testimony his own ambiguity, and through that listening, imagine the breaking of the frame of death that hegemonic masculinity holds on him. In that moment, the failure to be masculine can become a threshold into a new way of knowing or a new way of loving others.

## REFERENCES

Aaron, Michelle. "Cinema and Suicide: Necromanticism, Dead-already-ness, and the Logic of the Vanishing Point." *Cinema Journal*, 53 no 2 (Winter 2014): 71–92.

Agamben, Giorgio. *Remnants of Auschwitz: The Witness and the Archive*, translated by Daniel Heller-Roazen. New York: Zone Books, 2002.

Ashcroft, Bill, Gareth Griffiths, and Helen Tiffin. *Post-Colonial Studies: The Key Concepts*. New York: Routledge, 2000.

Atkinson, Joshua and Bernadette Calafell. "Darth Vader Made Me Do It! Anakin Skywalker's Avoidance of Responsibility and the Gray Areas of Hegemonic Masculinity in the Star Wars Universe." *Communication, Culture and Critique*, 2 no 1 (March 2009): 1–20. doi-org.proxy.lib.duke. edu/10.1111/j.1753-9137.2008.01026.x.

Barry, Ben. "The Toxic Lining of Men's Fashion Consumption: The Omnipresent Force of Hegemonic Masculinity." *Critical Studies in Men's Fashion*, 2 no 2–3 (September 2015): 143–161. dx.doi.org.proxy.lib.duke.edu/10.1386/csmf.2.2-3.143_1.

Bhabha, Homi, *The Location of Culture*. London: Routledge, 1994, 2004.

Bordwell, David. "Art Cinema as a Mode of Film Practice." In *Film Theory and Criticism: Introductory Readings*, 7th ed., edited by Leo Braudy and Marshall Cohen, 649–57. New York: Oxford University Press, 2009.

Broughton, Chad. "Migration as Engendered Practice: Mexican Men, Masculinity, and northward Migration." *Gender & Society* 22 no. 5 (October 2008): 568–589. DOI: 10.1177/0891243208321275.

Cline, Emma. "'The Virgin Suicides' Still Holds the Mysteries of Adolescence." *The New Yorker*, October 2, 2018. www.newyorker.com/books/second-read/the-virgin-suicides-still-holds-the-mysteries-of-adolescence.

Code, Lorraine. "Taking Subjectivity into Account." In *Feminist Epistemologies*, edited by Linda Alcoff and Elizabeth Potter, 15–48. New York: Routledge, 1993.

Connell, R.W., and James W. Messerschmidt. "Hegemonic Masculinity: Rethinking the Concept." *Gender & Society* 19 (2005): 829–59.

Doane, Sébastien. "Masculinities of the Husbands in the Genealogy of Jesus (Matt. 1:2–16)." *Biblical Interpretation* 27 no 1 (March 2019): 91–106. doi-org.proxy.lib. duke.edu/10.1163/15685152-00271P05.

Gutmann, Matthew C. *The Meanings of Macho: Being a Man in Mexico City*. Berkeley: University of California Press, 1996.

Häncl, Hilkje Charlotte and Mari Mikkola. "Feminist Philosophy and Pornography: The Past, The Present, and The Future." In *Beyond Speech: Pornography and Analytic Feminist Philosophy*, 1–20. Oxford: Oxford UP, 2017.

Handyside, *Sofia Coppola: A Cinema of Girlhood*. London: I.B. Tauris, 2017.

Haraway, Donna. "Situated Knowledges: The Science Question in Feminism and the Privilege of Partial Perspective." *Feminist Studies* 14 no. 3 (Fall 1988): 575–99.

Howson, Richard and Brian Yecies. "The Role of Hegemonic Masculinity and Hollywood in the New Korea." *Journal on Masculinities & Social Change*, 5 no 1 (February 2016): 52–69.

Jackson, Debra. "Answering the Call: Crisis Intervention and Rape Survivor Advocacy as Witnessing Trauma." In *Critical Trauma Studies: Understanding Violence, Conflict and Memory in Everyday Life*, edited by Monica J. Casper and Eric Wertheimer, 205–26. New York: New York University Press, 2016. ProQuest Ebook Central.

Jeffrey Eugenides on *The Virgin Suicides*." Abby Lustgarten, producer. New York: The Criterion Collection, 2018. DVD.

Langton, Rae. "Speech Acts and Unspeakable Acts." *Philosophy & Public Affairs*, 22 no 4 (Autumn 1993): 293–330.

Laub, Dori. "Bearing Witness and the Vicissitudes of Listening." In *Testimony: Crises of Witnessing in Literature, Psychoanalysis and History*, by Shoshana Felman and Dori Laub, 57–74. New York: Routledge, 1992.

Levi, Primo. *The Drowned and the Saved*, translated by Raymond Rosenthat. New York: Random House, 1989.

Luo, Wei. "Television's 'Leftover' Bachelors and Hegemonic Masculinity in Postsocialist China." *Women's Studies in Communication*, 40 no 2 (April 2017): 190–211.

Messerschmidt, James W. *Hegemonic Masculinity: Formulation, Reformulation, and Amplification*. Lanham MD: Rowman & Littlefield, 2018.

Revisiting *The Virgin Suicides*." Abby Lustgarten, producer. New York: The Criterion Collection, 2018. DVD.

Rogers, Anna Backman. "Imaging Absence as Abjection: The Female Body in Sofia Coppola's The Virgin Suicides." *Screening the Past* 43 (April 2018). www.screeningthepast.com/2018/02/imaging-absence-as-abjection-the-female-body-in-sofia-coppolas-the-virgin-suicides/.

———. *Sofia Coppola: The Politics of Visual Pleasure*. New York: Berghahn Book, 2019.

Shostak, Debra. "'Impossible Narrative Voices': Sofia Coppola's Adaptation of Jeffrey Eugenides's *The Virgin Suicides*." *Interdisciplinary Literary Studies* 15 no. 2 (2013): 180–202. www.jstor.org/stable/10.5325/intelitestud.15.2.0180.

Singh, Amardeep. "Mimicry and Hybridity in Plain English." Amardeep Singh Blog. May 8, 2009. www.lehigh.edu/~amsp/2009/05/mimicry-and-hybridity-in-plain-english.html.

Strange Magic by Tavi Gevison." Abby Lustgarten, producer. New York: The Criterion Collection, 2018. DVD.

Taylor, Charles. *Sources of the Self: The Making of the Modern Identity*. Cambridge: Cambridge University Press, 1989.

*The Virgin Suicides*. Sofia Coppola, director. New York: The Criterion Collection, 2018. DVD.

Woodhead, Hannah. "Body Woman is the Loneliest Creature: Growing up with *The Virgin Suicides*." *Bright Wall/Dark Room* 62, (August 2018). www.brightwalldarkroom.com/2018/08/22/woman-is-the-loneliest-creature-the-virgin-suicides/.

Wyatt, Justin. *The Virgin Suicides: Reverie, Sorrow and Young Love*. New York: Routledge, 2019.

Yadav, Anupam. "Epistemology Revisited: A Feminist Critique." *Journal of International Women's Studies* 19 no. 6 (2018): 374–381. vc.bridgew.edu/jiws/vol19/iss6/24.

## NOTES

1. Dori Laub, "Bearing Witness and the Vicissitudes of Listening" in *Testimony: Crises of Witnessing in Literature, Psychoanalysis and History*, by Shoshana Felman and Dori Laub (New York: Routledge, 1992), 59.
2. Ibid.
3. Ibid., 59–60, 61.
4. Ibid., 62.
5. Justin Wyatt, *The Virgin Suicides: Reverie, Sorrow and Young Love* (New York: Routledge, 2019), 48.
6. Debra Jackson, "Answering the Call: Crisis Intervention and Rape Survivor Advocacy as Witnessing Trauma," in *Critical Trauma Studies: Understanding Violence, Conflict and Memory in Everyday Life*, edited by Monica J. Casper and Eric Wertheimer (New York: New York University Press, 2016), 209, accessed July 24, 2020, ProQuest Ebook Central.
7. Ibid.
8. Ibid., 211.
9. Ibid., 212.
10. Ibid., 213.
11. Ibid., 217.
12. Dori Laub, "Bearing Witness and the Vicissitudes of Listening" in *Testimony: Crises of Witnessing in Literature, Psychoanalysis and History*, by Shoshana Felman and Dori Laub (New York: Routledge, 1992), 62.
13. Jackson, "Answering the Call," 217.
14. Laub, "Bearing Witness," 60.
15. Ibid.
16. Jackson, "Answering the Call," 224.
17. Laub, 72.
18. Ibid., 72.
19. Ibid., 73.
20. Primo Levi, *The Drowned and the Saved*, trans. by Raymond Rosenthat (New York: Random House, 1989), 55. Qtd. in Giorgio Agamben, *Remnants of Auschwitz: The Witness and the Archive*, trans. by Daniel Heller-Roazen (New York: Zone Books, 2002), 25.
21. Agamben, *Remnants of Auschwitz*, 26.
22. Ibid.
23. Wyatt, *The Virgin Suicides*, 48.
24. Michelle Aaron, "Cinema and Suicide: Necromanticism, Dead-already-ness, and the Logic of the Vanishing Point," *Cinema Journal*, 53 no 2 (Winter 2014): 78.
25. Jackson, "Answering the Call," 212.
26. James W. Messerschmidt, *Hegemonic Masculinity: Formulation, Reformulation, and Amplification* (Lanham MD: Rowman & Littlefield, 2018), 28.
27. R. W. Connell and J. W. Messerschmidt, "Hegemonic Masculinity: Rethinking the Concept" *Gender & Society* 19 (2005): 832.
28. Ibid.

29. Ibid.

30. Messerschmidt, *Hegemonic Masculinity*, 46.

31. Studies in hegemonic masculinity have made their way into disciplines as disparate as fashion studies and biblical studies. See for example, Ben Barry, "The Toxic Lining of Men's Fashion Consumption: The Omnipresent Force of Hegemonic Masculinity," *Critical Studies in Men's Fashion*, 2 no 2–3 (September 2015): 143–161, dx.doi.org.proxy.lib.duke.edu/10.1386/csmf.2.2-3.143_1. See Sébastien Doane, "Masculinities of the Husbands in the Genealogy of Jesus (Matt. 1:2–16)," *Biblical Interpretation* 27 no 1 (March 2019): 91–106, doi-org.proxy.lib.duke.edu/10.1163/15685152-00271P05. For samples of hegemonic masculinity studies in media and communication, see Wei Luo, "Television's 'Leftover' Bachelors and Hegemonic Masculinity in Postsocialist China," *Women's Studies in Communication*, 40 no 2 (April 2017): 190–211. See Richard Howson and Brian Yecies, "The Role of Hegemonic Masculinity and Hollywood in the New Korea," *Journal on Masculinities & Social Change*, 5 no 1 (February 2016): 52–69. See Joshua Atkinson and Bernadette Calafell, "Darth Vader Made Me Do It! Anakin Skywalker's Avoidance of Responsibility and the Gray Areas of Hegemonic Masculinity in the Star Wars Universe," *Communication, Culture and Critique*, 2 no 1 (March 2009): 1–20, doi-org.proxy.lib.duke.edu/10.1111/j.1753-9137.2008.01026.x.

32. Chad Broughton, "Migration as Engendered Practice: Mexican Men, Masculinity, and northward Migration," *Gender & Society* 22 no. 5 (October 2008): 572.

33. Ibid.

34. Ibid., 577. Messerschmidt, *Hegemonic Masculinity*, 67.

35. Messerschmidt, *Hegemonic Masculinity*, 67.

36. Ibid.

37. Ibid., 68.

38. Broughton, "Migration as Engendered Practice," 572.

39. Ibid. Messerschmidt, *Hegemonic Masculinity*, 46.

40. Charles Taylor, *Sources of the Self: The Making of the Modern Identity* (Cambridge: Cambridge University Press, 1989), 145.

41. Ibid., 17.

42. Lorraine Code, "Taking Subjectivity into Account," in *Feminist Epistemologies*, ed. Linda Alcoff and Elizabeth Potter (New York: Routledge, 1993), 16.

43. Anupam Yadav, "Epistemology Revisited: A Feminist Critique," *Journal of International Women's Studies* 19 no. 6 (2018): 375, vc.bridgew.edu/jiws/vol19/iss6/24.

44. Donna Haraway, "Situated Knowledges: The Science Question in Feminism and the Privilege of Partial Perspective," *Feminist Studies* 14 no. 3 (Fall 1988): 582.

45. Ibid., 581.

46. Amardeep Singh, "Mimicry and Hybridity in Plain English," Amardeep Singh Blog, May 8, 2009, accessed July 29, 2020, www.lehigh.edu/~amsp/2009/05/mimicry-and-hybridity-in-plain-english.html,.

47. Homi Bhabha, *The Location of Culture* (London: Routledge, 1994, 2004), 122, emphasis original.

48. Bhabha, *Location*, 122, emphasis original.

49. Bill Ashcroft, Gareth Griffiths, and Helen Tiffin, *Post-Colonial Studies: The Key Concepts* (New York: Routledge, 2000), 125.

50. Bhabha, *Location*, 107, 122, 123.

51. Singh, "Mimicry and Hybridity."

52. Ibid.

53. Bhabha, *Location*, 121–2. Ashcroft, Griffiths, and Tiffin, *Post-Colonial Studies*, 10.

54. Homi Bhabha, "Why Empires Fall," *The Institute of Art and Ideas*, accessed July 29, 2020, www.youtube.com/watch?v=9t82nbsoiqE.

55. Bhabha, *Location*, 123.

56. Ibid., 269.

57. Anna Backman Rogers, "Imaging Absence as Abjection: The Female Body in Sofia Coppola's The Virgin Suicides," *Screening the Past* 43 (April 2018), www.screeningthepast.com/2018/02/imaging-absence-as-abjection-the-female-body-in-sofia-coppolas-the-virgin-suicides/.

58. "Revisiting *The Virgin Suicides*," Abby Lustgarten, producer (New York: The Criterion Collection, 2018), DVD.

59. In feminist philosophy, Rae Langton's seminal essay "Speech Acts and Unspeakable Acts" guided feminist reflection on pornography for twenty years. She argued that pornography silences and subordinates women. See Rae Langton, "Speech Acts and Unspeakable Acts," *Philosophy & Public Affairs*, 22 no. 4 (Autumn 1993), 297. However, as feminist philosophers Hilkje Charlotte Hänel and Mari Mikkola note, "little agreement exists on many key issues," in the wake of Langton's essay, including basic questions like, "What is pornography? Does pornography in fact subordinate and silence women? Does pornography objectify women in harmful ways? Is pornography authoritative in the requisite sense to make good the speech act approach? How (if at all) is pornography speech?" Hilkje Charlotte Hänel and Mari Mikkola, "Feminist Philosophy and Pornography: The Past, The Present, and The Future," in *Beyond Speech: Pornography and Analytic Feminist Philosophy* (Oxford: Oxford UP, 2017), 11. While feminists debates about pornography is outside of the scope of this, Coppola implicitly takes up a position similar to Langton's anti-pornographic stance, or at least the stance that some forms of pornography subordinate and silence women (Hänel and Mikkola, "Feminist Philosophy," 9–10). Hence, our analysis reflects her and Langton's assessment.

60. Rogers interprets this scene as a potential rape. For more on her analysis see Rogers, *Sofia Coppola*, 38. Trip's metaphorical use of devouring language resonates with her claim.

61. "Jeffrey Eugenides on *The Virgin Suicides*," Abby Lustgarten, producer (New York: The Criterion Collection, 2018), DVD.

62. Emma Cline, "'The Virgin Suicides' Still Holds the Mysteries of Adolescence," *The New Yorker*, October 2, 2018, accessed August 18, 2020, www.newyorker.com/books/second-read/the-virgin-suicides-still-holds-the-mysteries-of-adolescence.

63. "Jeffrey Eugenides," DVD.

64. Ibid.

65. Hannah Woodhead, "Body Woman is the Loneliest Creature: Growing up with *The Virgin Suicides*," Issue 62 *Bright Wall/Dark Room* (August 2018), www.brightwalldarkroom.com/2018/08/22/woman-is-the-loneliest-creature-the-virgin-suicides/.

66. "Strange Magic by Tavi Gevison," Abby Lustgarten, producer (New York: The Criterion Collection, 2018), DVD.

67. Fiona Handyside, *Sofia Coppola: A Cinema of Girlhood* (London: I.B. Tauris, 2017), 67.

68. The reality of Lux's bleeding body works in contradistinction to the opening image of Lux, where she eats a red popsicle. Most commentators compare Lux's popsicle to the famous image of Stanley Kubrick's Lolita eating a red lollypop. Both connote the sexual availability of young girls.

69. Debra Shostak, "'Impossible Narrative Voices': Sofia Coppola's Adaptation of Jeffrey Eugenides's *The Virgin Suicides*," *Interdisciplinary Literary Studies* 15 no. 2 (2013): 196, accessed August 5, 2016, www.jstor.org/stable/10.5325/intelitestud.15.2.0180.

70. David Bordwell, "Art Cinema as a Mode of Film Practice," in *Film Theory and Criticism: Introductory Readings*, 7th ed., ed. Leo Braudy and Marshall Cohen (New York: Oxford University Press, 2009), 653.

71. Anna Backman Rogers, *Sofia Coppola: The Politics of Visual Pleasure* (New York: Berghahn Book, 2019), 44.

72. Ibid.

73. Ibid.

# PART II
*SEXUAL POLITICS*

*Chapter Three*

# A Limited Liberation

## Film Music, Suture, Feminism, and Anachronism in Marie Antoinette

Sofia Coppola's third film, *Marie Antoinette*, caused quite a bit of critical disagreement, particularly regarding her use of anachronisms. Film critic Roger Ebert praised the film's anachronisms saying, "Many characters in historical films seem somehow aware that they are living in the past. Marie seems to think she is a teenager living in the present, which of course she is—and the contemporary pop references invite the audience to share her present with ours."[1] Those anachronistic popular references include a wide range of cultural texts, from famous shoe designer Manolo Blahnik shoes, Converse "Chuck Taylor All Star" shoes, and 1980s New Romantic fashion to a wide range of 1970s and 1980s pop music, including The Strokes, The Cure, Siouxsie and the Banshees, Gang of Four, and Aphex Twin. Other critics dissented. For example, film critic James Berardinelli argued:

> Perhaps the most curious aspect of *Marie Antoinette* is Coppola's choice of music. Instead of the usual classical stuff we might expect (although there is some of that), she employs contemporary numbers by artists like Bow Wow Wow, The Cure, and Adam Ant and the Ants. This results in "Opus 23" being followed by "I Want Candy." To say it creates a *disconnect* is an understatement.[2]

This disagreement about anachronisms like film music is at the heart of our argument in this chapter. We should also acknowledge existing scholarship on Coppola's film, much of which concerns sartorial choices, which, alongside the musical selections, present intentional anachronisms. With this chapter, we intend to extend the findings of other prominent scholars, such as Heidi Brevik-Zender who studies the selections of costume, music, and language in *Marie Antoinette* through the lens of Walter Benjamin.

As we attend to anachronisms in *Marie Antoinette*, our reading of the film points to the ways white scholars can grapple more deeply with our racialized and limited understanding of liberation. To reach this conclusion, our chapter unfolds in five sections. We begin with a summary of the film's plot, which includes four main movements. Next, to clear the ground for our analysis of the film's music, we describe the basic functions of film music in classical narrative cinema, explain some essential terms, and define the concept of *suture*. Then, to contrast how the film's anachronistic music differs from its classical narrative music, we trace various forms of suture in relation to the film's use of an eighteenth-century composition, Antonio Vivaldi's Concerto alla Rustica. We examine a brief sequence, focusing on three scenes. Fourth, Anna Backman Rogers's feminist reading of the sequence, featuring Bow Wow Wow's "I Want Candy," offers a productive example of interpreting the film's anachronisms. Her reading emphasizes how the feminist concepts of masquerade, mimicry, and liberation are at play in the sequence and a few other moments in the film. Finally, we extend Rogers's reading, attending more closely to the anachronisms of music and fashion in the "I Want Candy" sequence. Our close reading of the anachronisms complicates masquerade and mimicry, producing a more nuanced account of the film. These complications lead us to the work of Chicana scholar Gloria Anzaldúa, through whom we conclude that what white scholars might take for liberation should, more rightfully, be understood as a limited liberation.

*Marie Antoinette* unfolds in four basic movements. First, the film opens just before the first meeting of the betrothed Austrian princess Maria Antonia (Kirsten Dunst) (hereafter Antoinette) to Louis Auguste, the dauphin of France (Jason Schwartzman) (hereafter Louis). Servants take Antoinette by coach to France, where she meets Louis, as well as his grandfather, King Louis XV (Rip Torn). The couple is married, and at their wedding feast, Louis XV toasts the new couple, articulating the key pressure that drives the first part of the film: "To the dauphin and dauphine of France: may you have many healthy children and produce an heir to our throne."[3] Louis Auguste, however, refrains from sexual contact with Antoinette, and members of the Versailles court blame her for the couple's childlessness. Louis prefers his hobby making keys and locks to Antoinette's interest or affections. Antoinette also finds the courtly etiquette at Versailles stifling, as the sequence of her morning dressing ceremony, a meal with her husband, and a religious service all attest.

After several frustrating attempts to have sex with her husband, Antoinette abandons the project and enters a period of lavish erotic, or bodily, delights. In one key sequence, during which the song "I Want Candy" blares on the soundtrack, Antoinette indulges in exotic clothes, expensive hairstyles, and ornate desserts. She also gambles and drinks with her ladies. She and her entourage then drag Louis to a masked ball in Paris. At the party, the dauphine catches the eye of Count Axel Fersen (Jamie Dornan), but Antoinette rejects his advances. Upon returning home, Antoinette and Louis discover that King Louis XV has died. Louis becomes Louis XVI, which makes Antoinette the new queen. During this period, Antoinette's brother, the Holy Roman Emperor Joseph II (Danny Huston) visits the royal couple, and during a short walk, he convinces Louis to have sex with Antoinette. Joseph fetishizes the act of copulation, comparing it to Louis's favorite hobby, locks and keys. The royal couple finally consummate their marriage, and Antoinette gives birth to Marie Theresa.

The third movement begins when Louis gives Antoinette a private house with its own gardens on Versailles property, a château called Le Petit Trianon. Here Antoinette abandons her self-indulgent partying in favor of a life of peace and becomes more deeply connected to the natural world. She and her entourage pick flowers, enjoy fresh fruit and milk, and read books in the luscious gardens. Antoinette gives birth to Louis-Joseph, the new dauphin. Though the court initially celebrates Antoinette's accomplishment, pamphlets attacking her lifestyle circulate. During this period, she has an affair with Count Fersen.

Finally, while dining one day, a messenger informs Louis and Antoinette that a mob has taken control of the Bastille prison. Soon a mob reaches Versailles, and Louis and Antoinette dismiss their entourages, opting to stay in Versailles's palace despite the danger. After the royal family is captured the following morning, several men escort them to a carriage. The couple leaves the palace. The final shot is a still image of a ransacked bedchamber.

## CLASSICAL NARRATIVE FILM MUSIC, (UN) NOTICED FILM MUSIC, AND SUTURE

To understand how anachronistic music functions in the "I Want Candy" sequence, we use three key insights from film music and film theory scholarship. In classical narrative cinema, film music tends to perform these basic functions: it interprets the image, encourages an emotional response, and establishes a film's setting or mood. Film studies scholar Claudia Gorbman notes that narrative film music interprets or pinpoints the so-called correct interpretation of images. For viewers of Steven Spielberg's *Jaws* (1975), for example, the "menacing 'shark' theme" that accompanies the opening credits helps viewers understand that the underwater images express an "advanced knowledge of the narrative threat."[4] For film studies scholar Royal S. Brown, film music can also encourage an emotional or affective response to the image. In the documentary *The Living Desert* (1953), Brown argues that "the doom-and-gloom music accompanying the snake making its kill" encourages the audience to take up a specific emotional disposition toward the snake.[5] It is not an animal acting according to its nature; rather, it is a villain, taking advantage of a weak, harmless mouse. In addition to interpretation and affect, film music can also establish the setting or mood of a film. James Horner's score to *Braveheart* (1995) evokes the film's Scottish setting, in part through Scotland's most notable instrument, the bagpipe. Similar to Brown, Gorbman concludes that music can evoke "the freshness of springtime, the seventeenth century, [or] menacing evil," situating the viewer to the narrative, emotion, time, place, and/or mood the filmmakers find preferable.[6]

The terms *diegetic* and *non-diegetic* name the relationship of film music to the audience and characters. Diegetic music, or source music, in films "theoretically comes from a source within the diegesis—a radio, a phonograph, a person singing, an orchestra playing."[7] Non-diegetic film music describes music that the audience alone hears. In this way, non-diegetic music relates to audiences much like voice-over narration, which orients the audience to the narrative.

Second, Gorbman discusses the audience's relationship to film music, highlighting that audiences generally do not notice the music. She explains that this phenomenon occurs because classical Hollywood film music tends to be subservient to a film's image and story. This is not to say that audiences do not register instances of film music—or film music "cues" as they are called in the industry—in meaningful ways. Rather, narrative film music immerses the spectator, "trance-like," in the world of the story, harmonizing or unifying the "auditor's ears . . . with the spectator's eyes."[8] Brown describes such film music as "consummated" to the image. In these cases, film music is "narrativized" or serves the film's narrative.[9] For Gorbman, such film music draws the audience into an "imaginary" realm, where they do not question the significance of the music.[10] Rather, an audience simply experiences the function of the music, be it interpreting the image, conveying emotion, or establishing the setting.

Audiences sometimes notice film music as "symbolic" or "unconsummated." Gorbman claims that when audiences notice film music, it becomes "symbolic" rather than imaginary. She implies that, in some way, noticed film music can encourage a viewer to wonder about the music's meaning or purpose.[11] If unnoticed music creates a trancelike unity, then noticed music calls the viewer out of the trance into an intellectualized awareness. Brown uses the term *unconsummated* to describe such a moment. His term connotes the possibility that film music can break with or work against the image in some way. By way of example, Brown suggests that Alain Resnais's holocaust documentary *Night and Fog* (1955) uses Harms Eisler's music to this effect.

"Eisler's score," he notes, "does not even attempt to join with the visuals and the voice-over narration," embodying the concept of "indifference."[12] In one key passage, Eisler composes a theme reminiscent of a Hollywood romance. Warm strings play a simple melody, one that might accompany two lovers kissing for the first time. However, in the voice-over, the narrator describes gas chambers, and Resnais presents photographs of naked concentration-camp victims walking into a chamber. For Brown, the music's indifference toward the image demonstrates "the brutal irony of the indifferent ordinariness that can mask unspeakable horrors."[13]

The insight that film music can go unnoticed raises a potential ethical concern regarding the ideological impact of film on viewers. If image and music can work on audiences in ways they do not notice, then a film might coerce audiences into ideological notions that could be unhealthy or unwanted. To return to Brown's example of *The Living Desert*, his analysis implies that the music's interpretation of the snake as a corrupt villain is simply a falsehood. It would be more constructive to interpret the snake as an animal who has the same desire to live as any other. To impose the interpretation of villain onto the snake makes as much sense as imposing the term *villain* onto the mouse the snake eats. In film theory, scholars have used the concept of suture to grapple with the phenomenon that films can coerce audiences into unhealthy interpretations of the world. And it is to this concept we now turn.

Like the sutures that medical professionals use to heal wounds, the term *suture refers to* how films make implicit offers to heal audiences of wounds or ruptures we carry around with us; however, film sutures more often harm rather than heal. The term *suture* originated in the psychological reflections of French scholar Jacques Lacan. Lacan noticed how his teacher, Sigmund Freud, used the term *castration* to describe the fear men have of being emasculated. Lacan took Freud's notion and used it to describe all people who exist in society. Lacan contended that as children grow up, they realize they are not the center of the world. As critical theorist Mari Rudi describes Lacan's insight, children learn that they are a "tiny cog" in society's "immense machinery," a machine over which they have "virtually no control."[14] Inside that lack of control, all people feel castrated, feel wounded, feel like some part of them has been removed or damaged, and all people long for that wound to be healed—that is, we long for that wound to be sutured.

Within film studies, scholars argue that suture functions as a metaphor for how the seamless whole of classical Hollywood cinema absorbs us into ideologies that promise to heal but only harm. On a technical level, narrative films are composed of many disjointed items. Hollywood films organize moments of acting, lighting choices, portions of story information, visual compositions, music, sound effects, and other such material into a whole that feels seamless, stable, and inevitable. That seamless whole is the metaphorical promise of healing. When viewers are drawn into the cinematic world, they are often unable to see how it has been sutured together. Because viewers are "unable to see the workings" of the film, they are "at its mercy."[15] Therefore, as the film absorbs the audience into the world of the film, the viewer also "absorbs an ideological effect without being aware of it."[16] For example, Hollywood films have and continue to present women in deeply dehumanizing ways—namely as passive, sexual objects that men gaze upon. The seamless whole of these stories offers a suture, or a false promise of wholeness, to women. If women could, like the women in classical narrative films, attract the gaze of men, then they too could experience the same wholeness and significance the films offer. Rudi claims that this account of suture helps explain how women are often seduced into "being a nonsubject—a passive object of desire."[17] Such sutures continue to offer healing but mainly serve to harm women.

Film studies scholar Alexander Binns suggests that music can participate in the work of suture, the work of absorbing viewers into an image:

> Imagine a scene in which we see a cornfield on a sunny day, whose crop is ready to harvest, gently swaying in the breeze. The visual clues give not only the impression of peace and tranquility but also of safety. Add to this a high-string pedal or a low pulsating figure in the musical underscore—perhaps also with the addition of dissonance—and a sense of impending danger is immediately suggested. In spite of the lack of visual clues, we believe the underscore without question; we assume it to be informing us of the film's truths.[18]

If, as Binn asserts, viewers readily accept musical significance "without question," then the same could hold true of ideological meanings. Music, no less than images, can perform the work of suturing.

The same can certainly be said of Coppola's sartorial choices in the film, which Brevik-Zender calls "[a] visual culture of fashionable phantasmagoria."[19] By aligning her comments with Walter Benjamin's cultural critique, *The Arcades Project* (1982), she asserts that various sartorial anachronisms represent interplay between femininity, female fashion, and Benjaminian formations of modernism. In her article, she rebuts previous descriptions of the costuming (and music) in *Marie Antoinette* as frivolous pastiche; she then details how Coppola's choices represent a transhistoric (thus contemporary) instantiation of Coppola's own identity in her protagonist. We would add that Coppola's sartorial selections additionally affect the cinematic suture, and much in the same way the filmmaker's musical selections: anachronism threatens suture, while selections that seem in accordance with the film's eighteenth-century setting tend to enable suture.

## CLASSICAL USES OF ANTONIO VIVALDI'S CONCERTO ALLA RUSTICA

To more clearly illustrate how the anachronistic song "I Want Candy" functions to disrupt cinematic sutures, we note how the film's use of Antonio Vivaldi's Concerto alla Rustica in G Major, RV 151 confirms to the classical film music techniques described above, including suture, evoking the setting, offering an interpretation, and representing emotion. The concerto is a short piece for strings and harpsichord, which usually takes approximately four minutes to perform. The concerto has three movements. The first movement is titled "Presto," which means that it is played very quickly. The second movement is performed very slowly, or "Adagio." The third and final movement is "Allegro," or rather quick. The film uses portions of all the movements, although it draws primarily on the first and third. The film's use of Vivaldi's Concerto alla Rustica not only conforms to the classical narrative film music norms but also uses suture in multiple ways to present the jagged compilation of various parts of the concerto as a seamless whole. The film uses the concerto in three scenes: Antoinette's dressing ceremony, a meal between Antoinette and Louis, and Antoinette attending a Catholic Mass. After a summary of the scenes and the film's use of Vivaldi's concerto, we turn to an analysis.

After Louis and Antoinette's uneventful first night together, the Comtesse de Noailles (Judy Davis) wakes Antoinette, the latter of whom is surprised to find herself alone in bed. The comtesse facilitates the morning dressing ceremony, and during the scene, the soundtrack plays passages from the first movement of Vivaldi's Concerto alla Rustica. The comtesse explains that the highest-ranking blood relative of the French crown is given the honor of dressing the dauphine. As her attendants undress her, new relatives arrive, leaving Antoinette naked and embarrassed in front of an increasingly large number of female strangers. As family members pass her undergarment to each other, the soundtrack transitions to the concerto's third movement. The piece comes to its harmonic resolution as a court member finally puts Antoinette's first garment on her. Exasperated, Antoinette tells the Comtesse de Noailles, "This is ridiculous," to which the comtesse responds, "This, Madame, is Versailles!"

The scene cuts to the newlywed couple awkwardly dining together, and Vivaldi's concerto plays, again with portions of the first and third movements. Servants and dignitaries surround the couple and stare at them, as though Antoinette and Louis are objects on display. When Antoinette asks the head servant for some water, he seems to ignore her and then strikes the ground with a large staff. The loud sound startles Antoinette, and the servant yells,

"Service pour le monsieur le dauphin!" The Comtesse de Noailles brings her a glass of water, waits awkwardly until Antoinette finishes, and takes the empty glass. As Antoinette turns to Louis, the music suddenly stops. "So," she inquires, "I've heard you make keys as a hobby?" Louis, barely acknowledges her but replies, "Yes." She asks, "And you enjoy making keys?" After her question, Louis responds in a dismissive manner, "Obviously." In the wake of his response, the film plays a short portion of the concerto's second movement, the "Adagio." After Antoinette internally processes his curt response, the first movement begins again. In the third scene, Antoinette sits in a religious service, a Catholic Mass. As the first movement transitions again into the third, the dauphine notices an old woman falling asleep. Antoinette giggles with her companion, and the music comes to its conclusion as the Comtesse de Noailles tries to silence her.

Three observations on suture are in order. Suture works in two ways: the film's music supervisor stitches together various parts of the concerto and makes alterations to the piece, all of which register as a seamless whole. The non-diegetic music also sutures over diegetic inconsistencies during the second scene. Next, the music evokes the aristocratic and eighteenth-century setting in which the film takes place. And the music offers the audience an emotional interpretation of these scenes, including Antoinette's sense of tedium in the first scene, her expectation and sadness in the second, and the court's indifference to her in the third.

As this and the tables below show, music supervisor Brian Reitzell sutures, or stitches together, disparate parts of Vivaldi's work to create a seamless whole. Here we focus on the first scene (see table 3.1). Of all the repetition of measures in these cues, Vivaldi intended only one set of repetition: the first nineteen measures of movement III. All other edits and repetitions are Reitzell's sutured choices. Some of these choices are fairly radical. For

Table 3.1. Analysis of Vivaldi's Concerto alla Rustica in G Major, RV 151, Antoinette's dressing ritual

| Movement | I: "Presto" (in 9/8) | | | III: "Allegro" (in 2/4) | | | | |
|---|---|---|---|---|---|---|---|---|
| Measures | 1–50 | 49–50 | 11 | 1–19 | 1–19 | 20–34 | 27–51 | 53 |
| Comments | | | | | Vivaldi intended this repetition | | Resolved harmony | Music paused for dialogue |
| Dialogue | | | | | | | | "This is ridiculous." "This . . . is Versailles." |

example, Reitzell connects two different movements in two different time signatures. The first movement has a rushing "three" pulse, but the third has a more relaxed or broader "two" feeling. Further, he repeats odd groupings of measures Vivaldi did not intend (for example, measures 49–50), transplants others (for example, measure 11), and omits large portions of the original piece (the entire second movement).

This cue evokes Versailles's eighteenth-century aristocratic setting and Antionette's emotional tedium at Versailles, the latter of which Reitzell signals through unusual changes to the composition's dynamics. Because only the extremely wealthy tended to have access to Vivaldi's music, the concerto connotes the high aristocracy of the court of France. Not only would such music have likely been heard at Versailles, but most people living in France would also have never heard this music. Vivaldi functioned as rarified, aristocratic music for so-called rarified, aristocratic people. Furthermore, the changes in dynamics (or volume changes for expression) Reitzell makes intensifies the emotional tedium Antionette experiences. In typical performances of the concerto, the harpsichord functions as an accompanying instrument, supporting the strings and the soloist. As a result, the harpsichord often plays at a lower volume than the other instruments. Also, most ensembles perform the work making subtle changes to the dynamic of the piece, playing some parts louder or quieter than others. On the soundtrack, the balance and dynamics of the instruments are different from typical performances. The harpsichord is unusually loud, and all instruments play with an intense *forte* (or, at a loud volume) throughout most of the piece. Reitzell's changes make the piece feel more tedious and overwhelming than the original, which reflects the overwhelming tedium Antoinette experiences in courtly life. Once the court dresses Antionette, the tedious music resolves just as the problem in the scene does. The dauphine summarizes her tedium: "This is ridiculous."

While the second scene and cue retain many of the elements from the first, the film incorporates an intensified musical suture (see table 3.2). In the dining scene, *Marie Antoinette* introduces on-screen, diegetic musicians; however, the non-diegetic Vivaldi cue creates an inconsistency, or a gap, that it simultaneously sutures, or closes. In the left corner of the screen, a small group of violin players and a harpsichord player play while the couple dines. One of the violinists conducts the group. However, both his conducting gestures and violinists' bow strokes indicate a slower tempo than the Vivaldi recording on the soundtrack. Furthermore, the on-screen musicians, who total approximately five in number, could not produce the soundtrack's volume or timbre. They also start playing after the music begins on the soundtrack. Despite these inconsistencies, the film insists on the concerto's non-diegetic function. The music fluctuates in volume, allowing for the audience to register the servant's declaration. Additionally, the music also lowers

Table 3.2 Vivaldi's Concerto alla Rustica in G Major, RV 151, Antoinette and Louis at a meal

| Movement | I: "Presto" (in 9/8) | | | | | III: "Allegro" (in 2/4) | | II: "Adagio" (in 3/4) |
|---|---|---|---|---|---|---|---|---|
| Measures | 1–10 | 23–50 | 49–54 | 11 | 1–18 | 19 | | 1–2 |
| Comments | Non-diegetic musicians and diegetic music differ | Music raises and lowers at various points, foregrounding the servant's dialogue and the awkward sounds of the cutlery | | | | Unresolved harmony | Music paused for dialogue | Harpsichord only |
| Dialogue | | | | | | | "So, I've heard you make keys." . . . "Obviously." | |

to emphasize the cutlery sounds, accentuating the awkward silence between the newly married couple. Nevertheless, most audiences likely do not question or notice the inconsistency or gap between music and image. Similar to Binns's example of ominous music over a quiet cornfield, the concerto both overpowers the image and remains unnoticed and consummated to the image. The gap between the musical source and the images speaks to the efficacy of the musical suture. Music creates a wound, an inconsistency with the image, which it simultaneously heals or sutures.

Reitzell also uses several changes to Vivaldi's score to register both the dauphine's expectation and her sadness. In the previous scene, the third movement ends with resolved harmony, mirroring the resolution of the dressing scene itself. In the second scene, however, Reitzell changes the original score so that measure 19 ends with unresolved harmony, which expresses Antoinette's sense of expectation and longing. Musicologists argue that auditors tend to experience unresolved harmony as suspenseful or as a metaphorical question yearning for a reassuring harmonic answer or resolution.[20] Because the cue ends unresolved, the music provides a feeling of anticipation in the silence before Antoinette speaks. It is as if the music, in asking its own harmonic question, anticipates the narrative reality that Antoinette is about to ask Louis a question. Additionally, Reitzell includes and alters a passage from the second movement, anticipating Antoinette's emotional reaction to Louis's rejection. Through her question, Antoinette wants to connect with her new husband; however, Louis rejects her in both his demeanor, one of disinterest, and his words, a condescending, "Obviously." Interpreting his rejection, the soundtrack plays a passage from Vivaldi's second movement. Unlike the bright sound of the first and third movements, the second movement sounds darker and sadder. This emotional interpretation appears before Antoinette's reaction. As the music plays, despondency slowly registers on her face. The slow tempo also contributes to her sense of bleakness and to the elongated emotional dead end that her husband now represents. In Vivaldi's score, the whole ensemble plays this passage; however, Reitzell gives these measures to a solo harpsichord. Like the other changes Reitzell makes, the solo harpsichord interprets the image. The solitary instrument reflects how isolated and alone the dauphine feels during this moment.

The last Vivaldi cue expresses, in conjunction with the sound design, how Versailles remains indifferent to Antoinette (see table 3.3). Unlike the previous scenes that have both music and synchronous sound, only Vivaldi plays on the soundtrack during this scene. In the previous scenes, Vivaldi's music interprets the manner in which Versailles' customs and Louis's disinterest pull the dauphine into a state of ennui. In the third scene, no synchronous sounds exist on the soundtrack. The music, then, represents Versailles' indifference to the dauphine. Although the elderly woman who falls asleep amuses Antoinette, the audience hears none of her joy or whimsy. It is as if Versailles has refused to listen to or accept her delight. Her joy persists until the end of the scene, when the comtesse quiets her. However, for the audience, the music expresses the dauphine's oppressed state. Although she lives in a beautiful, wealthy palace, she lives in a cage, a gilded cage that aims to restrain her body and emotions.

All the changes Reitzell makes to Vivaldi are quite radical and reveal the power of suture. Working at multiple levels, the music takes these disparate parts of the work and makes them sound like a seamless whole, perhaps most notably covering over inconsistencies between the music and the image. The music is so powerfully narrativized to the film that many audiences will instead process the way the music functions according to the norms of the classical narrative tradition. It serves the narrative through establishing the film's setting and interpreting the dispositions of the characters. Because sutures work to make these radical changes go unnoticed, when the film breaks the suture—that is, when audiences notice the music—they often struggle to make sense of it. The "I Want Candy" sequence offers such a break.

Table 3.3 Vivaldi's Concerto alla Rustica in G Major, RV 151, end of meal, Antoinette at Catholic Mass

| Movement | I: "Presto" (in 9/8) | | III: "Allegro" (in 2/4) | | | | |
|---|---|---|---|---|---|---|---|
| Measures | 51–53 | 11 | 7–13 | 16–19 | 42–47 | 50–51 | 53 |
| Comments | | | | | | | Resolved harmony |

## ROGERS' FEMINIST READING OF THE "I WANT CANDY" SEQUENCE

Film scholar Anna Backman Rogers interprets the "I Want Candy" sequence as a feminist critique of postfeminism. But her argument requires a bit of ground clearing on a few fronts, including first a summary of the "I Want Candy" sequence, the masquerade ball, and passages of Antoinette at the Le Petit Trianon, a description of postfeminism, and Luce Irigaray's concepts masquerade and mimicry. Rogers argues that the "I Want Candy" sequence engages in both masquerade and mimicry, presenting harmful ideologies of consumption while, at the same time, critiquing them. Rogers concludes her analysis by suggesting that Antoinette experiences moments of liberation while at her château, Le Petit Trianon.

The "I Want Candy" sequence occurs after Antoinette's sister-in-law, the Comtesse de Provence (Clémentine Poidatz), gives birth to a son. As Louis and Antoinette dine, the Comtesse de Noailles informs them that the birth has taken place. The couple arrives in the room, surrounded by onlookers, to congratulate the comtesse and her husband. Antoinette soon excuses herself and hurries down a hallway, attempting to escape the event. In the hallway, members of the court whisper about her as she passes by them, "It's barren. What do you expect? . . . When will you give us an heir? . . . I hear she's frigid." Antoinette finally reaches a room where she can be alone and breaks down crying. The handheld camera above her suggests her powerlessness, and the wide shot of the protagonist sitting on the floor emphasizes her isolation. While Antoinette has experienced exclusion and rejections throughout her time at Versailles, this moment is a breaking point for the dauphine. She responds with an extended period of erotic delight, particularly through her intense consumption of clothing, food, drinking, gambling, and partying.

This movement of the film begins with the "I Want Candy" sequence. The music begins with a loud Latin-inspired solo drumbeat, followed by bright, fuzz-tone guitar riffs. As opposed to the weeping, sadness, and isolation of the previous scene, the music evokes a celebratory tone. A row of shoes by Manolo Blahnik, a contemporary shoe designer, fill the screen. A woman tries on these shoes, with a pair of Converse brand Chuck Taylor All Stars sitting next to her. Servants parade an exquisite lineup of dresses, fans, and fabrics before Antoinette and her companions. The dauphine remarks upon one dress, "I like that pink. It's like candy." While rarely showing their faces, the montage implies that Antoinette and her companions engage in extended bodily delights. They gamble with playing cards and pastel-colored poker chips. An unending supply of pastries, champagne, necklaces, and chokers appear on screen, sometimes in elaborate geometric compositions. Léonard

(James Lance), the court hairdresser, arrives and gives Antoinette a hairdo so tall it nearly topples over. Her hair is filled with plumes of feathers, butterfly broaches, and bird figurines. Having looked at herself in a mirror, Antoinette bursts with delight, "Oh Léonard! You're the best!" Accompanying her massive hair, the dauphine wears excessive makeup, with garish rouge and lipstick. She wonders aloud to Léonard and a servant, "It's not too much, is it?" They reassure her that it is not.

Once the music concludes, the Duchesse de Polignac (Rose Byrne) suggests that Antoinette and her ladies attend a masquerade ball in Paris. Taking Louis with them, the ladies arrive at a lavish palace dressed in extravagant gowns and masks. While at the party, the duchesse and the queen notice Count Axel Fersen. Fersen talks to a woman, notices Antoinette, excuses himself, and approaches the dauphine. The duchesse sees the count approaching and whispers to Antoinette, "Have fun." Because Louis has failed to show sexual interest in Antoinette, the duchesse encourages the dauphine to obtain from the count what the dauphin will not give her. The count asks Antoinette, "Do I know you?" To which she responds, "No, I don't think so." After a brief interchange where the count reveals his identity, the dauphine refuses to reveal her own and walks away. The count grabs her by the hand. Antoinette stops, looks at him coyly, and walks away. Having refused the count's sexual advances, Antoinette and her company leave the party.

Rogers's reading of this sequence requires an understanding of postfeminism. As a reaction to second and third-wave feminism, postfeminism encourages women and girls to adopt traditional femininity (or girliness) as a means of liberation from patriarchy; however, those practices, scholars argue, only serve to trap women and girls inside patriarchal processes. In *The Rise of Enlightened Sexism: How Pop Culture Took Us from Girl Power to Girls Gone Wild* (2010), communication studies scholar Susan J. Douglas notes that, in a postfeminist age, women and girls engage in a "calculated deployment of their faces, bodies, attire, and sexuality" as a means to "gain and enjoy true power—power that is fun, that men will not resent."[21] As Rudi points out, postfeminism proves attractive to many women, because it connotes "activity and autonomy," where traditional femininity "signals passivity and submission."[22] However, through postfeminist practices, women participate in their own oppression. Douglas identifies such oppression in the phenomenon of women and girls "calling each other sluts and whores . . . and mocking girls whose clothes, hair, figures, or social status just aren't right."[23] Additionally, postfeminism ignores structural social inequalities and wrongly affirms that individual effort and capitalist consumption can solve the problem of women's oppression.[24]

In addition to postfeminism, the concepts of masquerade and mimicry require a brief exposition. Drawing on the work of feminist philosopher Luce

Irigaray, masquerade and mimicry occur when women engage in excessive displays of femininity but to radically differing effects, as the example of a hysterical woman demonstrates. Irigaray understands masquerade as "an alienated or false version of femininity" because the woman's "awareness of the man's desire" motivates her feminine display.[25] As a result, masquerade does not allow a woman to experience her desire as an act of liberation. Rather, masculine desire "permits" or "situates" her longings.[26] Her compensation for her excess of feminine display occurs when men choose her as "an object of consumption."[27] Mimicry (or mimesis), on the other hand, occurs when a "woman deliberately assumes the feminine style and posture assigned to her" as a means "to uncover the mechanisms" that exploit her.[28] By way of example, feminist scholar Ping Xu points out that "hysteria may well be a form of women's resistance to the repression or oppression forced on them in a male-dominated society."[29] In acting out masculine misperceptions of female irrationality, hysterical speech could say out loud what was both impossible and forbidden under a patriarchal regime.[30] As such, it might have functioned as one "path" a woman might take "to convert a form of subordination into an affirmation, and thus to begin to thwart it," without the woman being "simply reduced" to a subordinate role.[31]

Rogers argues that the "I Want Candy" sequence engages in both masquerade and mimicry. In her analysis of Antoinette's masquerade, Rogers emphasizes the sequence's excess of feminine consumption and display: lavish clothes, endless food and champagne, gambling, exaggerated hair and makeup. Rogers claims that this is an instance of "masquerade that affords Marie abatement from the constriction of her role"; however, "this critique can only take place within the confines of the very system that has bestowed upon her the paltry status of commodity."[32] Which is to say, in taking on the excesses of femininity, Antoinette inadvertently affirms the postfeminist notion of empowerment through consumption. However, Rogers suggests that the film's formal features trace how Antoinette "*becomes* a patriarchal subject."[33] Coppola achieves "a form of mimicry" and a critique of postfeminism.[34] In using anachronisms, the film "creates an impasse" or encourages a feeling of disruption that makes room for critique.[35] The montage, Rogers continues, prefigures our "superficial Instagram culture that features images of shoes and macaroons and abundance."[36] The film suggests "our 'progression' has been anything but progressive."[37]

Rogers concludes her reading of the "I Want Candy" sequence suggesting that Antoinette has a transitory but real experience of liberation during her time at Le Petit Trianon. Liberation, as Rogers means it, is an alternative way of life, one outside the strictures and patriarchy of Versailles. Focusing her analysis on the film's grainy structure, light saturation, and the improvisational quality of Antoinette's eighteenth birthday party and other scenes set at

Le Petit Trianon, Rogers claims these cinematic features enable viewers "to feel and identify with Marie's sense of her own liberation."[38] The scene that best exemplifies Antoinette's experience of liberation occurs when she and her friends watch the sun rise. During the sequence, Rogers notes that the dauphine "appears diminutive, luminescent and ghostlike at the very moment in which she passes into adulthood."[39] Such imagery reflects that her liberation is similarly fragile, delicate, and transitory. Nevertheless, her liberation is real because it takes "place outside of the court of Versailles," away from the forces that oppress her.[40]

## EXTENDING ROGERS' READING

In this final section of our chapter, we extend Rogers's reading of *Marie Antoinette*, offering a more detailed analysis of the anachronisms in the "I Want Candy" sequence, which complicate masquerade, mimicry, and liberation. We begin with the responses of some critics, which serve as representative examples of the manner in which some audiences are unwilling or unable to find productive meaning in the sequence's disruption. Drawing on Gorbman and Brown, we suggest that the concepts of masquerade and mimicry cannot fully account for the way Coppola displays Antoinette's femininity, primarily as an evasion of masculine sexual desire and the creation of an alternative identity. These complications lead us to the work of Gloria Anzaldúa, through whom we suggest that the liberation at Le Petit Trianon is limited to a personal liberation that is dependent on extravagant patriarchal resources. Taken together, our re-reading of the film and Anzaldúa suggests that white scholars need to more deeply understand the ways white liberation is a limited liberation.

While many viewers likely experience the "I Want Candy" sequence as a rupture or break, several film critics' reactions to the film document such feelings. Like Berardinelli's claim that the music "creates a *disconnect*," other film critics also found the anachronistic music unfitting for a period piece.[41] In *Time Out*, Dave Calhoun writes, "The music might be a hoot . . ., but the soundtrack—like the *distracting* costumes, cakes and production design—does . . . nothing to throw any light on the woman who gives the film its name."[42] Neil Miller of *Film School Rejects* suggests that Coppola "wanted to add her own flair as well to give the movie life, bright colors, a loud punk rock soundtrack and a cast that *doesn't fit* . . . a historical biopic. . . . Coppola's attempt at being original and edgy ends up being more of a missed opportunity."[43] Underlying each of these responses is the assumption that the anachronistic elements opens up a gap, a disruption, or a problem for the viewer.

Brown's and Gorbman's language of "unconsummated" and "symbolic" sheds light on the negative responses of these critics.[44] In Brown's analysis of *Night and Fog*, he argues that the score offers an ironic commentary on the images through the music's "indifference." Brown suggests that, as opposed to traditional narrative films where music is "consummated" to the image, Eisler's score remains "unconsummated." Likewise, unnoticed traditional film music, for Gorbman, works on the level of the "imaginary," where noticed film music poses a "symbolic" problem or meaning for audiences. The terms *unconsummated* and *symbolic* not only describe the function of the "I Want Candy" sequence in the film but also help explain the response of these film critics. When posed with the task of creating meaning outside of classical narrative norms, the critics discussed above seem unwilling or unable to enter into dialogue with the film's unconsummated or symbolic anachronisms as productive to the film's significance or meaning.

Counter to these critics and following Rogers's work as a model for engagement, we suggest that the "I Want Candy" sequence offers commentary on Antoinette's disposition of teenage rebellion, a commentary that some viewers reject as inappropriate. Reitzell affirms this reading of the anachronistic music, saying, "It would have been a lot harder to get across [Antoinette's] *teen angst* with a Masterpiece Theater type of soundtrack."[45] These anachronistic songs invite viewers to imagine an eighteenth-century teenager as having the responses appropriate to a late twentieth-century teenager. These critics' refusal to take up that invitation speaks to the power of suture. If music breaks the suture, some viewers will close the rupture through dismissing the anachronism as an inappropriate aesthetic choice.

Returning to Brevik-Zender's analysis of fashion through a Benjaminian lens in *Marie Antoinette*, she writes that Benjamin tends to disregard agency or subjectivity in the sartorial choices of women by asserting that the ability to decode "sartorial semaphores" is reserved for male critics alone.[46] Similarly, critics of Coppola's choices (nearly all male) neglect to consider the filmmaker's use of anachronism in fashion and music as hermeneutically constructive. Brevik-Zender views such maneuvers as "[an] intriguing example of herself, the appearance of a unique brand of contemporary woman filmmaker who uses cinema and its interplay with the haute couture industry to fashion herself as icon and writer/director alike."[47] Moreover, it appears equally conspicuous that Coppola selects music which for her is familiar and useful to represent her own identity within Brevik-Zender's construct of icon and filmmaker.

Assuming that Coppola's musical and fashion anachronisms are moments of productive meaning, our reading of the "I Want Candy" sequence depends on knowledge of the original song's intent. In the film, "I Want Candy" is the only song to appear in its entirety, hence, we suggest, the film draws on the meaning of the entire song. The song speaks about a woman who desires the sexual attention of a man. In the first verse and chorus, she refers to him and his sexual attention as "candy," singing, "I know a guy who's tough but sweet." The third verse clarifies that the singer does not possess the "candy" that she desires, hoping to make the "candy" hers someday. "Some day soon I'll make you mine/Then I'll have candy all the time." Hence, the singer sings from a perspective of one who is estranged from the man, his attention, and the sexual contact she desires. The film alters this primary meaning.

Within the context of the film, Antoinette evades heterosexual masculine sexual desire. "Candy," therefore, loses its euphemistic sexual meaning about which Bow Wow Wow sing. Antoinette surrounds herself with female friends and gay servants, seemingly disinterested in any heterosexual encounters. The most explicit reference to Antoinette's "candy" comes in her line about a dress, "I like that pink. It's like candy." Not limited to just clothing, her desire for "candy" encompasses cakes, pastries, jewelry, gambling, alcohol, and shoes. In an important sense, the film shares with the song in highlighting Antoinette's unfulfilled sexual desire for a man who has not expressed sexual interest in her. However, unlike the song, Antoinette refuses the task of seducing that man, her husband. She now indulges in an alternative set of erotic desires, in a decidedly non-heterosexual register. In fact, when Count Fersen shows sexual interest in Antoinette, she refuses him too. In so doing, Antoinette rebels against heterosexual masculine desire.

The disruption of the "I Want Candy" sequence also includes anachronistic fashion, particularly New Romanticism creation of alternative. Cultural studies scholar Stuart Borthwick and popular music scholar Ron Moy describe the New Romantic fashion movement in terms of punk's disruption and fashion's elitism. They note that the clothing industry profited from selling clothes to young people in the 1970s and 80s; however, the industry "had been . . . disrupted by punk (which was, in many ways, a form of 'anti-fashion' designed to disrupt conventional notions of fashionability)."[48] As a result, New Romanticism incorporated punk's anti-fashion sensibility through affiliations with punk-influenced musical groups. For example, London's New Romantic scene often hired punk-inspired bands to headline their fashion shows, including Bow Wow Wow. The influence of punk produced a "jumble sale," "mix-and-match" aesthetic, in which any article of low-priced clothing could be paired with any other.[49] New Romantic not only took up this mix-and-match aesthetic but also infused it with a sense of "elitism" through high-priced and rarified clothing.[50] Within this aesthetic, adherents formed alternative identities. Such alternatives took the form of gender bending and "cross-dressing,"[51] and examples include Culture Club's Boy George and the Eurythmics's Annie Lennox. Taken together, New Romanticism alternative identities combined the high and the low, the elitism of the fashion industry with low-budget punk aesthetics.

This exposition of New Romantic fashion suggests that Antoinette's "I Want Candy" rebellion is her attempt to create an alternative identity, in part through elements of high and low fashion. A key moment occurs with the inclusion of both Manolo Blahnik shoes and Converse brand Chuck Taylor All Star shoes. The All Stars were invented in 1917 as basketball shoes. However, they became a staple of the punk movement, associated with groups like The Clash. The shoes connote the low-budget, jumble-sale, mix-and-match sensibility of punk's influence on New Romanticism. Alongside these shoes, the film emphasizes the anachronistic Manolo Blahnik shoes. Coming to prominence in the late 1980s, Blahnik's designs became a staple of high-end fashion, and they featured prominently in shows like *Sex and the City* (1998–2004). Hence, the scene embodies New Romantic fashion, in depicting both low-budget All Stars and elitist Manolo Blahnik designs. Like the New Romantic emphasis on the creation of alternative identities, Antoinette's rebellion constitutes her attempt to form an alternative identity without reference to masculine desire. Antoinette surrounds herself with excesses of bodily desires. Instead of cross-dressing, she inhabits excessive femininity with her hair, makeup, and clothing. She also prioritizes the company of other heterosexual women and gay men and decenters her heterosexual male companions Louis and Count Fersen. While this attempt is ultimately not the way she chooses to live the remainder of her life, her rebellion is an attempt, albeit a fraught one, to try to imagine a new way of being in the world.

Based on this analysis, the concepts of masquerade and mimicry only partially describe Antoinette's feminine display during this period of the film. Antoinette's conspicuous consumption and partying can be ultimately characterized as the kind of alienation Irigaray describes, which could be why Antoinette eventually foregoes partying as unproductive. However, while Antoinette's motives are deeply related to Louis's sexual desire, she is not responding to his sexual longing for her. His lack of desire and the social isolation she experiences drive her actions. And she does not engage in feminine displays or any of the other erotic delights as a demand for Louis or any male to consume, love, or desire her. "I Want Candy" and her rejection of Count Fersen suggest that the dauphine both explores feminine excesses and evades masculine desire simultaneously. Inside of the system that turns her body into a commodity, she temporarily refuses the desires that commodify her. As a result, Antoinette's behavior only partially conforms to Irigaray's concept of masquerade. But neither does the dauphine engage in mimicry. The anachronistic music interprets Antoinette's behavior as a rebellion against the injustice of her situation. Therefore, in an important sense, she does engage in a critique of her plight through the excesses of femininity. However, Antoinette seems unable to name and expose the forces that subjugate her. She eventually finds her rebellion empty, hollow, and alienating, rather than a force of liberation.

While our close reading of the film complicates masquerade and mimicry, Chicana feminist Gloria Anzaldúa's understanding of El Mundo Zurdo (or, The Left-Handed World) complicates Rogers's account of liberation. The path to a liberated world begins when, Anzaldúa says, "we, the women here, take a trip back into the self, travel to the deep core of our roots to discover and reclaim our colored souls, [and] listen to the 'still small voice' . . . within us."[52] These acts of discovery, reclamation, and listening empower women "to create actual change in the world."[53] A changed world, then, is constituted of people with "a willingness to work with those people who would feel at home in *El Mundo Zurdo, the left-handed world*: the colored, the queer, the poor, the female, the physically challenged."[54] In the everyday world in which these people live, "words are not enough." Instead, "we must perform visible and public acts" through which women may become vulnerable to those who oppress them.[55] However, "our vulnerability," says Anzaldúa, "*can* be the source of our power," if women are willing to use it.[56] Liberation, therefore, runs two directions, "a going deep into the self and an expanding out into the world, a simultaneous recreation of the self and a reconstruction of society."[57]

Anzaldúa's reflections bring into relief the limited liberation that Antoinette experiences at Le Petit Trianon, first by way of a liberation that remains only personal. When Anzaldúa describes liberation, she connects the individual, liberated human to the larger, liberated world. The deep, personal reflections that individuals perform in relation to themselves, their history, their skin, and others is the starting point for the reconstruction of society. Each is implied in the other. The liberation of the individual, for Anzaldúa, demands the liberation of the world. In both *Marie Antoinette* and Rogers's reading, liberation begins and ends with the person of Antoinette. This is not to say that Antoinette does not experience liberation. Rather, her transient liberation does not result in visible, public action. We affirm with Rogers that Antoinette experiences real but transitory liberation while living at Le Petit Trianon. Through these moments, the film gestures toward an alternative way of life for the dauphine. However, her liberation lacks both the grounding of deep personal reflection and world reshaping. Antoinette bypasses, in a sense, Anzaldúa's insistence not only that the liberated person is changed deeply but that she also moves out into her world in action.

In addition, Antoinette's liberation appears limited due to its dependence on immense, patriarchal resources. She receives the Le Petit Trianon as a gift for giving birth to Louis's first child, after Antoinette fulfilled Versailles' and Louis's desire for progeny. Because she fulfilled her function as a commodity in the masculine economy of desire, Antoinette receives the château as payment for her objectification. The infrastructure for her liberation is, therefore, an affordance of patriarchal resources. While this does not diminish her feeling of liberation, it does limit it as not entirely outside of patriarchal desires, not entirely outside Versailles's way of life. Furthermore, Antoinette's liberation demands immense infrastructure—a château, servants, gardens, animals, and land. While Anzaldúa's account of liberation implies that masculine resources would be affected in some significant way, El Mundo Zurdo emphasizes a discovery of an alternative set of resources: history, self, skin, love, and relatedness with others and creation. Where Antoinette's liberation is dependent on masculine resources, Anzaldúa's emphasis rests on the resources the oppressed carry with them in their bodies, despite the world in which they live. Perhaps most importantly, Anzaldúa emphasizes that vulnerability is the source of liberating power. At Le Petit Trianon, Antoinette certainly experiences tenderness and connection but little vulnerability, and hence, little of the resources or power Anzaldúa claims are at the heart of liberation.

In extending Rogers's insights in this way, our reading of *Marie Antoinette* contributes to a more complicated understanding of concepts like masquerade, mimicry, and liberation. Bringing Coppola's and Anzaldúa's insights into conversation with white feminist reflection—and doing so at the site of film music—suggests limitations white scholars might consider. When we, white scholars, employ terms like masquerade, mimicry, and liberation, *Marie Antoinette* and Anzaldúa ask us to be increasingly critical about the imaginative horizons we carry with us. In part, we might need to question how resource-dependent white imaginations tend to be. If our imagining alternative worlds is both heavily resource dependent and ultimately personal, then we may need to consider whom our liberation excludes. And we may need to think more deeply about what we might need to divest if we are to imagine liberation for others and the world.

Perhaps most critically, Anzaldúa's conception of liberation presses white scholars to keep liberation connected both to moving into the world with public action and to drawing on the resources and power of vulnerability. Both in Antoinette's world and in our own, violent imperial powers continue to cause great and lasting harm. In this world, vulnerability is both resource and power, because it denies that violence will dictate what actions someone like Anzaldúa will perform with her own body. Vulnerability is both resource and power, because it implies that a new world is possible, a world where women like Anzaldúa and Antoinette can have a future liberated from the internalized violence of racism and the external violence of the state, be it the knee of redlining or the gift of Le Petit Trianon. Vulnerability is both resource and power, because it is not reserved for women of color. White women and men can become vulnerable. In such moments of vulnerability, perhaps what, in different ways, Marie Antoinette and Anzaldúa show us—the world as it is and as it could be.

## REFERENCES

Anzaldúa, Gloria E. "El Mundo Zurdo: The Vision." In *This Bridge Called My Back: Writings by Radical Women of Color*, edited by Cherríe Moraga and Gloria Anzaldúa, 195–96. New York: Women of Color Press, 1985.

———. "La Prieta." In *This Bridge Called My Back: Writings by Radical Women of Color*, edited by Cherríe Moraga and Gloria Anzaldúa, 198–209. New York: Women of Color Press, 1985.

Berardinelli, James. "Marie Antoinette (United States, 2006)." *ReelViews*, n.d. https://www.reelviews.net/reelviews/marie-antoinette.

Binns, Alexander. "The Development of Film Musicology: An Overview." In *Sound and Music in Film and Visual Media: An Overview*, edited by Graeme Harper, 725–38. New York: Continuum, 2009.

Borthwick, Stuart, and Ron Moy. *Popular Music Genres: An Introduction*. New York: Routledge, 2004.

Brevik-Zender, Heidi. "Let Them Wear Manolos: Fashion, Walter Benjamin, and Sofia Coppola's *Marie Antoinette*." In *Camera Obscura* 26, no. 3 (2011): 1–33.

Brown, Royal S. *Overtones and Undertones: Reading Film Music*. Berkeley: University of California Press, 1994.

Calhoun, Dave. "Marie Antoinette." *Time Out*, October 17, 2006. https://www.timeout.com/en_gb/film/marie-antoinette.

Coppola, Sofia, dir. *Marie Antoinette*. 2006; San Francisco, CA: American Zoetrope, 2007. DVD.

Dayan, Daniel. "The Tutor Code of Classical Cinema." In *Movies and Methods*, edited by Bill Nichols, 438–51. Berkeley: University of California Press, 1976.

Douglas, Susan J. *The Rise of Enlightened Sexism: How Pop Culture Took Us from Girl Power to Girls Gone Wild*. New York: St. Martin's, 2010.

Ebert, Roger. "Pretty in Pink." *RogerEbert.com*, October 19, 2006. https://www.rogerebert.com/reviews/marie-antoinette-2006.

Gorbman, Claudia. *Unheard Melodies: Narrative Film Music*. Bloomington, IN: University of Indiana Press, 1987.

Hubbert, Julie. "The Compilation Soundtrack from the 1960s to the Present." In *The Oxford Handbook of Film Music Studies*, edited by David Neumeyer, 291–318. New York: Oxford University Press, 2014.

Irigaray, Luce. *This Sex Which Is Not One*. Translated by Catherine Porter with Carolyn Burke. Ithaca, NY: Cornell University Press, 1985.

Meyer, Leonard B. *Emotion and Meaning in Music*. Chicago IL: University of Chicago Press, 1956.

Miller, Neil. "Marie Antoinette." *Film School Rejects*, October 20, 2006. https://filmschoolrejects.com/movie-review-marie-antoinette/.

Rogers, Anna Backman. *Sofia Coppola: The Politics of Visual Pleasure*. New York: Berghahn, 2019.

Rudi, Mari. *Feminist Film Theory and Pretty Woman, Film Theory and Practice*. New York: Bloomsbury Academic, 2016.

Sherman, Yael. "Neoliberal Femininity in Miss Congeniality." In *Feminism at the Movies: Understanding Gender in Contemporary Popular Culture*, edited by Hilary Radner and Rebecca Stringer, 80–94. New York: Routledge, 2011.

Silverman, Kaja. *The Subject of Semiotics*. Oxford: Oxford University Press, 1983.

Xu, Ping. "Irigaray's Mimicry and the Problem of Essentialism," *Hypatia* 10, no. 4 (Autumn 1995): 76–89.

## NOTES

1. Roger Ebert, "Pretty in Pink," *RogerEbert.com*, October 19, 2006, accessed June 3, 2020, www.rogerebert.com/reviews/marie-antoinette-2006.

2. James Berardinelli, "Marie Antoinette (United States, 2006)," *ReelViews*, n.d., accessed June 3, 2020, www.reelviews.net/reelviews/marie-antoinette (emphasis added).

3. Sofia Coppola, dir., *Marie Antoinette* (2006; San Francisco, CA: American Zoetrope, 2007), DVD.

4. Claudia Gorbman, *Unheard Melodies: Narrative Film Music* (Bloomington, IN: University of Indiana Press, 1987), 58.

5. Royal S. Brown, *Overtones and Undertones: Reading Film Music* (Berkeley: University of California Press, 1994), 27–28.

6. Gorbman, *Unheard Melodies*, 58.

7. Brown, *Overtones and Undertones*, 67.

8. Gorbman, *Unheard Melodies*, 7.

9. Brown, *Overtones and Undertones*, 30.

10. Gorbman, *Unheard Melodies*, 7.

11. Ibid.

12. Brown, *Overtones and Undertones*, 30–31.

13. Ibid., 31.

14. Mari Rudi, *Feminist Film Theory and Pretty Woman, Film Theory and Practice* (New York: Bloomsbury Academic, 2016), 26.

15. Kaja Silverman, *The Subject of Semiotics* (Oxford: Oxford University Press, 1983), 214.

16. Daniel Dayan, "The Tutor Code of Classical Cinema," in *Movies and Methods*, ed. Bill Nichols (Berkeley: University of California Press, 1976), 449. Quoted in Silverman, *Subject of Semiotics*, 215.

17. Rudi, *Feminist Film Theory*, 32.

18. Alexander Binns, "The Development of Film Musicology: An Overview," in *Sound and Music in Film and Visual Media: An Overview*, ed. Graeme Harper (New York: Continuum, 2009), 726.

19. Heidi Brevik-Zender, "Let Them Wear Manolos: Fashion, Walter Benjamin, and Sofia Coppola's *Marie Antoinette*," in *Camera Obscura* 26, no. 3 (2011): 1.

20. Leonard B. Meyer, *Emotion and Meaning in Music* (Chicago IL: University of Chicago Press, 1956), 26–30.

21. Susan J. Douglas, *The Rise of Enlightened Sexism: How Pop Culture Took Us from Girl Power to Girls Gone Wild* (New York: St. Martin's, 2010), 10.

22. Rudi, *Feminist Film Theory*, 84.

23. Douglas, *Rise of Enlightened Sexism*, 237.

24. Yael Sherman, "Neoliberal Femininity in Miss Congeniality," in *Feminism at the Movies: Understanding Gender in Contemporary Popular Culture*, ed. Hilary Radner and Rebecca Stringer (New York: Routledge, 2011), 90. Quoted in Rudi, *Feminist Film Theory*, 54.

25. Luce Irigaray, *This Sex Which Is Not One*, trans. Catherine Porter with Carolyn Burke (Ithaca, NY: Cornell University Press, 1985), 220.

26. Ibid.

27. Ibid., 84, 62.

28. Ibid., 220.

29. Ping Xu, "Irigaray's Mimicry and the Problem of Essentialism," *Hypatia* 10, no. 4 (Autumn 1995): 80, www.jstor.org/stable/3810206.

30. Irigaray, *This Sex Which Is Not One*, 164.

31. Ibid., 76.

32. Anna Backman Rogers, *Sofia Coppola: The Politics of Visual Pleasure* (New York: Berghahn, 2019), 136.

33. Ibid.

34. Ibid.

35. Ibid., 134.

36. Ibid.

37. Ibid.

38. Ibid., 137.

39. Ibid., 138.

40. Ibid., 137–38.

41. Berardinelli, "Marie Antoinette" (emphasis added).

42. Dave Calhoun, "Marie Antoinette," *Time Out*, October 17, 2006, accessed June 3, 2020, www.timeout.com/en_gb/film/marie-antoinette (emphasis added).

43. Neil Miller, "Marie Antoinette," *Film School Rejects*, October 20, 2006, accessed June 3, 2020, filmschoolrejects.com/movie-review-marie-antoinette/ (emphasis added).

44. See Gorbman, *Unheard Melodies*, 7 and Brown, *Overtones and Undertones*, 30–31.

45. Quoted in Julie Hubbert, "The Compilation Soundtrack from the 1960s to the Present," in *The Oxford Handbook of Film Music Studies*, ed. David Neumeyer (New York: Oxford University Press, 2014), 312 (emphasis original).

46. Brevik-Zender, "Let Them Wear Manolos," 8.

47. Ibid.

48. Stuart Borthwick and Ron Moy, *Popular Music Genres: An Introduction* (New York: Routledge, 2004), 132.
49. Ibid.
50. Ibid.
51. Ibid.
52. Gloria E. Anzaldúa, "El Mundo Zurdo: The Vision," in *This Bridge Called My Back: Writings by Radical Women of Color*, ed. Cherríe Moraga and Gloria Anzaldúa (New York: Women of Color Press, 1985), 195.
53. Ibid.
54. Ibid., 196, emphasis original.
55. Ibid., 195.
56. Ibid., 195, emphasis original.
57. Gloria E. Anzaldúa, "La Prieta," in *This Bridge Called My Back: Writings by Radical Women of Color*, ed. Cherríe Moraga and Gloria Anzaldúa (New York: Women of Color Press, 1985), 208.

*Chapter Four*

# Tables Turned

## *Hospitality, Phallogocentrism, and Virginity in* The Beguiled *(2017)*

This chapter unfolds in three sections. First, after a brief summary of the film, we examine the nature of hospitality, upon which Coppola's narrative is hinged. Our interest in hospitality concerns its potential to set up a politic vis-à-vis gender. We first look to Jacques Derrida, whose assertions on the nature of hospitality provide framework for both philology and etymology. As a source of comparison, we then turn to Virgil's *Aeneid*, which, although a text of mythological antiquity, provides insight in our examination of hospitality as it pertains to uneasy and problematic wartime relationships between host and guest. In the next section, we turn to the Civil War setting of *The Beguiled*, brimming with gender crises and destructive capitalist influences. We examine how misogynist propaganda exemplified in the ubiquity of patriarchal domination, especially in the Civil War South, from which the characters in the film likely sought a hermetic retreat. We then turn to the topics of womanhood, calling reference to the emblematicizing of women as representations of she-who-must-be-defended, as well as virginity, which carries various nineteenth-century religious and cultural implications. Finally, after a brief return to another text of antiquity, in this case the Hebrew Bible, we discuss the indelible effects of masculine intrusion into such feminine refuge and ways in which Coppola's *The Beguiled* engages in social commentary on the politics of gender.

Sofia Coppola's 2017 *The Beguiled* tells the story of Miss Martha Farnsworth's Seminary for Young Ladies, a southern all-girls boarding school in 1864 Virginia. While the exact location is not given, nearby combat suggests proximity to front line Civil War battle. The seminary has only a few students and teachers remaining: headmistress Martha Farnsworth (Nicole Kidman), teacher Edwina Morrow (Kirsten Dunst), and students Alicia (Elle Fanning),

Amy (Oona Laurence), Jane (Angourie Rice), Emily (Emma Howard), and Marie (Addison Riecke). The film opens with Amy picking mushrooms, when she discovers the wounded Union Corporal John McBurney (Colin Farrell). His accent and later conversation reveal that he is an Irish immigrant. The women and girls agree to take him in while he recuperates in their music room. One night, while the girls play music for McBurney, Confederate soldiers enter the home; Miss Martha asks whether any of the girls want to reveal McBurney's presence to them, but they each decline. Although he ingratiates himself with all the women and girls, Edwina and Alicia, in particular, vie for McBurney's attention and affection. Once McBurney is mobile, he tries to make himself helpful on the grounds, tending to the gardens. Eventually, he professes love for Edwina, though he consistently flirts with both Alicia and Miss Martha. One night, Edwina leaves her bed to meet with him, and finds him kissing Alicia in his bed. Edwina retreats. McBurney follows her, and as they scuffle, he falls down the stairs, greatly exacerbating his injury. In an effort to save his life, Miss Martha amputates McBurney's leg. Days later, he awakes in agony and enraged. He makes threats against the women and girls that escalate to the point where it becomes clear they will have to remove or kill him. While Edwina goes to his room to pacify him with sex, the others plot to poison him with mushrooms. Their plan is successful, and after McBurney dies at the dinner table, the women and girls sew him into a cloth body bag and leave his corpse outside the school's gate.

## HOSPITALITY (OR, HOSPITALITY BROKEN)

The evocative subject of hospitality, brimming with political and ethical nuances, brings to mind questions regarding how one might welcome a stranger, traveler, or migrant. By its own nature, it presents a dichotomous relationship between Self and Other, host and guest, secure and insecure, provided-for and in-need, etc. On a large scale, hospitality relates to national political realities, like the United States of America's historical and current exclusion of certain kinds of immigrants. On a smaller scale, the notion of hospitality has been, and likely will always be, a significant mode of concern within interpersonal political relations.

As the narrative of *The Beguiled* hinges upon Miss Martha's willingness to take McBurney in, we turn our analysis to the nature of hospitality in ancient literature as well as postmodern thought. On the subject of hospitality, philosopher Jacques Derrida points to paradoxical etymology of the Latin *hospes*. As an English cognate for "hospitality," *hospes* carries the dual and interchangeable meaning of both "host" and "guest," referring to both the host's identity and that of a guest, stranger, or visitor.[1] The interchangeability of the term sheds light on the ancient understanding that trust in both directions is necessary for proper hospitality.[2] In fact, Derrida suggests that such trust should lead to a radical posture. He asserts that all hosts should "say yes" to who or whatever arrives, be they "a foreigner, an immigrant, an uninvited guest, an unexpected visitor. Whether or not this new arrival, visitor, is the citizen of another country, human, animal or divine, a living or dead thing, male or female (*sic*)."[3]

Derrida's position here is one of unconditioned inclusion. Philosopher Shannon Hoff points out that a problem quickly arises at the onset of such openness. She writes,

> Other complicating considerations emerge: the place in which the guest is welcomed has an existence on its own terms, and for it to *be* a place for the guest it has to be able to define *itself*, protecting those resources that would allow it to persist. In so doing, however, it will effectively refuse to answer in an absolutely open way to the guest's terms and thus will be *in*hospitable in relation to them (emphasis in original).[4]

To welcome anyone, anytime, and providing any resources would be impossible, as it would strip the host of resources necessary to continue. Thus, Derridaean hospitality cannot be a truly practical hospitality. A possible solution, Hoff contends, is available only at the connection between absolute openness with that which retains a modicum of resources required to welcome a specific person according to their specific needs.[5]

Returning to etymology, and perhaps even further complicating Derrida's claims, the English term "hospitality" amalgamates *hospes* and the Latin verb *peto, petere* (to seek, desire, attack). Thus "hospitality" suggests a power dynamic in which one or both members carry potential for threat. So, true hospitality seems to also require a degree of circumspection: a host must not relinquish enough resources that the guest can overtake the host. The result would be a hospitality broken. While Coppola's *The Beguiled* could be read entirely as a mediation on hospitality, one could also describe it as a meditation on hospitality broken, as interaction between host (Miss Martha) and guest (McBurney) provide considerable dramatic focus.

As a source of comparison and to elaborate on the guest-host dynamic, we turn to Virgil's *Aeneid* and specifically to the interaction between Dido and Aeneas.[6] Aeneas, a Trojan soldier, having fled Troy while it was being destroyed by Greek forces, is shipwrecked on the African coast. He and his fellow sailors are rescued by Dido, the queen of Carthage, who had previously also escaped both war in Tyros and her brother, Pygmalion, who had murdered her fiancé. When a storm causes Dido and Aeneas to take shelter in a cave during a hunt, they make love, which signifies a marital bond for Dido, but not Aeneas.⁷ When Aeneas decides to set off for Italy, Dido becomes enraged. She orders that Aeneas's belongings be burned; she leaps onto the pyre and stabs herself with Aeneas's sword, cursing him and the other Trojans.

The story was commonly alluded to in ancient, medieval, and recent works, and one ancient author notes the importance of the concept of piety. In Book 3 of *Ars Amatoria*, Ovid reminds us that Aeneas's primary crime as Dido's guest was to bring violence and hostility within the Carthaginian court, "*et famam pietatis habet, tamen hospes et ensem / praebuit et causam mortis, Elissa, tuae*" [Though he may be famed for piety, however your guest Aeneas / provided the sword and the cause of your death, Dido]. *Pietas* (or what we translate as "piety") incorporates a wide range of postures, including affection, dutifulness, loyalty, and gratitude, which an original reader of Ovid would presuppose. The definition of *pietas* is more in line with our comparison to hospitality (or *hospitium*) in *The Beguiled*. Linking hospitality and *pietas*, classicist R. K. Gibson writes, "at the heart of *hospitium* . . . lay the ideals of duty, loyalty, reciprocity, and the exchange of services. *Pietas* includes, in this context, a reference to the guest's sense of, or actual fulfilment of, the duty to pay a proper return on the hospitality received."⁸

Similar to the ancient, mythological counterpart (Aeneas), Irish immigrants, like McBurney, fled famine and economic anxiety, seeking farm work. Ireland had historically struggled with colonial oppression and sectarianism, and such hostilities erupted in events like the 1848 Young Ireland Rebellion. After the rebellion, the United States received over three million immigrants between 1848 and 1860. Many Irish immigrants found themselves embroiled in a hegemonic regime, in which the culture of continental Europe was deemed superior to that of Ireland. A portion of these immigrants were recruited to join the Union army.

While it is not a justification for their violence against women, McBurney and Aeneas share a lower guest-status in relationship to a superior host, placing the guest in dependent relationship to the host's hospitality. When we first see him, Coppola's framing of the meeting between McBurney and Amy reflects McBurney's dependency via mise-en-scène. While picking mushrooms, Amy finds a butterfly, and she leans down to release it in an ostensibly better spot for it to thrive. She says to it, "Here you go," as she turns her hand over to release it. Abruptly seeing McBurney, she springs back and upright, startled, and looks down on him. McBurney lies on his back, looking up at her. The camera is behind her pointing down at McBurney. Having just seen Amy caring for a "wild and free" creature, we now see a pitiful creature in McBurney, destined to die, or at least suffer more greatly, without Amy's help.⁹ McBurney, however, already resists his dependency on Amy and asserts his dominance by limiting her speech by shushing her.

McBurney behaves as though his station, as a man and an adult, gives him the right to control Amy.

In this way, even at this point of physical vulnerability and emotional destitution, McBurney anticipates, to the point of taking for granted, violent hospitality. Though a trespasser and even enemy soldier, he sees Amy's youth and femininity as something to exploit, which he does with manipulative language. He says, "Are you frightened?" Amy responds, "No . . . Yes." McBurney admits, "So am I." This act of connection with Amy is certainly manipulative, since his immediate reaction is to silence her. However, Coppola's image reveals the opposite to be true. He is dependent on Amy and seeks to attach himself to her as *hospes* (read: guest). While Amy's acceptance of McBurney reveals her kindheartedness, even perhaps naiveté, she doubtless knows that his ultimate reception within the Farnsworth Seminary is entirely conditional upon Miss Martha's hospitality.

If McBurney's behavior is analogous to that of Aeneas, let us now consider Miss Martha as counterpart to Dido. Having fled her homeland of Tyros after her brother murdered her fiancé, Dido founded the city of Carthage, which prospered due to her industry, intelligence, and leadership. Virgil describes Dido as an industrious figurehead, having fled her home under threat of violence after losing a spouse, led a band of fugitives, sought to establish a new city, and provided guidance to her followers in various ways. Virgil refers to Dido as *dux femina facti* (I. 364), a rare instance of a female noun (*femina* [fem.], woman) affixed to a male noun (*dux* [masc.], a leader of military forces).[10] Historians Anke Gilleir and Aude Dufurne describe the significance of the double-gendered term: "a *woman* became the leader . . . Though ancient history and literature abound with unjust and tyrannical (male) rulers, 'dux femina' signals a state of exception, a disruption in the continuation of state power."[11] Like Dido, Miss Martha has taken refuge from war, and she uses her leadership ability to establish a sanctuary for others and places them in her care.

The film does not reveal the founding of the Farnsworth's Seminary for Young Ladies, but Miss Martha's creation of a safe haven for women and girls suggests three political conditions that life at the school preserves for the women and girls who live there. First, she shelters young women from the various eventualities of wartime savagery (we will discuss sexual violence during the Civil War later). Second, the school's placement in rural Virginia provides a unique opportunity to establish a self-sustaining environment, living on what they raise, grow, and gather. In this way, the women participants are no longer dependent upon the political apparatus of the Confederacy. Third, Miss Martha allows Edwina to challenge, in minor ways, patriarchal systems. One such example occurs when Edwina teaches French to her students. She neglects (or perhaps refuses) to include the masculine component of the third person singular conjugation of the verb *être*.[12] Like Dido's Carthage, Miss Martha's seminary is one of escape from violence of masculine interpersonal interactions.[13]

A telling masculine interaction occurs during the nighttime arrival of Confederate soldiers at the seminary; Miss Martha leaves the music room to answer the door, insisting that everyone remain there. Coppola creates suspense by enclosing the viewer and every character except Miss Martha within McBurney's bedroom. We (alongside the girls) hear loud footsteps and deep voices from the first floor: a concealed, chthonic presence, unpredictable and potentially harmful. The younger girls ask Edwina who and what the presence is, and as they hear someone climbing the steps, they recoil in fear. Miss Martha emerges and claims that the soldiers are "two of our own," simply there to offer assistance as the Confederate army prepares to leave the area. The ladies discuss whether to alert them to the presence of McBurney, and Miss Martha cunningly steers the girls to conclude that Christian charity should be considered, and all agree to conceal McBurney. Christian charity, for the girls at the seminary, seems to exist under the umbrella of piety.

In dealing with the Confederate soldiers, Miss Martha's *hospitium* diffuses masculine violence, ensuring safety of those in her charge. In the ancient world, *hospitium* often appears with repeated conventional elements, including the "arrival at destination, [the] description of the surroundings, the offer of a seat to the guest by the host, a feast, [the] identification of the guest, [an] exchange of information . . . [and] the bestowal of gifts by the host and departure of the guest."[14] We discuss the first four elements early on, and we will refer to the final element later. Miss Martha invites them into the home (arrival), discusses with them the situation (surroundings), offers them a place at her table (seat), feeds them (feast), identifies them as "our boys" (identification), and exchanges information, though only in part. Miss Martha withholds McBurney's presence, because it would engender masculine hostility into the female environment.

When Miss Martha sends the girls to bed, Emily asks, "Can we go greet the soldiers?" to which Miss Martha declines, saying, "I do not want to put temptation in their way." Her response is telling of her assumption that the soldiers would see young ladies and/or girls as targets of sexual violence and be less able to control themselves and their potential aggression.[15] After the young ladies and girls leave, Miss Martha tells McBurney of the soldiers' statement that, "There is nothin' more frightenin' than a startled woman with a gun," a not-so-subtle reminder of her *dux femina facti*; like Dido, Miss Martha is the armed figurehead of her domain. She continues, as if to celebrate her victory at keeping hostilities in check by denying the male soldiers (including McBurney) opportunity to act according to what Virgil might describe as *ferocia corda* ("savage instincts," I. 302), and she asks McBurney whether he would care to join her for a brandy. Her speech is deliberate and positive, with a rare smile. Her success in this manner frees her to express *mentem benignam* ("kindly mind," I. 304) towards McBurney and the Confederate soldiers, but only as it suits the regulations of her home and domain.

While McBurney continues to ingratiate himself with all the women and girls in the house, he speaks in lofty and overly sentimental language, even while lying. For example, he confesses a deep love for Edwina, having only interacted with her a handful of times. As Backman Rogers describes his speech, "McBurney's utterly spurious declaration of love . . . 'I love you' may be a cliché, a pregiven sentiment," which he uses to "cruel and pernicious" effect.[16] We see similar empty and overly sentimental features in Aeneas's supplication towards Dido (I. 605–609): "What happy age gave birth to you? What parents produced such a child? Your honor, name and praise will endure forever, whatever lands may summon me, while rivers run to the sea, while shadows cross mountain slopes, while the sky nourishes the stars."

Like his ersatz love for Edwina, McBurney's interactions with Amy first appear as innocent *hospes* (guest) but eventually turn violent. When he wakes for his first full day in the house, Amy enters the music room to check on him. They have a brief conversation in which Amy asks if McBurney likes birds. Echoing their first meeting, he says, "Oh, I love them. Anything wild I love—wild and free." Amy initially accepts McBurney's attempt to ingratiate himself to her. Film scholar William Brown points out that in a later scene, Amy accepts a gift from McBurney, a button from his military as "a sign of his esteem and, taken with his flattery, she treats the button as some kind of talismanic object worthy of saving in a tin box alongside other childish objects of seemingly numinous import."[17] Though claiming to love anything "wild and free," McBurney's method of tending to the garden suggests that he desires the opposite. As William Brown notes, McBurney "wishes to prune roses and to trim bushes; that is, he wishes to stop the growth of, and to control, that which is wild and free."[18] After his amputation and in fits of rage, his violence against Amy is an especially cruel act, in which he kills "her most prized possession (her tortoise Henry) by dashing his delicate body on the stone floor of the kitchen."[19] Amy demonstrates hospitality closer to Derrida's idealistic description than any other character; perhaps this is due to her youth or naiveté. However, one might rather assert that her boldness early on as she rescues McBurney is indicative of an active desire to express a pure, Derridaean hospitality. His ultimate betrayal against Amy, however, occurs in his response to her interminable kindness with violent *hospes* against her community.

As Miss Martha reaches a full understanding of McBurney's intentions and instability, she, like Dido, ultimately renounces *hospitium*, saying, "We have to rid ourselves of him. We're not safe here, while he's in the house." We see a similar renunciation of *hospitium* in Dido's final speech as she takes her life; Dido entreats her followers to dismiss Aeneas and his family line saying, "Then, O Tyrians, pursue my hatred against his whole line and the race to come, and offer it as a tribute to my ashes. Let there be no love or treaties between our peoples" (IV. 622–624). After Miss Martha's renunciation, and while McBurney and Edwina are alone in the music room (which we will discuss later), Miss Martha and the others sit and listen to what occurs. The girls begin to suggest means of McBurney's removal. Some of the girls suggest leaving McBurney in the woods or hanging him, but Miss Martha insists that they not resort to brutality. Such brutality, from the perspective of Miss Martha and those in her charge at the seminary, is precisely the kind of violent masculine interpersonal interaction they have painstakingly avoided. When Marie points out the McBurney loves mushrooms, this becomes the ideal solution, as it resists the masculine *ferocia corda*. Miss Martha's rejection of *hospitium* is a primarily feminine choice: Backman Rogers reminds us that "poison is often considered to be the female weapon of choice."[20] Moreover, it ironically encapsulates the final stage of *hospitium*, the bestowal of gifts by the host and departure of the guest. In Miss Martha's *hospitium*, the gifts are culinary, and the means of the guest's departure (read: death) are of his ostensibly favorite dish.

## PHALLOGOCENTRISM AND SEXUAL ASSAULT

Women in literature and most especially in mythologies (including Virgil) are often represented negatively to uphold patriarchal ideologies. The importance of female authorship, which feminist philosopher Hélène Cixous calls *écriture féminine,* for films like *The Beguiled* offer a feminine position to address such imbalances.[21] This is especially pertinent as it might pertain to intertextual discourse with such misogynist antiquitous writings as Virgil's *Aeneid*. For this reason, we now turn to phallogocentrism in the known-and-literary world, about which female authors (and screenwriters) implement their craft as a means to negotiate it.[22] Phallogocentrism, Derrida's term for a system that privileges the masculine as a linguistic symbol, has been adopted by feminist critics (e.g., *écriture feminine* authors Cixous and Catherine Clément).[23] The term contains within it the hegemonic ideals of patriarchal culture, simply from the nature of the evolution of languages having stemmed from those cultures. As phallogocentric structures are embedded in language and culture from antiquity, these structures etymologically transverse emerging cultures (and cultures having emerged) through linguistic construction; according to Cixous we are "born into language and language speaks (to) us [and] dictates its law."[24] The resulting nature of language has been phallogocentric, privileging the masculine in symbols and linguistic components. Cixous urges female authors to shatter what she calls the "framework of institutions" by challenging masculine paramountcy via appropriation and adaptation.[25] Coppola's film, especially due to its narrative and subject matter (which we will discuss in more detail later) lends itself to an examination of female authorship as a challenge to phallogocentrism. In this way, we might view Edwina's neglect of the masculine iteration of *être* as an act of defiance as opposed to simply removing the superfluous.

As we consider Coppola's authorship as a challenge to phallogocentricm, we should also examine her use of filmic language, especially concerning aural language. Coppola's variegated uses of music in films are common subjects in this and other scholarly works, but unlike each of Coppola's other feature films, *The Beguiled* offers little in terms of music. The one recurring piece of music throughout the film, however, is the Civil War era song, "Lorena." We first hear Amy humming it in the woods in the opening scene. Later the girls sing it to McBurney, with Jane at the piano, until they are interrupted by the arrival of the Confederate soldiers knocking on the door. The lyrics of "Lorena," originally a poem written in 1856 by Henry D. L. Webster, describe the end of a relationship, telling the story of a woman who eludes the love, or more rightly the control, of a man.[26] Although published by a Northerner, the song's inherent nostalgia engendered its popularity in North and South alike.

Musicologist Kelsey Murphy notes that the love story served as a nationalist metaphor, mirroring "what the Confederate veterans were feeling regarding the loss of their 'nation.'"[27] Murphy points out that the sentimentality of the song emboldened the Confederate-desired function "to recall an idyllic past" that was threatened by a "shared white brotherhood of pain and loss."[28] Thus, "Lorena" was a reminder of "male hegemonic pre-War womanhood that carried into the Civil War era."[29] She continues, "these tropes from the antebellum era carried into wartime they were given a new function in song due to the context of the war. Domesticity, piety, purity, and submissiveness were no longer just facets of true womanhood, they were a patriotic necessity."[30] The song was banned in several Confederate army camps after causing, or, rather, being blamed for, homesickness and desertion.[31] Its use in Coppola's film not only reflects the Civil War temperament of dislocation and despondency but enlivens discourse regarding gender disharmony.

The ban of "Lorena" due to its nostalgic properties that threatened the war resolve of Confederate soldiers bears a resemblance to Miss Martha's denial of the girls' request to greet the Confederate soldiers in their house.

By assuming the soldiers' sense of dislocation from their homes (and perhaps love interests from their homes), she presupposes that they might look at the young ladies and girls in her charge as wartime substitutes to be assailed, and certainly that if they were to harm the girls, punishment for such actions would be improbable in Civil War circumstances. As we mentioned in the section on *hospitium,* Miss Martha denies the girls' request, saying, "I do not want to put temptation in their way." Such a statement not only works to exemplify Miss Martha's power over soldiers, young ladies, and girls, but it points towards her understanding of the precariousness of wartime gender interactions. Ultimately, her trepidation will be realized in McBurney's victimization of Edwina.

African American studies scholar Crystal N. Feimster relates the ubiquity of sexual assault during wartime and specifically the American Civil War. She writes that wartime rape, an issue of both ancient and contemporary hostilities, is evident not only in recent reports from Yugoslavian wars of secession and Rwandan genocide, but in accounts from the Hebrew Bible, Homer, Greek/Roman mythologies, and various medieval chronicles.[32] She writes, "evidence seems to suggest that whenever and wherever men go to war, rape and the threat of sexual violence against women are inevitable, even strategic components of warfare."[33] After detailing several court cases involving Civil War-time rapes that were prosecuted, Feimster continues that "most rapes . . . likely went unreported because many women, especially women of the planter elite, considered sexual assault a fate worse than death. Because a white woman's virtue represented her most valuable commodity, much was at stake in making public a crime understood to tarnish that virtue."[34]

Perhaps one of the most telling results of gendered hostility among white Southerners occurred after Union General Benjamin Butler's infamous "General Orders No. 28" on May 15, 1862 in Union occupied New Orleans. The order reads:

> As the officers and soldiers of the United States have been subject to repeated insults from the woman (calling themselves ladies) of New Orleans in return for the most scrupulous non-interference and courtesy on our part, it is ordered that hereafter when any female shall by word, gesture, or movement insult or show contempt for any officer or soldier of the United States she shall be regarded and held liable to be treated as a woman of the town plying her avocation.[35]

While Butler would later claim that the order was not a specific license or call to rape, "he clearly believed that threatening sexual violence was a justifiable means of subduing southern women."[36] Regardless, from the Southern female perspective, men from both Union and Confederate armies alike imbued threats of sexual violence. Both factions use political or propagandist memoranda to manipulate and disconcert women for their own purposes. As capital, women are at the behest of male control; Butler's declaration intensifies the gender crisis via capitalist language, "woman of the town," that is, sex worker.

News of Butler's order spread through the South quickly, so one can easily assume Virginians in 1864 to be aware of it. In light of this, upon the arrival of McBurney at the Farnsworth Seminary, victimization of one or more of the girls might almost be anticipated. McBurney's presence, like that of the Confederate soldiers, constitutes masculine intrusion into feminine space. Their space, free of masculine presence for an untold duration previous to these events, presents a unique target for masculine desire: a place of solace and gratification. Backman Rogers writes, "McBurney wishes for these women to become handmaidens, attendant only to his distinctly masculine libido."[37] One could surmise that Miss Martha had painstakingly removed herself and her female charges from the violent, masculine sphere of Civil War Virginia out of awareness that for many women, dislocation and vulnerability were the norm. Historian Susan-Mary Grant writes:

> For southern women during the American Civil War, the concept of home front and battlefront was often a distinction without a difference. What had been domestic space became, over the course of the conflict, military, medical and memorial space. As their homes became hospitals and their gardens, graveyards, many found themselves adrift. Whether as white refugees, fleeing the invading armies, or as slaves, fleeing toward freedom, theirs was a dislocated world, positioned between home front and battlefront, between slavery and freedom.[38]

Without masculine intrusion, the young ladies and girls at Farnsworth's seminary experience both physical and psychological security that masculine presence would ultimately threaten. Such an orientation bolsters the prescience of Miss Martha's refusal to "put temptation in [the soldiers'] way," as she recognizes violent instability to potentially exist in any man, especially during the precariousness of wartime and most especially in this now-exposed female space. Though Miss Martha dismisses the Confederate soldiers with ease, the seminary's entrenchment with McBurney is clearly more problematic. Even at the onset of McBurney's arrival, when the ladies are carrying the limp, wounded soldier into the house, Jane forewarns the group, "You know they rape every Southern woman they come across." By "they," Jane clearly means Union soldiers, and the inclusion of the word "Southern" in Jane's prediction, evinces an acute cognizance of rape as war-time weapon, if not a vivid comprehension of political elements such as Butler's order. That McBurney's intemperate and eventually aggressive behavior slowly crescendos during his stay at the Farnsworth Seminary seems indicative of the accuracy of Jane's warning. McBurney's belligerence seems consistently phallic in nature; Backman Rogers calls attention to his attachment to the gun that he inveigles away from Miss Martha.[39]

Moreover, McBurney's encounters with Alicia and Edwina quickly become sexually driven. We see this when Edwina discovers Alicia in McBurney's bed, as well as his chasing Edwina to defend his actions (calling her "darling," and "lovely Edwina"). He repeats her name several times, as Edwina backs away from the music room into the hallway. The image here is almost entirely negative space; Coppola's nearly pitch-black mise-en-scène allegorizes Edwina's disbelief in what she (barely) sees. Like Edwina, we as viewers know little of McBurney's intent or even momentary physical presence and disposition. Finally, the two reach the hallway and are backlit by the window, which projects enough light to make their bodily profiles visible. Gasping and emotional, Edwina begins to say and repeat "no," and when McBurney tries to embrace her, she begins to strike him. He tries to control her with his arms, and she pushes him. Ultimately, McBurney's failure as seductor of both women ultimately exacerbates his injury via his falling down the stairs, but more significantly, it reveals his desperation to dominate this feminine space.

McBurney's façade is removed when, days later, he wakes screaming from the pain of his amputation. Edwina rushes to his side to comfort him and apologize, but he continues screaming; when Miss Martha enters, he calls her "the butcher." Miss Martha relates that she had no choice, and that amputation was the only means to save his life. He responds, "You didn't have a choice, or you wanted to punish me for not going into *your* room!" His question sounds more declarative than inquisitive, revealing his assumption that Miss Martha wanted to have a sexual relationship with him; with this declaration, McBurney reveals his intent to dominate each interaction with female members of the house and to do so on his phallocentric terms. When Edwina defends Miss Martha, McBurney shouts, "You're worse than she is! Did you plan this together? Now you have me at your beck and call!" As the ladies leave to retrieve alcohol to numb his pain, he winces, "You didn't tell me it was a house of mad women." Such a statement, including the unknown pronoun "you" (who? God? Miss Martha?), further divulges McBurney's phallogocentrism by repositioning Miss Martha's clearly adept medical and surgical skills as "mad." He immediately perceives that by removing his leg, Miss Martha fundamentally displaces him on his (assumed) phallogocentric plane, which presupposes women to be at men's "beck and call," rather than the inversion he now perceives. Moreover, his grouping off all the ladies and girls as "mad women" unsexes them, based upon his preconceived expectation of woman's cordial disposition (read: handmaidens), and that this space is, for him, one of solace and gratification.[40] In McBurney's view, by neglecting her duty to maintain the clean, organized, and gracious care of a proper nurse, Miss Martha forsook her feminine role to nurture and provide for male members (or guests) of her domicile. The "butcher," a "mad woman," or no woman at all, damages the male body and forces it to become the submissive body, the opposite to its phallogocentric positioning. Thus, he self-diagnoses as no longer a man (castration, which he mentions later).

McBurney psychologically tortures all women and girls in the seminary, screaming and breaking fragile items, grabbing Alicia's hair and demanding she retrieve the music-room key, and pressuring Jane to intercede for him with Miss Martha. Finally, he emerges in the kitchen and asks, "What are you lovely Southern ladies learnin' today? The art of castration?" When Miss Martha entreats Amy to tie a blue ribbon to the gate (which would alert outside soldiers of an intruder), McBurney tears it away and chases her into a barn, where he terrorizes her with questions at gunpoint. After Miss Martha coaxes him away, claiming to have more bourbon in the cellar, the three reenter the house, where he forces them to gather in a sitting room. He shouts:

> I never meant any harm to any of youse. And look at me, really look what you've done to me. I'd rather be dead than be a man without a leg, hobblin' around . . . I'm not even a man anymore! I took your kindness and I trusted you, and ya, ya toyed with me, and ya butchered me!

McBurney's claim that he is "not even a man anymore," a self-diagnosed "castration," underscores how bodily lack, castration, and/or impotence are elements of phallic economy and thus entirely the province of patriarchy and its insistence upon phallocentric and phallogocentric sustainability. McBurney's intensified anger and aggression are misguided attempts to suture (physically) what he perceives (psychologically) as lacking, i.e., the bleeding wound/amputation. Ironically, he forgets that an injury was the only bodily component able to grant him admission to the female-hegemonic space of the seminary. Backman Rogers points out that "McBurney's error is to believe that he still occupies a position of power within this environment when he is, in fact, a "'most unwelcome visitor.' There simply is no space set aside to accommodate him in this world."[41] Taking Backman Rogers's comment further, not only was McBurney never in a position of power, as Miss Martha demonstrates during the incident with the Confederate soldiers' arrival, but the women's healing of McBurney's injuries would have been the very act to nullify his ingress in the first place. His toxic behavior, sexually preying on those around him, which leads to his literal and psychological downfall, actually reinforces his belief that he is indeed a "most welcome visitor," as it behooves all women to provide solace and comfort in such situations.

## A SACRIFICIAL VIRGIN

Historian Stephanie McCurry writes that in the antebellum/Civil War Confederacy, the citizen was male, the state female.[42] She writes,

> In the late antebellum Southern states, the female figure of the state took many forms–genius of liberty, old lady in hoop skirts–but none more commonly than mother, the better, presumably, to summon the loyalty of her sons . . . Images of the political mother proliferated secessionist discourse in the upper and lower South states, feeding into a larger theme of politics as filial piety, and rooting the political and martial duties of male citizens, not in the abstraction of the state but the intimate body of the mother, "the soil which gave him birth," as one put it. We must be "united at home as a band of brothers ready to defend the honor of an insulted mother."[43]

Such imagery of mother and sons engendered a powerful dynamic within the discourse of the Confederate ethos. State-as-woman became, for Southern men, emblematic of the vulnerability of wives, daughters, and brides, and more importantly, the virtue of these. The resulting state-as-bride correlative brought alongside it a religious quality, at least to those in the Confederacy with claims of devout Christianity. New Testament authors Paul (2 Cor. 11:1–4; Eph. 5:22–33) and John (John 3:25–30; Rev. 19:7–9; 21:1–3, 9–10; 22:17) use images of marital relations to express the relationship between Jesus Christ and the Christian church; Christian ministers recall such imagery likely to foster piety by describing ideal devotion to be intimate.[44] By channeling the state-as-bride analog, Southern men were called upon, within the social-religious construct, to protect the new Confederate state(s) as one would protect the virtue of a new bride.

At the apogee of Coppola's film, what is at stake for Edwina goes beyond sacrifice of self (body), via sex with McBurney, though already this is no small offering. McBurney's assault sets forth a distortion, or massacre, of the virginal. After terrorizing the women with Miss Martha's gun, McBurney shoots the chandelier, knocking it to the ground, threatens the women and girls with the next gunshot, and wanders off. Resolute and determined, Edwina follows him, despite protest from Miss Martha, and enters the music room. Despite any potential, cursory observation that Edwina may actually desire McBurney, or even that the resulting assault could be viewed as remotely consensual, the environs of the music room and pertinacious disposition of Edwina clearly counter such notions. This is not a romantic scene. Coppola describes it as "raw," "violent," and notes, "it was really important that they didn't kiss. It was important that it had to be angry."[45] Rather, the scene is a near-ceremonial self-sacrifice: Edwina resigns her state(hood)-as-woman(hood); in her world, she proffers to the violator (North) "the dishonor which is infinitely worse than death." Backman Rogers notes the "ritualistic" manner in which she lays "herself out on the bed like a sacrificial object dressed in a virginal gown," and the brutality of the way he "takes her . . . tearing asunder her clothes and scattering pearl buttons across the wooden floorboards."[46]

Virginity in nineteenth-century America, writes literature scholar Julie Noel Durling Smith, is "the one commodity that a woman lacking monetary assets could use as a bargaining tool on the marriage market."[47] Edwina's sacrifice of body consequently diminishes her worth within the patriarchal hegemonic system. Perhaps more germane is the homology between Edwina's victimization and countless other unreported domiciliary sexual assaults in the Civil War South. Though women were restricted to the home to protect against assailants, the wartime backdrop of such assaults relates how women's bodies often resemble a terrain on which the war has been repeatedly waged throughout history.[48] Historians E. Susan Barber and Charles F. Ritter report that between 1992 and 2000, only 63 percent of rapes and 65 percent of attempted rapes in contemporary American society were reported to law enforcement.[49] They surmise that "this must have been even more the case in mid-nineteenth-century America when white women's purity was a highly prized commodity and a woman's disclosure of such a crime risked her own character being exposed to a high level of scrutiny for evidence that she was somehow complicit in the attack."[50]

Barber and Ritter's comment that a woman's sexual purity was to be understood as a "highly prized commodity" references (among countless other sources) Barbara Welter's 1966 landmark article "The Cult of True Womanhood: 1820–1860," in which Welter claims sexual purity was "as essential as piety to a young woman, its absence as unnatural and unfeminine. Without it she was, in fact, no woman at all, but a member of some lower order."[51] Such a categorization certainly befits a comparison with the language of Butler's "General Orders No. 28," in which the women deemed inhospitable should be "treated as a woman of the town plying her avocation," and thus "a member of some lower order." Religious studies scholar Sara Moslener describes the virtue of "purity" as a uniquely feminine "asset" and its role as part of the larger project to alleviate Protestant anxieties about personal wealth.[52] Furthermore, Moslener claims, the control of sexuality through evangelical Christian education remains a dominant strategy for retention of cultural capital, as "women's ability to maintain the virtues of religious piety and sexual purity allowed white, middle-class men to pursue economic success and thus reassure white middle-class Protestants of their cultural dominance."[53]

Edwina's sacrifice, ostensibly successful in pacifying McBurney's savagery, provides her with two options: accept her assailant as potential inamorato in the unspecified future or accept the full loss of her social and cultural capital. Coppola demonstrates this in the brief but telling moment later that night when the two join hands at the dinner table, just before the other ladies murder McBurney. Coppola contrasts the climactic dinner scene with a similar scene prior to McBurney's new injury. As the group (including McBurney) are gathered for dinner, Edwina wears a shoulderless dress. Alicia complains that she is not allowed to wear such revealing clothing, and Miss Martha tells Edwina to draw her shawl to cover up. In the latter scene, as McBurney and Edwina join the others for dinner, we see her bare shoulders; Edwina, no longer a virgin, is no longer censured by Alicia or Miss Martha, suggesting that everyone present knows what occurred in the music room (though perhaps without the grisly details). McBurney's postcoital afterglow seems to have temporarily nullified his sense of castration, as he reinstated his manhood in brutal conquest of the virginal female body. He proffers an unctuous assertion to reinstate non-threatening *hospitium*, "Thank you for excusing my . . . my outburst. I'd like to thank you for all this as well. It looks, uh, it looks just about the finest meal I've ever seen."

After he pours wine for Edwina, in a transparently obsequious servile position demonstrative of his postcoital resignation of manly power, he offers her mushrooms and calls her by the oleaginous, flattering moniker "Miss Morrow," as if to intimate that their erotic connection (rather, his phallic performance) has now elevated her to his societal equal. He continues, "I'm not gonna stay here much longer. [McBurney and Edwina join hands] But, um, while I'm here, I wanna do my best to make it up for, you know, all the unfortunate things that happened."

His retreat from culpability via passive voice both evinces McBurney's sense of justification for hostility within female surroundings and his continued lack of awareness of his own vulnerability. His demise rests upon this dissolution: McBurney, unwilling to perceive his vulnerability and insisting upon assumed phallic dominance, results in his lack of inhibition or suspicion, even in the "house of mad women." His victory, now a pyrrhic one, reveals him to be "the beguiled" in the film's most hermeneutic sense; he sits across from the tableau of "mad women," striated out from Miss Martha, whose sober female gaze watches him fall to his death. Edwina's initial confusion about McBurney's demise evidences her predicament to be a Hobsons's choice: to be with McBurney (as long as he'll have her) or to have nothing (having lost social and cultural capital). Thus, we recognize her bodily sacrifice to be even more poignant: Edwina's solitude, now a forgone conclusion, while having freed her from McBurney's further abuse, likely negates her agency and cultural capital in future life. Coppola's mise-en-scène complements this reading, as Miss Martha joins hands with the rest of the young ladies and girls, leaving Edwina out of the untainted, maidenly circle.

For our final comparative reading of an antiquitous text, we turn to the story of Dinah from Genesis 34 in the Hebrew Bible. The story of Dinah, a young migrant woman, begins with her visiting women near where her family has settled. She is spotted by Shechem, the son of local prince named Hamor. Shechem seizes Dinah and rapes her. After the assault, he professes love for her, returns home and tells Hamor to acquire Dinah as his wife. Dinah's father, Jacob, and her brothers learn of the attack and confront Hamor, who requests that Dinah and Shechem be married; he further suggests their families should intermarry ("Give your daughters to us, and take our daughters for yourselves"),[54] as well as that the families share land and supplies. Jacob agrees, on the condition that the men in Hamor's family all be circumcised. They agree, and as they are healing from circumcision, Dinah's brothers attack their camp, murder the men, and take their women, children, and supplies. Throughout the story, Dinah is voiceless. She is effectually anonymized, as her position on marriage to Shechem is never considered. Thus, she resembles a form of cultural capital to be traded in accordance with patriarchal tradition.

As scholars and religious leaders have retained this androcentric historiography (likely in support of patriarchal hegemony) for centuries, the text of Genesis 34 serves as a fitting comparison for our reading of McBurney's conquest of Edwina, for two reasons. First, McBurney's actions and statements liken those of Shechem, and second, the text provides fertile ground to consider the problematic guest-host dynamic.

The text is problematic in two ways. First the reader is told nothing about Dinah's reaction to the assault or other events. She has lost her virginity to a man whom her brothers murdered, so her future is uncertain and likely grim. Second, Dinah has no voice; while hers is the violated body, the author focuses on male experience and bias. In this way, and like many antiquitous narratives, Dinah's story is not only phallogocentric but also entirely androcentric, focused on men and issues solely affecting them, often to the detriment of non-males. Still, the chief narrative element is the sexual assault of Dinah. Moreover, religious tradition seems to have consistently retained the story's androcentrism; according to Old Testament scholar Susanne Scholz, "The story of Dinah is one of the most contested rape stories in the Hebrew Bible. During its extensive history of interpretation, Jewish and Christian interpreters mainly ignore Dinah."[55] Religious scholar Gina Messina-Dysert posits that exegetical focus of Dinah's story has been "the men of the story, the tribal connotations, [and] literary–historical composition."[56] Male scholars have even asserted Shechem's actions to be innocuous. For example, Stuart West refers to Dina's story as the "conquest of Shechem." He describes Shechem in a positive light, claiming that he "was man enough to do the 'right' thing by offering to marry [Dinah].[57] Indeed, the vast majority of scholars, according to Caroline Blythe, have tended to read Dinah's story as "the narrator's initial attempt to rehabilitate Shechem's character, by portraying him as a man who has replaced aggressive action with powerful and deep-seated sentiments of love for the object of his initially abusive attentions."[58]

Shechem, having just raped Dinah, could have left her alone; as son of the prince with land belonging to his family, he is not held responsible for attacking a migrant girl, provided he can stave off her family's retaliation. Choosing to marry her, and especially by doing so without asking her, essentially anonymizes her, relegating her to cultural capital to be bought or traded per androcentric purposes. Similarly, while McBurney's "spurious declaration of love" (again borrowing Backman Rogers's language) does occur before his assault of Edwina (though Shechem's occurred immediately after), the power dynamic at work is the more pressing issue. Edwina's dependence on McBurney has been made secure by the assault; he has the power to keep her and ostensibly to take her with him after he leaves the seminary. Alternately, he can simply leave without her, which one might expect. Either way, Edwina has become his cultural capital within his phallogocentric perspective. Moreover, by leaving the issue of marriage entirely out of conversation, McBurney similarly anonymizes Edwina. In this way, we could view his oleaginous identification of her as "Miss Morrow" to be a rejection; he may intend to leave the next day in secret. On the other hand, this identification could be genuine, as McBurney certainly appears to be. Either way, by granting her a name, he controls her anonymization, or lack thereof, via phallogocentric perspective.

Like *The Beguiled,* Dinah's story is suffused by sexual politics and hospitality throughout. Dinah, as part of a migrant family, is a guest on Hamor's land. After Shechem rapes her, Hamor takes it upon himself to "right the wrong" via commerce. When Jacob and Dinah's brothers approach, Hamor says, "The soul of my son Shechem longs for your daughter. Please give her to him to be his wife. Make marriages with us. Give your daughters to us and take our daughters for yourselves. You shall dwell with us, and the land shall be open to you. Dwell and trade in it, and get property in it."[59] Shechem then speaks up, saying, "Let me find favor in your eyes, and whatever you say to me I will give. Ask me for as great a bride-price and gift as you will, and I will give whatever you say to me. Only give me the young woman to be my wife."[60] Neither Hamor or Shechem use Dinah's name, nor does Jacob's party. The entire negotiation reinforces Dinah's anonymization. Her guest-status is unequivocal in that her future is being arranged by others. More significantly, Hamor's offer involves sharing his host-status with his male guests (Jacob's migrant family). The group not only positions Dinah's body as capital within the negotiation but extends this positioning to other female family members. Jacob's sons' counteroffer is one of shared bodily identification (circumcision, with its religious connotations), but more importantly, as an act that only males can perform, the counteroffer that secures the negotiation is phallogocentric (and literally phallocentric!). To achieve *hospitium*, Jacob and Hamor's families must self-identify as marked by circumcision to achieve shared host status. More significantly, the offer to intermarry, using the women as capital and their bodies as a shared genetic pool, would have secured host status for generations to follow.

Like Dinah, Edwina's role is determined by phallogocentric means. Her host status within the seminary is removed once her body is violated, which we see in her absence from inclusion in the handholding image. Edwina sits between Jane (on her left) and McBurney's empty place after he dies. The others join hands, but Jane raises her right hand to the table, leaving Edwina alone. By taking her virginity, McBurney has relegated her to guest status. McBurney's death secures her guest status permanently, not unlike Shechem's death by her brothers' hands does for Dinah. Both women lack a male provider, which in the religious societies of nineteenth-century America and ancient Israel, causes them to depend on others (read: hosts).

By way of conclusion, we return to *hospitium* in *The Beguiled*. For Miss Martha, *hospitium* is an overly successful project, as she wields it based on needs of the female-centered household. As she masterfully commands the men within her walls (Confederate soldiers and McBurney), McBurney's toxic disposition and bellicose actions cause *hospitium* to be revoked but only on her terms. The nadir (or zenith) of Miss Martha's *hospitium* occurs at the point she agrees to use the mushrooms, therefore negating her gracious hospitality in favor of a power-based politic.

Returning to the crucial dinner scene, the young ladies set the table, observing the ritual of *hospitium,* and sit in their places and wait on their (now two) guests, Edwina and McBurney. When they emerge, McBurney pulls Edwina's chair out for her, another act of sham gentility (though in line with *hospitium* ritual). Miss Martha greets McBurney and says, "We'd like you to know that we harbor no ill feelings, and we've prepared this meal in commemoration of your journey ahead." Here we see the final iteration of *hospitium*: "bestowal of gifts by the host and departure of the guest."[61] After McBurney's feigned apology, they pray, and the wine is poured. Miss Martha, in control of her weapon, keeps the mushrooms closest to her, and when offering them to McBurney, we see the mushrooms' ritualistic passage from Miss Martha to Emily, to Alicia, to Marie, and finally to McBurney: a demonstration of shared female agency and sororal intent.

While Miss Martha controls *hospitium* within the house, the project is a shared one. Against the backdrop of male-centric conflict (over the right to own other people of all things), female hegemony at Farnsworth Seminary is communal and collaborative. As in Coppola's *Marie Antoinette, The Beguiled* gestures towards what would have made history better—women with genuine agency. Some viewers of each, or both, of these films might see allohistory, or an intentionally false and speculative history since allohistorical films have been recently voguish.[62] Coppola's Antoinette was not the version that Cannes viewers expected, and perhaps *The Beguiled*'s localized female insurrection against patriarchal violence and phallogocentrism is equally aberrant. However, as Backman Rogers notes, *The Beguiled* provides Lux Lisbon (et al.) an opportunity for retribution in intertextual space (Backman Rogers connects both Kirsten Dunst roles in Coppola films), we might consider the film a depiction of reprisal for unnamed victims of masculine aggression in quasi-allohistoric space. Furthermore, by exploring conflicts between sociocultural discourses and female expressions of desire and agency, Coppola's female-centric representation of *hospitium* signals the potential of post-capitalist, post-patriarchal, post-male-hegemonic existence; the language of *The Beguiled*, having reconstructed (or deconstructed!) *hospitium* by displacing antiquitous phallogocentrism, demonstrates female articulation of agency and control.

Derrida's quixotic posture (say "yes" to everyone) is ultimately dangerous, perhaps because it is, albeit unintentionally, phallogocentric (Derrida's own term). For such a stance to really work, it should likely only be addressed to those in power, i.e., men, who in such a wartime setting, should not be allowed carte blanche access women's homes and resources. In Coppola's film, without Miss Martha's ability to control *hospitium* by subduing or preventing hostilities, the acceptance of such a stance would have been even more disastrous for the women and young girls at the seminary. Indeed, *The Beguiled* works as a meditation on hospitality broken. Like Dido's acceptance of Aeneas, Miss Martha accepts McBurney to her own (and more significantly, Edwina's) detriment. Still, Miss Martha's control via female hegemony functions as a buffer or, using Hoff's solution, a retention of resources. While Edwina's body is sacrificed, the women and girls survive the ordeal, and they do so on their own terms: Rejecting masculine *ferocia corda*, they remove McBurney from their home using poison, "the female weapon of choice," as their final stage of *hospitium*, the bestowal of gifts.

The final image of McBurney's body, shrouded in the street, demonstrates the success of Miss Martha's *hospitium*: her seminary has removed the intruder and reinstated female collaboration. She is still host to her younger guests, though without masculine intrusion. Moreover, the image of an unnamed corpse fully encased in white sheets functions to anonymize McBurney, an ultimate reversal of gendered power struggle and culmination. Though Edwina has been anonymized via religious and sexual politics, McBurney becomes a nameless victim of Civil War hostilities to be carried off and forgotten.

*The Beguiled*, a meditation on hospitality (or broken hospitality), stands as a repudiation of androcentric cinema. The tables are essentially turned on the masculine intruder, and his aggression towards women is examined from their perspective rather than his. Unlike the stories of Dido and Aeneas, Dinah, and countless literary and cinematic examples of actions against women being addressed from phallogocentric viewpoints, Coppola's film repositions the power dynamic so often visible in film language configured towards male hegemony.[63] By channeling female agency through Miss Martha's navigation of *hospitium*, *The Beguiled* questions patriarchal historiography in a similar vein to Coppola's *Marie Antoinette*. Though arguably her most violent film to date, *The Beguiled* reframes violence to inculpate the violator. By anonymizing him, his body instantiates all masculine aggressors, thereby reclaiming the value of female name and agency, even in a setting as hostile as a war fought to protect the rights of men to own bodies of others.

## REFERENCES

Backman Rogers, Anna. "And That I See a Darkness: The Stardom of Kirsten Dunst in Collaboration with Sofia Coppola in Three Images." *Film-Philosophy* 23, no. 2 (2019): 114–136.

———. *Sofia Coppola: The Politics of Visual Pleasure*. New York: Berghan Books, 2019.

Barber, Susan E., and Charles F. Ritter. "Dangerous Liaisons: Working Women and Sexual Justice in the American Civil War." *European Journal of American Studies* 10, no. 1 (2015): 1–15.

Barstow, Ann L., ed. *War's Dirty Secret: Rape, Prostitution, and Other Crimes against Women*. Cleveland: Pilgrim Press, 2000.

Blyth, Caroline. "Redeemed by His Love? The Characterization of Shechem in Genesis 34." *Journal for the Study of the Old Testament* 33, no. 1 (2008): 3–18.

Bowler, Alexa L. "'Killing Romance' by 'giving birth to love': Hélène Cixous, Jane Campion and the language of *In the Cut* (2003)." *Feminist Theory* 20, no. 1 (2019): 93–112.

Brown, William. "A (Mush)room of One's Own: Feminism, Posthumanism, and Race in Sofia Coppola's *The Beguiled*." *Aniki: Portuguese Journal of the Moving Image* 7, no. 1 (2020): 71–95.

Cixous, Hélène. "Castration or Decapitation?," trans. Annette Kuhn. *Signs*, 7, no. 1 (1981): 41–55.

———. "The Laugh of the Medusa," trans. Keith Cohen and Paula Cohen. *Signs* 1, no. 4 (1976): 875–893.

Coppola, Sofia. "Sofia Coppola Talks Teen Girls, Sexual Desire and Her New Film 'The Beguiled.'" Interview by Hannah Ewens, *Vice,* Vice Talks Film, July 10, 2017. https://www.youtube.com/watch?v=6xv95k4VmJc&list=PLwGlqbbep5Mp2vygutWn4vRdxmWNe_5Ms&index=9.

Derrida, Jacques. *Of Hospitality*, trans. Rachel Bowlby. Palo Alto: Stanford University Press, 2000.
Durling Smith, Julie Noel. *The Fallen Woman in the Nineteenth-Century American Novel*. Ph.D. diss., University of Kansas, 2003.
Erbsen, Wayne. *Rousing Songs and True Tales of the Civil War*. Asheville: Native Ground Books and Music, 1999.
Enloe, Cynthia. *Maneuvers: The International Politics of Militarizing Women's Lives*. Berkeley: University of California Press, 2000.
Feimster, Crystal N. "General Benjamin Butler & the Threat of Sexual Violence during the American Civil War." *Dædalus* 138, no. 2 (Spring, 2009): 126–134.
Gibson, R. K. "Aeneas as *Hospes* in Virgil, *Aeneid* 1 and 4." *Classical Quarterly* 49, 1 (1999): 184–202.
Gilleir, Anke, and Aude Defurne. "*Dux Femina Facti*: Gender, Sovereignty, and (Women's) Literature in Marie Antonia of Saxony's *Thalestris* and Charlotte von Stein's *Dido*." In *Realities and Fantasies of German Female Leadership: From Maria Antonia of Saxony to Angela Merkel*, edited by Elisabeth Krimmer and Patricia Anne Simpson, 97–112. Suffolk: Boydell & Brewer, 2019.
Grant, Susan-Mary. "When the Fires Burned Too Close to Home: Southern Women and the Dislocations of the Home Front in the American Civil War." *Women's History Review* 26, no. 4 (2017): 568–83.
Hamington, Maurice. "Toward a Theory of Feminist Hospitality." *Feminist Formulations* 22, no. 1 (2010): 21–38.
Hoff, Shannon. "Translating Principle into Practice: On Derrida and the Terms of Feminism." *Journal of Speculative Philosophy* 29, no. 3 (2015): 403–414.
Lichtenwalner, Andrew L. *The Church as the Bride of Christ in Magisterial Teaching from Leo XIII to John Paul II*. Ph.D. diss., The Catholic University of America, 2012.
Marsten, Kendra. *Postfeminist Whiteness: Problematising Melancholic Burden in Contemporary Hollywood*. Edinburgh: Edinburgh University Press, 2018.
McCurry, Stephanie. *Confederate Reckoning: Power and Politics in the Civil War South*. Cambridge: Harvard University Press, 2010.
Messina-Dysert, Gina. *Rape Culture and Spiritual Violence*. Abingdon: Routledge, Taylor & Francis Group, 2015.
Moslener, Sara. *Virgin Nation: Sexual Purity and American Adolescence*. Oxford: Oxford University Press, 2015.
Murphy, Kelsey E. *Civil War Song and Womanhood: Mediating Myth, Reality, and Memory*. M. M. thesis, West Chester University of Pennsylvania, 2014.
Radmacher, Earl D. *The Nature of the Church*. Hayesville: Schoettle, 1996.
Saucy, Robert. *The Church in God's Program: Handbook of Bible Doctrine*. Chicago: Moody Press, 1972.
Scholz, Susanne. *Sacred Witness: Rape in the Hebrew Bible*. Minneapolis: Fortress Press, 2010.
Tara, Mary Beth. *The Erosion of Protestant Pastoral Identity in American Evangelicalism*. M.A. thesis, Trinity Evangelical Divinity School, 2020.
*The Beguiled*. Directed by Sofia Coppola. 2017: Universal City CA: Focus Features.

Welter, Barbara. "The Cult of True Womanhood: 1820–1860." *American* Quarterly 18, no. 2 (Summer, 1966):151–174.

West, Stuart. "The Rape of Dinah and the Conquest of Shechem." *Dor le Dor* 8, no. 3 (Spring, 1980): 144–156.

# NOTES

1. The same is true for Derrida's language (French, having evolved from Latin): *hôte*, meaning both "guest" and "host." *Hospes* also etymologically stems from the Latin *hostis* (enemy).

2. Derrida contends that no "guest" exists without a host providing hospitality, while no "host" exists without a "guest" present to receive it. See Maurice Hamington, "Toward a Theory of Feminist Hospitality," *Feminist Formulations* 22, no. 1 (2010): 21–38.

3. Jacques Derrida, *Of Hospitality*, trans. Rachel Bowlby (Palo Alto: Stanford University Press, 2000), 77.

4. Shannon Hoff, "Translating Principle into Practice: On Derrida and the Terms of Feminism," *Journal of Speculative Philosophy* 29, no. 3 (2015): 406.

5. Ibid.

6. Dido is sometimes called "Elissa."

7. Cupid, son of Venus, had cast a love spell on them. While relationship and interactions with gods are a crucial component of Virgil's poem, we have left this out simply for clarity, and as such interactions are not relevant to our comparison. For example, Aeneas had been shipwrecked by the goddess Juno but was favored by Venus, his mother, along with Cupid.

8. R. K. Gibson, "Aeneas as *Hospes* in Virgil, *Aeneid* 1 and 4," *Classical Quarterly* 49, 1 (1999): 184.

9. We will address the characterization of "wild and free" later.

10. The two words are conjoined with the participle *facti* (having been made), a masculine iteration (explanatory genitive singular), as the proper feminine would be *factae*. The parenthetical "I. 364" refers to book 1 of the Aenead, line 364. We have marked subsequent passages the same way.

11. Anke Gilleir and Aude Defurne, "*Dux Femina Facti*: Gender, Sovereignty, and (Women's) Literature in Marie Antonia of Saxony's *Thalestris* and Charlotte von Stein's *Dido*" in *Realities and Fantasies of German Female Leadership: From Maria Antonia of Saxony to Angela Merkel,* eds., Elisabeth Krimmer and Patricia Anne Simpson (Suffolk: Boydell & Brewer, 2019): 98 [emphasis in original].

12. Anna Backman Rogers makes this point as it illustrates the assumption that the seminary has no space for masculine interaction, thus the need for the masculine "*il est.*" McBurney's attempt to force himself into the female environment, according to Rogers, is destined to fail, rendering him both impotent and thus increasingly hostile. See Anna Backman Rogers, "And That I See a Darkness: The Stardom of Kirsten Dunst in Collaboration with Sofia Coppola in Three Images," *Film-Philosophy* 23, no. 2 (2019): 114–136.

13. We should also mention that Carthage became a major supplier of agricultural goods to the Greek and Roman states; similarly, the North in the American Civil War conflict depended upon the agrarian South. In this way, Miss Martha's haven mirrors Dido's established city: both women found fertile land to suit their escapist purposes.

14. Gibson, "Aeneas," 186.

15. Miss Martha does, as Backman Rogers points out, protect young ladies from masculinity as well. She notes that "McBurney's body has such an effect on Miss Martha as she is focusing on the act of bathing him that she proceeds to shut and lock the door to the music room in which he sleeps; in other words, she views his physicality and charm as a contagious force that needs to be contained." Anna Backman Rogers, *Sofia Coppola: The Politics of Visual Pleasure* (New York: Berghan Books, 2019), 61. We will discuss further implications of Miss Martha's statement about temptation in the next section.

16. Backman Rogers, *Politics*, 131–132.

17. Ibid.

18. William Brown, "A (Mush)room of One's Own: Feminism, Posthumanism, and Race in Sofia Coppola's *The Beguiled*, *Aniki: Portuguese Journal of the Moving Image* 7, no. 1 (2020): 83.

19. Backman Rogers, *Politics*, 59.

20. Ibid, 50.

21. Hélène Cixous, "The Laugh of the Medusa," trans. Keith Cohen and Paula Cohen, *Signs*, 1, no. 4 (1976): 875–893. Cixous's seminal essay posits that female authors should aim to establish literary works that deviate from traditional masculine styles. She argues that via traditional, phallocentric writing, women have been taught to view themselves as valuable only as they are loveable by men. She claims that a "New Woman" must be liberated from the "Old" by women writing about female experience outside of masculine points of view.

22. Cixous developed *écriture féminine* from Lacan's notion that structure of language is centered by the Phallus (phallocentric). In "The Laugh of the Medusa," Cixous argues that the subject position of "woman" or "feminine" is de-centered, i.e., less firmly anchored and controlled by the Phallus. She argues that "woman" has always been in a position of otherness and alterity in Western phallogocentric culture.

23. "Phallogocentric" is a portmanteau of "phallocentric," i.e., a system in which the masculine perspective is standard/dominant due to the presence of the phallus (penis), which, based on Freudian psychoanalysis represents the only visible (and valuable) sex organ and possession of the phallus is crucial to Oedipus-complex-basis of the ego; and "logocentric," philosopher Ludwig Klages's term for the Western practice of using language as fundamental expression of the known world by centering logic as the guarantor of identity.

24. Hélène Cixous, "Castration or Decapitation?," trans. Annette Kuhn. *Signs* 7, no. 1 (1981): 44.

25. Cixous, "Laugh," 888. See also Alexia L. Bowler. "'Killing Romance' by 'giving birth to love': Hélène Cixous, Jane Campion and the language of *In the Cut* (2003)," *Feminist Theory* 20, no. 1 (2019):93–112.

26. Brown, "(Mush)room," 79.

27. Kelsey E. Murphy, *Civil War Song and Womanhood: Mediating Myth, Reality, and Memory* (M. M. thesis, West Chester University of Pennsylvania, 2014), 15.
28. Ibid.
29. Murphy, *Civil War Song,* 1.
30. Ibid.
31. Wayne Erbsen, *Rousing Songs and True Tales of the Civil War* (Asheville: Native Ground Books and Music, 1999), 47.
32. Crystal N. Feimster, "General Benjamin Butler & the Threat of Sexual Violence during the American Civil War," *Dædalus* 138, no. 2 (Spring, 2009): 126–127.
33. Ibid.
34. Ibid, 127. We will turn to Kendra Marsten's seminal work on postfeminist whiteness in film in our concluding chapter. We intend to echo Marsten's comment that white female characters in Coppola films are heralded for various feminine qualities; but one "integral feature of Coppola's cinema" is that her "protagonists who are [racialized] as white and socio-economically empowered are incapable of decentering their experience to see, hear, or otherwise relate to subjects [racialized] as non-white—especially in so far as these subjects are positioned below them in status and class hierarchies." See Kendra Marsten, *Postfeminist Whiteness: Problematising Melancholic Burden in Contemporary Hollywood* (Edinburgh: Edinburgh University Press, 2018), 163–164. Due to its publication date, Marsten's book does not address Coppola's *The Beguiled*, but clearly her comment here is germane as it regards the women in the school. The Versailles Court restricts Antoinette's liberty and agency much like the Civil War backdrop and McBurney behavior limits all the women and girls in *The Beguiled*.
35. Feimster, "General Benjamin Butler, 128–129.
36. Ibid.
37. Backman Rogers, *Politics*, 61.
38. Susan-Mary Grant, "When the Fires Burned Too Close to Home: Southern Women and the Dislocations of the Home Front in the American Civil War," *Women's History Review* 26, no. 4 (2017): 568.
39. Backman Rogers, *Politics,* 58.
40. Feimster also finds the term "unsexing" in the correspondence of Union General Thomas Williams, as he describes the unruly behavior of Southern women in Union occupied areas. He claims, "such venom one must see to believe. Such unsexing was hardly ever before in any cause or country so marked and so universal. I look at them and think of fallen angels." Feimster, "General Benjamin Butler," 128.
41. Backman Rogers, *Politics*, 58.
42. Stephanie McCurry, *Confederate Reckoning: Power and Politics in the Civil War South* (Cambridge: Harvard University Press, 2010), 25.
43. Ibid, 26.
44. Mary Beth Tara relates how these New Testament texts draw upon Old Testament prophetic tradition and how historically, marital language describes situations in which Ancient Israelites were viewed by Torah/Biblical authors as committing infidelity when behaving outside of God's law. See Mary Beth Tara, *The Erosion of Protestant Pastoral Identity in American Evangelicalism* (M.A. thesis, Trinity

Evangelical Divinity School, 2020). See also Earl D. Radmacher, *The Nature of the Church* (Hayesville: Schoettle, 1996); Robert Saucy, *The Church in God's Program*: *Handbook of Bible Doctrine* (Chicago: Moody Press, 1972); Andrew L. Lichtenwalner, *The Church as the Bride of Christ in Magisterial Teaching from Leo XIII to John Paul II* (Ph.D. diss., The Catholic University of America, 2012).

45. Vice, "Sofia Coppola Talks Teen Girls, Sexual Desire and Her New Film 'The Beguiled,'" *VICE Talks Film*, www.youtube.com/watch?v=6xv95k4VmJc&list=PLwGlqbbep5Mp2vygutWn4vRdxmWNe_5Ms&index=8.

46. Backman Rogers, *Politics,* 57–59. Backman Rogers connects this assault with that of Trip Fontaine's sexual conquest of Lux Lisbon in *The Virgin Suicides*. While such an intertextual connection is indeed valuable, we are limiting our inquiry only to this event in *The Beguiled*. Still, Backman Rogers's observation could reveal even more about Edwina's victimization here. Moreover, while the film is ambivalent regarding whether Edwina was a virgin prior to this assault, her "virginal" attire noted by Backman Rogers, as well as her previous hesitance to be physical with McBurney, tend towards the interpretation that she was. More significantly, the intertextual relationship between Dunst-Lux and Dunst-Edwina, also noted by Backman Rogers, further solidifies the perception.

47. Julie Noel Durling Smith, *The Fallen Woman in the Nineteenth-Century American Novel* (Ph.D. diss., University of Kansas, 2003), 35.

48. See Cynthia Enloe, *Maneuvers: The International Politics of Militarizing Women's Lives* (Berkeley: University of California Press, 2000). See also Ann L. Barstow, ed., *War's Dirty Secret: Rape, Prostitution, and Other Crimes against Women* (Cleveland: Pilgrim Press, 2000).

49. Susan E. Barber and Charles F. Ritter. "Dangerous Liaisons: Working Women and Sexual Justice in the American Civil War," *European Journal of American Studies* 10, no. 1 (2015): 3.

50. Ibid.

51. Barbara Welter, "The Cult of True Womanhood: 1820–1860," *American Quarterly* 18, no. 2 (Summer, 1966): 154. We should mention that Welter's connection of Christian piety and purity is fundamental to American Christian views of female sexuality, especially in the nineteenth century. While the other components in "The Cult of Womanhood" that Welter observes, "submission" and "domesticity" are relevant in comprising the wholeness of the "True Woman," the hand-in-hand collaboration of piety and purity seems essential to Welter's remarks.

52. Sara Moslener, *Virgin Nation: Sexual Purity and American Adolescence* (Oxford: Oxford University Press, 2015), 16–17.

53. Ibid.

54. Gen 34:9, ESV.

55. Susanne Scholz, *Sacred Witness: Rape in the Hebrew Bible* (Minneapolis: Fortress Press, 2010), 32.

56. Gina Messina-Dysert, *Rape Culture and Spiritual Violence* (Abingdon: Routledge, Taylor & Francis Group, 2015): 8.

57. Stuart West, "The Rape of Dinah and the Conquest of Shechem" *Dor le Dor* 8, no. 3 (Spring, 1980): 151.

58. Caroline Blyth, "Redeemed by His Love? The Characterization of Shechem in Genesis 34," *Journal for the Study of the Old Testament* 33, no. 1 (2008): 8.

59. Gen 34:8–10, ESV.

60. Gen 34:11–12, ESV.

61. Gibson, Aeneas, 186.

62. For example, recent films of Quentin Tarantino delve into allohistory (*Inglourious Basterds* (2009), *Django Unchained* (2012), *Once Upon a Time in Hollywood* (2019).

63. On the other hand, one might assert that Coppola's *The Virgin Suicides* behaves in an androcentric manner. But a male narrator and male do not default to androcentrism; Coppola's debut film does not dismiss the Lisbon sisters' experience but rather highlights them.

# PART III
## *BODIES*

*Chapter Five*

# A Bodily Desire

## (Micro)celebrity, Celebrity Culture as Parareligion, and the Erotic in The Bling Ring

When reflecting on Coppola's fifth feature film, *The Bling Ring* (2013)—a film about a group of wealthy teenagers who break into celebrities' homes and steal personal items—several scholars and journalists make an unusual connection. They implicitly link the film with religion. Using the religious language of "cults" and capitalism, film scholar Sara Pesce notes that the film "reflects and . . . fosters a cult and exploitation of personal image and of the strategic creation of an identity to be endorsed and sold to others."[1] Likewise, film studies scholar Fiona Handyside links the implicitly religious language of iconography to sexual desire. She claims that "clothing seems to take on an iconic role in *The Bling Ring*. By this I mean that the importance of clothing is not what it can point to, or demonstrate, but simply that it once belonged to a celebrity and therefore is worthy of fetishization."[2] Film scholar Maryn Wilkinson extends Handyside's insight on sexuality with reference to an immaterial, spiritual reality. "Commodity fetishism," she argues, "can only be fulfilled by direct mimesis; these teens don't want a blouse like Paris [Hilton]'s, i.e., the same one she wears; they want the actual one she wears, with the aura of celebrity . . . it carries."[3] In a slightly more detailed register, film scholar Anna Backman Rogers describes the characters' inability to escape a "world of surfaces," because they are "steeped in a culture that dictates a quasi-religious worship of objects through strategic proliferation of iconic . . . images."[4] Film reviewer A.O. Scott claims that the film "occupies a vertiginous middle ground between banality and transcendence."[5] And in his reflections on *The Bling Ring*, *Spring Breakers* (2012), and *The Great Gatsby* (2013), he suggests that the films not "only eroticize wealth and its accoutrements; they spiritualize it, too."⁶ In each case, however, the writer makes the connection in passing and quickly moves on to other issues. Counterintuitively, perhaps, this chapter expands these passing references into a sustained religious reading of the film, one that focuses upon materiality and bodies.

Such a reading might be considered counterintuitive because, in the early twenty-first century, the language of religion seems increasingly irrelevant, especially since the academy and the film industry are, arguably, secular spaces in which religion is mostly absent. While a full account of secularization is outside of the scope of this chapter, a brief word should suffice to justify why religion might still be relevant to secular society. Sociologists of religion have noted that, even though societies like those in the United States are becoming increasingly secular, significant religious participation persists. Sociologists perceive religious persistence as a problem within the field, because, in the middle of the twentieth-century, predictions abounded that religion would soon be a thing of the past. Sociologist Mohita Bhatia states the problem clearly and succinctly when she recounts that "Many academics," like sociologists Peter Berger, Thomas Luckmann, and Bryan R. Wilson, "analysed the relationship between secularism and secularization, assuming that both are engendering a 'modern' world by replacing religion. This thesis received a setback when evidence pointed to not just the prevalent religiosity among people in Western and non-Western landscapes, but also to the dialogic and entwined nature of the interaction between the 'secular' and the 'religious.'"⁷ While the nature of that dialogic and entwined relationship is an ongoing debate, our chapter takes that discussion as a point of departure, claiming that *The Bling Ring* represents celebrity culture in an age of social media in such a way that, metaphorically, reflects aspects of bodily desire and religious practice.⁸

We argue that *The Bling Ring* offers a meditation on religious aspects of celebrity culture, taking relics and bodily desire as central to religious experience. Our argument unfolds in three sections. First, the Bling Ring behave in ways consistent with accounts of microcelebrity. They submit themselves to the established celebrity hierarchy, using social media to display their proximity to and their aspiration toward the wealth and lifestyle of celebrities. Members of the Bling Ring also express an awareness that they both lack and need traditional means, like mainstream media, to achieve celebrity status. However, the concept of microcelebrity does not explain why the Bling Ring both reveres and harms celebrities. Christian theologian Pete Ward's parareligious account of celebrity helps answer that question. Celebrity culture functions as a metaphor of religious experience, one that can incorporate relics that have been near to celebrities as a means of possessing the power of that celebrity's extraordinariness and freedom. Fans also identify with celebrities in contradictory ways, which can take the form of rites of ascent and decent. The Bling Ring sees the celebrities they target as possessing an extraordinary capacity for fashion and a freedom to behave badly. To take possession of that power, the Bling Ring elevates themselves through a rite of ascent. They take relics from celebrities' homes. That rite also demands a sacrifice or a scapegoat: harming the celebrities themselves. The group also uses these possessions to inhabit moments of ecstasy. Like many celebrities, the Bling Ring eventually facilitate their own descent. Although the language of rites and relics helps explain how the Bling Ring transfer power onto themselves, a Christian account of the erotic sheds further light on the embodied nature of their veneration. Eroticism is an expanded, inclusive account, and includes a wide range of physical and emotional comportments, as both Christian art and historical examples illustrate. The Bling Ring display the erotic in their reaction to celebrity relics. Several members of the group attach sexual desire to their break-ins to Paris Hilton's home or to a gun from Megan Fox's house. Of all the Bling Ring members, the leader, Rebecca (Katie Chang), reaches the apex of religious eroticism during the break-in of her fashion icon, Lindsay Lohan. By way of conclusion, we offer implications our analysis has for secular society, social media, bodily human desire, and boredom.

*The Bling Ring* unfolds in a series of extended flashbacks, but a brief chronological summary will orient the analysis below. The film begins with the arrival of Marc Hall (Israel Broussard) at his new school, Indian Hills High School, which is located in the greater Los Angeles area. He befriends Rebecca Ahn (Katie Chang), who invites him to a party. As they leave the party, she persuades Marc to join her in opening unlocked cars and stealing the cash and valuables they find. Later, Rebecca asks Marc if anyone he knows is out of town. Marc tells her about an acquaintance, Evan, who is in Jamaica with his family. They go to Evan's vacant house, and like the cars, Rebecca finds an open door. The two enter the house, and Rebecca steals cash, a handbag, and the owner's car. Marc is hesitant but goes along with her. After a day of shopping with their stolen money, the two meet Rebecca's friends at a nightclub: Chloe (Claire Julien), Nicki (Emma Watson), and Sam (Taissa Farmiga). Chloe explains that Nicki and Sam are not sisters. Nicki's mother, Laurie (Leslie Mann), adopted Sam. Laurie homeschools them both and they practice a religion based on Rhonda Byrne's best-selling book, *The Secret* (2006). Marc is amazed when he sees Paris Hilton (playing herself) at the club, but the girls take little notice, since she is there often.

A few days later, Marc discovers that Hilton is out of town for an engagement. Rebecca and Marc go to her home, find her house keys under her door mat, and enter through the front door. They walk around the house and are amazed at her wealth. Eventually, Rebecca steals a few items, including a diamond tennis bracelet. Rebecca and Marc recount their exploits to Chloe,

Nicki, and Sam, and Rebecca shows the group the tennis bracelet she stole. The Bling Ring forms when all five return to Hilton's home, each stealing a few items. Marc, for example, steals a pink pair of Hilton's shoes. Soon, they begin to target other celebrities, like Megan Fox, each when they learn that the celebrity is out of town. When Marc and Rebecca break in to Audrina Patridge's home, CCTV captures their images. As their break-ins escalate, so does their use of illegal drugs and alcohol. When they break into the home of Orlando Bloom and Miranda Kerr, Marc steals several Rolex watches, which he later sells. Although a news report emerges with footage of the Patridge break-in, Rebecca remains undaunted and insists they continue their spree. They return to Hilton's house numerous times, once with Sam's boyfriend Rob (Carlos Miranda), who steals a box of jewelry. The Bling Ring eventually invade Rebecca's ultimate "fashion icon": Lindsay Lohan.

The police are able to apprehend the Bling Ring, because the group brags openly about their exploits at parties, posts images of stolen items and of themselves in their victims' homes on social media, and has stolen items in their possession. The police arrest all five members, as well as Rob. Marc tells the police everything, enabling a harsher sentence for himself and Rebecca. Before their incarceration, a *Vanity Fair* journalist named Kate (Annie Fitzgerald) interviews Marc and Nicki. Marc shows remorse, but Nicki blames the other members of the Bling Ring. After her release from prison, Nicki gives an interview in which she insists that she has her own version of the story. She looks directly into the camera and tells viewers to follow at her website.

## CELEBRITY AND MICROCELEBRITY

Communication scholar Alice Marwick describes the new breed of celebrity known as microcelebrity, noting its differences from traditional celebrity. Developing the term from performance studies scholar Theresa M. Senft,[9] microcelebrity is a practice in which social media users share personal information in an effort to increase attention and expand their number of followers. "In the broadcast era," Marwick explains, "celebrity was something a person was; in the Internet era, microcelebrity is something people *do*."[10] Both celebrities and microcelebrities participate in the wildly popular trend of self-photographs, or selfies, that dominate social media outlets like Instagram. Selfies allow users to "show glimpses of their lives to others,"[11] "strategically revealing information to increase or maintain this audience."[12] Marwick also notes important differences between celebrity and microcelebrity. Social media certainly provides opportunities for users outside of traditional mass media and politics. However, "these opportunities are typically limited, fleeting, and unaccompanied by the financial resources available to the traditionally famous."[13] Therefore, Marwick argues that microcelebrities, such as Cayla Friesz, an Indiana high school sophomore, can have substantial followings. However, she is not famous "in the Paris Hilton sense that she has access to mainstream media's star-making machine."[14] All Friesz can do on her platform is attract attention. Without access to Paris Hilton's resources, her fame is short-lived. At the time of Marwick's 2015 publication, Cayla had 31,000 followers. In early 2021, she had a little over 15,000 and serves as "Brand Ambassador for @thespinsterz," a company that sells hula-hoops and other flow toys.[15] The spinsterz Instagram account, which supports a traditional capitalist venture, has over 40,000 followers.[16] Marwick's point here is not that Instagram users cannot generate enormous amounts of wealth; rather, she argues that wealth and fame are often only sustainable when coupled with the traditional capitalist practices associated with celebrity.

Microcelebrities also tend to traffic in aspirational ways of life that often resembles celebrity fame and wealth. As a result, microcelebrity is not as egalitarian as it might appear. It "reinforces an existing hierarchy of fame, in which the iconography of glamour, luxury, wealth, good looks, and connections is reinscribed in a visual digital medium."[17] Within that hierarchy, traditional mass media sometimes grant microcelebrities a degree of legitimacy, especially when a microcelebrity approaches the tropes of celebrity glamour and wealth. For example, Marwick discusses Kane Lim, a fashion student from Singapore who studied at the Fashion Institute of Design and Merchandising. He posts photos of his "expensive couture clothing; photos of his collections of designer shoes, clothes, and jewelry; and selfies with Singapore socialites."[18] As a result, several fashion blogs featured him for his "luxe style."[19] In 2015, Lim's Instagram account existed in a space between Cayla Friesz and Paris Hilton, expressing both the aspirational quality of many microcelebrities and the perfunctory display of celebrity wealth.[20] However, unlike Cayla, Lim possess connections to traditional capitalist structures that support his extreme wealth. Those connections eventually facilitated his entry into mass media. In early 2021, he describes himself as a "Real Estate Developer/Investor/Philanthropist," appears on Netflix's reality television show *Bling Empire*, and has almost 450,000 Instagram followers.[21]

In Coppola's film, Marc and the rest of the Bling Ring behave in at least two ways consistent with microcelebrity. First, they submit themselves to the established celebrity hierarchy. In the *Vanity Fair* interview, Kate asks Marc why he thought Rebecca, and by proxy the rest of the Bling Ring, shared an obsession with these particular celebrities and their fashion, such that they would steal from them. Marc replies that he thought they "wanted to be a part of, like, the lifestyle. Like, the lifestyle that everybody kind of wants." Marc's statement implies that their desires existed in submission to the established celebrity hierarchy. The Bling Ring focuses their attention on someone like Paris Hilton, who lives and works within the upper echelons of the celebrity hierarchy. Likewise, when Nicky's mother, Laurie, homeschools the girls on character development, she encourages them to make a vision board with examples of people with good character. The example she offers them is of Hollywood actor, director, and producer Angelina Jolie. Beyond lifestyle, Jolie epitomizes for Laurie the highest way of being ethical in the world. Film scholar Delphine Letort notes, "The physical resemblance between the girls of the Bling Ring also testifies to the pervasive influence of stereotypical celebrities, who embody a type of femininity characterised by long hair, high-heeled shoes, sunglasses, slim trousers, etc."[22] Her comment underscores how their aspiration to look like celebrities not only confirms the hierarchical relationship the Bling Ring has to celebrities but also shows up at the site of their bodies. Marc also articulates mental health struggles in relationship to Hollywood standards of beauty. In the same interview, Marc connects his feelings of self-loathing and anxiety to the fact that he "felt . . . ugly." Kate insists that he is not ugly. He responds, "I never saw myself as an A-list looking guy." Whether the celebrity lifestyle, good character, their bodies, or Marc's self-understanding, characters behave in ways that affirm the existing celebrity hierarchy.

Second, Marc's social media postings show glimpses of their lives that both display their proximity to and their aspiration toward the wealth and lifestyle of celebrities. During many of their activities together, the Bling Ring take photographs of themselves, some of which are selfies. For example, after Rebecca and Marc steal the car from Evan's home, she drives the stolen car. As she is driving, she poses for a photo that Marc takes of her. During night club scenes, selfies dominate the photographs they post on social media. The Bling Ring also take photos of themselves at celebrities' homes and with their stolen merchandise. Likewise, whether they party in a nightclub or at Paris's nightclub room, they, at least temporarily, live the lifestyle and behave in ways they perceive celebrities do. And when achieved, their aspiration brings them satisfaction. After a brief montage where Marc posts some of these photos to Facebook, he relaxes in bed. In a single medium shot, he smiles, as if he is pleased. He has momentarily achieved, in an existential way, the lifestyle of celebrities, and like a celebrity, he displays his proximity to and intimacy with celebrity status on social media.

As a further example of their aspiration toward and proximity to celebrity, the Bling Ring livestream an impromptu fashion show with their stolen goods. After Rebecca and Marc invade Audrina Patridge's home, several Bling Ring members spend time trying on the items they have stolen, mixing and matching clothing and accessories. Their behavior mimics ways they likely imagine Paris Hilton or Audrina Patridge might behave before going out at night. They choose items from an orgy of clothes and accessories. After Marc takes a photograph of Nicki, she walks over to her dresser and puts on lip gloss. She leans down, as if she is looking at her reflection in a mirror. Coppola cuts to a point of view shot of where the mirror would be, except it is a low resolution video image. The reflection in Nicki's sunglasses suggests that instead of a mirror, she is looking at a computer screen, implying that the Bling Ring are livestreaming their impromptu fashion show. Soon Sam and Marc join Nicki, and the three dance with each other, gazing at themselves in the screen. It is as if the Bling Ring are broadcasting their own reality television show, perhaps as an emulation of Paris Hilton or Audrina Patridge's reality shows.

Despite these enactments of microcelebrity, members of the Bling Ring express an awareness that, at present, they both lack and need traditional capitalistic means to achieve the celebrity status of their victims. Early in the film, Marc, Rebecca, and Chloe sit on the beach smoking marijuana. Rebecca says that she wants to attend the "Fashion Institute of Design" (and Merchandising), the same school Kane Lim attended. Her justification for going to school there is "*The Hills* girls all went there." Audrina Patridge, one of their victims, was a star on the reality TV show, *The Hills*, a show about young women pursuing careers in the fashion industry. Marc, of course, understands her line of thinking and suggests that she could, then, serve as an intern at *Teen Vogue*, a publication focusing on fashion and beauty style, politics, entertainment, and identity.[23] Rebecca continues the fantasy, donning a faux accent of sophistication, saying that she would "have my own line, and fragrance, host my show." Taking a more serious tone, Marc responds, "I'd like to have my own lifestyle brand." Both Rebecca and Chloe smile and respond affirmatively. This interchange suggests that neither Rebecca nor Marc simply desires a version of microcelebrity akin to Indiana sophomore Cayla Friesz. Rather, they understand that, to be a celebrity like Hilton or Patridge, they need connections to traditional forms of capitalism, here the fashion, lifestyle, and mass media industries. To this end, their criminal activity, whether it is taking money to buy clothing or stealing fashion items, constitutes their attempt to acquire the materials needed to practice, at the site of their bodies, their fashion sensibilities. Although it is misguided, their crimes are organized around their long-term goals of pursuing a career in the fashion, lifestyle, and media industries. For example, after Rebecca and Marc first steal items from cars together, they take the money and spend it on clothing. When they steal from celebrities, the Bling Ring appropriate celebrities' fashion sensibilities for their personal sartorial, or clothing, collections. And they put to use their fashion know how with the items that fashion makers use to craft their own style. Their criminal practices are, in part, providing the material so they can prepare themselves for the rigors of traditional celebrity.

Like Rebecca and Marc, Nicki also displays a desire to achieve celebrity through the legitimizing function of mainstream media. In one scene early in the film, Nicki walks into the courthouse for her trial (though chronologically this occurs after their break-ins). Like a movie star, a group of media surrounds her. Midstride, she turns to them and delivers this speech: "I am a firm believer in Karma, and I think this situation was attracted into my life as a huge learning lesson for me—to grow and expand as a spiritual human being. I want to lead a huge charity organization. I want to lead a country one day for all I know." Aside from the way Coppola uses these words, which the real life member of the Bling Ring, Alexis Neiers, actually said,[24] this is not the first time she has delivered a speech of this kind. During her *Vanity Fair* interview, she convinces her lawyers to let her deliver a prepared statement. "I think this situation was attracted into my life as a huge learning lesson for me to grow and expand as a spiritual human being. I believe that I am an old soul." Chronologically, this interview occurs before her day in court, so here Nicki is workshopping and rehearsing material she plans to deliver at her court date, not unlike a speech a celebrity might do. Nicki's final monologue, which ends the film, functions in a similar way. In a television interview, she recounts elements of her personal life, particularly her version of events with relationship to the Bling Ring and her time in prison. In the film's last shot, she looks directly into the camera and says, "You can follow everything about me and my journey at nickimooreforeverdot com." Like a microcelebrity, she attempts to reveal aspects of her personal life to garner attention. Like a celebrity, she understands that she needs traditional forms of mass media to sustain that attention.[25]

Even though the distinctions between celebrity and microcelebrity help describe the world through which members of the Bling Ring knowingly move, the film still leaves open questions as to contradictions the characters inhabit. On the one hand, celebrity and microcelebrity help explain the agency the Bling Ring bring to their ways of moving through the world. While they do not make life choices that work out for themselves in positive ways, neither does the film present them as naïve microcelebrities. Likewise, when they steal clothing and jewelry and use them to approximate a celebrity lifestyle, they are preparing themselves, albeit in criminal ways, for the life of a celebrity. Celebrity, they understand, is not something that simply happens. Celebrity must be practiced bodily. On the other hand, questions remain as to why the Bling Ring simultaneously reveres celebrities and dismisses or harm them. For example, in the first nightclub scene, Rebecca introduces Marc to Chloe, Nicki, and Sam. He sits between Chloe and Rebecca, taking in the activity in the nightclub. Marc notices Paris Hilton across the room. He says to the group, "Oh, my God, that's Paris Hilton!" Nicki responds dismissively, "Yeah, she's here a lot." Taking Nicki's dismissal together with the reality that the Bling Ring harms celebrities they wish to emulate, microcelebrity, as a theoretical apparatus, does not adequately provide an explanation as to the contradiction between emulation and harm. A religious or, more accurately, a parareligious account of celebrity helps answer that question.

## CELEBRITY CULTURE AS A PARARELIGION

In his analysis of celebrity culture, Christian theologian Pete Ward argues that celebrity culture functions as a metaphorical religious experience, what he calls a parareligion. He notes the long history linking celebrities with religious language. In popular discourse, "Film stars," Ward says, "have been likened to the gods . . . Female singers have regularly been spoken of as divas . . . In the 1960s, spray-painted graffiti appeared all around London, calling Eric Clapton a god."[26] Additionally, "Pop singers are regularly referred to as icons or idols."[27] Ward also offers examples of similar scholarly reflection. Semiotician Roland Barthes describes film star Greta Garbo's face as through it undergoes *theosis*, or "the metamorphosis of a human into the divine."[28] Feminist scholar Camille Paglia analyzes pop singer Madonna's music videos using the ancient Greek gods as points of departure.[29] Literature scholar John Frow draws on religious notions of sacredness to describe pop singer Elvis Presley and Princess Diana as god-like figures in human form.[30] Ward is careful to say, however, that both popular and scholarly discourse around celebrity does not mean that celebrity culture is a literal religion. The term parareligion suggests that celebrity culture fills a gap left by wider societal movements toward secularization. Although religion may not hold a central place in public life, celebrity provides a loose, "functional equivalent" to religion.[31]

Within that equivalency, Ward suggests that celebrity culture contains "religious elements" that fans "experience as a kind of contradiction"; celebrity culture contains rules that resist "stability," and therefore express fundamental "ambiguities."[32] As a parareligion, celebrity culture serves two ambiguous purposes, the first of which is an intimacy between fans and celebrities. Media regularly invite fans into intimacy with the celebrity, but it is an intimacy at a distance.[33] In early Hollywood, for example, studios leaked private, intimate information about their stars to the public. Social media intensifies this insider look into the private lives of public figures. Intimate information, however, occurs within the context of a massive distance between fans and celebrities, both physical and economic. Similar to Marwick's observations about microcelebrity, the distance between fans and a celebrity serves an aspirational function, offering a form of life that fans may want to inhabit for themselves.

In a more detailed account of intimacy and aspiration, sociologist Chris Rojek draws on Shamanistic traditions to claim that intimacy offers to fans the power of a celebrity's freedom and extraordinariness. Acknowledging the divergent range of beliefs and practice, Rojek notes Shamanisms tend to share a commitment that spiritual power can manifest in material reality, be it in human beings (like the shaman) or in physical objects, be they natural (like a rock) or human made (like a totem).[34] Shamans are traditionally thought to be extraordinary, touched by a spirit or divinity.[35] In popular culture, celebrities often display such shamanistic qualities. Hollywood celebrities represented, for many, unusually intense economic and moral freedom. Stars are "self-made individuals who . . . received a king's ransom for their labour. Moreover, in the highly public reporting of the sex lives of Hollywood celebrities, Middle America sat goggle-eyed at the freedom from moral restraint."[36] Stars were also extraordinary, even magical, people who performed amazing acts on screen, "like John Wayne, Robert Mitchum, Harrison Ford, Bruce Willis, Mel Gibson and Pierce Brosnan."[37] Intimacy with or proximity to stars who possess freedom and extraordinariness offers to fans access to that power.

Because the Shamanistic power of the celebrity can reside in physical objects, fans often collect objects in close proximity to celebrities. As a result, fans often construct "celebrity reliquaries."[38] In the early Hollywood days, fans collected "film stars' soap, a chewed piece of gum, cigarette butts, lipstick, tissues, and even a blade of grass from a star's lawn."[39] Fans also purchase personal objects that stars once owned, be they from Andy Warhol, Jacqueline Kennedy, or Princess Diana. Fans also "covet autographs and signed photographs of celebrities, preferably delivered with a 'personal' message to the fan. The Hard Rock Café chain displays rock memorabilia and rotates them between branches."[40] Fans may also engage in pilgrimages to celebrity gravesites, a practice common among religious peoples. In a digital age, social media platforms offer reliquaries of so-called "direct, unmediated relationships with fans," providing "the impression of candid, unfettered access."[41] Whether through a physical object or social media, reliquaries provide fans proximity to stars and their powers, while still retaining the distance between them.

In addition to intimacy, Ward notes a second parareligious feature of celebrity culture, an ambiguous identification of the fan to the celebrity, which can take the form of rites. Celebrity culture invites fans to both identify and disidentify with celebrities. When identifying with celebrities, fans use them as "significant models for lifestyle and behavior."[42] Disidentification occurs when fans "disapprove of the choices made by celebrities."[43] Disapproval can take a variety of reactions, including irreverence, disdain, or the "deep pleasures in seeing how celebrities mess up and fail."[44] For Rojeck, identification and disidentification can take the form of rites of ascent and decent. Ascension rites occur, for example, when a shaman sacrifices an animal, and the sacrifice enables the shaman to ascend spirituality to the heavens or physically up mountains or trees. Rites of descent often involve mortification through bodily discipline, like fasting, or harm, such as self-cutting.[45] Celebrity culture possesses analogous rites. Ascension often occurs when media elevate celebrities, especially when celebrities promote a new product, like an album or film, or display their wealth, status, and luxury. Both promotion and display function as "symbols of success in market society."[46] Because celebrities demand so much public honor, status, and envy, fans sometimes desire or delight in their downfall, a form of *Schadenfreude*.[47] Celebrities sometimes facilitate their own descent, including bodily mortifications, like anorexia, weight gain, phobias, or social mortifications, like law breaking. "The mortification of the [celebrity's] body," Rojeck concludes, "brings the celebrity down to earth," down to where fans reside.

In line with the parareligions aspects of celebrity culture, the Bling Ring sees the celebrities they target as possessing an extraordinary capacity for fashion and a freedom to behave badly. In his *Vanity Fair* interview, Marc reports that Lindsay Lohan was Rebecca's "ultimate fashion icon." The term "ultimate" implies that all of Rebecca's targets were icons to her. The film hints at this reality when, before the Audrina Patridge break-in, Rebecca reports how much she loves her style. Likewise, prior to breaking into several star's homes, including Megan Fox and Patridge, Coppola inserts montages of the stars they target, from images (accompanied by sounds of keyboard clicking, representing internet research) in magazines or on (fictional) fashion websites, like "I Heart Celebrities." In addition, the Bling Ring's reaction to Paris Hilton's home confirms her extraordinariness. Upon witnessing her personal possessions, the group can only speak in exclamations and obvious statements, as if Hilton's extraordinariness confounds their linguistic capacity. On their initial break-in, Rebecca and Marc tend to utter phrases like, "Oh, my God," "Whoa," or "It's amazing." They are also reduced to statements of fact that double as statements of amazement. Rebecca, for example, puts on a pair of Hilton's sunglasses and states their brand name, "These are Alexander McQueen." On their next visit, the rest of the Bling Ring respond similarly. They utter phrases like, "Oh, my God," "This is sick," "It's so cute," and state the brand name of the famous shoe designer, "Look at all her Louboutins." In addition to extraordinary fashion sensibilities, the Bling Ring note the freedom celebrities have to behave in self-destructive and/or illegal ways. Marc and Rebecca mention Mischa Barton's and Lindsay Lohan's DUIs, as well as Lohan's time in prison for jewelry theft. Given the power celebrities have for freedom and extraordinariness, the language of rites helps explain how the Bling Ring attempt to take possession of that power.

When Rebecca and Marc recount the story of their first break-in to the rest of the group, their discourse suggests that the break-in is a ritual of ascent, through which they display their own freedom to break the law and take possession of Hilton's extraordinariness. While Marc and Rebecca are still in Hilton's nightclub room, Coppola cuts suddenly to Rebecca, Marc, Nicki, Sam, and Chloe at a party. The director elides the moment when Rebecca tells the group that she and Marc broke into Hilton's home. The scene begins with Nicki exclaiming that she wants to go to Hilton's home. Rebecca responds with restrained excitement, "We hung out in her nightclub room. I got this." She extends her right wrist to the group, showing them a diamond tennis bracelet she stole. The group responds with shock, amazement, and disbelief. With an air of sophistication, Rebecca says, "Isn't that beautiful?" The bracelet bears two forms of extraordinariness. First, the bracelet was, until Rebecca stole it, in possession of a fashion icon. Second, Rebecca's appraisal of the item's beauty implies that the object expresses Hilton's extraordinary power. When she displays the bracelet, Rebecca ascends, not unlike the way celebrity displays of wealth function as rites of ascension. Likewise, Rebecca and Marc break the law not unlike the celebrities they aspire to be like. When Sam questions how they got into Hilton's home, Marc tells them that the key was under the doormat and says, "We just walked in." The simplicity of their solution elicits shock from the other characters. Marc and Rebecca closed the distance between themselves and Hilton to an incredibly thin space, and their intimacy with her is a direct result of their law-breaking and lack of moral restraint. And they also do it with ease. In all, Rebecca and Marc link their freedom to break the law ("We just walked in") with an intimacy to Hilton's extraordinary fashion ("Isn't that beautiful?").

Their linking of extraordinariness and freedom implies that, like Rojeck's account, this rite of ascension demands a sacrifice or a scapegoat: the celebrities themselves. Aside from their acts of criminality, an interaction between Marc and Rebecca demonstrates their understanding that their ascent demands a sacrifice. After they break into Megan Fox's home, Marc asks Rebecca, "If I ever became not your friend anymore, would you rob me?" Which is to say, with all of his extraordinary objects, would Rebecca sacrifice him for her own ascent? She responds, "I would never do that to you." She would never sacrifice him the way they sacrificed Megan Fox. However, later in the film, Marc cooperates with police, thereby mortifying or bringing himself, Rebecca, and the rest of the Bling Ring low.

Furthermore, intimacy with a celebrity's possessions becomes a pathway to achieve another form of freedom, self-destructive and law-breaking behavior. Once the entire Bling Ring enter Hilton's home, they place themselves in intimate connection with her possessions. They try on her shoes, look through her clothes and jewelry, find cash and sexual photographs. They also party in her nightclub room, dancing on her stripper pole, listening to music through her sound system, drinking her alcohol and spilling it on the floor. After they invade Hilton's home, the Bling Ring return to the club, and with the cash they stole, toast the night with more drinks. In the next scene, Chloe is driving. The entire scene plays out in a single shot. The camera peers into the car from Marc's front passenger seat window. Chloe and Rebecca slur their words, as if they are drunk. The rapper M.I.A.'s "Bad Girls" plays on the car's sound system. Chloe and Marc sing the words to the chorus along with the recording, "Live fast, die young/Bad girls do it well." As if in a self-conscious display, Chloe behaves as if her proximity to Hilton's possessions has facilitated her capacity to "live fast" like a "bad girl." While she sings, she turns to Marc, taking her eyes off the road, and she does not see the car that crashes into them. In that moment, her "bad girl" behavior nearly caused her to "die young." Coppola cuts from the car to Chloe's mug shots, echoing the DUI's and mug shots of celebrities like Lohan and Barton have. The next day, she continues to inhabit the law-breaking, self-destructive "bad girl" persona. She brags to Rebecca and Marc that her alcohol levels were excessive and dangerous. She says that the people who tested her "didn't know how I was driving, let alone still alive."

The trajectory of the film suggests that relics exist in an associative, not a cause-effect, relationship to a celebrity's extraordinariness and freedom. Clearly, the Bling Ring must break the law (i.e., sacrifice Hilton) into order to bring themselves into intimacy with her relics. Like Rebecca and Marc's story, it is the entanglement or association of law breaking and intimacy with Hilton's extraordinary objects that produce for the Bling Ring their ascent. Which is to say, it is not the infrastructure or materiality of the lifestyle—wearing high fashion dresses and shoes, drinking and dancing where celebrities do—but their response to these relics that seems to suggest their Shamanistic power. Once they leave Hilton's home, they carry that power with them, and from this break-in, the group creates an ever-expanding celebrity reliquary. As their reliquary expands, their bad behavior expands, including escalating drug use and selling stolen goods. This is not to say that the members of the Bling Ring have not behaved badly up to this point or broken the law. Rather, it is the escalation of this bad behavior to that of a Barton or a Lohan, which flows from the group's invasion of Hilton's home. Here again, the effect is not necessarily causal. Coppola associates the extraordinary power of celebrity relics to their freedom to break the law.

In addition to behaving badly, relics enable the Bling Ring to inhabit the ecstasy of their own extraordinariness. After Marc steals several Rolexes from Orlando Bloom's home and sells them, Coppola presents the entire Bling Ring in a brief series of slow motion shots at the night club. Having received bottle service from the bar, the group sits on a couch and intense techno music blasts over the soundtrack. Marc pulls out the $5,000 in cash he received from the sale of Bloom's watches. The group poses with each other, flashing the money toward their cell phones as the waitress pours their drinks. The music climaxes just as Chloe's camera phone flashes, suggesting that the moment is one of ecstasy. In the next shot, the music continues, and Nicki and Sam dance back to back. Coppola puts them in a close-up shot. They smile, and Nicki's right arm is raised, triumphantly. Although there is no synchronous sound, Nicki opens her mouth as if she screams in delight. Coppola cuts to Marc, also in close up, who jumps up and down with the crowd. Like Nicki, he thrusts his arm in the air. In this scene, their lives have reached a moment of intense exaltation. While he is still dancing, Marc's voiceover explains. "When we went out, we got in everywhere and everyone loved us. We had so many gorgeous, beautiful things." Marc's statement implies the Shamanistic power of their celebrity possessions. His statement links the extraordinariness of their beautiful things with the extraordinary ability to inhabit any nightclub they wanted, not unlike the celebrities they target.

Nevertheless, like other examples of a celebrity's descent, the Bling Ring facilitate their own mortification, through which Nicki and Marc inhabit a form of celebrity status. The police apprehend the Bling Ring, because Marc has appeared on a CCTV recording from their Patridge break-in and because the Bling Ring posted photographs of themselves on social media. In those photographs, they appear with stolen goods and sometimes at celebrity homes. But, their descent also facilitates an opportunity for celebrity status. After his arrest, Marc recounts in his *Vanity Fair* interview, "On my Facebook page recently, I had 800 friend requests. I accepted them all. I didn't even look at them. Then I noticed someone had created a fan page for me . . . It's kinda showing that America has some sick fascination with a Bonnie and Clyde kind of thing." The friend requests and fan page signal that celebrities like Bonnie and Clyde (or Rebecca and Marc) can be celebrities for the same reasons that Hilton is a celebrity: extraordinariness and freedom. While Marc's language of "sick fascination" denotes his ambivalence toward his microcelebrity status, Nicki takes an opposite approach. She attempts to use her downfall to promote her own life story. Hence, the film ends with her direct address to camera and her encouragement to the audience to follow her journey at her website.[48] Although the language of rites and relics helps explain how the Bling Ring transfer power onto themselves, elements of the Christian tradition shed further light on the embodied nature of relics.

## SAINTS, RELICS, AND THE EROTIC

Expanding on Rojek's account of shamanism, the Christian cult of the saints and the veneration of relics provides a more detailed account of how the Bling Ring engage with celebrity relics. In the Middle Ages, the cult of the saints became an important part of embodied Christian practice throughout Europe and the Middle East. Saints were usually martyrs, Christians who were executed, sometimes publicly, for their faith. Although death separated the saint from their communities, Christians believed saints to be alive spiritually with God. In that spiritual state, saints could connect with living Christians, particularly, to use Rojeck's language of spiritual ascent, to aid them "in the way of salvation."[49] As a means both to commune with the dead saint and to embrace spiritual edification, living Christians venerated relics. Relics could be objects that came in contact with saints before their death, like clothes, (not unlike celebrity memorabilia or autographs) or could be the complete bodies or partial bodily remains of the saints themselves (not unlike celebrity grave sites). In and of themselves, saints and relics do not add anything new to Ward or Rojeck's parareligious account of saints. However, the Christian notion of bodily, erotic desire does.

A Christian account of the erotic is an expanded, inclusive account, which both includes and exceeds sexualization. The pre-modern Christian tradition understood *eros* as a wide spectrum of bodily desires, appetites, comportments, reactions, and affections. Theologian Sarah Coakley argues that the erotic includes a bodily craving for "food, drink, comfort, intimacy, acknowledgement, power, pleasure, money, relaxation, rest, etc., as well as physical sex."[50] In this expansive sense, the erotic appears in all kinds of human phenomena, like the manifestation of emotional reactions in one's body; experiencing empathy; or the feeling of unity communities create when participating in embodied social phenomena, such as music, sports, theater, dancing, etc. Hence, sexuality and other forms of bodily desire—even spiritual affections—are, at least in the Christian tradition, continuous and sometimes coterminous with each other.

It should be no surprise that the Christian tradition includes accounts of physical and emotional comportments consistent with this expanded account of erotic desire, within both Christian art and historical examples of Christians venerating relics. In Christian art, Italian artist Gian Lorenzo Bernini's sculpture "Ecstasy of Saint Teresa" expresses a version of erotic. Teresa was a spiritual mystic and died having an sexual, spiritual connection with Jesus. Historian and religious studies scholar Carlos M. N. Eire describes the statue, saying, "Teresa is a virgin experiencing a encounter with Christ; she is ecstatic, suspended between heaven and earth."[51] Historian Peter Brown also recounts several examples suggestive of erotic desire at work in acts of veneration. Of the Carthaginian noblewoman named Megeti, it was recorded that, when she venerated relics housed in a shrine, "she beat against it [the shrine], not only with the longings of her heart, but with her whole body so that the little grille in front of the relic opened at the impact. . . . [She] pushed her head inside and laid it on the holy relics resting there, drenching them with her tears."[52] Gregory of Nyssa, a fourth century Cappadocian Christian, described Christians who venerated relics as bringing their entire person and passions to the act. "[T]hey bring eye, mouth, ear, all the senses into play, and then, shedding tears of reverence and passion," and they speak to the saint as though they were present in body.[53] Likewise, the late fourth and early fifth century Christian, Jerome, recounts how his mood or temperament produces bodily reactions when he enters into proximity to the relic: "Whenever I have been angry or had some bad thought upon my mind, or some evil fantasy has disturbed my sleep," he notes, "I do not dare to enter the shrines of the martyrs. I quake with body and soul."[54] In these examples, erotic desire includes a wide variety of embodied responses, like sexualized spirituality, physical violence, destruction of property, emotional outpourings, involuntary physical reactions, and the release of bodily fluids. They demonstrate that the range of erotic responses to relics shows considerable complexity—sometimes violent, negative, passionate—but all suggesting that the act of veneration awakens the whole, embodied person and a wide range of responses. Some of these responses are evident in Marc, Nicki, Sam, and Rebecca's reaction to celebrity relics.

Coppola links Marc's sexual desire to the violence of the break-ins and to Hilton's shoes. After a day of school, Rebecca asks Marc if he knows anyone who is out of town. He says that he knows a kid named Evan, who is in Jamaica with his family. She asks where Evan lives and how well Marc knows him. He claims that they had "met up" a few times, then says, "He's pretty hot." While the interchange does not verify a sexual encounter, Marc refers to Evan's attractiveness, suggesting Marc's erotic attraction to him. Marc and Rebecca's break-in connects his sexual attraction to violence—entering Evan's house and stealing items. Coppola develops Marc's eroticism in their second invasion of Hilton's home. With the entire Bling Ring in Hilton's closet, Marc enters wearing a pair of bright pink high heels. The girls fawn over him. Nicki exclaims, "He looks hot," and, in response, Marc bites his finger in a sexually suggestive manner. In these moments, Coppola entangles Marc's erotic desire to sites of violence.

However, Marc hides other aspects of sexuality from the other members of the Bling Ring. After Chloe's car accident, Marc sits alone in his room and at his computer. Like the livestream images, Coppola sets the camera at the height of Marc's computer screen. In addition to the height of the camera, the quality of the image implies that it is a webcam: it is a low-resolution, noisy, black and white image. Marc smokes marijuana and dances to singers Ester Dean and Chris Brown's song, "Drop It Low." Marc smiles and sings along to the male singing voice, "Drop it, drop it low, girl." When the song reaches the female-lead lyrics—"He say he like the way my booty, booty, booty popped/ He say he like the way my booty, booty, booty rocked"—Marc turns his back to the camera, lowers his pants slightly, and shakes his backside back and forth. When he faces the camera, Marc smiles. Apart from his sexually suggestive dancing, he takes directives from the male singer as though he identifies with the "girl," in the song, behaving in a way that might be attractive to men. This is similar to Chloe's car crash scene, where he sings along with Chloe as though he was one of the "bad girls," too. In this scene, however, he performs this display in private and never behaves in quite this manner in front of the rest of the Bling Ring.

Hilton's pink shoes appear again in a similar moment where he hides his sexuality. Marc sits alone on his bed looking at his phone. He wears Hilton's pink shoes. Because the shoes do not match his outfit, he likely does not intend to wear them in public. His mother knocks at his door and tells him to come to dinner. He is startled and asks his mother to wait. He quickly removes the high heels and puts them in a case he hides beneath his bed. While his immediate motive to take off the shoes might be to not get caught with them, his response suggests that he might be ashamed of wearing them, precisely because they are displays of his bodily desire for sex. In both of these scenes, Marc saves his most intense sexual performances for the privacy of his room. Taking his privacy together with his admission to the journalist that he does think he is attractive, it is possible he fetishes Hilton's shoes, redirecting his anxiety about his attractiveness into the shoes and the positive reception of his attractiveness he received from other members of the Bling Ring.

The other members of the Bling Ring also display erotic comportments to Hilton's relics, including sexual desire. When Nicki and Sam walk into Hilton's shoe closet for the first time, their mouths are agape; they squeal and hold each other, as though they need the embodied grounding of touch just to bear witness to Hilton's extraordinary relics. Nicki, especially, displays the erotic dispositions of delight and excitement. She jumps up and down on several occasions. Everyone comes in intimate contact with Hilton's shoes, clothes, jewelry, and cash, touching them not unlike Christians who came in bodily contact with relics. Nicki and Sam stand before Hilton's clothes, and her dresses are full of sparkles. The hangers are at least a foot above the heads of the girls, so they look up at the dresses, not unlike the manner in which people gaze at the stars. They stand in physical postures of awe, yet sexuality is also at play. Rebecca finds Polaroid-style photographs of Paris Hilton. Later in the film, a police officer refers to them as "personal photographs."

In commenting on the photos, Marc implies the sexual nature of the photographs, noting the inordinate amount of bronzer on Hilton's body. Sexuality also extends to their behavior in Hilton's nightclub room. At the center of the room is a table with a pole that reaches from the floor to the ceiling. Nicki dances on the pole similar to the way a dancer at a strip club might dance. Having observed the photograph of Hilton's sexuality and touched her relics, Nicki engages in sexualized behavior, presumably at the site at which Hilton performs similarly sexualized behavior.

The film also links Sam's eroticism and violence with one relic in particular, a gun from Megan Fox's house. Following Nicki's dance in Hilton's nightclub room, the Bling Ring return to the nightclub. While the rest of the Bling Ring toast Hilton, Coppola cuts away from the group to Nicki. She stands against a wall and kisses her boyfriend, Rob. Like Nicki and Marc, Coppola links Sam's sexuality with the rite of ascent they perform. The director develops this connection during the Megan Fox break-in. The scene plays out in a long, single take. Nicki finds a box with a gun in it. She calls out to Sam, who takes the gun and waves it around. She takes the bodily comportment of delight and exaltation. She holds the gun, points it at the sky and herself, and spins in circles, as if she is physically dancing with the weapon. When Marc approaches her, she engages in a rite of descent against him. She points the gun at him, belittling and controlling him. Unlike Rebecca, who insists that she would never sacrifice him, Sam performs a sacrifice (demeaning Marc and threatening violence against him) within a sacrifice (committing violence against Fox). She smiles and laughs. She notes how heavy the gun feels and voices her erotic attraction to the relic, "I actually like it a lot." Sam then sneaks into Rob's window with the gun in hand. She stands on the bed above him, looks down and points the gun at him. Rob slowly reaches up to her and violently pulls her down to the bed. In shock, she screams and accidentally fires the weapon. But immediately, he quiets her, pushes the gun out of her hand, and intertwines his fingers with hers in a sexualized gesture. He kisses her. Like her behavior with Marc, here she performs a sacrifice (threatening violence against Rob) within a sacrifice (violence against Fox), precisely at the site of the relic.

Of all the Bling Ring members, Rebecca's display of eroticism is, perhaps, the most subtle. The apex of Rebecca's eroticism occurs during the break-in of her fashion icon, Lindsay Lohan. In a medium, slow motion, single shot of Rebecca, mostly in profile, she stands in front of her victim's vanity mirror, and ethereal, ambient music plays on the soundtrack. The music begins with a low rumble, but soon, smooth high pitched sounds emerge. There is no synchronous sound, and so the music envelops her. Taken together, the slow motion photography and ambient music present Rebecca as though she is having a transcendent religious experience, perhaps not unlike St. Theresa.

Rebecca picks up Lohan's perfume and stares at it. She removes the lid and opens her mouth slightly before bringing the nozzle to her nose. She breathes in what Lohan must smell like. Then, Rebecca sprays Lohan's scent onto her neck, first her right side then her left. Only her left side is visible to the camera, but the spot of perfume glistens, almost sticky in the low light of the scene. Once she sets the perfume down, she leans into the mirror, her eyes fixed on her own image. As she adjusts her hair, her eyes fill with hope and possibility, and eventually she smiles at herself in a moment of sheer satisfaction. The eroticism of this moment is reminiscent of the eroticism of the examples of Christian responses to relics—at once bodily, emotional, religious, and violent. Unlike her peers, however, there is little, if any, explicit sexuality. She displays the erotics of bodily identification with her victim, experiencing upon her own body what she likely envisions Lohan's body to experience. This moment is not unlike an earlier and more muted scene from Hilton's home. In a similar medium shot, Rebecca stands in front of Hilton's bathroom mirror. She picks up Hilton's lipstick, looks at herself in the mirror, and spreads the celebrity's lipstick on her lips. While there is no slow motion or ethereal music, the intimacy is palpable. Rebecca connects with Hilton's body. Her lips now touch what Hilton's lips touch. Physicality and desire merge at the sites of these relics, relics that represent far more intimacy with the bodies of celebrities than mere clothes or jewelry.

By way of conclusion, we offer implications our analysis has for secular society, social media, bodily human desire, and boredom. First, even though, broadly speaking, the West is a secular and secularizing society, religious language still has the capacity to shed light on what might appear to be non-religious, physical experience. This is not to colonize non-religious experiences. Rather, the usefulness of such language underscores two functions. Not unlike the claims of Ward and Rojek, portions of secular society retain, at least metaphorically or analogically, echoes or remnants of a religious past. Those remnants persist, as Bhatia notes, in a dialogic relationships to secularity. This is the case in *The Bling Ring*. The content of religious life may have vanished, but structural aspects of religion remain, like the embodied eroticism of relics and violence.

Second, Coppola's film suggests that religious metaphors are relevant to the realm of social media. If elements of social media experience are, indeed, religious in character, then such a reality might attenuate some scholarly anxieties about technological developments. Media Ecologists—as someone like Neil Postman might represent—often overemphasize a pessimistic account of how technology has harmed, or perhaps ruined, Western society.[55] Such an appraisal should not to diminish the strong analytic work of some Media Ecologists or underestimate the reality that technologies like the printing press, television, or the internet have had important impacts on the world and social relationships. However, if people use social media as reliquaries, not unlike the way medieval Christians used their own, then perhaps, as an ancient religious sage once observed, "There is nothing new under the sun."[56] Social media may simply reveal that certain aspects of human practice remain consistent over long periods of time. And the language of religious reflection helps clarify those consistencies and attenuate pessimistic appraisals.

Third, like the language of religion, Christian reflection, on *eros* and bodily desire specifically, remains useful as well. There is no doubt that Christianity has produced significant physical and social harm throughout the world. From the Doctrine of Discovery, in which the Church underwrote the expansion of colonial violence,[57] to the high numbers of Christians who supported the openly misogynist and white supremacist president of the United States, Donald Trump,[58] to the millions of white Evangelical Christians who refuse to receive the COVID-19 vaccine,[59] Christians have posed and continue to pose a threat to the flourishing of the world. Within that broad understanding, elements of Christian reflection have explanatory power. This is, again, not to say that desire and the erotic, as a topic of scholarly reflection, is the sole province of Christian reflection.[60] Desire, however, understood as linked to the body in reference to a wide variety of appetites, be they sexual or otherwise, has the potential to contribute to scholarly reflections on embodiment more broadly. The usefulness of such contribution is, by and large, yet to be made, but the potential remains. For example, sociologist of media and culture Nick Couldry and scholar of information systems Jannis Kallinikos argue that the ontology of social media is "an ephemeral, real-time attuned, and perpetually changing 'everyday' that reorders the trivial pursuits and habits of individuals" into data that corporations use to generate "revenue."[61] *The Bling Ring* suggests that part of what is reordered into revenue—far from trivialities or mere habits—is the eroticism that users perform at the site of social media. And, far from a disembodied experience, these capitalist processes mediated through social media cannot be divorced from bodily existence and formation.

Finally, our reading of *The Bling Ring* suggests how unusual the film is, not only among Coppola's films, but in relationship to teen films more broadly, particularly in relation to the experience of boredom. Many of Coppola's films can be described as films about characters captured in so-called gilded cages. While the Bling Ring live in a gilded world, they are not trapped in the sort of cages evident in her previous films. For example, in *The Virgin Suicides* (1999), the Lisbon sisters experience boredom and ultimately commit self-destructive behavior, but they do so because of their entrapment. In *Somewhere* (2010), Johnny experiences boredom and engages in self-destructive behavior, but he does so because he feels trapped. By contrast, the Bling Ring engage in self-destructive behavior and are free to do so, but they do so because they are bored. With boredom as a cause of conflict or one of the problems characters desire to overcome, *The Bling Ring* opens territory rarely covered in teen films. Unlike Nicholas Ray's *Rebel Without A Cause* (1955) or John Landis' *Animal House* (1978), the Bling Ring do not rage against generational differences. Like Richard Linklater's *Dazed and Confused* (1993), characters engage in substance use to deal with their boredom. But unlike the characters in Linklater's Texas high school film, the Bling Ring commits felonies. Unlike Bo Burnham's *Eighth Grade* (2018), the Bling Ring are neither being bullied nor do they bully other teenagers. Unlike Amy Heckerling's *Clueless* (1995), the Bling Ring arenot concerned with romantic love. And unlike Mark Waters' *Mean Girls* (2004) or Olivia Wilde's *Booksmart* (2019), the Bling Ring are not primarily concerned with friendships. That teenagers claim to be bored seems too obvious to say. But our reading of the film turns the commonplace statement into an interesting meditation on the religious implications of boredom. Perhaps boredom is an embodied, spiritual condition, one that the characters attempt to alleviate within the structure of religious experience. If, as Bhatia suggests, the religious and the secular are entwined with one another, then these implications suggest they are intertwined at the site of everyday life, our bodies, our boredoms, and our technologies.

## REFERENCES

A L E X I S H A I N E S, "itsalexishaines," *Instagram*, accessed April 18, 2021, www.instagram.com/itsalexishaines/?hl=en.

Bhatia, Mohita. "Secularism and Secularisation: A Bibliographical Essay." *Economic and Political Weekly* 48, no. 50 (December 14, 2013): 103–10. www.jstor.com/stable/24479051.

Brown, Peter. *The Cult of the Saints: Its Rise and Function in Latin Christianity*. Chicago: University of Chicago Press, 1981.

Bulgokov, Surguis. "The Virgin and the Saints in Orthodoxy." In *Eastern Orthodox Theology: A Contemporary Reader*, 2nd ed., edited by Daniel B. Clendenin, 65–75. Grand Rapids, MI: Baker Academic, 1995.

Butler, Judith. *Subjects of Desire: Hegelian Reflections in Twentieth-Century France*. New York: Columbia University Press, 1987.

Carr, Nicholas. *The Shallows: What The Internet Is Doing To Our Brains*. New York: W.W. Norton, 2010.

Coakley, Sarah. *The New Asceticism: Sexuality, Gender, and the Quest for God*. London: Bloomsbury, 2015.

*The Bling Ring*. Directed by Sofia Coppola. 2013; New York: A24.

Couldry, Nick and Jannis Kallinikos. "Ontology." In *The SAGE Handbook of Social Media*, edited by Jean Burgess, Alice Marwick, and Thomas Poell, 146–59. Los Angeles: Sage Publications, 2018.

Deleuze, Gilles and Felix Guattari. *Anti-Oedipus: Capitalism and Schizophrenia*. Translated by Robert Hurley, Mark Seem, and Helen R. Lane. Minneapolis, MN: University of Minnesota Press, 1983.

Dias, Elizabeth and Ruth Graham. "White Evangelical Resistance Is Obstacle in Vaccination Effort." *The New York Times*, April 5, 2021. www.nytimes.com/2021/04/05/us/covid-vaccine-evangelicals.html.

Eire, Carlos M. N. "Ecstasy as Polemic: Mysticism and the Catholic Reformation." *Irish Theological Quarterly* 83, no. 1 (December 2017): 3–23.

Foucault, Michel. *The History of Sexuality, Volume 1: An Introduction*. Translated by Robert Hurley. New York: Vintage, 1990.

Friesz, Cayla. "caylafriesz." *Instagram*, www.instagram.com/caylafriesz/?hl=en.

Handyside, Fiona. *Sofia Coppola: A Cinema of Girlhood*. London: I.B. Tauris, 2017.

Hanes, Alexis. "Recovering from Reality with Alexis Hanes." Accessed April 18, 2021. www.recoveringfromreality.com/.

Jo Sales, Nancy. "The Suspects Wore Louboutins." *Vanity Fair*, March 2010, archive.vanityfair.com/article/share/e9cc0cc3-dbf1-4fab-8367-5fc7c05608e6.

Letort, Delphine. "The Cultural Capital of Sofia Coppola's *The Bling Ring* (2013): Branding Feminine Celebrity in Los Angeles." *Celebrity Studies* 7, no. 3 (2015): 1–14.

Lim, Kane. "kanelk_k." *Instagram*, www.instagram.com/kanelk_k/?hl=en.

Lorde, Audre. "Uses of the Erotic: The Erotic as Power." In *Sister Outsider: Essays and Speeches by Audre Lorde*, 53–9. Berkeley, CA: Crossing Press, 1984.

Lovett, Ian. "White Evangelicals Resist Covid-19 Vaccine Most Among Religious Groups." *The Wall Street Journal*, July 28, 2021. www.wsj.com/articles/white-evangelicals-resist-covid-19-vaccine-most-among-religious-groups-11627464601.

Marwick, Alice E. "Instafame: Luxury Selfies in the Attention Economy." *Public Culture* 27 (2015): 137–60.

Marwick, Alice E. *Status Update: Celebrity, Publicity, and Branding in the Social Media Age*. New Haven, CT: Yale University Press, 2013.

Newcomb, Steven. *Pagans in the Promised Land: Decoding the Doctrine of Christian Discovery*. Golden, CO: Baylor University Press, 2008.

Pesce, Sara. "Ripping off Hollywood Celebrities: Sofia Coppola's *The Bling Ring*, Luxury Fashion and Self-Branding in California." *Film, Fashion and Consumption* 4, no. 1 (2015): 5–24.

Postman, Neil. *Amusing Ourselves to Death: Public Discourse in the Age of Show Business*. New York: Viking Press, 1985.

———. *Technopoly: The Surrender of Culture to Technology*. New York: Vintage Books, 1992.

Pulkkinen, Levi. "White Evangelical Churches and the Crisis of Vaccine Hesitancy." *U.S. News and World Report*, August 10, 2020. www.usnews.com/news/health

-news/articles/2021-08-10/white-evangelical-churches-and-the-crisis-of-vaccine-hesitancy.
*Pretty Wild*, performances by Alexis Neiers and Tess Taylor (2010, Los Angeles: E!).
Rogers, Anna Backman. *Sofia Coppola: The Politics of Visual Pleasure*. New York: Berghahn, 2019.
Rojek, Chris. *Celebrity*. London: Reaktion Book, 2001.
Sales, Nancy Jo. "The Suspects Wore Louboutins." *Vanity Fair*, March 2010. archive.vanityfair.com/article/share/e9cc0cc3-dbf1-4fab-8367-5fc7c05608e6.
Scott, A. O. "Gatsby, and Other Luxury Consumers." *The New York Times*, May 16, 2013. www.nytimes.com/2013/05/19/movies/the-luxe-life-in-gatsby-bling-ring-and-other-films.html.
———. "Twinkly Totems of Fame, Theirs for the Taking." *The New York Times*, June 13, 2013. www.nytimes.com/2013/06/14/movies/a-bling-ring-lusting-after-celebrity-trinkets.html
Senft, Theresa M. *Camgirls: Celebrity and Community in the Age of Social Networks*. New York: Peter Lang Publishing, 2008.
Smith, Gregory A. "White Christians Continue to Favor Trump over Biden, but Support has Slipped." *Pew Center Research*, October 13, 2020. www.pewresearch.org/fact-tank/2020/10/13/white-christians-continue-to-favor-trump-over-biden-but-support-has-slipped/.
Spinsterz, The. "thespinsterz." *Instagram*, www.instagram.com/thespinsterz/?hl=en.
Teen Vogue. Accessed April 17, 2021, www.teenvogue.com/.
Turkle, Sherry. *Alone Together: Why We Expect More from Technology and Less from Each Other*. New York: Basic Books, 2011.
Ward, Pete. "Celebrity Worship as Parareligion: Bieber and the Beliebers." In *Religion and Popular Culture in America*, 3rd ed., edited by Bruce David Forbes and Jeffrey H. Mahan, 313–27. Oakland: University of California Press, 2017.
Ward, Pete. "Gods Behaving Badly: Celebrity as a 'Kind of' Religion." *The Other Journal: An Intersection of Theology and Culture*, October 22, 2010. theotherjournal.com/2010/10/22/gods-behaving-badly-celebrity-as-a-kind-of-religion-2/.
———. *Celebrity Worship*. New York: Routledge, 2020. iBooks.
———. *God Behaving Badly: Media, Religion, and Celebrity Culture*. Waco, TX: Baylor University Press.
Wilkinson, Maryn. "Leisure/Crime, Immaterial Labor, and the Performance of the Teenage Girl in Harmony Korine's *Spring Breakers* (2012) and Sofia Coppola's *The Bling Ring* (2013)." *Journal of Feminist Scholarship* 12 (Spring 2018): 20–37. digitalcommons.uri.edu/jfs/vol12/iss12/3.

## NOTES

1. Sara Pesce, "Ripping off Hollywood Celebrities: Sofia Coppola's *The Bling Ring*, Luxury Fashion and Self-Branding in California," *Film, Fashion and Consumption* 4, no. 1 (2015): 7.

2. Fiona Handyside, *Sofia Coppola: A Cinema of Girlhood* (London: I.B. Tauris, 2017), 144.

3. Maryn Wilkinson, "Leisure/Crime, Immaterial Labor, and the Performance of the Teenage Girl in Harmony Korine's *Spring Breakers* (2012) and Sofia Coppola's *The Bling Ring* (2013)," *Journal of Feminist Scholarship* 12 (Spring 2018): 29, digitalcommons.uri.edu/jfs/vol12/iss12/3.

4. Anna Backman Roger, *Sofia Coppola: The Politics of Visual Pleasure* (New York: Berghahn, 2019), 141.

5. A. O. Scott, "Twinkly Totems of Fame, Theirs for the Taking," *The New York Times*, June 13, 2013, www.nytimes.com/2013/06/14/movies/a-bling-ring-lusting-after-celebrity-trinkets.html.

6. A. O. Scott, "Gatsby, and Other Luxury Consumers," *The New York Times*, May 16, 2013, www.nytimes.com/2013/05/19/movies/the-luxe-life-in-gatsby-bling-ring-and-other-films.html.

7. Mohita Bhatia, "Secularism and Secularisation: A Bibliographical Essay," *Economic and Political Weekly* 48, no. 50 (December 14, 2013): 103. www.jstor.com/stable/24479051.

8. Because our analysis focuses on the metaphoric function of religion, we do not explore formal or institutional religion, which the film represents through a religious affiliation to Rhonda Byrne best-selling book *The Secret* (2006). Our reading suggests that the most profoundly religious moments in the film appear as thoroughly secular in nature.

9. Theresa M. Senft, *Camgirls: Celebrity and Community in the Age of Social Networks* (New York: Peter Lang Publishing, 2008), 25.

10. Alice E. Marwick, "Instafame: Luxury Selfies in the Attention Economy," *Public Culture* 27 (2015): 140, emphasis original.

11. Ibid., 142.

12. Alice E. Marwick, *Status Update: Celebrity, Publicity, and Branding in the Social Media Age* (New Haven, CT: Yale University Press, 2013), 117.

13. Marwick, "Instafame," 142.

14. Ibid., 149.

15. Cayla Friesz, "caylafriesz," *Instagram*, accessed April 18, 2021, www.instagram.com/caylafriesz/?hl=en.

16. The Spinsterz, "thespinsterz," *Instagram*, accessed April 18, 2021, www.instagram.com/thespinsterz/?hl=en.

17. Marwick, "Instafame," 141.

18. Ibid.

19. Ibid.

20. Ibid.

21. kane lim, "kanelk_k," *Instagram*, accessed April 18, 2021, www.instagram.com/kanelk_k/?hl=en.

22. Delphine Letort, "The Cultural Capital of Sofia Coppola's *The Bling Ring* (2013): Branding Feminine Celebrity in Los Angeles," *Celebrity Studies* 7, no. 3 (2015): 5.

23. *Teen Vogue*, accessed April 17, 2021, www.teenvogue.com/.

24. Nancy Jo Sales, "The Suspects Wore Louboutins," *Vanity Fair*, March 2010, archive.vanityfair.com/article/share/e9cc0cc3-dbf1-4fab-8367-5fc7c05608e6.

25. The legitimizing function of media and capitalism is even more evident in the character on whom Nicki is based, Alexis Neiers (now Alexis Haynes). In real life, police arrested Alexis Neiers for her involvement with the Bling Ring while she was shooting her reality TV show, *Pretty Wild*, which co-starred Tess Taylor, the woman on whom Sam is based. After recovering from drug addiction in her teens, Alexis Haynes currently works as a Recovery Advocate at Alo House Recovery Center. Like Paris Hilton, Haines also sells a lifestyle, except instead of wealth and fashion, she sells a lifestyle of "recovery" and "wellness." See A L E X I S H A I N E S, "itsalexishaines." On her website, "Recovering from Reality," her audience can purchase a copy of her book; listen to her podcast; take courses; buy merchandise; and see glimpses of life after recovery and her relationship with her mother, husband, and children. She is supported by a handful of boutique beauty sponsors. See Alexis Hanes, "Recovering from Reality with Alexis Hanes," accessed April 18, 2021, www.recoveringfromreality.com/.

26. Pete Ward, *Celebrity Worship* (New York: Routledge, 2020), iBooks.

27. Pete Ward, "Celebrity Worship as Parareligion: Bieber and the Beliebers," in *Religion and Popular Culture in America*, 3rd ed., ed. Bruce David Forbes and Jeffrey H. Mahan (Oakland: University of California Press, 2017), 315.

28. Ward, *Celebrity Worship*, iBooks.

29. Ibid.

30. Ibid.

31. Pete Ward, "Gods Behaving Badly: Celebrity as a 'Kind of' Religion," *The Other Journal: An Intersection of Theology and Culture*, October 22, 2010, accessed February 23, 2020, theotherjournal.com/2010/10/22/gods-behaving-badly-celebrity-as-a-kind-of-religion-2/.

32. Pete Ward, *God Behaving Badly: Media, Religion, and Celebrity Cutlure* (Waco, TX: Baylor University Press), 80–1.

33. Ward, "Celebrity Worship as Parareligion," 320–1.

34. Chris Rojek, *Celebrity* (London: Reaktion Book, 2001), 53–4.

35. Ibid., 55.

36. Ibid., 73.

37. Ibid., 77.

38. Ibid., 62.

39. Ibid., 58.

40. Ibid., 59.

41. Marwick, "Instafame," 139.

42. Ward, "Celebrity Worship as Parareligion," 321.

43. Ibid.

44. Ibid.

45. Rojek, *Celebrity*, 55.

46. Ibid., 75.

47. Ibid., 79.

48. In real life, Alexis Haines, the character Nicki is based on, does something similar. She promotes her own story via social media, her website, and podcast. After her recovery from drug addiction, she uses her platform to promotes her wellness lifestyle.

49. Surguis Bulgokov, "The Virgin and the Saints in Orthodoxy," in *Eastern Orthodox Theology: A Contemporary Reader*, 2nd ed., ed. Daniel B. Clendenin (Grand Rapids, MI: Baker Academic, 1995), 70.

50. Sarah Coakley, *The New Asceticism: Sexuality, Gender, and the Quest for God* (London: Bloomsbury, 2015), iBooks.

51. Carlos M. N. Eire, "Ecstasy as Polemic: Mysticism and the Catholic Reformation," *Irish Theological Quarterly* 83, no. 1 (Dec, 2017): 13.

52. Peter Brown, *The Cult of the Saints: Its Rise and Function in Latin Christianity* (Chicago, IL: University of Chicago Press, 1981), 88.

53. Ibid.

54. Ibid.

55. While a full account of media ecology, especially its strengths and weaknesses, is outside the scope of this chapter, a brief list of works should suffice to establish that media ecology has a distinctly pessimistic strain. See, for example, Neil Postman, *Amusing Ourselves to Death: Public Discourse in the Age of Show Business* (New York: Viking Press, 1985); Neil Postman, *Technopoly: The Surrender of Culture to Technology* (New York: Vintage Books, 1992); Sherry Turkle, *Alone Together: Why We Expect More from Technology and Less from Each Other* (New York: Basic Books, 2011); Nicholas Carr, *The Shallows: What The Internet Is Doing To Our Brains* (New York: W.W. Norton, 2010).

56. Ecc. 1:9, NRSV.

57. Steven Newcomb, *Pagans in the Promised Land: Decoding the Doctrine of Christian Discovery* (Golden, CO: Fulcrum, 2008), 125–8.

58. Gregory A. Smith, "White Christians Continue to Favor Trump over Biden, but Support has Slipped," *Pew Center Research*, October 13, 2020, accessed May 7, 2021, www.pewresearch.org/fact-tank/2020/10/13/white-christians-continue-to-favor-trump-over-biden-but-support-has-slipped/.

59. Elizabeth Dias and Ruth Graham, "White Evangelical Resistance Is Obstacle in Vaccination Effort," *The New York Times*, April 5, 2021, www.nytimes.com/2021/04/05/us/covid-vaccine-evangelicals.html. Levi Pulkkinen, "White Evangelical Churches and the Crisis of Vaccine Hesitancy," *U.S. News and World Report*, August 10, 2020, www.usnews.com/news/health-news/articles/2021-08-10/white-evangelical-churches-and-the-crisis-of-vaccine-hesitancy. Ian Lovett, "White Evangelicals Resist Covid-19 Vaccine Most Among Religious Groups," *The Wall Street Journal*, July 28, 2021, www.wsj.com/articles/white-evangelicals-resist-covid-19-vaccine-most-among-religious-groups-11627464601.

60. While outside the scope of this chapter, the language of the erotic and desire appear in the work of many scholars. See for example: Michel Foucault, *The History of Sexuality, Volume 1: An Introduction*, trans. Robert Hurley (New York: Vintage, 1990), 70 and 81; Gilles Deleuze and Felix Guattari, *Anti-Oedipus: Capitalism and Schizophrenia*, trans. Robert Hurley, Mark Seem, and Helen R. Lane (Minneapolis,

MN: University of Minnesota Press, 1983), 119–20; Judith Butler, *Subjects of Desire: Hegelian Reflections in Twentieth-Century France* (New York: Columbia University Press, 1987), 24–5; Audre Lorde, "Uses of the Erotic: The Erotic as Power," in *Sister Outsider: Essays and Speeches by Audre Lorde* (Berkeley, CA: Crossing Press, 1984), 53–9.

61. Nick Couldry and Jannis Kallinikos, "Ontology," in *The SAGE Handbook of Social Media*, ed. Jean Burgess, Alice Marwick, and Thomas Poell (Los Angeles: Sage Publications, 2018), 156.

*Chapter Six*

# An Embodied Joy

## *Carnivalesque Subversions and Grotesque Bodies in* A Very Murray Christmas *(2015)*

In interviews supporting the release of her 2015 Christmas special, *A Very Murray Christmas*, Sofia Coppola described the impetus for the film with two references: Bill Murray's singing and the emotional response of joy. Referring to Murray's "Nick the Lounge Singer" character in the early years of the long-running sketch comedy show, *Saturday Night Live* (1975–) (*SNL*), she claims to have always "love[ed] hearing Bill sing."[1] For the film, she wanted him to sing at the Café Carlyle, a lounge at the famous New York City hotel, the Carlyle Hotel. In conversations with the film's producer Mitch Glazer, he pointed out how no one produces old television Christmas specials anymore. Hence, Coppola's desire to hear Murray sing met Glazer's suggestion to produce a Christmas special. Coppola also spent time with holiday specials by the musical group, The Carpenters, a band composed of a brother-sister duo, Richard (piano, vocals) and Karen Carpenter (drums, vocals). She said she was "inspired by the Carpenters' Christmas special from the '70s,"[2] like their 1977 special *The Carpenters at Christmas*, adding that she wanted "to do something joyful."[3] Part of what is unusual, or perhaps counterintuitive, about *A Very Murray Christmas*'s relationship to *The Carpenters at Christmas* is that Coppola captures the qualities of "love" and "joy" through acts of subversion.

Historically, many enactments of subversion and irreverence have used irony. Artists often reuse "old forms," of literature, television, or stereotypes, "in order to . . . reactivate their ability to promote critical awareness,"[4] subverting some features and upholding others. However, critics have pointed out that recent iterations of irony and subversion are not without problems.

In the last few decades, humorists, especially, have displayed this disposition, as the example of *The Colbert Report* (2005–14) demonstrates. In his ironic portrayal of a conservative talk show host, Steven Colbert both satirized conservative politics while portraying a character who engaged in sexist, racist, and homophobic discourse. This form of humor has led critics, like communication studies scholar Jonathan P. Rossing, to claim that such acts are complicit in the problems they attempt to critique.[5] Although Colbert takes an ironic posture, Rossing argues that what the comedian affirms (here sexism, racism, and homophobia) limits his ability to subvert the problems within conservativism.

Within this context, it might be reasonable to expect that Coppola would deploy subversive irony in a similar way. Netflix's promotion of the special could be taken to make this precise implication. The company describes the film in this manner, "Bill Murray rounds up an all-star cast for an evening of music, mischief and barroom camaraderie in this *irreverent* twist on holiday variety shows."[6] Here, the use of the term "irreverent" suggests that Netflix wants to communicate clearly to their audience that this is not going to be a typical Christmas special. There will be significant differences from what their audience might expect. However, it is precisely the film's lack of irony that makes the film's use of subversion so curious. As film critic David Biancully rightfully argues, the most unusual feature of *A Very Murray Christmas*, its "twist," is that it exists "without irony. This isn't Bill Murray in the guise of his smug nightclub crooner from *Saturday Night Live*. This is Bill Murray in the guise of Bill Murray, enjoying himself with friends . . . They're having fun, but they're not being sarcastic."[7] This chapter explores how Coppola subverts the television Christmas, especially specials like the 1970s Carpenters' special, in such a way that points to the realities related of embodiment and joy.[8]

After a brief summary, we begin with a generic analysis of the film. Taking *The Carpenters at Christmas* as a fulfillment of the Christmas television special, *A Very Murray Christmas* both affirms and subverts elements of the genre. However, the methodology of genre analysis fails to fully name the ways Coppola subverts the genre. To compensate for that shortcoming, Russian literary theorist Mikhail Bakhtin's notion of the carnivalesque offers better ways of describing how the film engages in acts of subversion. Although Bahktin's work offers many ways of discussing the carnivalesque, his notion of the seven series appears prominently in this film, specifically food, drink, and sex, subverting the disembodiment of Christmas specials more broadly. And Coppola's use of hybridized, grotesque bodies of singers subverts the professionalism of Christmas specials. We close the chapter with reflections on joy and equity.

*A Very Murray Christmas* opens on a snowy Christmas Eve in New York City. Bill Murray (as himself) stands at the window in his hotel room, overlooking Central Park, as Paul Schaffer (as himself) plays piano. Murray recognizes the song and sings "Christmas Blues." He, however, is not in the Christmas spirit. He has plans to perform a live, television Christmas special in the Café Carlyle at the Carlyle Hotel with an all-star audience, including celebrities like Brad Pitt, Angelina Jolie, George Clooney, Paul McCartney, and Pope Francis. Unfortunately, a snowstorm has paralyzed the city, and without any transportation, not a single celebrity will attend the performance. Murray wants to cancel the performance, but his producers Liz (Amy Poehler) and Bev (Julie White), inform him that his contract will not permit a cancellation. They leave the hotel room and walk to the café. Reluctantly, Schaffer and Murray begin the performance, but soon Murray insists that he cannot perform and walks off the stage and into the lobby. There he runs into comedian Chris Rock (as himself). Murray convinces Rock to perform with him, and they sing a duet. At the end of the performance, the storm causes an electrical blackout. Because a blackout fulfills an "act of God" clause in their insurance contract, the producers immediately cancel the show. Murray and Schaffer retire to the bar.

Seated at the piano, The Waitress (Jenny Lewis) brings Murray a drink, and the two sing a duet of "Baby, It's Cold Outside." The Waitress hears a disturbance in the kitchen and rushes off with Murray in tow. The Chef (Thomas Mars) and his crew (the band Phoenix) are distressed, because the wedding reception they catered has been cancelled. Murray insists that the night need not be ruined. Rather, the food and drink can now become a feast for everyone in the bar. On their way to the bar, they pass The Bride (Rashida Jones) who sits alone in the hallway. She and Elliot the Groom (Jason Schwartzman) had to cancel her wedding because of the storm, and she is inconsolable. Although Murray invites her into the bar, she refuses. Back in the bar, Murray convinces the Chef and his crew to perform a song. Murray drags Elliot the Groom to the drums, and the band, along with Schaffer and Murray, performs "Alone on Christmas Day." After the song, Murray tells Elliot the Groom to reconcile with The Bride and then walks away. Immediately, The Lounge Singer (Maya Rudolf) appears and forces him to drink a drink called a "Soiled Kimono." She tells him to listen to the song she will sing. Backup singers dressed like wait staff accompany her. Moved by the performance, Elliot the Groom speaks with The Bride. Murray joins them and facilitates their reconciliation. In response and as an act of celebration, Murray pours drinks for the entire bar. Everyone drinks, including Murray, and gathers around the piano to sing, "A Fairytale in New York," including The Bartender (David Johansen) who begins the song. At the end of the song,

Murray, having drunk too much, passes out of the floor. In his drunken stupor, he dreams about performing in a traditional Christmas special.

In his dream, he appears on a white colored stage, with large Christmas trees in the background. Schaffer and the band are dressed in white tuxedos, while Murray wears a black one. He sings "Sleigh Ride," and soon Miley Cyrus, wearing a strapless, red mini-dress, and George Clooney, dressed in a black tuxedo, arrive on a sled, a group of dancers accompanying them. Later, Murray and Clooney leave the stage, and Cyrus and Schaffer perform a bluesy arrangement of "Silent Night." Coppola transitions to the band performing "Santa Clause Wants Some Lovin.'" Murray sings the verses, while Clooney pops out from behind the Christmas trees to sing the choruses. The dream sequence ends with "Let it Snow." Murray wakes on Christmas morning. Schaffer is playing "We Wish You a Merry Christmas" at the piano. Having recovered the Christmas spirit, Murray performs "We Wish You a Merry Christmas." The film ends as the protagonist walks to the window, looks out over a sunny Central Park, and says, "Merry Christmas, everyone."

## AFFIRMING AND SUBVERTING THE CHRISTMAS TELEVISION SPECIAL

To give an account of how *A Very Murray Christmas* subverts the Carpenters' Christmas specials and Christian television specials more broadly, we offer a genre analysis, taking *The Carpenters at Christmas*, as a point of comparison. After a brief history of Christmas specials and a summary of *The Carpenters at Christmas*, the analysis offers special attention to four generic elements: the spirit of Christmas, a Scrooge figure, Christmas carols, and the tenor of frivolity.[9]

Because early television drew heavily on successful radio programming, the first Christmas special that appeared on television in the United States was an original Christmas opera entitled *Amahl and the Night Visitors,* "composed by Gian-Carlo Menotti especially for NBC television in 1951."[10] Although operas and Christmas specials were popular on the radio, *Amahl and the Night Visitors* was not a success. What turned out to be very successful were one-off Christmas specials, the first of which was a Walt Disney production of Richard Wallace's *One Hour in Wonderland* (1950).[11] The program featured a ventriloquist and promoted Clyde Geronimi, Wilfred Jackson, and Hamilton Luske's animated film *Alice in Wonderland* (1951). Soon other specials followed featuring a wide variety of performances and formats, including ice skating, music, and animation. Some half-hour animated specials remain popular to this day, such as Larry Roemer's *Rudolph, the Red-Nosed Reindeer* (1964), Bill Melendez's *A Charlie Brown Christmas*

(1965), and Chuck Jones and Ben Washam's *How the Grinch Stole Christmas* (1966).[12] Oher specials, like *The Carpenters at Christmas*, went out of style.

*The Carpenters at Christmas* opens on a pre-recorded performance of the Christmas carol, "Sleigh Ride." The performance occurs on a large sound stage, with extravagant white décor and Christmas trees in the background. Once the ensemble finishes the musical number, the program shifts to a "behind the scenes" story and establishes the central conflict. Karen invites everyone to her Christmas party later that night, but Richard does not want to go. In a state of ennui, Richard wanders from location to location and meets other characters, played by past and present television stars. At a bowling alley, Richard meets comedian Harvey Korman (playing himself), who appeared on *The Carol Burnett Show* (1967–78). Korman joins Richard on his wanderings, and outside the bowling alley, the two meet the child actor Kristy McNichol (playing herself). She appeared on several 1970s television shows like *The Love Boat* (1977) and *The Bionic Woman* (1976). McNichol reveals that her parents have left her alone on Christmas. Richard has pity on her and invites her to Karen's party. After McNichol leaves the scene, Richard and Korman wander into a park and find a puppet show. The puppeteer, Burr Tillstrom, performs the characters Kukla and Ollie, who both appeared on the television show *Kukla, Fran, and Ollie* (1947–57). Korman, Kukla, and Ollie convince Richard to attend Karen's party. Richard and Korman pick up the puppets' stage and carry it to the party.

The program incorporates musical performances. In many cases, character fantasies motivate the songs. For example, when McNichol realizes that Richard is the famous performer Richard Carpenter, she wishes she could sing a song with Karen. This desire motivates a slow iris wipe to McNichols and Karen singing the Buddy Kaye and Jules Loman composition "Christmas Alphabet." Likewise, when Kuklka and Ollie ask Richard to sing his favorite Christmas song, their question motivates a fantasy, where Richard plays a highly technical piano arrangement of the traditional Christmas carol "O, Holy Night." During the performance, a large orchestra accompanies him, all on a large sound stage. However, not all songs are fantasies. In the bowling alley, Korman performs the Irving Berlin composition, "Top Hat, White Tie, and Tails." And at home, Karen performs Robert Wells and Mel Tormé's, "The Christmas Song." Once Richard, Korman, Kukla, and Ollie join the party, she and the group of attendants sing a festive song about New Year's Resolutions. The program concludes with a somber rendition of Domenico Bartolucci and Ray Charles' collaboration on "Christ is Born."

Communication scholar Stephen J. Lind points to four features of the Christmas television specials genre, the first of which is a universal and non-religious spirit of Christmas. This spirit of Christmas is, for Lind, best stated on a Christmas episode of *The Red Skelton Show* (1951–71). The actress Greer Garson (playing herself) claims that the "true spirit of Christmas" occurs when we make Christmas "a happy occasion for so many others."[13] In *The Carpenters at Christmas*, Karen expresses an identical but more elaborate sentiment. In a direct address to the camera, she says, "Christmas is a time for friends and family. It really is a special time. And I think that is why it is my favorite holiday of all." Similarly, in McNichol and Karen's performance of "Christmas Alphabet," the duo confirms that the "H" in Christmas represents "Happiness with all the family."

*A Very Murray Christmas* begins by subverting such familial Christmas spirit. In his hotel suite, Murray's phone rings, and both he and his producers hope it is George Clooney confirming his arrival for the special. Murray's anger toward the caller suggests that this is not the case. Once Murray hangs up the phone, he admits that the caller was his sister. As opposed to the happiness the Carpenters associate with family, Murray behaves in ways that promote the opposite.[14] It is, in fact, the success of the special that takes precedence over the happiness of family. Nevertheless, the film later affirms the spirit of Christmas through happiness, through a character claiming Christmas is their favored holiday, and through connection with others in a found family. Before singing "Baby, It's Cold Outside,"[15] The Waitress brings a drink to Murray, and he expresses his happiness because of her gift. She then explains that Christmas Eve is her "favorite night" of the year, because while it is cold outside, it is "warm" and "cozy" in the bar. Likewise, once Murray discovers that The Bride and Elliot the Groom have cancelled their engagement, he goes through considerable effort to reunify them and the new family they are forming together. And, perhaps most importantly, Murray unifies everyone in a found family at the bar, primarily through group singing—the precise elements present in the New Year's resolution number in *The Carpenters at Christmas*. While Murray undercuts the notion of family and happiness, he also displays happiness, reunifies a family, and encourages the creation of a found family.

Lind also notes the inclusion of a Scrooge character in Christmas specials, based on the famous Ebenezer Scrooge character in Charles Dickens' novella *A Christmas Carol* (1843). The Scrooge character is often presented as sad, depressed, curmudgeonly, and in some cases, the commercialization of Christmas contributes to the character's negative disposition. This dissatisfaction exists in tension with the reality that the program itself has commercial sponsorship. By the end of the episode, "this character is consistently reformed" in such a way that they can now "enjoy the universalized 'good'" of the Christmas spirit.[16] In *The Carpenters at Christmas*, Richard is the primary Scrooge character. Not only does he not want to attend Karen's

Christmas party, but, as he reveals in a scene with Korman, Richard is experiencing "a hint of the blues," and says "I really can't get into the Christmas spirit." Korman affirms Richard's response, saying, "Yeah, me neither. It's too commercial." However, like Lind notes, this sentiment exists in tension with the fact that, on several occasions, the program reminds the viewer that both Kodak and Timex are sponsors. By the end, Richard and Korman are reformed, primarily through the participation in the festivities at Karen's party.

*A Very Murray Christmas* begins with Murray taking up the role of the Scrooge character. In his hotel suite, Murray's first song is Sammy Cahn and David Holt's "Christmas Blues." Murray is not in the Christmas spirit, because a snowstorm has hit New York City. This means, in part, that no celebrities will be able to make his live Christmas special performance. Murray is so distraught that he cannot perform and weeps openly on stage. At the end of the program, Murray is indeed reformed. He wakes on Christmas morning, notes that Christmas is "good," sings the traditional English carol, "We Wish You a Merry Christmas," and offers Shaffer and Dimitri Dimitrov (as himself) a "Merry Christmas." The film concludes when he looks out of the window, precisely where he stood at the beginning of the film, says, "Merry Christmas, everyone," and smiles. However, unlike *A Christmas Carol*, Murray's reform does not occur only at the end of the film. Rather, in the middle of the film, his mood brightens through the reunification of The Bride and Elliot the Groom. He also brings festivities and Christmas merriment to the bar. The protagonist is both one who is reformed and the bringer of Christmas spirit to the bar.

Third, Lind observes that Christmas specials use both secular and sacred songs. Not only are carols common, but they may also tend to appear as aesthetic devices, with little motivation, commentary, or contextualization. "They may be meaningful to the characters, live studio audience members, or home viewers," but songs rarely "move the plot along"; rather they tend to serve emotional responses of the program, like "joyous and somber scenes."[17] *The Carpenters at Christmas* conforms to Lind's characterizations. The program uses carols like "Sleigh Ride," "The Christmas Song," and the lesser known "Christmas Alphabet." *The Carpenters at Christmas* also uses one non-Christmas song, Harvey Korman's performance of "Top Hat, White Tie, and Tails." The program also ends, not on the merriment from the party, but on incredibly the somber rendition of "Christ is Born," in which nearly every performer, with the exception of Karen, is dressed in black.

Like the Carpenters' special, *A Very Murray Christmas* incorporates both Christmas and non-Christmas songs. Coppola uses popular carols like "Let it Snow!," "Silent Night," and "Jingle Bells." It also employs one non-Christmas song, the 1970s Todd Rundgren hit, "I Saw the Light (Only You)." However, the film uses Christmas songs that subvert traditional representations of the

Christmas spirit. The film opens on Murray's performance of "Christmas Blues." Phoenix also performs the unreleased Beach Boys song, "Alone on Christmas Day." Finally, the found family concludes their time at the bar with a group sing-along to the unsentimental 1980s hit, "Fairytale of New York," by the Celtic punk band The Pogues. Like many Christmas specials, Coppola uses these songs primarily as aesthetic devices. However, their presence suggests that the universal notion of Christmas spirit cannot contain what actually transpires on the holiday. But the film does not sustain this critique. By the end, Murray reaffirms the goodness of Christmas, albeit without the kind of sentimentality of specials like *The Carpenters at Christmas*.

Finally, Christmas specials tend to traffic in frivolousness, particularly through lighthearted entertainment and a longing for the past. As cultural historian David Budgen notes, Christmas specials are "frivolous, appealing to a broad audience, conveying a warm sense of nostalgia rather than cutting-edge entertainment."[18] *The Carpenters at Christmas* presents itself as unrelentingly lighthearted. Its frivolity is, perhaps, most acute in Richard's Scrooge persona. Unlike Dickens' Scrooge, who performs cruelties on others, Richard's sadness takes the form of a childish pout. After rejecting Karen's invitation, he walks to a bowling alley and orders a cup of coffee to "think . . . a little more" and admits to having "a hint of the blues." Richard's cruelty reaches its apex in his interaction with Korman. When the comedian says that Richard might recognize him from his previous work in show business, Richard responds, "I don't watch cartoon shows." And, what eventually motivates Richard to attend Karen's party is nostalgic, silly merriment: an old vaudevillian style act that puppeteer Burr Tillstrom's performs with his Kukla and Ollie characters, characters who had not appeared on television for almost twenty years. Hence, frivolity and nostalgia intersect in this sequence and become the means that reform Richard. *A Very Murray Christmas* certainly embraces frivolity and nostalgia. Coppola's film presents its most lighthearted moments in its fantasy sequence. Here, Murray, Cyrus, and Clooney perform Christmas carols on a sound stage, emulating the opening white decorations in *The Carpenters at Christmas*. Coppola also presents nostalgia, albeit in a more muted form. Several of the performers reached their artistic and commercial peak in the years prior to *A Very Murray Christmas*. Paul Shaffer, for example, was best known for his decades' long role as musical director for *Late Night with David Letterman* (1982–1993) and *The Late Show with David Letterman* (1993–2015). Likewise, David Johansen was best known as front man for the 1970s punk band The New York Dolls.

While the film affirms and subverts these elements of television Christmas specials, this mode of generic analysis is limited. It cannot grapple with several unstated assumptions embedded withing the genre, assumptions that Coppola subverts, namely disembodiment and professionalism. Embodiment and a lack of professionalism create the conditions for joy. In order to explain how joy becomes manifest in the film, we will make use of literary theorist Mikhail Bakhtin's notion of carnival as a critical framework.

## THE CARNIVALESQUE

Mikhail Bakhtin was born in 1895 to a Russian family of minor nobility. His work has influenced scholars from a wide variety of disciplines, including literature, linguistics, anthropology, theology, political science, but most relevant to this chapter, cinema, television, and communication theory.[19] Bakhtin wrote primarily about Western literature (like sixteenth-century French writer François Rabelais and 19th-century Russian author Fyodor Dostoevsky) and philosophy. Bakhtin's interest in art and philosophy was not an attempt to escape into the abstract realm of academic ideas. He was primarily interested in the realm of daily life, in the "prosaic" nature of the "everyday,"[20] precisely because both life and literature assume that authors, like people, have a responsibility to others.[21] Hence, scholars often read Bakhtin's work as having distinct and substantial contributions to ethical reflection and on what makes for healthy everyday existence. In making these ethical claims, Bakhtin often turned to unlikely sources, like medieval carnival rituals.

While precursors for carnivals reach back to the Dionysian and Saturnalian festivals of the Greeks and Romans, Bakhtin focuses on the pre-Lenten festivals of the High Middle Ages as the ritualistic precursor for what appears in Western literature. Muted aspects of the carnivalesque appear in present day pre-Lenten festivals such as New Orleans' Mardi Gras or in Carnivals throughout the Caribbean and South America; however, Bakhtin understands that the true social power of the medieval ritual was to turn the world of the participants temporarily upside down. Readers of Bakhtin, like film scholar Robert Stam, often interpret the carnival as holding radical, political possibilities. Stam notes, "carnival represented . . . the ludic undermining of all norms," in which "all that is marginalized and excluded—the mad, the scandalous, the aleatory—takes over the center."[22] The literary embodiment of the ritual, according to Bakhtin, displays a host of tropes and features that critique social norms that harm the marginalized. For example, the carnivalesque celebrates the "lower bodily stratum"[23] and represents abnormal psychic states.[24] Such features centralize what typical hierarchies of the Middle Ages usually ignored. Crucially, the carnivalesque leads to life-giving regeneration, like celebration, joy, and poking fun at the difficulties of life.

In cinema and television, the carnivalesque can take a wide variety of forms. In films such as *Blazing Saddles* (1974), American filmmaker Mel Brooks uses bodily humor as a regenerative force. In the famous bean-eating scene, where several characters "blech" and "pass gas," "the lower body stratum" brings the film's villains "down to the earth."[25] The scene is regenerative because, "To laugh at these corporeal commonalties, to acknowledge them, is to make everyone equal."[26] In Tim Story's film *Barbershop* (2002), similar carnivalesque features are at work, particularly through Eddie's (Cedric the Entertainer) demeaning of others. Humor brings "those individuals down to earth who have positioned themselves as superior" to others.[27] "Hence, "friendly 'abuse' cements communality," because it restores the equality of all who are part of the group.[28] Likewise, in the 1950s, television performer Maila Nurmi used her "Vampira" persona on hosted horror television shows as "a public space for resisting social hierarchies and dominant values."[29] Nurmi mixed elements of humor and bondage/discipline sexuality that "parodied everyday life, which in the mid-1950s ranged from domestic values to prevailing modes of television presentation."[30] Paul Feig's *Bridesmaids* (2011) offers a more recent iteration of these elements. The group of mostly middle-class bridesmaids eat lunch before visiting an upper-class, high-end bridal shop. Unbeknownst to the women, they have nearly all contracted food poisoning from lunch, and the scene ends with most of the women uncontrollably vomiting or defecating in, on, and around high-end dresses. Because the women are mostly middle class, their presence represents an aspiration to rise from middle to upper-class life. In the scene, lower bodily functions, in part, bring low the pretentions of and aspirations to upper-class culture.

Bakhtin makes clear, however, that the elements of the carnival in literature appear in muted and metaphorical form. What Bakhtin points out about literature is true of cinema and television. The carnivalesque is merely the trace or echo of the ritual.[31] Nevertheless, there are at least two echoes of the carnival in *A Very Murray Christmas*, the seven series and the grotesque body. These elements subvert two deeper generic features of the Christmas special: disembodiment and professionalism, respectively.

## THE SEVEN SERIES AND (DIS)EMBODIMENT

In the novels of Rabelais, Bakhtin identifies seven elements of the lower-stratum affiliated with the carnivalesque: the body, clothing, food, drink, sex, death, and defecation.[32] The medieval world often seems to have understood bodies negatively, as objects of decay and vulnerability.[33] In contrast, Rabelais represents the human body and physiological functions as a way to affirm the complexity, depth, and significance of life.[34] Of all the objects Rabelais brings into contact with the body, food and drink dominate,[35] particularly in excessive, lengthy, detailed representations of feasts or banquets.[36] Often, gluttony and drunkenness point out the hypocrisy of the so-called ascetic, disciplined existence of Christian monastic life in the period.[37] Through defecation, whether through themes of "arse-wiping" or urination, Rabelais brings low the high and wealthy.[38] Sexuality may take a range of forms, "from the bawdy joke and anecdote to . . . marriage,"[39] and sexual acts create new life that "destroy[s] the established hierarchy of values."[40] Within this affirmative stance toward bodily existence, Rabelais presents the threat that death poses to the body as a matter about which audiences should laugh.[41] He presents life as triumphant, embracing death, laughter, food, sex, and the body in a new, integrated whole. In the seven series, the lower bodily functions affirm not only life but also represent a new, holistic view of the human body, a view absent from both the Middle Ages and Romantic and post-Romantic literature. In fact, this holistic view of the body would eventually give way to Romanticism's non-holistic, disembodied view of life.[42]

Of these seven series, *A Very Murray Christmas* includes the elements of sex, food, and drink in five sequences or scenes. In the first sequence, a moment of sexual humor appears in Murray and The Waitress' performance of "Baby, It's Cold Outside." The song was likely intended as a cute interaction between two consenting adults, a man who wants his woman companion to stay longer. She, however, wants to go home. Many twenty-first-century interpreters have taken the song as the documentation of the woman's lack of consent. The line the woman sings, "Say what's in this drink?," suggests that the man has drugged her beverage, a tactic common to incidences of sexual assault. Contrary to these readings, Murray and The Waitress perform the song with a charming, humorous, and frivolous affect. Also, instead of singing all the written lyrics, Murray improvises bawdy sex jokes along the way, rendering him less of a sexual threat. Early in the song, he takes The Waitress' hand and notes, "Your hands are like ice!" Later, he takes her presumably cold hand, places it under his arm, and says, "This is the second warmest spot on the human body," and proceeds to say that this "trick" can keep The Waitress' fingers from freezing, turning black, and falling off. Murray's introduction of warm armpits, along with frostbitten fingers, diffuses his character's sexual interest in The Waitress. Furthermore, he references his underarms as the body's second warmest spot, implying that the groin is the first. He does not use the reference as a sexual invitation. The joke's purpose is sheer (perhaps frivolous) fun, delight, and refreshment rather than a threat. We are not convinced that this use of humor successfully diffuses the song's misogyny. However, the performance clearly draws on playful sexual comedy.

Sexual humor also appears in Murray's fantasy sequence, particularly in "Santa Claus Wants Some Lovin.'" Originally made famous by the blues guitarist and singer Albert King, the song is from the perspective of a father who know that Christmas day is for his children. However, "right now Mama it's Christmas Eve/Come make your papa happy please." In a heterosexual familial context, Murray declares his desire for sex with the mother of their children. Like his previous performances in the film, Murray engages in a variety of silliness and improvised jokes that distract from a threatening form of sexuality. For example, during the instrumental break of the song, a group of women dancers surround him, and they are much younger and more beautiful than he is. As they dance around him, he marvels at them, "Now, holy-moly . . . " Because the context of the song has established his desire for sexual contact, the exclamation, on its own, suggests that he is marveling at them as sexual objects. However, the punch line of the joke diffuses such a reading, "What size shoe is that anyway? Is that a seven-and-a-half, eight? . . . You're awful fine, but I don't think you're mine." He does not marvel at their bodies but at the size of their feet, and then rejects them as potential sexual partners. And during the chorus, Clooney sticks his head out from behind the Christmas trees and, in a clearly unprofessional singing voice delivers the lines, "Santa Claus wants some lovin'." Although Clooney represented for many years a sexy, A-list Hollywood star, here his unprofessional singing voice does not make the lines sexy in any regard. Rather, his embodiment of sexuality, here in bad singing, is not unlike Murray's interaction with The Waitress. It is sexuality as sheer fun, silliness, and frivolity.

Third, during the bar sequence, the film exploits drinking, drunkenness, and death as a feature of revelries. After the power goes out and Shaffer and Murray retire to the bar, the revelries begin when The Waitress brings the two men drinks. During the beginning of the banquet, Murray encourages The Bartender to pour champagne for everyone. When Murray and The Lounge Singer encourage Elliot the Groom to reconcile with The Bride, The Lounge Singer forces Elliot the Groom to drink a "Soiled Kimono." As the bar sequence concludes, the protagonist pours the group shots of vodka and tequila. They all sing "Fairytale of New York," which opens with lines that link drunkenness and Christmas. The Bartender sings, "It was Christmas Eve, babe/In the drunk tank." Like sexuality, drunkenness violates the typical representation of Christmas spirit. The scene in the song opens with a singer, arrested for public intoxication on Christmas eve. The singer continues, this time adding the death sequence, "An old man said to me/won't see another one." Again, death subverts the frivolity of Christmas specials and the Christmas spirit, but here Coppola links them together. Despite this dark beginning, the song eventually ends with an uplifting sense of optimism. The group sings with passion "And the bells were ringing out on Christmas day." However, the drunkenness and death at the beginning of the song counters typical Christmas frivolity. The sequence also ends with Murray, drunk, passing out on the floor. Unlike any of the musical numbers in *The Carpenters at Christmas*, Murray's drunkenness motivates the dream sequence with Cyrus and Clooney.

Finally, during the bar sequence, several scenes surrounding Elliot the Groom and The Bride bring together the elements of sex, food, and drink. While no sex jokes or sexual acts appear in this sequence, Bakhtin understands marriage to be fundamentally sexual in nature. So, the marriage sequence carries with it the implication of sexual consummation and the creation of a new (in this case, heterosexual) family. The sequence begins with the couple estranged, and the marriage celebration in ruins. The Waitress takes Murray into the bar's kitchen. There, the Chef expresses his despair to Murray, because the wedding was called off. All the food he made for the wedding reception will go to waste. Murray, in an act that aims to lift their despair, orders the Chef and his crew to bring the food and drink into the bar, creating a banquet for everyone. The banquet, along with the songs that follow, becomes the means to create a new community, not a reunion of an estranged family (like Richard and Karen) but the creation of a found family.

Moreover, one of the most intense scenes in the seven series is The Lounge Singer's "Soiled Kimono" joke. The "Soiled Kimono" refers to a sketch written and performed by the first *SNL* head writer, Michael O'Donoghue, whom Murray knew since he was one of *SNL*'s founding cast members.[43] *A Very Murray Christmas*'s producer Mitch Glazer also had a long-time relationship with O'Donoghue, including their co-written 1988 Christmas film, *Scrooged*, in which Murray starred.[44] While on *SNL*, O'Donoghue wrote and performed a recurring sketch, "Mr. Mike's Least-Loved Bedtime Tales," in which he would recount demented stories including "The Soiled Kimono." The piece begins with Mr. Mike (O'Donoghue) tending bar, and a drunken patron (Laraine Newman) begs him for a Least-Loved Bedtime Tale. He will provide her with one, but only on the condition that she sings an aria from the opera *Madame Butterfly* (1904). While she sings, the text of two items scrolls on the screen: a recipe for a Soiled Kimono and the story of its origin, the latter of which involves an angry American solder throwing the ingredients of the drink at an unfaithful lover.[45] After the lover exclaims that the drink is delicious, she kisses the soldier and then kills the soldier, "hit[ting] him in the lungs with a gardening tool."[46] Upon O'Donoghue's death in 1994, Murray delivered a comedic eulogy on *SNL*, during which "The Soiled Kimono" sketch was replayed in its entirety. Murray concluded the eulogy, offering a toast to the writer's widow with a Soiled Kimono in his hand.[47] The eulogy and Glazer's relationship with O'Donoghue suggest that the Soiled Kimono joke has the sketch and its author in mind.

Given the history of the sketch, its use in the film constitutes a particularly intense intersection of sexuality and drink. After Murray encourages Eliot the Groom to reconcile with The Bride, The Lounge Singer walks up to Eliot the Groom and says, "You ever try a Soiled Kimono?" When he protests, she responds, "Just drink it." She places the glass on his mouth, lifts his chin back into a posture of submission, and forces him to ingest the entire drink. The alcoholic beverage evokes Bakhtin's drink series. However, it also draws on the sexuality of common cocktail names, like "Sex on the Beach" or "Dirty Banana." The "soiled" descriptor in the name of the drink evokes sexuality, perhaps a sexual act that soils or sullies the kimono.[48] This scene bears some similarities but also very important differences to queer cultural studies scholars Lauren Berlant and Michael Warner's description of a performance of erotic vomiting. In the performance, a "top" force fed a "bottom" an assortment of "milk" and "foods."[49] As the name of the act suggests, the scene reaches its climax with the top forcing the bottom to vomit. Berlant and Warner write, "Finally, as the top inserts two, then three fingers in the bottom's throat, insistently offering his own stomach for the repeated climaxes, we realize that we have never seen such a display of trust and violation."[50] This moment in the film is clearly not built around the complexity or consensuality of the erotic vomiting that Berlant and Warner observe. However, like the performance, this moment links sexuality and food. In the sketch, violence, drink, and sexuality occur at the site of the lovers' bodies. This film's joke echoes these features. The Lounge Singer forces Eliot the Groom to drink, and while it is not an explicitly sexual act, it does evoke the top and bottom roles present like in like public displays of erotic vomiting.

The range of these carnivalesque examples suggest that part of what *A Very Murray Christmas* subverts in the Christmas special is the non-holistic representation of the body, or more to the point, the disembodiment that shows like *The Carpenters at Christmas* assume. Bakhtin argues that, through features like the seven series, Rabelais presents a healthy, holistic, affirmative stance toward bodily life. That life is ultimately triumphant and integrated, because it embraces the so-called lower features of the body, like death, laughter, food, sex, and the like. To the extent that *A Very Murray Christmas* embraces elements of the seven series—sex, food, and drink—and does so without irony and with laughter and delight, it represents an affirmative, carnivalesque embodiment. *The Carpenters at Christmas*, by comparison, suffers from a disembodied view of life.[51] By denying lived experiences like sex, food, and drink, *The Carpenters at Christmas* disassociates itself from the bodies of their performers and artists. Certainly, that disassociation is not absolute. In the recording studio, performers sang and played instruments, which they pretend to do during filming. Performers also dance on screen. All of these features are embodied practices. Yet, in denying the lower bodily stratum, the program denies the fullness of holistic bodily life. And it is precisely the body, or to be more precise, the grotesque body, that Coppola presents as a mechanism of joy.

## HYBRIDIZED-GROTESQUE BODIES AND PROFESSIONALISM

The work of communication scholar Leslie Baxter and her colleagues focuses primarily on interpersonal relationships; however, her interpretation of Bakhtin offers a constructive way to understand features of *A Very Murray Christmas*. Baxter implies that a grotesque body is a hybridized body, filled with dichotomies of opposition. Beginning with Bakhtin's notion of dialogue, Baxter argues that the dialogic is, fundamentally, a "contradiction-ridden" reality favoring a "both/and" dialectic.[52] As a result, dialogue foregrounds "the struggle of competing discourses"[53] and does not "presuppose a center."[54] Baxter frames the competition between discourses as a dichotomy between oppositional states. The carnivalesque has within it these same dialogic dichotomies of opposition, filled with the tensions between the "sacred" and "profane," the "lofty" and the "low," the "great" and "insignificant," the "wise" and the "foolish."[55] In interpersonal encounters, Baxter claims that such dialectical oppositions abound. She notes, for example, the tensions between the individual and community[56] or between connection with others and autonomy from them.[57] Because ongoing tensions, or flux between these oppositions, is what defines relationships, Baxter suggests that relationships may take a hybridized form. "A hybrid," she insists, "is a construction in which the formerly competing discourses are still identifiable yet are repositioned as compatible. Think of hybrids as salad dressing made by mixing oil and vinegar. The discourses (oil, vinegar) are distinct, yet they combine to form a new meaning—salad dressing."[58] *A Very Murray Christmas* takes up the hybridized, dichotomy of oppositions in Coppola's choice of singers. This group of singers, and sometimes individual singers, represent what Bakhtin describes as a grotesque body.

For Bakhtin, the grotesque body is a hybridized dichotomy of oppositions that serves a specific purpose, takes a particular form, and subverts standard notions of beauty, all as a means to produce joy. Like the seven series, a grotesque body degrades, or lowers, whatever is "high, spiritual, ideal, abstract," to the place of materiality or the earth.[59] The grotesque presents material bodies as mixed or ambivalent bodies, sometimes presenting two or more bodies in a single body.[60] By way of example, Bakhtin points to the image of the pregnant hag. Present in ancient Greek terracotta figurines, these women are not only old and senile, but they are full of life and often laugh. This grotesque body "is ambivalent . . . There is nothing completed, nothing calm and stable," nothing final in a such a body.[61] Grotesque bodies also subvert conventional standards of beauty. From the perspective of "'classic' aesthetics,"—perhaps from the ancient or medieval perspective, which views the beautiful body as a unified, complete figure—the ambivalence and contradictions of the grotesque appear as "ugly," "monstrous,"[62] "hideous and formless."[63] But in subverting these aesthetic norms, the materiality of the grotesque body presents a holistic body, "[a]nd this whole" insists Bakhtin, "is gay and gracious."[64] Which is to say, the degradation that a hybridized body represents as monstrous, ugly, and hideous can function as a means of joy.

Like the non-holistic disembodiment of Romanticism, contemporary instances of the grotesque body tend toward weak manifestations of their medieval predecessors, albeit not without the possibility of a renewed vitality. In an almost pessimistic register, Bakhtin notes that "almost nothing has remained of the ambivalent meaning" of the grotesque body; rather, "bare cynicism" persists.[65] As a result, older expressions of the grotesque tend to be alien to contemporary representations of the body.[66] "The entire field of realistic literature of the last three centuries," Bakhtin opines, "is strewn with the fragments of grotesque realism."[67] Hence, what is true of literature is evident in cinema. Films like John Landis' *National Lampoon's Animal House* (1978), Bob Clark's *Porky's* (1981), or Todd Phillips' *The Hangover* (2009) do represent grotesque moments, but such moments are cynical, mean-spirited, and reinforce contemporary notions of beauty. They lack ambivalence, wholeness, graciousness, and joy. However, Bakhtin holds out the possibility that some contemporary examples of the grotesque "are not mere remnants of the past but manifest a renewed vitality."[68] A grotesque mechanism of joy is part of what is at play in passages of *A Very Murray Christmas*, and it is at play in at least two ways.

First, Coppola centralizes Bill Murray and his hybrid performance as a "bad-good" or "unprofessional-professional" singer. Murray's performance is not unique. It comes from a tradition within American popular culture. "Bad-good" singers in American popular music appear, for example, in the discourse around singer-songwriter Bob Dylan's voice. Critics have noted that he possesses a "bad" singing voice, and yet many still laud his "good" singing; which is to say, he can convey artistic and musical significance through his "broken" instrument.[69] This type of voice, in Bakhtinian terms, is a grotesque embodiment of a "bad-good" singer. While a full discussion of this hybridized voice is outside the scope of this chapter, it is enough to note that Dylan acknowledges not only his critics but also other singers within this tradition of grotesque embodiment.

> Critics say I can't sing. I croak. Sound like a frog. Why don't critics say that same thing about Tom Waits? Critics say my voice is shot. That I have no voice. Why don't they say those things about Leonard Cohen? Why do I get special treatment? Critics say I can't carry a tune and I talk my way through a song.

Really? I've never heard that said about Lou Reed. Why does he get to go scot-free?[70]

Not unlike Dylan, Waits, Cohen, or Reed, Murray has long embodied this grotesque means of performance.

Albeit in a comic register, it is this tradition of "good-bad" singing in which Murray participates, perhaps most notably during his time on *SNL*. His character "Nick the Lounge Singer" demonstrates that he cannot sing with the technical proficiency of "good" or "professional" singers, like Aretha Franklin, Whitney Houston, or Ariana Grande. In those performances, which Shaffer also accompanies, Murray's character inhabits grandiose excesses. In one *SNL* sketch, he begins with a rendition of Richard Strauss' "Also Sprach Zarathustra, Op. 30."[71] Murray not only sings at the high end of his register and cannot accurately hit those pitches, but he is also performing at a run-down ski lodge. He performs Strauss' composition with other science fiction movie themes, and Murray is likely referencing director Stanley Kubrick's use of the composition in his science fiction classic *2001: A Space Odyssey* (1968). The comedy here works on disparity, contrasting the pretentious ambition of human achievement and capacity (present in both Strauss and Kubrick) with Murray's inability to perform it well and the lowliness of the locale. And yet, within or perhaps because of his significant limitations—his limited vocal range or his inability to always sing pitches accurately—he proves an effective performer, not unlike those Dylan names above in this tradition of "bad-good" singers. It is likely this hybridization, this tension between Murray's incapacities and his capacities, that provokes from viewers like Coppola positive reactions, like love or pleasure.

When compared to Nick the Lounge Singer, Murray's performance in *A Very Murray Christmas* offers a more attenuated embodiment of "bad-good" singing. The film opens with Murray's rendition of "Christmas Blues." The vocal range of the song is limited, and Murray does not struggle to accurately perform any of those pitches, especially early in the song. His voice is aged and embodies the sadness and disappointments of Christmas. After the bridge section of the song, the lyrics bestow blessings on the listener, "May all your days be merry/Your seasons full of cheer," and he sings these lines in the same tenor of resigned sadness. However, he sings the next lines, "But 'til it's January/I'm gonna go disappear," with a different affect. He closes his eyes, lifts his hands in the air, as if in disappointment, and sings the last line behind the beat, evoking an exaggerated sadness. All of these gestures suggest a comical sense of self-loathing, the most extreme musical and emotional choices in the song so far. It is not that Murray makes technical mistakes in this song, like he does with his performance of Strauss decades earlier. Rather, this performance accepts his limitations as a "bad" singer, a performer with bodily limitations. Those limitations open up creative possibilities for an effective or "good" performance, particularly with the emotional and comedic affect. Hence, the sadness of the song becomes a site of joy, perhaps not for the singer, but for the audience, who can delight at his exaggerated sense of self-loathing on Christmas eve.

Second, in addition to Murray's embodiment of a grotesque "bad-good" singer, Coppola presents a group of singers singing as a mixed body of "unprofessional-professional" singers. The film has performances by unambivalently "professional" singers, which make up the majority of the singers who appear on screen. Although she has had a solo career, Jenny Lewis (as The Waitress) was, most notably, the lead singer and guitarist for the indie rock band Rilo Kiley. Thomas Mars (as Chef) is the lead singer of the French Pop band, Phoenix. And known primarily for her solo musical career, Miley Cyrus (as herself) was also star of the hit Disney television show *Hanna Montana* (2006–11), where she played a pop singer living a double life. Maya Rudolf's backup singers (Cindy Mizelle, Tawatha Agee, and Rachele Cappelli) also sing like "professional" singers. While not an unambivalent "professional" singer, Rudolf performs with the technical acumen approaching these professional singers. Against this backdrop of professional singers, Murray and former The New York Dolls front man David Johansen participate in the tradition of "bad-good" singing. The film presents Chris Rock (as himself), Rashida Jones (as The Bride), and Jason Schwartzman (as Elliott the Groom) as unambivalently "unprofessional" singers. Hence, taken as a whole, the cast is a grotesque, hybridized body of "unprofessional-professional," "bad-good" singers.

The focal point of the ugly or hideous singing of this grotesque body is most evident in the group's performance of "Fairytale in New York." Coppola includes Jenny Lewis, Maya Rudolf, the backup singers, Murray, David Johansen, Rashida Jones, and Jason Schwartzman. On the final chorus of the song, everyone performs live, some singers singing in unison and others in harmony. What this grotesque group of "unprofessional-professional" singers produces is a wide range of intonation inaccuracies, inconsistencies, and other ugly sounding mistakes, hideous by professional standards. These errors violate the contemporary aesthetic of recorded music, which prioritizes perfection and achieves perfection for all singers through technologies like pitch correcting software.[72] Coppola not only leaves these mistakes in the film, but the sound mix also deemphasizes singers who might make fewer mistakes, like the backup singers, who are virtually inaudible. What this hideous-sounding, grotesque body represents is an inclusive "gay and gracious"[73] space, a space of joy and forgiveness. So-called mistakes in this context are not counted against singers. In effect, they are forgiven, and more importantly, function as markers of inclusion. Perfection is not the goal of this moment. Rather, because the plot of the film presents these characters as a found family, inclusion into the family yields this hybridized, grotesque body.

The grotesqueness of these errors makes clear, as a genre, that Christmas specials' assume professionalism. When compared to *The Carpenters at Christmas*, *A Very Murray Christmas* celebrates the grotesque bodies of "bad" singing, whereas *The Carpenters at Christmas*, and other Christmas specials like it, prioritize perfection, what Bakhtin might call a televisual version of classic aesthetics.[74] This means, in part, that the genre of Christmas specials are inherently exclusionary, elitist spaces, played out at the site of musical performance. Only a select few are welcome into the performance of universal Christmas spirit and the affirmation of family.

The grotesque bodies that perform imperfections carry in their music a politics of inclusion, but, in the case of *A Very Murray Christmas*, it is an inclusion that lacks equality. Immediately, the singing of performers like Chris Rock, Jason Schwartzman, Rashida Jones, and other "bad" singing signals that perfection or professionalism need not be the sole criterion that qualifies one to participate in the familial aspect of the universal Christmas spirit. In fact, their inclusion suggests that the so-called universal Christmas spirit was never fundamentally universal in character. Relatedly, up until Coppola's most recent film, *On the Rocks* (2020), *A Very Murray Christmas* has her most racially diverse cast. The Bride (Rashida Jones), Chris Rock (as himself), Maya Rudolf (The Lounge Singer), two backup singers (Cindy Mizelle and Tawatha Agee), three dancers (only one of whom is identifiable as Jenny Laroche), and one musician (drummer Steve Jordan) present as racialized minorities or identify as bi-racial. Given that her previous films are virtually all populated by white actors (and a handful of Japanese actors in the case of *Lost in Translation*), that increased diversity is, unfortunately, a relatively low bar.

However, the inclusion of persons of color implies several limitations of Coppola subversion of the Christmas special. For all the participants in the film, some version of professionalism is essential to inclusion in this diverse space. Minor characters of color in the film are professional in their particular field. For the unprofessional singers of color, they are successful professionals in some other field. In as much as *A Very Murray Christmas* subverts the politics of professionalism, it also upholds it. Furthermore, there is no compelling reason to not include more people of color, whether they are professional singers or professional musicians or dancers. Finally, because the majority of singers who appear on screen are professional, the film presupposes a "center" of professionalism, around which "unprofessional" singers can be included. Taken together with the reality that the majority of the cast presents as white, there is inclusion in the film, but it is an inclusion that exists without equity. White professionalism is the center around which inclusion must take place.

By way of implications, we conclude this chapter with a reflection on joy and equity. The film suggests that joy is only possible if the body and its lower, grotesque realities are affirmed and included. If joy is present in *The Carpenters at Christmas*, it can be described as a positive emotional state of happiness or a pleasant state.[75] Likewise, joy functions as an emotional response to situations of connection, not unlike joy in other situations, such as "watching your kids playing kindly with each other, having an otherwise unexceptional meal with your family, [or] running in a field on a sunny spring day."[76] To these descriptions of joy, *The Carpenters at Christmas* places limiting conditions. The act of singing serves as the metaphorical representation of those conditions. Like musicologist Christopher Small points out, musical performances embody ideals that communities hold valuable, whether it is the rough unprofessionalism of punk rock music or the perfectionism of high art concert music.[77] In *The Carpenters at Christmas*, the perfection and professionalism suggest that the many voices of a choir, party, or orchestra must conform to a set of standards and expectations. The effect of those standards is the production of a homogenous community. In a limited way, *A Very Murray Christmas* suggests that another version of joy is possible. Embodiment, as opposed to the overwhelming disembodiment of *The Carpenters at Christmas*, serves as a prerequisite for joy. Joy needs bodies. Furthermore, joy does not demand perfection. If joy is that positive state akin to happiness, a deep connection with the self and others, then an embodied joy can facilitate the inclusion of those with so-called capacity and incapacity. In this context, incapacity is, in many ways, more foundational to joy than any other criteria. Which is to say, it is not mere bodily or lower bodily existence that has to be affirmed and included for joy to be a possibility. But what communities perceive (rightly or wrongly) as weaknesses or incapacities must also be affirmed and included for social spaces to have the possibility of the fullness of joy. These so-called lower, grotesque, embodied realities are, in fact, prerequisites for the possibility of joy.

In addition to the condition of bodily weakness or incapacity, Coppola's film suggests that, like Bakhtin, whatever is the center of a hierarchical society must be decentered for equity to exist. When Coppola presents "bad" or "good-bad" singers as sites of joy, she signals the possibility that the grotesque body can be a body of equality. That *A Very Murray Christmas* presents inclusion without equality, however, is illustrative. If, like Small implies, social ideas (and their corresponding problems) are embodied in musical performance, then what is at play in *A Very Murray Christmas* is a system not unlike what Isabel Wilkerson describes as caste. "If we have been trained," writes Wilkerson, "to see humans in the language of race, then caste is the underlying grammar ... Caste, like grammar, becomes an invisible guide ... the autonomic calculations that figure into a sentence without our having to think about it."[78] In *A Very Murray Christmas*, the center of the caste system is white professionalism. If the Bakhtinian grotesque body is an ambivalent body without a center, then *A Very Murray Christmas* demonstrates that inclusion, in and of itself, will never produce equity. While the unquestioned center is, perhaps, part of what keeps Coppola's films from providing more radical social critiques, her failure is only reflective of larger societal failures. At the conclusion of her book, Wilkerson writes,

> The fact is that the bottom caste, though it bears much of the burden of the hierarchy, did not create the caste system, and the bottom caste alone cannot fix it. The challenge has long been that many in the dominant caste, who are in a better position to fix caste inequity, have often been least likely to want to.[79]

What Coppola's unquestioned center demonstrates is that, for those of us in the dominant caste, there is considerable work left to perform, and unless we perform it, no amount of our subversions will ever produce anything like a true, fulsome, embodied joy. Our next chapters, on *Lost in Translation* and *On the Rocks*, turns from joy to another way of being in the world—to the possibility of love.

## REFERENCES

*A Very Murray Christmas*. Directed by Sofia Coppola. Los Gatos, CA: Netflix.www.netflix.com/title/80042368.

Bachor, Kenneth. "A Very Murray Christmas Director Sofia Coppola: I Wanted To Do Something 'Joyful.'" *Time*, December 4, 2015. time.com/4132069/sofia-coppola-a-very-murray-christmas/.

Bakhtin, Mikhail M. *Art and Answerability: Early Essays by M. M. Bakhtin*. Translated by Vadim Liapunov. Austin, TX: University of Texas Press, 1990.

———. *Rabelais and His World*. Translated by Helene Iswolsky. Bloomington, IN: Indiana University Press, 1984.

———. *The Dialogic Imagination: Four Essays by M. M. Bakhtin*. Translated by Caryl Emerson and Michael Holquist. Austin, TX: University of Texas Press, 1982.

Baxter, Leslie A. "A Tale of Two Voices: Relational Dialectics Theory." *The Journal of Family Communication* 4, no. 3 and 4 (2004): 181–92.

———. *Voicing Relationships: A Dialogic Perspective*. Los Angeles: Sage Publications, 2010.

Baxter, Leslie A. and Barbara M. Montgomery. *Relating: Dialogues and Dialectics*. New York: The Guilford Press, 1996.

Baxter, Leslie A. and Kristen M. Norwood. "Relational Dialectics Theory: Navigating Meaning From Competing Discourses." In *Engaging Theories in Interpersonal*

*Communication: Multiple Perspectives*, edited by Leslie A. Baxter and Dawn O. Braithwaite, 279–291. Thousand Oaks, CA: Sage 2015.
Belarmino, Melanie and Melinda R. Roberts. "Japanese Gender Role Expectations and Attitudes: A Qualitative Analysis of Gender Inequality." *Journal of International Women's Studies* 20 no. 7 (August 2019): 272–288.
Berlant, Lauren and Michael Warner. "Sex in Public." In *The Cultural Studies Reader*, 2nd ed., edited by Simon During, 354–367. New York: Routledge, 1999.
Biancully, David. "Netflix Wishes You A 'Murray Christmas' In A Cheerful, Irony-Free Holiday Special." *Fresh Air*, December 3, 2015, www.npr.org/2015/12/03/458303447/netflix-wishes-you-a-murray-christmas-in-a-cheerful-irony-free-holiday-special.
"Bill Murray's Eulogy for Michael O'Donoghue (delivered on *Saturday Night Live* the week he died, in 1994)." Special feature in *Mr. Mike's Mondo Video*. Directed by Michael O'Donoghue. 1979; Burbank, CA: New Line Cinema. DVD.
Bonnstetter, Beth E. "Mel Brooks Meets Kenneth Burke (and Mikhail Bakhtin): Comedy and Burlesque in Satiric Film." *Journal of Film and Video* 63, no. 1 (Spring 2011): 18–31.
Bordo, Susan. *Unbearable Weight, Feminism, Western Culture, and the Body*. Berkeley, CA: University of California Press, 1993.
Bowie, David. "Song for Bob Dylan." Track 9 on *Hunky Dory*. RCA Records, 1971, Apple Music.
Bowler, Gerry. *The World Encyclopedia of Christmas*. Toronto, ON: McClelland & Stewart, 2000.
Budgen, David. "'Halfway Out of the Dark': Steven Moffat's *Doctor Who* Christmas Specials." In *The Eleventh Hour: A Critical Celebration of the Matt Smith and Steven Moffat Era*, edited by Andrew O'Day, 89–105. London: I.B. Tauris, 2014.
*The Carpenters at Christmas*. Directed by Bob Henry. 1977; New York, The American Broadcasting Company.
Carson, Tom. "Mr. Mike's 'SNL' Nightmare." *Grantland*, August 22, 2014. grantland.com/features/michael-odonoghue-snl-saturday-night-live-mr-mike/.
Carter, Bill. "Michael O'Donoghue, 54, Dies; Writer for *Saturday Night Live*." *The New York Times*, November 10, 1994. www.nytimes.com/1994/11/10/obituaries/michael-o-donoghue-54-dies-writer-for-saturday-night-live.html.
Chappell, Ben. "Bakhtin's Barbershop: Film as Folklorist." *Western Folklore* 64, no. 3–4 (Summer-Fall 2005): 209–229.
Coy, Maddy. "This Body Which Is Not Mine: The Notion of the Habit Body, Prostitution and (Dis)embodiment." In *Embodied Selves*, edited by Stella Gonzalez-Arnal, Gill Jagger, and Kathleen Lennon, 101–118. New York: Palgrave Macmillan, 2012.
Di Martino, Loredana. "Postmodern Irony." In *Encyclopedia of Humor Studies*, edited by Salvatore Attardo, 589–592. Los Angeles: Sage Reference, 2014.
Ellsworth, Phoebe C. and Craig A. Smith. "Shades of Joy: Patterns of Appraisal Differentiating Pleasant Emotions." *Cognition and Emotion* 2, no. 4 (1988): 301–331.

Eve, Martin Paul. "Sincerity." In *The Routledge Companion to Twenty-First Century Literary Fiction*, edited by Daniel O'Gorman and Robert Eaglestone, 36–47. London: Routledge, 2018.

Hirschberg, Lynn. "A Very Murray Christmas." *W* 44, no. 10 (December 2015/January 2016): 103.

Holquist, Michael. *Dialogism: Bakhtin and his World*, 2nd ed. New York: Routledge, 1990.

Hutchinson, Phillip J. "Frankenstein Meets Mikhail Bakhtin: Celebrating the Carnival of Hosted Horror Television." *The Journal of Popular Culture* 53, no. 3 (2020): 579–599.

Johnston, Derek. "Christmas Television." *Journal of Popular Television* 6, no. 1 (2018): 81–84.

Jonze, Tim. "Bob Dylan: 'Critics Have Been Giving Me A Hard Time Since Day One.'" *The Guardian*, February 9, 2015. www.theguardian.com/music/2015/feb/09/bob-dylan-critics-have-been-giving-me-a-hard-time-since-day-one.

Latson, Jennifer. "How Karen Carpenter's Death Changed the Way We Talk About Anorexia." *Time*, May 23, 2016. time.com/3685894/karen-carpenter-anorexia-death/.

Lebold, Christophe. "A Face like a Mask and a Voice that Croaks: An Integrated Poetics of Bob Dylan's Voice, Personae, and Lyrics." *Oral Tradition* 22, no. 1 (2007): 57–70.

Lind, Stephen J. "Christmas in the 1960s: *A Charlie Brown Christmas*, Religion, and the Conventions of the Television Genre." *Journal of Religion and Popular Culture* 26, no. 1 (Spring 2014): np. dx.doi.org.proxy.lib.duke.edu/10.3138/jrpc.26.1.1.

Lott, Eric. "'Love and Theft' (2001)." In *The Cambridge Companion to Bob Dylan*, edited by Kevin J. H. Dettmar, 167–173. Cambridge: Cambridge University Press, 2009.

Morson, Gary Saul and Caryl Emerson. *Mikhail Bakhtin: Creation of a Prosaics.* Stanford, CA: Stanford University Press.

"Nick The Lounge Singer Sings Star Wars Theme—SNL." *Saturday Night Live*. www.youtube.com/watch?v=ljiVRV5B5i8.

Prisco, Jacopo and Andrew Stewart. "The Invention that Changed Music Forever." *CNN*, May 27, 2015. www.cnn.com/2015/05/26/tech/autotune-inventor-mci.

Restad, Penne L. *Christmas in America: A History*. Oxford: Oxford UP, 1998.

Rossing, Jonathan P. "An Ethics of Complicit Criticism for Postmodern Satire." *Studies in American Humor* 5, no. 1 (2019): 13–30.

*Scrooged.* Directed by Richard Donner. Written by Mitch Glazer and Michael O'Donoghue. 1988; Los Angeles CA: Paramount Pictures. DVD.

Shelton, Robert. *No Direction Home: The Life and Music of Bob Dylan*. London: Omnibus Press, 2011.

Small, Christopher. *Musicking: The Meaning of Performing and Listening*. Hanover: Wesleyan UP, 1998.

Stam, Robert. *Subversive Pleasures: Bakhtin, Cultural Criticism, and Film*. Baltimore, MD: The Johns Hopkins University Press, 1989.

Sterritt, David. "The Diabolic Imagination: Hitchcock, Bakhtin, and the Carnivalization of Cinema." *Hitchcock Annual* 1 (1992): 39–67.

Telling, Gillian. "Sofia Coppola." *Entertainment Weekly*, December 11, 2015, 50.
Van Cappellen, Patty. "The Emotion of Joy: Commentary on Johnson." *The Journal of Positive Psychology* (2019): 40–43.
Wilkerson, Isabel. *Caste: The Origins of Our Discontents*. New York: Random House, 2020.

## NOTES

1. Gillian Telling, "Sofia Coppola," *Entertainment Weekly*, December 11, 2015, 50.

2. Lynn Hirschberg, "A Very Murray Christmas," *W* 44, no. 10 (Dec 2015/Jan 2016): 103.

3. Kenneth Bachor, "A Very Murray Christmas Director Sofia Coppola: I Wanted To Do Something 'Joyful,'" *Time*, December 4, 2015, time.com/4132069/sofia-coppola-a-very-murray-christmas/.

4. Loredana Di Martino, "Postmodern Irony," in *Encyclopedia of Humor Studies*, ed. Salvatore Attardo (Los Angeles: Sage Reference, 2014), 591.

5. Jonathan P. Rossing, "An Ethics of Complicit Criticism for Postmodern Satire," *Studies in American Humor* 5, no. 1 (2019): 27–29.

6. *A Very Murray Christmas*, dir. Sofia Coppola (Los Gatos, CA: Netflix, 2015), www.netflix.com/title/80042368, accessed January 5, 2021, emphasis ours.

7. David Biancully, "Netflix Wishes You A 'Murray Christmas' In A Cheerful, Irony-Free Holiday Special," *Fresh Air*, NPR, December 3, 2015, www.npr.org/2015/12/03/458303447/netflix-wishes-you-a-murray-christmas-in-a-cheerful-irony-free-holiday-special.

8. In reflecting on writers responding to postmodern irony, scholars sometimes claim that authors like David Foster Wallace, Dave Eggers, Jennifer Egan, George Saunders, Rachel Kushner and Jonathan Franzen turn away from irony toward a so-called "(New) Sincerity." Martin Paul Eve, "Sincerity," in *The Routledge Companion to Twenty-First Century Literary Fiction*, eds. Daniel O'Gorman and Robert Eaglestone (London: Routledge, 2018), 36–39. As we hope will become clear below, we believe the elements of carnival at play in the film provide a better account for the subversions at work rather than sincerity. However, as Wallace knows, the risk an artist's sincerity poses is the perception of sentimentality. "Whether or not this is the case," Eve argues, "will depend, of course, upon how cynical you yourself are as a reader." Eve, "Sincerity," 42–44. To the extent that Coppola's film might be considered sentimental, it might appear that she succumbs to similar artistic dangers.

9. Stephen J. Lind, "Christmas in the 1960s: *A Charlie Brown Christmas*, Religion, and the Conventions of the Television Genre," *Journal of Religion and Popular Culture* 26, no. 1 (Spring 2014): np, dx.doi.org.proxy.lib.duke.edu/10.3138/jrpc.26.1.1.

10. Penne L. Restad, *Christmas in America: A History* (Oxford: Oxford UP, 1998), 169.

11. Gerry Bowler, *The World Encyclopedia of Christmas* (Toronto, ON: McClelland & Stewart, 2000), iBooks.

12. Ibid.

13. Lind, "Christmas in the 1960s," np.

14. As the next characteristic states, this moment might be interpreted as a feature of a Scrooge character. However, Scrooge's disaffection toward Christmas takes aim primarily against his employees and not family.

15. Our analysis below deals directly with the implications of sexual assault in the song.

16. Lind, "Christmas in the 1960s," np.

17. Ibid. In the Western musical tradition, this use of music is nothing new. In Opera, for example, arias express characters' emotional states, while recitatives move plot along. In nineteenth-century Italian opera, singers occasionally requested to have their favorite arias from previous works inserted to new staged productions. These additions could be nicknamed "suitcase" or "trunk arias" [*Arie di baule*]. Author Giorgio Migliavacca writes, "In the Bel Canto era, an opera star's baggage typically included a special little trunk containing the sheet music of favorite arias the singer could draw upon, ad libitum, for use as showstoppers in operas or as highlights and encores at concerts . . . Although the tradition eventually died out, remnants of it still turn up now and then, as in a certain tenor's habit of ending his concerts with 'Nessun dorma.'" Giorgio Migliavacca, "Mariella Devia: 'La morte di Didone' e Arie di baule," *Opera Quarterly* 15, no. 2 (1999): 356.

18. David Budgen, "'Halfway Out of the Dark": Steven Moffat's *Doctor Who* Christmas specials," in *The Eleventh Hour: A Critical Celebration of the Matt Smith and Steven Moffat Era*, edited by Andrew O'Day (London: I.B. Tauris, 2014), 91. Quoted in Derek Johnston, "Christmas Television," *Journal of Popular Television* 6, no. 1 (2018): 82.

19. Literary scholar Michael Holquist notes that scholars have produced so many articles and books about Bakhtin that there is a "Bakhtin industry," or "a thriving business . . . of transnational global commerce with outposts all over the world." Michael Holquist, *Dialogism: Bakhtin and his World*, 2nd ed. (New York: Routledge, 1990), 180.

20. Gary Saul Morson and Caryl Emerson, *Mikhail Bakhtin: Creation of a Prosaics* (Stanford, CA: Stanford University Press), 15 and 22.

21. Mikhail M. Bakhtin, *Art and Answerability: Early Essays by M. M. Bakhtin*, trans. Vadim Liapunov (Austin, TX: University of Texas Press), 1.

22. Robert Stam, *Subversive Pleasures: Bakhtin, Cultural Criticism, and Film* (Baltimore, MD: The Johns Hopkins University Press, 1989), 86.

23. Ibid., 93.

24. Ibid., 98.

25. Beth E. Bonnstetter, "Mel Brooks Meets Kenneth Burke (and Mikhail Bakhtin): Comedy and Burlesque in Satiric Film," *Journal of Film and Video* 63, no. 1 (Spring 2011): 23.

26. Ibid.

27. Ben Chappell, "Bakhtin's Barbershop: Film as Folklorist," *Western Folklore* 64, no. 3–4 (Summer-Fall 2005): 216.

28. Ibid., 216–17.

29. Phillip J. Hutchinson, "Frankenstein Meets Mikhail Bakhtin: Celebrating the Carnival of Hosted Horror Television," *The Journal of Popular Culture* 53, no. 3 (2020): 580.
30. Ibid., 585.
31. Holquist, *Dialogism: Bakhtin and his World*, 96.
32. Mikhail M. Bakhtin, *The Dialogic Imagination: Four Essays by M. M. Bakhtin*, trans. Caryl Emerson and Michael Holquist (Austin, TX: University of Texas Press, 1982), 193.
33. Ibid., 171.
34. Ibid., 170.
35. Ibid., 178.
36. Ibid., 180.
37. Ibid., 185.
38. Ibid., 187.
39. Ibid., 190.
40. Ibid., 192.
41. Ibid., 193–4.
42. Ibid., 199. By way of illustrating this non-holistic, non-affirmative carnivalesque view of the body, film critic David Sterritt devotes special attention to the seven series in Alfred Hitchcock's 1948 film *Rope*, and how the series appears without regeneration. In the film, two characters, implicitly presented as lovers, Brandon Shaw (John Dall) and Phillip Morgan (Farley Granger) murder a former classmate, David Kentley (Dick Hogan). They store the body in a trunk and serve a dinner to a group of guests close to David from that trunk. Sterritt observes that the film begins on a close up of Brandon and Phillip strangling David (the body series). Although his corpse is hidden in the trunk, its presence is constant throughout the film (the death series), and the murderers serve dinner from a trunk containing a corpse (the food and death series). Sterritt links the killers' implicit homosexuality with the sex and defecation series (implying their engagement in anal sex). Throughout the dinner, alcohol weakens Phillip's nerves (the drink/drunkenness series). And the film makes some limited use of the socially correct clothing all the characters wear to the dinner (the clothing series). Sterrit notes an important deviation from the carnivalesque in the film. Where the carnivalesque uses gaiety and mirth as regenerative devices, Hitchcock's carnivalism is "morbid and dystopian . . . more Halloween than mardigras." David Sterritt, "The Diabolic Imagination: Hitchcock, Bakhtin, and the Carnivalization of Cinema," *Hitchcock Annual* 1 (1992):40. Which is to say, Hitchcock revels in an ironic posture of subversion. He uses "destabilizing and norm-breaching practices . . . gleefully undermining decorum" not only of his characters but also "of Hollywood cinema itself." Sterritt, "The Diabolic Imagination," 45.
43. Tom Carson, "Mr. Mike's 'SNL' Nightmare," *Grantland*, August 22, 2014, grantland.com/features/michael-odonoghue-snl-saturday-night-live-mr-mike/; Bill Carter, "Michael O'Donoghue, 54, Dies; Writer for *Saturday Night Live*," *The New York Times*, November 10, 1994, accessed April 1, 2021, www.nytimes.com/1994/11/10/obituaries/michael-o-donoghue-54-dies-writer-for-saturday-night-live.html.

44. Richard Donner, dir., *Scrooged*, written by Mitch Glazer and Michael O'Donoghue, Hollywood, CA: Paramount Pictures, 1988. DVD.

45. "Bill Murray's Eulogy for Michael O Donoghue (delivered on Saturday Night Live the week he died, in 1994)," Michael O'Donoghue, dir., *Mr. Mike's Mondo Video*, Burbank, CA: New Line Cinema, 1979. DVD.

46. Ibid.

47. Ibid.

48. The image of the kimono also evokes patriarchal stereotypes, especially of Japanese women. Because kimonos are often made of delicate silk fabric, the joke also works from patriarchal assumption about the perceived delicacy of women's bodies, which are easily "ruined" by sexual activity. But perhaps even more troubling, the joke seems to also assume the hyper-sexualization of Japanese women, here possibly in the role of "comfort women," in which Japanese women served soldiers' sexual desires during World War II, a practice many consider a form of sex slavery. See, for example, Melanie Belarmino and Melinda R. Roberts, "Japanese Gender Role Expectations and Attitudes: A Qualitative Analysis of Gender Inequality," *Journal of International Women's Studies* 20 no. 7 (August 2019): 273–4.

49. Lauren Berlant and Michael Warner, "Sex in Public," in *The Cultural Studies Reader*, 2nd ed., ed. Simon During (New York: Routledge, 1999), 366.

50. Ibid., 367.

51. Jennifer Latson, "How Karen Carpenter's Death Changed the Way We Talk About Anorexia," *Time*, May 23, 2016, time.com/3685894/karen-carpenter-anorexia-death/. While space does not permit a full treatment of Karen Carpenter's eating disorder, it is important to note how such experiences intersect with the notion of disembodiment and feminist reflections on mind-body dualisms. In philosopher Susan Bordo's analysis of anorexia, she links the manner in which women who suffer from anorexia to the mind-body dualisms of Plato, Augustine, and Descartes. Susan Bordo, *Unbearable Weight, Feminism, Western Culture, and the Body* (Berkeley, CA: University of California Press, 1993), 144. Likewise, women's studies scholar Maddy Coy notes how some women who experience the violence of objectification as sex workers may engage in dissociative bodily practices, which she uses as a near synonym for (dis)embodiment. Maddy Coy, "This Body Which Is Not Mine: The Notion of the Habit Body, Prostitution and (Dis)embodiment," in *Embodied Selves*, eds. Stella Gonzalez-Arnal, Gill Jagger, and Kathleen Lennon (New York: Palgrave Macmillan Limited, 2012), 110. Taken together, mind-body dualism is the fountainhead out of which disembodied practices flow, perhaps as ways of exerting control over one's body (as Bordo argues about anorexia) or one's bodily objectification (as Coy observes about practices like drug use). That Karen Carpenter suffered from anorexia and appeared in a Christmas special that represented the body as a non-holistic body might be coincidence. But perhaps there is a link between eating disorders and the assumptions of Christmas specials—they both have as a source the disembodied, mind-body dualisms of the Western tradition.

52. Leslie A. Baxter, *Voicing Relationships: A Dialogic Perspective* (Los Angeles: Sage Publications, 2010), 33.

53. Ibid, 42.

54. Leslie A. Baxter, "A Tale of Two Voices: Relational Dialectics Theory," *The Journal of Family Communication* 4, no. 3 and 4 (2004): 186.
55. Baxter, *Voicing Relationships*, 34.
56. Ibid., 55–57.
57. Leslie A. Baxter and Barbara M. Montgomery, *Relating: Dialogues and Dialectics* (New York: The Guilford Press, 1996), 95.
58. Leslie A. Baxter and Kristen M. Norwood, "Relational Dialectics Theory: Navigating Meaning From Competing Discourses," in *Engaging Theories in Interpersonal Communication: Multiple Perspectives*, eds. Leslie A. Baxter and Dawn O. Braithwaite (Thousand Oaks, CA: Sage 2015), 285.
59. Mikhail M. Bakhtin, *Rabelais and His World*, trans. Helene Iswolsky (Bloomington, IN: Indiana University Press, 1984), 19.
60. Ibid., 26.
61. Ibid., 25.
62. Ibid.
63. Ibid., 29.
64. Ibid., 19.
65. Ibid., 28.
66. Ibid.
67. Ibid., 24.
68. Ibid.
69. Christophe Lebold, "A Face like a Mask and a Voice that Croaks: An Integrated Poetics of Bob Dylan's Voice, Personae, and Lyrics," *Oral Tradition* 22, no. 1 (2007): 64–65. Artists and critics alike have described his voice as "tubercular," like "gravel," or like "sand and glue." See Robert Shelton, *No Direction Home: The Life and Music of Bob Dylan* (London: Omnibus Press, 2011), iBooks. See Eric Lott, "'Love and Theft' (2001)" in *The Cambridge Companion to Bob Dylan*, ed. Kevin J. H. Dettmar (Cambridge: Cambridge University Press, 2009), 171. See David Bowie, "Song for Bob Dylan," track 9 on *Hunky Dory* (RCA Records, 1971).
70. Tim Jonze, "Bob Dylan: 'Critics Have Been Giving Me A Hard Time Since Day One,'" *The Guardian*, February 9, 2015, www.theguardian.com/music/2015/feb/09/bob-dylan-critics-have-been-giving-me-a-hard-time-since-day-one.
71. "Nick The Lounge Singer Sings Star Wars Theme—SNL," *Saturday Night Live*, www.youtube.com/watch?v=ljiVRV5B5i8, accessed March 15, 2021.
72. For one reflection on the impact of pitch correcting software, like Celemony Melodyne or Antares Auto-Tune Pro, on the music industry, see Jacopo Prisco and Andrew Stewart, "The Invention that Changed Music Forever," *CNN*, May 27, 2015, www.cnn.com/2015/05/26/tech/autotune-inventor-mci.
73. Bakhtin, *Rabelais and His World*, 19.
74. Ibid., 25.
75. Phoebe C. Ellsworth and Craig A. Smith, "Shades of Joy: Patterns of Appraisal Differentiating Pleasant Emotions," *Cognition and Emotion* 2, no. 4 (1988): 326.
76. Patty Van Cappellen, "The Emotion of Joy: Commentary on Johnson," *The Journal of Positive Psychology* (2019): 1.

77. Christopher Small, *Musicking: The Meaning of Performing and Listening* (Hanover: Wesleyan University Press, 1998), 13.

78. Isabel Wilkerson, *Caste: The Origins of Our Discontents* (New York: Random House, 2020), 18.

79. Ibid., 380.

# PART IV
*LOVE*

*Chapter Seven*

# A Liminal Love

## Charles Taylor's Malaise and Chela Sandoval's Decolonial *Love in* Lost in Translation

This chapter picks up on a theme from our reading of *The Virgin Suicides*. From Coppola's first film, we highlighted a form of masculinity at work in the lives of the neighborhood boys, a masculinity that unwittingly linked love with violence. In this chapter, Coppola's characters are capable of loving each other outside of realms of violence and even, in certain ways, beyond the central causes of violence in the Western tradition.

*Lost in Translation* represents love as a liminal love, between a Western, dichotomous love and a decolonial love. Supporting this claim, our chapter unfolds in three main sections. First, we describe philosopher Charles Taylor's understanding of malaise as a loss of meaning, a result from the shifts from a premodern to a modern world. In the film, Charlotte (Scarlett Johansson) and Bob (Bill Murray) experience malaise through layers of alienation, including alienation from their own bodies; from relationships with others; from Japanese culture and language; and from meaningful work. Second, against the dichotomies that undergird Western notions of love, Chicana scholar Chela Sandoval claims that decolonial love creates affiliations across lines of difference that can lead to social transformation. Decolonial love can move in three stages: disruption, attachment, and a return to drifting, albeit with a sense of ease and wholeness. If disruption is a puncture in ordinary life, Bob and Charlotte experience each other as a puncture in their alienation. Together they experience humor, delight, and a connection to their own bodies. If attachment is a non-dualistic way of being in the world that includes acts of gift-giving, then Bob and Charlotte experience attachment through an intimacy that binaries like father/daughter or lover/beloved cannot contain.

They also exchange the gifts of vulnerability. And finally, if drifting involves a state of wholeness and being at ease in the world, then Bob and Charlotte return to their lives in a different state—relieved and centered.

Finally, this analysis suggests an important limitation to the love Bob and Charlotte experience: it exists as a liminal love between Western love on one hand and decolonial love on the other. Bob and Charlotte's love lacks social transformation and remains unaware of how colonial, global capital enables the love they share. We conclude with two implications. Our analysis, first, suggests that Taylor's failure to understand colonialism as internal to the modern world is a serious deficiency. And, second, while many white settlers are beginning to come to terms with colonial realities, we, like Bob and Charlotte, need not only experience personal transformation. Social transformation will only occur if we are prepared to imagine and live a different form of life.

## MALAISE

For Charles Taylor (1931–), the shift from a premodern, enchanted world to a modern, disenchanted world produced for many individuals a loss of personal meaning and significance. In a premodern world, the Canadian philosopher suggests in *The Malaise of Modernity* (1991) people, especially in the West, found significance and meaning through a grand, hierarchical, "cosmic order, a 'great chain of Being,' in which humans figured in their proper place along with angels, heavenly bodies, and our fellow earthly creatures."[1] This premodern world was also an enchanted world, filled with gods, angels, cosmic forces, and spirits—both good and bad. The hazard of an enchanted world meant that humans were vulnerable to these forces; however, it provided a powerful, shared horizon of meaning and significance. The modern world, however, disenchanted that premodern world, jettisoning the hierarchal cosmic order for a flattened, imminent world. In this world, people lose their vulnerability to "evil spirits, cosmic forces or gods."[2] However, the loss of the hierarchy and vulnerability produces another loss, what "we might call a loss of meaning."[3] Taylor continues, "Sealed off from enchantment, the modern . . . self is also sealed off from significance, left to ruminate in a stew of its own ennui."[4] Ennui, which can be understood as that feeling of boredom, listlessness, or even despair, has, for Taylor, a particularly modern character. In emphasizing the phenomenology of this loss of meaning, Taylor claims, "My point is not that everybody feels this, but rather . . . that many people do."[5]

Taylor describes the ennui modern people experience in their loss of meaning—what he calls a malaise of modernity—as a lack and as a fragility of significance. The experience of malaise means that "our actions, goals, achievements, and the like, have a lack of weight, gravity, thickness, substance."⁶ By way of example, he points to the common experience of people in their young adulthood and midlife. Many experience a crisis of meaning or identity. In the everyday experience of many humans in the modern world, our actions have a point, whether we are traveling to work or purchasing groceries. However, those same individuals, be they in young adulthood or midlife, can reflect on those everyday experiences in such a way that promotes ennui and loss. We "can stop and ask why we're doing these things," and the question, if taken seriously, can produce "a crisis, where we feel that what has been orienting our life up to now lacks real value, weight."⁷ Or, in a differing register, all those structures of meaning which have worked, satisfied, and mattered now, in a crisis of meaning, fail to work, satisfy, and matter.⁸ As a result, a mid-career doctor may leave a highly paid job to "go off with Médecins Sans Frontières to Africa, with a sense that *this* is really significant."⁹ However, our responses to the crisis of meaning are also fragile and uncertain.¹⁰ What will the doctor do, for example, when work in Africa fails to provide meaning?

*Lost in Translation* follows two characters, Charlotte and Bob. The film introduces Bob as he wakes in the back of a cab, which is taking him from an airport to a hotel. In the cab, he rubs his eyes, initially because he has jet lag. However, as he looks at the bright lights and massive buildings of Tokyo, Japan, he also rubs his eyes in disbelief. Bob is an action movie star who is past his prime. His visit to Japan is not one that will rekindle his career. Rather, he is making advertisements for Suntory whisky. At the high-rise, luxury Park Hyatt Hotel, his Suntory handlers greet him with gifts. He also receives a faxed message from his wife, Lydia (Nancy Steiner). In the message Bob learns that he has forgotten his son's birthday. Her terse, passive aggressive statement at the end of the fax, "I'm sure he will understand," suggests that they are having relational difficulties, too. Charlotte and her husband John (Giovanni Ribisi) are staying at the same hotel. John is in Japan working as a photographer, shooting a band for a record label. While John is working, Charlotte wanders aimlessly through her days. Sometimes she behaves like a tourist, visiting famous sites. At other times, she sits in her hotel room staring out the window or listens to a self-help CD (entitled *A Soul's Journey: Finding Your True Calling*). Overall, she experiences Japanese culture as strange and impenetrable.

In the opening movement of the film, Charlotte and Bob experience malaise through layers of alienation,¹¹ including alienation from their own bodies and from meaningful connections with their spouses. Suffering from jet lag, Charlotte and Bob's inability to sleep alienates them from their bodies. That first night Bob lies in bed, unable to fall asleep, and then goes down to the bar to get a drink. Charlotte stares out her hotel window, looking down at the city. Both characters also cannot connect in a meaningful way with their spouses. When Charlotte cannot sleep, she sits in the windowsill. She stares at John, troubled by the sound of his snoring. She returns to bed and wakes John, trying to connect with him. Instead, he puts his arms around her, tells her to go back to sleep, and then begins snoring again. She is physically trapped in his embrace and emotionally alienated from him. Likewise, at 4:20 am, Bob is still awake in his bed, but the loud sound of the fax machine in his room disturbs him. He raises his head and looks at the fax, which is from his wife. Bob's study is undergoing renovations, and Lydia wants to know what shelves he wants installed. With a sense of frustration, Bob lays his head back in bed. Like Charlotte's failed attempt to connect with her husband, the banality of the message suggests their lack of connection. Lydia does not show interest in his travel or how he is doing, nor is she considerate of the time difference. In a state where Bob cannot sleep and where he has forgotten his child's birthday, the topic of shelving units foregrounds the alienation he experiences with his wife.

Bob also experiences other forms of bodily and relational alienation. In addition to his inability to connect meaningfully with his wife and child, he refuses to connect with other Americans. When Bob first tries to sleep and cannot do so, he goes down to the bar to smoke a cigar and drink whisky. A red-headed lounge singer (Catherine Lambert) sings while two men (Gregory Pekar and Richard Allen) a few seats down recognize Bob from his films. They gush over how wonderful he was in one film in particular, in part because Bob performed all his own driving stunts. They ask him what he is doing in Japan, and Bob lies, saying that he is visiting friends and eventually leaves the conversation. The lie suggests that Bob is already alienated from the work he is going to perform. Once a successful action star, he has now been reduced to peddling alcohol. He seems unwilling or unable to admit this reality to these fans and leaves, alienated and alone. Likewise, Bob's height alienates him from Japanese norms. In the elevator up to his room, Bob stands head and shoulders above everyone in the elevator. In the shower the next morning, he raises the showerhead to its apparent maximum height, which is too short for his stature. He awkwardly lowers his body to get it beneath the stream of water, and the film plays the awkwardness to comedic effect. He does, however, experience one slight connection with another person. On his way to work the next morning, Bob and Charlotte ride the same elevator. They eventually notice each other and exchange smiles.

Nevertheless, Bob continues to experience alienation from Japanese culture, which renders meaningful work impossible. One of the main forms of cultural alienation that Bob experiences at work occurs through poor translations.[12] In one scene, the director of a commercial (Diamond Yukai) speaks to Bob in Japanese. He delivers his direction with passion and intensity. He also speaks for a very long time. When the translator (uncredited) turns to Bob, she delivers the most perfunctory direction, "He wants you to turn and look in camera." Confused, Bob asks if that was all the director intended. The translator reassures him that the director said nothing else. After a series of similar miscommunications, it becomes clear to Bob that the linguistic gap between what the director wants and what the translator says traps him into a performance that will lack quality and integrity. The next day, Bob's handlers say that a famous talk show host has invited Bob to be on his show, the "Johnny Carson of Japan." Having already experienced layers of alienation, Bob tells his agent on the phone, "I gotta get out of here as soon as I can." He brings that frustration into the photo shoot.

During the shoot, the photographer speaks in broken English to Bob, directing him to imitate the Rat Pack and James Bond. At first, Bob tries to capture the essence of these mid-twentiethth century icons, but soon his frustration takes over. The photographer (Tetsuro Naka) asks, "Are you drinking?" Bob replies, "Am I drinking? As soon as I'm done." Unable to act in the way the photographer wants, Bob reveals his frustration. He bites his tongue, as if in physical pain, and stares at the ceiling. The scene ends with a disappointed smirk on Bob's face, having given up on trying to make the shoot a meaningful endeavor. In both the commercial and photo shoot, the cultural distance between himself and the Japanese crew produces an alienation that he cannot overcome. It becomes clear to him that his work will lack meaning and significance. As he says to Charlotte in a later scene, he could be performing in a play but instead he is here, trapped inside of layers of alienation, not unlike the way Charlotte is trapped inside her husband's embrace. If Taylor's mid-career doctor quit her job to work in Africa as a way of grasping personal significance, Bob has made the opposite decision, making his work meaningless and painful.

Charlotte's alienation is similar. Like many tourists, she takes public transit through the city. After deciphering the subway map, she boards a train and observes a man reading a pornographic manga (comic book) in public. Since she does not speak Japanese, all she can do is observe the strangeness of this overt and public display of the objectification of women's bodies. She eventually arrives at the Jugan-ji Temple and observes monks chanting in a religious ceremony. Like her interaction on the subway, Charlotte simply observes the impenetrability of the event. Back in her hotel room, she brings her alienation out into the open. She calls an American friend (uncredited) on the phone and weeps during the entire call. Through her tears, she describes her reaction to the ceremony, "I didn't feel anything. You know?" Her response to the ceremony leads abruptly into differing topics, which underscores her alienation: "I even tried ikebana, and John is using these hair products. I just . . . I don't know who I married." Her friend, however, is distracted, excuses herself from the call momentarily and then returns. Charlotte does not have the energy to deal with her friend's distraction, so she quickly gets off the phone. Once she hangs up, she continues to cry and wipe her own tears.

During the phone call, Charlotte links her alienation from Japanese culture with the alienation she experiences from her husband. In her reading of this scene, film scholar Anna Backman Rogers points out that Charlotte's "I didn't feel anything" response is rooted in a problematic cultural expectation. She wrongly believes "that she must feel something in response to a culture that is extrinsic to her (a culture that is frequently misappropriated by Western culture for bankrupt forms of nebulous 'spirituality')."[13] Therefore, while her feelings of alienation are real, her response reveals an unintended exploitation of Japanese spirituality. She expects that the monks should provide her some religious feeling or experience. However mistaken her expectation is, it drives, in part, the emotion she experiences on the phone, which she links to her relational alienation from her husband. John does not appear to experience alienation. Unlike John's use of hair products, Charlotte attempted ikebana, the Japanese tradition of flower arranging, but implies that the practice did not have a positive, life-giving effect on her. Her assumption, like that of her expectation about religious feelings, suggests an expectation that ikebana will provide for her some form of connection. When compared to her husband's experience, her alienations lead her to conclude, "I don't know who I married." Taken together, her speech suggests that she cannot find meaning in anything or anybody in her life. Even her friend on the phone is too distracted to listen to and connect with her.

Charlotte's alienation from her husband and from Japanese culture continues, which she exacerbates through her use of humor. In her hotel room, Charlotte performs mundane tasks. She puts on lipstick, hangs paper flowers, knits a scarf, lounges in her underwear, smokes, and stubs her toe. The film contrasts her idleness to John's activity. John appears in the hotel room for only a moment, but he speaks passionately about his job. Charlotte tries to interest John in her scarf, but he ignores her. John also reprimands Charlotte, when he notices a burning cigarette; and as he puts it out, he scolds her. Soon, John packs up his camera gear and leaves. Where John's work energizes him, Charlotte experiences ennui and idleness. John also aggravates her alienation from him through reprimanding her. Furthermore, humor intensifies Charlotte's relational and cultural alienations. As Bob will make clear later, Charlotte rarely smiles. But when she does, it often reveals her sense of superiority to others. For example, John and Charlotte meet an actress that John has worked with previously, Kelly (Anna Faris). The film presents Kelly as a Hollywood stereotype: beautiful, blonde, and vapid. Once Kelly leaves, Charlotte smiles and makes fun of her. She expects John to participate in her form of humor, but John refuses, saying, "Why do you have to point out how stupid everyone is all the time?" Later in the film, she visits a video arcade. While she walks around, she smiles with condescension at a young Japanese man, who is dressed like a rock star with a cigarette hanging out of his mouth. He is playing a Guitar Hero-style video game. In both of these scenes, Charlotte's humor becomes part of the means by which she lacks meaningful connection with others.

Taylor's account of malaise, particularly a loss of meaning, is at play in both Charlotte and Bob's life. Their lack of meaning and significance takes the primary form of alienation, particularly alienation from meaningful connection to their bodies and to others. However, Bob and Charlotte both reflect the ages at which Taylor insists ennui is common. Bob, as Charlotte jokes, is experiencing a midlife crisis where, primarily, his work is meaningless. Like the doctor, who leaves a high paying job for work for Médecins Sans Frontières, Bob has the exact same experience but makes the opposite choice. He would rather perform in a play, but instead, he is in Japan making an extraordinary amount of money for meaningless and alienating work. Likewise, Charlotte does not know what she is going to do for meaningful work. But perhaps the clearest signal that she experiences a fragility of significance is her self-help CDs. As a philosophy major from an Ivy League university, she should be, as the film will later suggest, above self-help drivel. Like Bob, she is in a state of malaise.

Both characters eventually connect with each other, particularly over their experiences of malaise and alienation. Later, when Charlotte is unable to sleep and does not want to watch television, she sits next to Bob at the bar, and the two strike up a conversation. She asks him what he is doing in Japan. Perhaps frustrated from his continued experiences of alienation and malaise, he responds with vulnerability and honesty. "Taking a break from my wife, forgetting my son's birthday, and getting paid $2 million to endorse a whisky when I could be doing a play somewhere." He asks her the same question. She responds with her own experiences of alienation and malaise, "My husband is a photographer, so he's here working. I wasn't doing anything, so I came along. And we have some friends that live here." They joke that Bob might be having a midlife crisis. When he asks what she does for work, she admits that she is not sure, perhaps because she "just graduated last spring" with a philosophy degree. They then admit to each other their shared bodily alienation: Charlotte reveals that she cannot sleep, and Bob reciprocates. They sit in silence for a moment before the scene ends. While their connection is slight, it is, by and large, their only meaningful ones. While this scene does not solve their malaise, it sets the stage for the love they experience with each other, a love that bears some similarity to a decolonial love.

## DECOLONIAL LOVE

Early in *Methodology of the Oppressed* (2000), Chicana Studies scholar Chela Sandoval reflects on colonialism, the insights of US third-world feminists of color, and the notion of love as a means to resist colonialism's ongoing harms. Although she never defines colonialism directly, her treatment throughout the text implies a historical and political understanding of the term. First, colonialism describes the historical period, from the late fifteenth century through to decolonizing movements of the post-World War II period. During this half-millennium, European empires used exploitation and violence to expand their holdings, in places that would become known as the Americas, Australia, New Zealand, and Africa. While the colonial period might be over, in a political way, colonialism remains present, for Sandoval, through the exploitative processes of global capitalism. "Western colonial explorations," Sandoval observes, "opened up other world geopolitical regions, making available vastly different languages, cultures, and riches for Western consumption."[14] In the context of consumption and exploitation, she takes as given the wisdom of US third-world feminists of color—like Angela Davis, Alice Walker, Mitsuye Yamada, Audre Lorde, Gloria Anzaldúa, Nellie Wong, Cherríe Moraga, Toni Morrison, Paula Gunn Allen, bell hooks, and others—who claim that the dominant colonial culture of the West poses a threat to poor, women of color. She also, throughout her book, reflects on their work in order to find resources to decolonize themselves (their minds, bodies, practices, ways of life) and the world in which they live.[15] Her response to these colonial forces reaches its climax in her account of love, or, as she calls it sometimes, decolonial love.

But before turning to decolonial love, Sandoval describes Western, dichotomous love as that which bears within it the binaries of either/or, possessor/possessed, and active/passive. If at the heart of colonialism is the dichotomy of the colonizer (European settler) and the colonized (Indigenous peoples and their land), then Western love can be colonized with similarly dichotomous relationships.[16] For example, when one falls in love with another, lovers usually finds themselves with an either/or relationship to the beloved. Either lovers have "hope" that the beloved loves them back, or the lover has no hope of the beloved returning their love.[17] Likewise, Western love can also work within the dualistic rule of possession. The lover, in some real way, possesses the beloved, because as is often the case, "one loves what one owns."[18] The possessor/possessed dichotomy fuels stereotypical responses lovers are often expected to perform. For example, if a lover violates the possessor/possessed dichotomy, an "injury" might take place.[19] In such situations, stereotypical lovers are supposed "to be jealous, neglected, frustrated—like everyone else."[20] Sandoval also relates active and passive linguistic constructions to the dichotomies that fuel Western love.[21] Such binaries are, properly understood, evidence of the subject/object binary. One is either a subject who acts upon an object (as in the sentence, "Dick loves Jane"). Or, one is a passive object who is acted upon (as in the sentence, "Jane is loved by Dick"). Sandoval's analysis suggests that Western love functions as a metaphor for social life. Such love reflects and preserves the dichotomous status quo of the colonial West.

Sandoval argues that decolonial love can be an apparatus for the social transformations and affirmative connections necessary for decolonization to occur. Early in the book, she claims that love is, fundamentally, an apparatus or "technology for social transformation,"[22] composed of the "body of knowledges, arts, practices, and procedures," that decolonizes "the self and the world."[23] If western binaries produce, in part, an "apartheid," or a division, by "race, sex, class, gender, and identity," then love overcomes such divisions, through affirmative connections with others.[24] Love encourages all peoples, "regardless of social class,"[25] to recognize difference,[26] and to create an "alliance and affection across lines of difference."[27] Affirmative connection is a key mechanism that permits the transformation of the social, the self, and the world.

Although Sandoval's account of love is not necessarily linear, it possesses at least five aspects: disruption; attachments; drifting, ease, and wholeness; connections "from below"; and social transformation. Our initial analysis focuses on the first three aspects. The last two features, however, are absent, and we address those in the following section. But first, we turn to how Bob and Charlotte experience disruptions to their alienation.

## DISRUPTION

Decolonial love can produce in the lover an experience of disruption, or a puncture or rupture in one's ordinary life; the rupture opens up the possibility for the lover to engage in a non-controlling way of moving, or drifting, through the world. Decolonial love, for Sandoval, is "a synchronic process that punctures through traditional, older narratives of love, that ruptures everyday being."[28] If scholars use the term "diachronic" to trace how language of love changes over time, then Sandoval uses the term "synchronic" to focus on the moment of disruption. Whatever the state of one's everyday life, or ordinary way of being, love punctures through the status quo. Love is a "'breaking' through whatever controls," or a "break . . . from the ties that bind."[29] When lovers fall in love, they not only submit to what is "intractable," or impossible to control, but they also release control over others.[30] Unlike Western lovers, who possess and actively assert themselves over others, those who fall in love refuse such control. Without the practices of control, love "permits crossing over to another" way of being, to a "gentle abyss," a no-place "where everything is possible."[31] Lovers can enter a state of drifting, where they can "pick, graze, convert, cruise, [or] low-ride" through alternative ways of being in the world.[32] Bob and Charlotte's connection with each other is that which disrupts their ordinary lives of alienation.

A few days after their first conversation, John leaves for a few days to work on a photoshoot. That day, Charlotte and Bob meet accidentally in a hallway, and Charlotte invites him out with some friends. Bob accepts her invitation. That night, Charlotte is getting ready in her bathroom, when Bob knocks on the door. He raps rhythmically and loudly on the door, which amuses Charlotte. She opens the door and laughs at Bob's shirt—it has a camouflage design but its colors are bright orange, yellow, brown, and black. She says, "You really are having a midlife crisis, huh?" Bob responds with a self-deprecating, "Yeah. I was afraid of that." He walks into the bathroom, turns the shirt inside out, and asks Charlotte to cut off the tag. Because Bob is taller than Charlotte, she reaches up to cut off the tag and comments on his height, "You're too tall." He says, "Anybody ever tell you, you may be too small?" She laughs at his joke. While he sits down, he notices Charlotte's self-help CD *A Soul's Journey: Finding Your True Calling*. He asks her whose CD this is. She is embarrassed and lies to him. He places the CD back on the table and says, "I have that." Again, Charlotte laughs. Once she removes the tag, he puts on his coat and asks her a series of playful questions regarding all the things she will need before they leave: her shoes, her hotel key, her bag. His tone seemingly plays on their age difference; Bob imitates the words that a parent or guardian might say to a child when they are getting ready to leave their place of residence. Like Charlotte has responded throughout the entire scene, Bob's behavior amuses her. She smiles as he rushes out the door.

Before Charlotte completely exits her hotel room, Coppola cuts to a bar. Large white spheres hang from the ceiling and projectors display mesmerizing patterns on them. Dance music blasts over the soundtrack. Bob meets Charlotte's friend (Fumihiro Hayashi), who goes by the name Charlie Brown. Charlie introduces Bob to his friends. Coppola suddenly cuts to another bar, where Bob speaks in broken French to a Japanese man (Akimitsu Naruyama). Charlotte comes up to Bob to chat, but in the background, Charlie has an altercation with the bartender. The bartender reveals a stun gun and chases them out of the bar. Bob and Charlotte run through a video arcade and eventually find Charlie. They ride off in a cab together. Coppola cuts suddenly to an apartment where Charlie takes a picture of Charlotte. Bob and Charlotte meet more people, chat, drink, listen to music, and dance.

Cutting from the apartment, the group has moved to a karaoke room, where Charlie sings the Sex Pistols' "God Save the Queen." In response to Charlie's exaggerated performance, everyone smiles, enjoying themselves. Bob sings Elvis Costello's "(What's So Funny 'Bout) Peace, Love and Understanding." Everyone claps and cheers. Charlotte has put on a faded pink wig, and she sings the Pretenders' "Brass in Pocket," making intentional and sustained eye contact with Bob. She sings, "I'm gonna make you see/[There's] nobody else here, no one like me." In the call and response portion of the song, Charlotte sings, "I'm special," and Bob sings back to her "Special." Cutting to a later moment, Bob sings "More than This," by Roxy Music. In the chorus, he sings "More than this/You know there's nothing, more than this . . . " He turns and looks at Charlotte while he sings. She smiles, slightly embarrassed and looks away, but then she turns back and the two lock eyes. Coppola cuts again, to later in the evening. Outside the karaoke room, Charlotte sits alone and smokes a cigarette. Bob walks out of the room and sits next to her. He pulls the cigarette from her fingers, takes a drag, and gives it back to her. She lays her head on his shoulder. Bob folds his hands and rests them on his knee.

In this sequence, the protagonists experience two initial disruptions, or ruptures. Humor provides the first rupture. Throughout the scene in Charlotte's hotel room, humor functions as their primary form of connection. As Bob will point out later in the film, Charlotte rarely smiles. When she does smile, she usually denigrates others, like Kelly or the Japanese video game player dressed like a rock star. In this scene, Bob's humor has the opposite function. Rather than demeaning Charlotte, Bob's interactions with her—whether he knocks on the door, comments about her height, nags her like a parent, or rushes out the door—are non-coercive acts of connection. Bob also uses humor to care for Charlotte. When Bob discovers Charlotte's self-help CD, she responds with embarrassment. Bob's humor dispenses with her negative feelings. Once he jokes that he has the same CD, her anxiety disappears into laughter. The second rupture occurs through Charlie Brown. Rather than experience alienation from Tokyo, he guides the protagonists through the city, introduces them to new people, and grants them entry into places would likely never have access, like a private home of a stranger. If alienation is Bob and Charlotte's status quo, lack of alienation, or positive contact, ruptures their daily life.

In addition to these disruptions, Bob and Charlotte drift through their evening, through what Sandoval calls a "gentle abyss," where new possibilities of delight open up to them.[33] Unlike Bob's alienations at work or Charlotte's alienations as a tourist, Charlie ushers these Americans into many different physical spaces, never staying long at one place in particular. Following Charlie, neither Bob nor Charlotte attempts to control the movements or responses of others. In fact, they move from space to space with little or no expectations of what the night might hold. They drift through Tokyo, as though the city and the night are a gentle abyss. In this realm of possibility, the film envelops the protagonists with an array exhilarating sensual experiences. Coppola presents the first bar as a place of visual and aural wonder. The projection on the hanging balls mixed with the infectious dance music produce an atmosphere of delight, merely through their inhabitation of the space. Likewise, Bob delights at the peculiar and bizarre experience of speaking French with a Japanese interlocutor. The entire evening, they simply drift from one place and experience to the next.

In addition to delight, Coppola represents their drifting through montage-like editing, often cutting the middle of actions or events. For example, at the bar, Coppola cuts from the middle of a loud musical phrase (using a gentle fade) into the middle of a conversation between Bob and the Japanese French speaker. Rather than music, this scene foregrounds the conversation as the primary auditory element, and the volume of a new song is quite low on the soundtrack. A similar technique occurs in the next scene. After Charlotte, Bob, and Charlie find their way into a cab, Coppola cuts from the moving cab into the middle of an action in the next scene. At an apartment, Charlie leans down, out of frame, to pick up a camera. He then turns and takes a photograph of Charlotte. The abruptness of these cuts, in the middle of actions or musical phrases, suggests a breaking, that the drifting has an excitement, energy, and possibility that their daily lives of alienation do not. Throughout the scene, the film also drifts from fragments of one conversation to another—partial introductions; other conversations in Japanese; a surfer talks about a camping experience; Bob asks about marijuana. From these fragments, Coppola suddenly cuts to a different moment in the apartment: Charlie dancing to loud music. During the song, the protagonists "cruise" or "low-ride" through time. In one shot, Bob dances with Charlotte, then she cuts to Bob dancing with a Japanese woman, and Charlotte is in the background of the frame. In the middle of a musical phrase, Coppola cuts again, this time to Charlie, who leans into the camera in a close up, singing karaoke. In these scenes, Bob and Charlotte drift, cruise, or low-ride through their evening.

Through these driftings, Bob and Charlotte experience other bodily and relational ruptures. If both Bob and Charlotte's everyday life includes bodily alienations, these scenes present them as connected to their bodies. From the second bar, both protagonists run from the bartender, holding hands as they move through the arcade. In the apartment, Bob and Charlotte dance intensely with each other and other Japanese characters. And at the karaoke room, they sing and respond to others singing. One clear synchronic rupture of connection between Bob and Charlotte occurs during Bob's rendition of "More Than This." When Bob sings "More than this/You know there's nothing, more than this . . . " he and Charlotte gaze at each other. In that moment, his song claims, there is nothing else that matters as significant than this look they share. The punctum of connection occurs in the intimacy and stillness of a look and a song. The next scene affirms the connection. Out on the hallway, Charlotte lays her head on his shoulder, and the two simply sit, at rest with one another.

In a cab on their way home, after significant jet lag, Bob has finally fallen asleep. Charlotte looks at him and smiles. From the cab, Coppola cuts to a hotel hallway. Bob carries Charlotte in his arms. Like a child, Charlotte leans her head against his shoulder. Her arms are wrapped around his neck. Bob opens her room, places her in bed, takes off her shoes, and covers her with the comforter. She raises her eyelids slightly, smiles at him, and then closes her eyes, as if she is going to sleep. Bob rolls his eyes slightly in response to her lack of gratefulness. He turns off her light, touches her shoulder, and leaves the room. Back at his room, Bob calls his wife in an attempt to connect with her. He talks to her about the renovation to his office and tries to tell her about his evening. However, with the time difference, it is morning in Los Angeles, and Lydia struggles to get their daughter to eat breakfast. Their daughter interferes with the connection he is trying to make with his wife. Lydia ends the conversation abruptly, insisting that she has to get the kids to school. Bob winces in frustration. He tries to tell Lydia that he loves her, but she hangs up before he can get the words out. He hangs up the phone and says, "That was a stupid idea." His attempt to connect with his wife only ends in alienation.

The final rupture of the sequence occurs in their ability to rest with one another. In the cab, after all his jetlag, Bob finally sleeps, if only for a moment. Likewise, Bob cares for Charlotte, carrying her to the hotel room and putting her to bed. After all her jetlag, she finally rests. Coppola underscores the power of these ruptures with Bob's failed attempt to connect with his wife on the phone. Some alienations remain. But Bob and Charlotte have experienced disruptions to their everyday alienations and malaise, and they do so drifting together.

In drawing on Sandoval's account of drifting, our reading of this sequence bears some similarities to and some differences from two other readings. First, Rhetorical and media scholar Brian L. Ott and communication studies scholar Diane Marie Keeling argue that this sequence marks a shift in the film. "The sense of alienation and dislocation that dominates the first third of the film," they write, "is replaced by a feeling of intensity, energy, electricity, and engagement, which is sustained by total sensory immersion (envelopment)."[34] They name that feeling of immersion and envelopment with the phrase, "choric connection—a profound sense of oneness with the world."[35] This state is not unlike the state of the infant experiences in the womb,[36] an experience of "oneness with the mother's sounds, touch, warmth, and bodily rhythms."[37] Such connections are important in the wake of the wider sense of social alienations that technology produces. As our analysis implies above, we agree with Ott and Keeling that this sequence marks an important shift, from alienation to something like connection, energy, engagement—a clear disruption of their status quo. However, the connection we see them experience is not to be one with the world. For example, Bob and Charlotte still have trouble communicating with people they meet. Their linguistic alienation has not changed. But what has changed is the way they relate to each other, to spaces they inhabit, and to their own bodies. They seem less like infants in the womb and more like teenagers being introduced to something simultaneously strange and familiar.

Next, our reading also bears some similarities to and differences from that of Anna Backman Rogers. Drawing on the work of literary scholar Leo Charney, Rogers notes that in the early twentieth century, there was a widespread desire to intellectually make meaning, not of the past, but of the present moment. However, the present cannot be captured intellectually; it must be felt. Therefore, "the only way in which one can experience the present . . . is through drift."[38] When Rogers defines drifting, she defines it like an amalgam of Ott and Keeling and Sandoval. Drifting is an immersion of "oneself in the fabric of the world," and a bodily wandering, a flowing movement from place to place.[39] For Rogers, Bob and Charlotte are unable to drift[40] until the end of the film, where Bob and Charlotte drift in separate directions.[41] We agree that Bob and Charlotte drift, but Sandoval has convinced us that they begin that process in this sequence, not merely at the end of the film. And, while they experience connection, it seems less a connection with the world more broadly and more a connection to each other, particular spaces, and their own bodies. In both cases, as well, the aim of such connections and driftings is less about technology or modernity and more about coloniality.

## ATTACHMENT

In addition to drifting and rupture, Sandoval's account of love allows lovers to engage in non-dualistic attachments, or a third way of being in the world, for which the ancient middle voice of the verb serves as an illustration. Although drifting is an important component of love, love also enables attachments "with something else" or "to another system of knowledge."[42] In Western love, attachments between lovers have clear rules, which foster stereotypical responses, like jealousy. However, what Sandoval has in mind is an attachment that defies binary configurations.[43] Love, therefore, offers ways of relating that "do not easily slip into either side of a dominant binary opposition."[44] Outside of binaries, Sandoval argues that third ways of being in the world are possible. Referring to active and passive verbs, Sandoval offers the ancient linguistic form of the middle voice of the verb as an illustration of a third way. In ancient Greek, heterosexual marriage used two different verbs, one for men and one women. "*Gamein* is an active verb form—that is reserved for males—which means 'to marry,' while *gamesthai*, the same verb but in the middle voice, is reserved for women, and means 'to wed.'"[45] The active voice retains the distinction between the subject (man) and the object (woman). However, in the middle voice, which applies only to the woman, "the distinction between subject and object is obliterated" or "conflated."[46] The middle voice exists outside of the binaries of active/passive and subject/object to form an "an interrelating set of subjectivities."[47]

Furthermore, the practice of gift-giving can facilitate Sandoval's decolonial love, precisely through enabling lovers to accept and touch one another without recourse to binaries. Through dichotomies like colonizer and colonized, the process of colonialism produces dehumanization, i.e., colonized peoples are no longer people. Colonization aims to reduce those persons to passive objects, in what colonial theorist Franz Fanon calls *the damned*.[48] In French, the term damned (*damné*) is related to the term giver (*donner*). Through this linguistic link, Latino and Caribbean studies scholar Nelson Maldonado-Torres concludes that part of what colonialism "aims to obliterate" in those it curses as *damned* is "gift-giving and generous reception as a fundamental character of being-in-the-world."[49] In response, Hispanic Studies scholar Cornelia Gräbner argues that gift-giving contributes to love, because it suggests that acceptance can exist outside of the Western dichotomies like possessor/possessed or active/passive.[50] In Gräbner's analysis, while lovers can gift one another stories as acts of reciprocity, one of the most important and foundational gifts is trust.[51] As Maldonado-Torres points out, "This is the precise meaning of decolonization: restoration of the logic of the gift," such that lovers might be able "to touch the other, to feel the other, to explain the other to myself."[52] The logic of gift-giving helps lovers resisting the damaging work that colonial dichotomies perform. Third ways and gifts are at play in one scene in particular, the scene where Bob and Charlotte fall asleep.

The night after they sing karaoke, Charlotte cannot sleep. Soon, someone slips a note under her door, a message from Bob that asks, "Are you awake?" She smiles. In the next shot, Charlotte and Bob sit in his room, watching Federico Fellini's Western art film masterpiece *La Dolce Vita* (1960). While the film plays, Charlotte and Bob recount their memory of their first meeting. Eventually, they lie back on the bed, side by side, looking up at the ceiling. In a wide shot, Charlotte appears on screen left—Bob, screen right. Having taken these bodily comportments of intimacy, Charlotte shares a vulnerability that has been evident from the beginning of the film. She says to Bob, "I'm stuck," and asks, "Does it get easier?" Bob equivocates at first, "No. Yes. It gets easier," and then elaborates, "The more you know who you are and what you want, the less you let things upset you." Charlotte says that she does not know what she is supposed to be in life. She hates what she writes.

Her photographs are mediocre. But Bob comforts her, "You'll figure that out. I'm not worried about you." Charlotte then turns on her side and looks at Bob. The camera presents her face in profile, suggesting a disposition of earnestness. "But I'm so mean," she says. Bob laughs and comforts her again, "Mean's okay." He turns on his side to face her and places his right hand behind his head. He appears relaxed. She asks, "What about marriage? Does that get easier?" Bob's eyes dart in a slight panic. He pauses and then pulls back slightly, and says, "That's hard."

Bob says that he and Lydia enjoyed each other earlier in their marriage. She would accompany him when he made films, and they laughed together. Now, she stays home with their children. "It gets a whole lot more complicated when you have kids," he concludes. Charlotte notes how frightening the reality of children must be. Bob confirms her suspicion and continues, "It's the most terrifying day of your life the day the first one is born." Feeling the weight of the reality and thankful for his honesty, Charlotte says, "Nobody ever tells you that." But Bob lightens the tension with a half-joke, "Your life, as you know it, is gone," he smiles, "Never to return." Charlotte looks at him with an overwhelmed look but then relents with a smile. Bob continues, "But they learn how to walk, and they learn how to talk, and you want to be with them. And they turn out to be the most delightful people you will ever meet in your life." She relaxes and smiles. Bob rubs and closes his eyes, as if he is tired. He lies flat on his back. She also closes her eyes. As they fall asleep, Charlotte curls her legs so that she lies in the fetal position. Her toes touch his hip. He places his hand on her foot and lightly taps her with his fingers. As they fall asleep, he says, "You're not hopeless."

In the DVD featurette, "A Conversation with Bill Murray and Sofia Coppola," Murray comments on Bob and Charlotte's bedroom scene saying:

> [T]here's a romantic-encounter structure [in cinematic storytelling] that we are all familiar with. And usually it gets to the point where the writing . . . makes a choice to go one way or another. And usually both ways are . . . not true. . . . [P]eople [or, characters] either have an affair and consummate an affair, or they . . . turn on each other. . . . [W]hen you get to a point where you have the possibility to consummate an affair usually people will belittle their other life.[53]

Murray makes clear the either/or dualism the filmmakers self-consciously faced in tracing Bob and Charlotte's relationship. Either the couple consummates the affair (and diminish their married lives) or they turn on each other. Neither of which, Murray explains, is true. What Murray makes plain in his commentary on the scene is what Sandoval claims about decolonial love: Charlotte and Bob experience love as a third way of being in the world.

Bob and Charlotte's third way can be described, at least initially, through the ways it both affirms and denies binary configurations. For example, there are some elements of a father/daughter relationship between Bob and Charlotte. In Charlotte's hotel room, Bob asks her about all the things she needs for the evening, joking upon the way a father might interact with his daughter before they leave the home. Also, Bob acts like a father when he carries Charlotte to her room and puts her to bed. However, unlike the father/daughter binary, what they share with one another is not fully platonic. There are moments in which they behave the way lovers might. Exemplary is the karaoke scene where, through looks and lyrics, Charlotte and Bob flirt and sing intimately to one other. Charlotte communicates to Bob that she wants his attention, not unlike that of a romantic lover. She expresses this desire when she sings, "I'm gonna make you see/[There's] . . . [n]o one like me." In a similar gesture, Bob sings to Charlotte about the intimacy of the moment they share. As they gaze at one another, he sings, "You know there's nothing, more than this." However, what the bedroom scene articulates, which Murray's commentary confirms, is precisely the reality that they are not stereotypical lovers. They share a physical and emotional intimacy, but they do not consummate their vulnerability and erotic connection in a stereotypical sexual encounter. Hence, Sandoval might say, their relationship "do[es] not easily slip into either side of a dominant binary opposition."54

In this non-dualistic attachment, Bob and Charlotte exchange the gifts of vulnerability, acceptance, and touch. In this scene, Charlotte is vulnerable, and she shares two realities in her life: her malaise and her cruelty to others. Bob accepts her vulnerability as a gift, because he engages in an act of reciprocity. In response, he affirms her capacity to find significance in her work, her capacity to have meaningful relationships with others, and a disposition toward a hopeful future for her. His affirmation evades the dualism of active/passive or possessor/possessed. Bob does not treat Charlotte like a problem to be solved. He does not possess answers for her. He is not the older, wiser, active male that fixes the young, naïve, passive female. Out of his own subjectivity, all he can do is express what he experiences: he is not worried about her. He encourages her to keep writing. In his experience, being mean is not the end of relationality with others. His affirmation is a reciprocal, not a colonial, form of superiority. Inside of the practices of gift-giving and acceptance, they touch one another. When they lie on the bed together, they do so with intimacy and openness but unlike stereotypical sexual encounters. Charlotte's body suggests an alternative relational space. She rests in the fetal position, much like the safety and intimacy of her mother's womb, and it is in their shared maternal space that they touch one another. Their gifts produce, not a heterosexual binary, but a feminine space where life and rest take place. If what Maldonado-Torres argues is correct, that decolonization is the capacity to touch, feel, and explain the other to the self, then something very close to that is precisely what the protagonists share.

In reference to Murray's commentary, Bob's gifts to Charlotte are his own vulnerability and intimacy, which do not pose a threat to their marriages, much less demean their spouses. While he presents the difficulties of marriage and children with tenderness and humor, Bob claims, implicitly, that his children ended the good relationship he once had with his wife. Whether or not his assessment is accurate is, in effect, besides the point. Bob gifts Charlotte his vulnerability, refusing to hide the difficult truths of his experience. To further support the claim that their relationship refuses binaries of Western love, this scene and the remainder of the film confirm that their relationship does not constitute a threat to their marriages. It is, certainly, difficult to imagine their spouses would understand or approve of their intimacies, vulnerabilities, acceptance, and touch. However, they do not diminish their spouses. Those relationships are real and important. What they share together does not change those realities. This scene suggests the binaries that define most Western forms of love are, to a significant degree, "obliterated" in an unconventional, non-dualistic attachment.[55]

The day they fall asleep together, Charlotte takes a tourist trip to Kyoto. Meanwhile, Bob appears on a talk show with the "Johnny Carson of Japan" (Takashi Fujii). He loathes and endures the appearance. That night, Bob sits alone at the bar and smokes a cigar. After the red-headed lounge singer finishes her set, she sits next to Bob, orders champaign, and makes obvious eye contact with him. After Bob looks at her, Coppola cuts to the next morning. Bob wakes to find an empty bottle of champagne and hears the lounge singer singing in his bathroom. He rolls his eyes and lays his head back, pained at his drunken choice to sleep with her. As Bob loathes himself, Charlotte knocks at his door. Bob rushes out of bed and answers the door shirtless, his hair tousled. Charlotte jokes that he had a rough night and invites him out to lunch. Then, she hears the lounge singer singing. With a smile that is both condescending and hurt, she says, "Yeah, I guess you're busy." She forces one more smile before she turns her head with a look of woundedness. Over lunch, the two fight. Charlotte demeans him with insults like, "[S]he *is* closer to your age," and "maybe she liked the movies you made in the 70s, when you were still making movies" [emphasis added]. Bob looks hurt and insults her, "Wasn't there anyone else there to lavish you with attention?" Charlotte scowls at Bob and picks up her menu to avoid him. Once they order, Charlotte folds her arms and glares at him.

Both Bob and Charlotte's reaction conforms to Western binaries and suggests that, although they may have experienced aspects of decolonial love, their formation inside of stereotypical, Western love remain intact. The first signal that jealousy is at work is Bob's reaction to Charlotte at his door. He wants to hide the lounge singer's presence from her. Clearly, Bob knows that his sleeping with the lounge singer would provoke in Charlotte a negative reaction. Charlotte experiences his choice as an injury. Bob committed an infidelity against his wife, but Charlotte reacts as though he has committed an infidelity against her. The two protagonists' behavior also suggests at least two dichotomies. Charlotte implicitly expects to possess or control Bob's body in a real way. Although they never discussed it, she makes clear, in her hurt reaction and in her cruelty toward him over lunch, that he cannot stay in a relationship with her and sleep with whomever he desires. Similarly, during their lunch, she demeans his age and failed career with her humor. In response, Bob reciprocates with a demeaning insult of his own—that she is a spoiled child. Their demeaning behavior suggests that both Bob and Charlotte have been formed inside the norms of Western, colonial love, and they carry that formation with them. If Western, dichotomous love is the norm that we inhabit, then it should be of little surprise that Bob and Charlotte would both respond in this way. While they may have experienced a third way of being in the world, that single encounter did not prove sufficient to overcome a lifetime of Western, colonial formation.

## DRIFTING, EASE, AND WHOLENESS

That night, after their fight over lunch, a fire alarm causes everyone to vacate the building. Outside, Bob sees Charlotte and walks over to her. They avoid talking directly about their fight. Instead, they joke about how terrible their meal was. They look at each other apologetically. Charlotte asks when Bob will leave, and he says he leaves tomorrow. She tells him that she will miss him. At the bar, they share a sake, hold hands, look into each other's eyes, and make jokes. During the elevator ride to their respective floors, they gaze at each other. When Charlotte leaves the elevator, Bob kisses her, partly on her cheek and partly on her mouth. The next day, Bob walks through the hotel lobby to leave for his flight. He stops at a lobby phone and calls Charlotte's room, but she does not answer. He leaves a message for her, hoping that she would return his jacket. Out in the lobby, Bob's Japanese handlers take photos with him. Surprisingly, Charlotte arrives with his jacket. They share an awkward goodbye, which lacks the intimacy of their drink the previous night and their physical contact in the elevator. His handlers take pictures with Bob, but he cannot pay attention to them. His attention is drawn to her as she leaves the hotel. He tries to force a slight smile for the photograph, but his interaction with Charlotte has left him saddened.

Outside the hotel, he gets into a car that will take him to the airport. When the car stops at an intersection, he sees Charlotte walking. Bob immediately tells the car to wait. He exits the vehicle, chases after her, and stops her on the street. When she turns, her eyes are glassy, as though she has been holding back tears. They lock eyes and hug each other. Although she does not cry, within their embrace, her eyes suggest that she is overcome with emotion. He whispers something inaudible in her ear and kisses her on the mouth. The only words that are audible are his "Okay?" and her response, "Okay." They exchange goodbyes and kiss one another. As he walks away, he turns to look at her, and they both smile. As she walks away, into Tokyo, she smiles as though the interaction both emotionally moved and relieved her. He gets into the car and instructs the driver to proceed. When he first enters the car, his breath is heavy, likely from the emotional intensity of the interaction. But soon he settles, smiles slightly, and looks intently around the world outside of the car, filled with wonder. The film ends with shots similar to Bob's introduction: a car moving through the streets of Tokyo.

As this final sequence illustrates, in addition to rupture and attachment, lovers can also experience a renewed sense of drifting and being at ease in the world. If lovers can embrace a third way, Sandoval claims that one response to a world filled with dichotomies is an existence that remains in a state of "constant 'drifting' to a somewhere else."[56] Given what Sandoval says about attachments, drifting does not necessarily imply an absolute sense of detachment from others. Drifting is not confined to an either/or dichotomy. Rather, it exceeds such dualisms. In this sense, drifting after one has fallen in love constitutes a drifting in a renewed register. A quality of that renewed sense of drifting includes what Argentinian philosopher María Lugones (1944–) describes as "ease." In her article "Playfulness, 'World'-Travelling, and Loving Perception" (1987), Lugones offers a taxonomy of ease. For example, in various social spaces, one can be "a fluent speaker," or "know all the norms . . . words . . . and moves," of a particular community.[57] Such knowledge or competencies evoke from lovers a sense of ease. Or, most pertinent to film, one can be at ease when one has "a history with others that is shared."[58]

In a similar register, Chicana Studies scholar Gloria Anzaldúa claims that disruption can conclude with a sense of wholeness, which includes a personal centering and lack of loneliness. In a phenomenological register, Anzaldúa describes the experience of disruption coming to a close. "And suddenly," she says, "I feel everything rushing to a center, a nucleus. All the lost pieces of myself come flying from the deserts and the mountains and the valleys, magnetized toward that center. *Completa* [Complete]."[59] If alienation is that mechanism that pulls people from others and the individual from herself, then love yields a reunion, a whole, centered self. Anzaldúa's experience of centeredness makes another phenomenon possible, a lack of loneliness. In that moment, she claims, something "pulsates in my body, a luminous thin thing that grows thicker every day. Its presence never leaves me. I am never alone . . . And I am not afraid."[60] Anzaldúa does not specify what that presence or pulsation is, but she implies that it is an internal, organic phenomenon. She describes this attachment as a bright and small presence within her that grows over time. But most importantly, that presence outflanks her experience of alienation, even alleviating her fear. Fearless attachment within the individual is at least one end (or goal) of decolonial love.

Like the ending of *Somewhere*, *Lost in Translation* does not end with a clear resolution to the problems characters face; rather, both films present characters on the precipice of alternative ways of being in the world. *Lost in Translation* presents a renewed sense of drifting and ease. First, in the same sense that Charlotte and Bob do not consummate their relationship in any conventional way, they do not join themselves together in an ongoing relationship. Rather, they return to their individual lives, in a renewed sense of drifting. The film leaves Charlotte much like it has presented her throughout the film. She takes the posture of a tourist in Tokyo. However, her experience of love, intimacy, vulnerability, and physical embrace leaves her in a different state. She no longer appears alienated from herself. The final image of her suggests that she is relieved in some way, not unlike Anzaldúa's sense of inner wholeness. By implication, her experience of love opens up the possibility that she does not have to experience Japan's difference as alienating. Love can enable her to be who she is in a different way, grounded and with a sense of wholeness she did not experience at the beginning of the film. The world has not changed, but love has changed her. She is alone but not lonely. She can now drift from location to location, and she carries her attachment to Bob with her. The same can be said of Bob.

The film leaves him in a setting similar to the one that introduced him. Bob sits in the back of the car, drifting through Tokyo. Like Charlotte, he now carries with him a wholeness. None of his circumstances has changed. He still has a difficult relationship with his wife. His career is not what it once was. But his connection with Charlotte has changed him. In his last gesture of the film, he reaches out to Charlotte, not in a grand Hollywood gesture of romance, but in a minor one. He stops her on the street, embraces and kisses her. Most importantly, he gives her unknown words. This intimate but mysterious gesture provides Bob with a sense of wholeness; her reaction suggests that the same is true for Charlotte. His physical and emotional gestures are erotic but an eroticism typical of Hollywood films. Like Charlotte, Bob's wholeness mirror's Anzaldúa's. He is alone at the film's end, but he is not lonely, not alienated from himself.

The film's closing images emphasize Bob's experience of ease and centeredness. The ease he experiences is not one of cultural competency or knowledge. His time in Japan has not provided him with the skills to be a fluent Japanese speaker or to know all the norms, words, or moves within

Japanese culture. What he does inhabit, however, is a shared history with Charlotte. The words they utter to one another, "Okay," are an instantiation of what that shared history has produced. They are going to be okay. They will be at ease in the world. Bob's ease here takes the form of a physical centeredness. As Bob enters the car, he carries the intensity of emotion with him. He breathes heavily. But soon, he settles and centers. His breathing slows, which gives way to an awareness of the world around him. In the opening of the film, he rubbed his eyes because he was jet lagged, alienated from his body. Here, he no longer exists in a dreary disembodied alienation. His eyes scan the world. Ease and centeredness have made him alive to the world, as if he is intensely aware of it for the first time.

## A LIMINAL LOVE

Key to Sandoval's decolonial love is a connection to the lived experience of U.S. third world feminists of color. Their self-described social location is the "standpoint of the subjugated" or the social location of those "from below."[61] The language of subjugation or below-ness evokes a metaphor of social power that is hierarchical, vertical, or pyramidal. There are those who hold social locations that carry with them forms of power, like "the capitalist upper classes, white races, male genders, or dominant sexualities," over and against those who do not share those social locations.[62] However, what U.S. Third World feminists of color insist on is that those from below carry "their own unsettling, ominous, and equal accesses to forms of power," that has the potential to threaten vertical forms of power, like Western, dichotomous love.[63] But to function fully in that manner, love from below must be "recognized as a site of multidimensionality,"[64] which is "generated by affinity through difference,"[65] or as an "alliance and affection across lines of difference."[66] A full sense of decolonial love, therefore, must both engage difference and enable access to subjugated points of view from below.

If decolonial love, in its fullest sense, is dependent on affinity, alliance, and affection with those who see the world from below, then Bob and Charlotte's love exists in the liminal space between Western, dichotomous love and a decolonial love. This is not to say that Bob and Charlotte's love does not cross some lines of difference. They are of different genders, ages, and likely differing strata of the upper class. And they move, with the help of Charlie Brown, in and through various facets of Japanese life and culture, developing affections and affiliations that differ from the alienations they experienced previously. However, as film and media scholar Geoff King argues, the film's presentation of Bob and Charlotte "is all carried out within a very privileged arena."[67] They exist, as many of Coppola's characters do, in a rarefied world of wealth. Bob was a major movie star. He is paid $2 million for a few days' work. Charlotte attended Yale and earned a philosophy degree. Her husband works freelance for a record label that has enough resources to send him and his wife to Japan. Bob and Charlotte's love exists against the backdrop of the Park Hyatt Tokyo, one of the most exclusive and expensive high-rise luxury hotels in Japan. At nowhere in the film do they encounter any of the social or economic subjugation or below-ness that Sandoval describes as integral to decolonial love. While their love exists in a legitimate rendering of a third-space or middle-voice, it is trapped inside immense wealth. Their love, therefore, resists many of the dichotomies of Western love. They approach decolonial love, but they cannot leave that liminal place between the West and decolonization.

Furthermore, Sandoval insists that decolonial love leads to social transformation. In differentiating U.S. third world feminism from other liberative movements (like mainstream white feminism), Sandoval claims that the former refused to hold any single ideological position that could be used as "the single most correct site where truth can be represented."[68] Liberative movements that do embrace single, ideological correctness reproduce the colonial logics they fight against and become "trapped inside a drive for truth that ends only in producing its own brand of dominations."[69] Women of color offer a tactical and responsive way of moving through the world, shifting between sets of insights as situations demand. This act of shifting enables a form of love that can serve as a "technology for social transformation."[70] Decolonial love transforms the social sphere into a postcolonial sphere.

Bob and Charlotte's love is liminal, in part, because it embraces personal instead of social transformation. Clearly, the love Bob and Charlotte share violates aspects of Western, dichotomous love present in most Hollywood films. Their eroticism and attachments do not conform to the either/or Hollywood romance that Murray criticizes. One of Coppola's major accomplishments is to produce a romance that is both a romance and a way of relating that shifts and evades stereotypical love, like parental or romantic love. However, trapped inside their social location, unaffected by those "from below," the transformation Bob and Charlotte experience is purely personal. There is no sense, at the end of the film, that much else in their worlds will change as a result of their experience together. This is not to undermine the importance of the personal. Personal transformation, as Sandoval and other Chicana writers emphasize, is a vital component of social transformation. However, without social transformation, the love Bob and Charlotte experience is not decolonial.

Finally, Bob and Charlotte's love exists as a liminal love, because they lack a self-awareness of the colonial context that facilitates their love, particularly the mechanism of global capitalism. Film scholar Todd McGowan observes, "The excessive nature of global capitalism becomes visible in the sequence depicting Bob's arrival in Tokyo at the beginning of film."[71] He argues that Bob and Charlotte "see through" the excess of "Tokyo and of global capitalism" to critique their own American culture.[72] What both Coppola and McGowan leave unquestioned, however, is Bob and Charlotte's own participation in the colonial, global capitalism that enables them to be in Japan. Bob is an international movie star, working in Japan. Charlotte is a unemployed Yale graduate, whose husband is working in Japan. While, as McGowan suggests, they might be able to "see through" Tokyo, they show little awareness that the West brought capitalism to Japan. In effect, the global capitalism that enables Bob and Charlotte to approach decolonial love is the same mechanism that keeps them from encountering those whom Sandoval describes as "from below."

In addition to global capitalism, their experiences of alienation and inability to "see through" themselves links Bob and Charlotte to the colonial invaders who came before them. The couple do not arrive in Japan with weapons or religious oppression; however, like the invaders that came before them, they experience Japan as exotic and alienating. And it is precisely their colonial experience of alienation that facilitates their liminal love. If they could, perhaps, see through themselves in the same way McGowan suggests they can see through American culture, then perhaps they would do more than use their alienation to experience personal transformation. Or, as American Studies scholar Aaron Nyerges argues in relation to *Lost in Translation*, "The task is for the colonizing or imperializing population to examine the conduct, motives, desires, and consequences of the imperialist history that has formed its own subjectivity."[73] If Bob and Charlotte loved in such a way that understood the history of their own subjectivity, then perhaps they could touch someone from below, through whom they might see themselves even more clearly and receive a deep sense of the limits of their love. This lack of self-awareness is the film's most important limitation when it comes to the film's representation of decolonial love.

Based on our reading of this film, we offer two implications. First, malaise, in the way Taylor describes it, is a necessary but insufficient aspect of modernity. What he is missing, as Sandoval and other Chicana scholars imply, is the colonial stratification that marks the modern period. Any fulsome account of malaise demands an understanding of the phenomenon that takes into account the experience of Black, Indigenous, and other people of color. Until further evidence can be marshaled, what Taylor is describing should be properly understood as a "white malaise of modernity." While we take this as an obvious shortcoming, the fact that many of Taylor's critics fail to take someone like Sandoval seriously means, for us, this obvious shortcoming needs to be said aloud and repeatedly by people like us—white, male scholars.

Second, we briefly recount Coppola's representation of masculinity and love from the first section of the book, as a means to illustrate the shortcomings many white, settler colonists experience in our contemporary moment. *The Virgin Suicides* presents a hegemonic form of masculinity that, in part, links love with violence. The men who narrate the film are unable or unwilling to see the world of violence the Lisbon sisters inhabit. *Somewhere* traces how a masculine figure, engaged in cycles of toxic behavior, can come to the threshold of an alternative way of being a man, a way that embraces features including delight, vulnerability, play, and rest. If *The Virgin Suicides* presents a world where love can be a domain in which violence takes place, *Somewhere* demonstrates that the work of untangling love from violence includes attending to features like the formation of peoples through *habitus*, through disrupting the nexus of toxic cycles, harmful bodily acts, and the forms of materiality that facilitate those cycles and behaviors. *Lost in Translation* presents yet another progression. Bob and Charlotte inhabit a liminal space beyond hegemonic or toxic masculinity. They experience a form of love approaching decolonial love, a love that exists beyond many damaging Western binaries. When read in this order, *Lost in Translation* offers a massive, imaginative leap for the manner in which Coppola represents the possibilities of men (and women) to live outside of hegemonic and toxic masculinities.

However, because Bob and Charlotte only seem able to love in the liminal space between Western and decolonial love, their love suggests problems that many white settlers have not fully confronted. This is, in many ways, one of the key pressing questions for the white settlers who, as a group, benefit from the colonial project of global capitalism Sandoval means to critique. Like Bob and Charlotte, the world, in some very important ways, works for white people, especially if they are descendants of settlers in lands like the United States, Canada, New Zealand, Israel, or Australia. While many have refused to acknowledge these colonial realities, some settlers have begun the process of coming to grips with realities like genocide and land theft. As is often the case, these settler folks perform acts like "Land Acknowledgements" where, before a public event, a white settler stands and names the Indigenous peoples who were first on the lands they now stand. Perhaps those same folks write public critiques, teach differently, or support Indigenous movements like the Idle No More or Wet'suwet'en protests in Canada; or the Standing Rock or Thirty Meter Telescope protests in the United States. However, something deeper is needed. Decolonial love means that white settlers are going to perform the challenging work of imagining and living a different form of life. What shape that differing form of life should take is an open question. But that is the question that needs to be pressed, imagined, and lived for not only Sandoval to experience freedom, but also for white settlers to experience it too.

## REFERENCES

"A Conversation with Bill Murray and Sofia Coppola." *Lost in Translation*. Los Angeles, CA: Universal Pictures Home Entertainment, 2003. DVD.
Andersen, Kara Lynn. "My Stockings. Lip Them: Consuming Japan Through Film and Video Games." *Post Script—Essays in Film and the Humanities*, 28 no. 2 (Winter 2008): 82–91.
Anzaldúa, Gloria. *Borderlands/La Frontera: The New Mestiza*, 4th edition. San Francisco: Aunt Lute Press, 2007.
Cardullo, Bert. "Love Story, or Coppola vs. Coppola." *The Hudson Review*, 57 no. 3 (Autumn 2004): 463–470.
Chen, Kuan-Hsing. *Asia as Method: Toward Deimperialization*. Durham: Duke University Press, 2010.
Gräbner, Cornelia. "'But how to speak of such things?': Decolonial Love, the Coloniality of Gender, and Political Struggle in Francisco Goldman's *The Long Night of White Chickens* (1992) and Jennifer Harbury's *Bridge of Courage* (1994) and *Searching for Everardo* (1997)." *Journal of Iberian and Latin American Studies*, 20 no. 1 (2014): 51–74.
King, Geoff. *Lost in Translation*. Edinburgh: Edinburgh University Press, 2010.
*Lost in Translation*. Directed by Sofia Coppola. Los Angeles, CA: Universal Pictures Home Entertainment, 2003. DVD.
Lugones, María. "Playfulness, 'World'-Travelling, and Loving Perception." *Hypatia*, 2 no. 2 (Summer 1987): 3–19, www.jstor.org/stable/3810013.
Maldonado-Torres, Nelson. "On the Coloniality of Being." *Cultural Studies*, 21 no. 2–3 (2007):240–270.
McGowan, Todd."There is Nothing *Lost in Translation*." *Quarterly Review of Film and Video*, 24 no. 1 (2007): 53–63.
Nyerges, Aaron. "Orienting the Coppolas: A New Approach to U.S. Film Imperialism." *Sydney Studies in English*, 40 (2014): 1–20. openjournals.library.sydney.edu.au/index.php/SSE/article/view/8317/8453.
Ott, Brian L. and Diane Marie Keeling. "Cinema and Choric Connection: *Lost in Translation* as Sensual Experience." *Quarterly Journal of Speech* 97 no. 4 (2011): 363–386.
Rogers, Anna Backman. *Sofia Coppola: The Politics of Visual Pleasure*. New York: Berghahn Book, 2019.
Sandoval, Chela. *Methodology of the Oppressed*, Theory Out of Bounds vol. 18. Minneapolis: University of Minnesota Press, 2000.
Smith, James K. A. *How (Not) to Be Secular: Reading Charles Taylor*. Grand Rapids, MI: Wm. B. Eerdmans Publishing, 2014. iBooks.
Takemura, Masaaki. "Sofia Coppola, *Lost in Translation* (2003)." *Markets, Globalization & Development Review*, 2 no. 4 (2017): 1–7.

Taylor, Charles. *The Malaise of Modernity*. Scarborough, ON: HarperCollins Canada, 1991. iBooks.

———. *The Secular Age*. Cambridge MA: The Belknap Press of Harvard University Press, 2007.

Veracini, Lorenzo. "Introducing Settler Colonial Studies." *Settler Colonial Studies* 1 no. 1 (2011): 1–12.

Wright, George. "Hit Film Gets Lost in Racism Row." *The Guardian*, February 27, 2004. www.theguardian.com/world/2004/feb/27/oscars2004.usa.

## NOTES

1. Charles Taylor, *The Malaise of Modernity* (Scarborough, ON: HarperCollins Canada, 1991), iBook.
2. Charles Taylor, *The Secular Age* (Cambridge, MA: The Belknap Press of Harvard University Press, 2007), 303.
3. Taylor, *The Malaise of Modernity*, iBooks.
4. James K. A. Smith, *How (Not) to Be Secular: Reading Charles Taylor* (Wm. B. Eerdmans Publishing: Grand Rapids MI, 2014), iBooks.
5. Taylor, *The Secular Age*, 302.
6. Ibid., 307.
7. Ibid.
8. Ibid.
9. Ibid., 308. Author's emphasis.
10. Ibid.
11. Like Brian L. Ott, Diane Marie Keeling, and Geoff King, we also note the alienation characters experience in the film. Our reading extends their observations. See Brian L. Ott and Diane Marie Keeling, "Cinema and Choric Connection: *Lost in Translation* as Sensual Experience," *Quarterly Journal of Speech* 97 no. 4 (2011): 363. See Geoff King, *Lost in Translation* (Edinburgh: Edinburgh University Press, 2010), 126.
12. Several writers have noted that these jokes are problematic. In his commentary on the racist nature of these jokes, Geoff King says, "The lack of any other motivation for such examples makes them appear to be egregious cases of crude stereotyping, in search of cheap laughs. The film also has a tendency to emphasize the 'crazy' or 'extreme' nature of some aspects of Japanese culture, including the 'premium fantasy' prostitute who visits Bob in his hotel room and the oddball chat-show host with whom Bob appears on television, among several others." King, *Lost in Translation*, 132. Similarly, Bert Cardullo argues that the film "is very funny, yes, but at the expense of the Japanese people." Bert Cardullo, "Love Story, or Coppola vs. Coppola," *The Hudson Review* 57 no. 3 (Autumn 2004): 466. Masaaki Takemura notes, "some Japanese critics felt a sense of malaise and discomfort about this film, seeing it as a crass stereotype." Masaaki Takemura, "Sofia Coppola, *Lost in Translation* (2003)," *Markets, Globalization & Development Review* 2 no. 4 (2017): 2. Kara Lynn Andersen argues that, despite "Coppola's best intention to depict Japanese culture," her film

fails to "escape charges of racism." Kara Lynn Andersen, "My Stockings. Lip Them: Consuming Japan Through Film and Video Games," *Post Script—Essays in Film and the Humanities* 28 no. 2 (Winter 2008): 82. Additionally, during Oscar season, an organization called the Asian Media Watch advocated for members of the Academy of Motion Picture Arts and Sciences to not vote for the film. See George Wright, "Hit Film Gets Lost in Racism Row," *The Guardian*, February, 27 2004, accessed December 13, 2020, www.theguardian.com/world/2004/feb/27/oscars2004.usa.

13. Anna Backman Rogers, *Sofia Coppola: The Politics of Visual Pleasure* (New York: Berghahn Book, 2019), 77.

14. Ibid., 7.

15. Chela Sandoval, *Methodology of the Oppressed*, Theory Out of Bounds vol. 18 (Minneapolis: University of Minnesota Press, 2000), 2.

16. Ibid., 141.

17. Ibid., 142.

18. Cornelia Gräbner, "'But how to speak of such things?': Decolonial Love, the Coloniality of Gender, and Political Struggle in Francisco Goldman's *The Long Night of White Chickens* (1992) and Jennifer Harbury's *Bridge of Courage* (1994) and *Searching for Everardo* (1997)," *Journal of Iberian and Latin American Studies*, 20 no. 1 (2014): 53.

19. Sandoval, *Methodology of the Oppressed*, 142.

20. Ibid.

21. Ibid., 155.

22. Ibid., 2.

23. Ibid., 4.

24. Ibid.

25. Ibid., 140.

26. Gräbner "'But how to speak of such things?'," 53.

27. Sandoval, *Methodology of the Oppressed*, 170.

28. Ibid., 141.

29. Ibid., 140.

30. Ibid., 142.

31. Ibid., 140.

32. Ibid., 145.

33. Ibid., 140.

34. Ott and Keeling, "Cinema and Choric Connection," 372.

35. Ibid., 365.

36. Ibid., 366.

37. Ibid. 374.

38. Rogers, *Sofia Coppola*, 83.

39. Ibid., 87.

40. Ibid., 84.

41. Ibid., 88.

42. Ibid., 146.

43. Ibid., 147.

44. Ibid., 150.

45. Ibid., 156.
46. Ibid., 156.
47. Ibid., 144.
48. Nelson Maldonado-Torres, "On the Coloniality of Being," *Cultural Studies* 21 no. 2–3 (2007): 257–8.
49. Ibid., 258.
50. Gräbner, "'But how to speak of such things?'," 54, 56, and 53.
51. Ibid., 60.
52. Maldonado-Torres, "On the Coloniality of Being," 260.
53. "A Conversation with Bill Murray and Sofia Coppola," *Lost in Translation* (Los Angeles, CA: Universal Pictures Home Entertainment, 2003), DVD.
54. Sandoval, *Methodology of the Oppressed*, 150.
55. Ibid., 156.
56. Ibid., 144. Here we also affirm what Rogers notes about how Bob and Charlotte drift at the end of the film. Rogers, *Sofia Coppola*, 83.
57. María Lugones, "Playfulness, 'World'-Travelling, and Loving Perception," *Hypatia* 2 no. 2 (Summer 1987): 12, www.jstor.org/stable/3810013.
58. Ibid.
59. Gloria Anzaldúa, *Borderlands/La Frontera: The New Mestiza*, 4th edition (San Francisco: Aunt Lute Press, 2007), 73.
60. Ibid.
61. Sandoval, *The Methodology of the Oppressed*, 174–5.
62. Ibid., 75.
63. Ibid.
64. Ibid., 76–77.
65. Ibid., 174.
66. Ibid., 170.
67. King, *Lost In Translation*, 138.
68. Sandoval, *The Methodology of the Oppressed*, 59.
69. Ibid.
70. Ibid., 2.
71. Todd McGowan, "There is Nothing *Lost in Translation*," *Quarterly Review of Film and Video* 24 no. 1 (2007):54.
72. Ibid.
73. Quoted from Kuan-Hsing Chen, *Asia as Method: Toward Deimperialization* (Durham: Duke University Press, 2010), 3. Aaron Nyerges, "Orienting the Coppolas: A New Approach to U.S. Film Imperialism," *Sydney Studies in English* 40 (2014): 18, openjournals.library.sydney.edu.au/index.php/SSE/article/view/8317/8453.

*Chapter Eight*

# A Managed Love

## *Emotional Labor, Exhaustion, and Unhappiness in* On the Rocks *(2020)*

For her seventh feature, Coppola made a film inspired by classic Hollywood cinema. She wanted to produce a film in the style of the Myrna Loy and William Powell vehicle *The Thin Man* (1943), in which the two main characters drink martinis and try to solve a mystery. She also reflected on a conversation she had with her father, the famed filmmaker Francis Ford Coppola. Sofia was trying to deal with someone she liked but who ignored her. Her father informed her that "a [playboy] can be like air traffic control, and women are the planes that have to be managed."[1] Both of these features come together in *On the Rocks*. Laura (Rashida Jones) and her playboy father, Felix (Bill Murray), drink martinis and solve the mystery of whether or not her husband, Dean (Marlon Wayans) is having an affair. In reflecting on the film, film reviewer Owen Gleiberman notes that part of the struggle Laura finds herself in is if she should trust Felix's playboy way of seeing the world. Because he is a philanderer investigating a potential philanderer, Laura wonders if Felix's "flawed rapscallion way" of seeing men and women is accurate, or "does he see what he wants to see?"[2] Eventually, Gleiberman says, Laura and Felix learn "who they are through the lens of . . . love."[3] The significance of managing others and love is precisely what is at stake for Laura and Felix, but the film explores them through an unusual device: emotional labor.

Through Laura's and Felix's experiences of emotional labor, exhaustion, and unhappiness, *On the Rocks* points to both a critical and constructive account of love. Our argument unfolds in three sections. First, if emotional labor is the task of managing the emotions of the self and others, then Laura and Felix are constantly engaged in such tasks. Within the absence of Laura's romantic and sexual connection with Dean, he generates emotional labor for her through his odd behavior and his lack of appreciation. And her emotional labor occurs within the context of an unrelenting and emotionally monotonous daily routine. Where Laura is simply trying to survive, Felix's emotional labor is productive, primarily producing in others the experiences of recognition and affirmation. Next, emotional labor is, however, not without hidden costs, such as emotional laborers unable to process the impacts of exhaustion on the body. Such exhaustion can weaken or debilitate. Laura's relationships with her extended family and friend Vanessa (Jenny Slate) exhaust her to states of immobility. By contrast, however, Laura experiences Felix as both exhausting and energizing in ways others do not.

Finally, Laura experiences unhappiness, and cultural studies scholar Sara Ahmed's account of the (un)happy housewife illuminates her experience. The image of the happy housewife appears in eighteenth-century philosopher Jean-Jacques Rousseau. He claims that a housewife must align her happiness to the happiness of others, and he substantiates his claims from a self-justifying appeal to nature. Ahmed claims that Rousseau's account of happiness is a fantasy, and unhappiness or so-called "killjoys" can critique that fantasy. Like Rousseau, Felix's misogyny is self-justifying, including his desire for control, his denigration of marriage, and his appeal to nature. At first, Laura experiences only ephemeral flashes of unhappiness, but with Felix she explores her unhappiness more deeply, in moments of vulnerability and as an angry killjoy. Because Laura and Felix's vulnerability suggests a more expansive definition of emotional labor, we conclude the chapter with a critical and constructive account of the love Felix and Laura experience together.

*On the Rocks* opens on a black screen. Felix tells Laura that, as her father, she will always be his until she marries, and then she will still belong to him. Coppola cuts to Laura and Dean's wedding day. Dean and Laura leave their reception to swim in a pool together. A few years later, Laura and Dean are the parents of two children, Maya (Liyanna Muscat) and Theo (Alexandra and Anna Reimer). Dean has recently started a business and is away on a trip. Laura cleans up after the children and then lies in bed, watching a routine by comedian Chris Rock. Late that night, Laura is asleep and Dean, who had taken a sedative on the plane, slips into bed and passionately kisses Laura. Once Laura pulls away, Dean looks at her oddly, rolls over, and passes out. Dean's odd behavior troubles Laura, but the next day she goes through her morning routine: she gets the kids ready for the day; takes Maya to school, where she interacts awkwardly with Vanessa; goes home to put Theo to bed and attempts but fails to write the novel she is working on. Distracted by Dean's behavior, she calls a friend for advice but also calls Felix. He confirms her worst fears and claims that Dean thought she was someone else. Later that day, she makes a discovery that causes her to suspect that Dean might be having an affair. Laura discovers a woman's toiletry bag in his luggage. When she asks Dean about the bag, he says that he carried it for a co-worker, Fiona (Jessica Henwick), who did not have room in her luggage. That weekend, she spends the day with her family, and they also insinuate that Dean might be cheating on her, much like Felix cheated on Laura's mother. A few days later, Felix shows up at Laura's apartment and the two have lunch. Felix convinces Laura that they should find out if Dean is having an affair with Fiona.

Though Dean is on a business trip during Laura's birthday, he, Maya, and Theo give her a gift, a Thermomix, a high-end kitchen device. The gift disappoints her. Later that night, Felix shows up unannounced and insists that Laura go out with him for her birthday. His presence distresses Laura, but she relents. He gives her a gift she loved as a child, Felix's watch. He shares that he has been following Dean, who recently purchased an item from Cartier, a French luxury brand known for exquisite jewelry. This news distresses Laura, because she did not receive jewelry for her birthday gift. Dean comes home and the family is delighted to see him. But, when Dean takes Laura to a wine bar for a belated birthday, the interaction ends awkwardly. A few days later, Dean has a work dinner. Felix picks up Laura in a sports car to follow him. Dean leaves the restaurant with three other people, two men and Fiona. The two men leave in a cab, whereas Fiona and Dean get into a cab together. Their action implies Dean is, indeed, having an affair with Fiona. Felix races after their cab, but, since he was speeding, the police pull him over and he talks his way out of ticket. Felix and Laura have martinis at a bar, where she expresses her deepest sadness: a single tear falls into her drink.

Soon, Felix discovers that Dean is taking a suspicious trip to Mexico. Laura, saddened even more by the news, walks alone on the street. Later that night, Dean confirms his trip and that Fiona is going with him. Felix convinces Laura to go to Mexico, hoping to get to the bottom of what is happening. In Mexico, Laura and Felix very difficult conversation over dinner, having to do with Felix's sexual infidelities with her mother. After dinner, they spy on Dean's room and see Fiona there. But they discover that Dean gave Fiona and her girlfriend his room. He returned to New York early. In part because Fiona is lesbian, Laura becomes convinced that Dean is not having an affair. Infuriated, after rushing back to her room and yelling angrily at Felix, Laura returns home and tells Dean everything. A few days later, Felix half-heartedly apologizes to Laura. The film closes with Dean and Laura at dinner. He did buy her a watch from Cartier. She takes off her father's watch and puts on the one Dean gave her.

## EMOTIONAL LABOR

Sociologist Arlie Russell Hochschild's neologism "emotional labor" emerged from a response she had to sociologist C. Wright Mills. As a graduate student, Hochschild was entranced by Mills' book *White Collar* (1951), particularly a chapter entitled "The Great Salesroom." However, when Mills narrated the toll that the act of selling had on salespeople, Hochschild sensed that "something was missing."[4] Years later, she argued that what was missing was the "emotional labor" the salesperson performed.[5] Emotional labor occurs when an individual presents or restrains certain emotions as a means of inducing in others an emotion, feeling, or state of being. People put their emotions to work when, for example, they "create a publicly observable facial and bodily display."[6] Because this labor can be sold, it has market value. Even though she writes about the male-dominated field of bill collectors, Hochschild puts considerable emphasis on the female-dominated work of flight attendants. If flight attendants go to work in a state of sadness, for example, emotional labor describes the work they must do to smile at the customers whom they serve. Other forms of emotional labor might include being polite when a customer is rude, complimenting someone's clothes, or laughing at a joke that is not funny.[7] In essence, emotional labor occurs where there is a disjunction or estrangement between how a worker feels and how the worker presents or expresses emotion. Such conditions discourage emotional transparency and vulnerability. Emotional labor is labor, in a negative sense, because the labor inhibits who the person authentically is or what the person authentically feels.[8]

Hochschild draws attention to emotional labor, because corporations often ignore the negative impact emotional labor has on workers, especially invisibility. When flight attendants discover Hochschild's work, they often share negative and alienating experiences—of acting cheerful when they were depressed, of suppressing feelings of fear, or of responding to rudeness with humor. But, she notes, "Much of the anguish I heard was linked to the sheer invisibility of emotional labor."[9] Hochschild offers the example of a nurse who recounted to her:

> how galling it felt to give loving care daily to needy dying patients and be ignored by emotionally obtuse surgeons, for whose absence of bedside manner she was quietly making up. "The surgeons take the cancer out," she explained, "but medically and emotionally, we nurses get the patients through the ordeal. Why can the world see and credit what the doctors do, but not what the nurses do?"[10]

The quotation implies a few realities about emotional labor. Inasmuch as nurses work to manage the emotional well-being of their patients, their work is, in part, emotional labor. Calming a patient after a negative interaction with a surgeon is work. Also, she illustrates the cost of invisible or overlooked emotional labor. Hochschild's nurse, for example, is not necessarily asking to be paid more for labor. The nurse simply expresses a desire that her work be recognized as work, that her work is important, and that her work compensates for the failure of more visible workers. Hence, emotional labor is not only labor, but when individuals or corporations refuse to recognize it as labor, workers experience such invisibility negatively. *On the Rocks* presents these facets of emotional labor, particularly through Laura and Felix.

Partly because Laura is a stay-at-home mother, her emotional labor occurs within the loss of a romantic and sexual connection with Dean. Coppola establishes Laura's loss and labor with two contrasting shots. At Laura and Dean's wedding reception, the two slip away to indulge in a romantic moment on their own. Coppola points the camera down at the floor, tracking to reveal the clothes and shoes that they have removed, the shot ending on Laura's wedding dress. Coppola cuts to Dean sitting in a pool. With a nod, he invites her in. Laura stands on the edge of the pool with her veil still on, and in a wide shot, she jumps in the pool. The director then cuts to the title card, "On the Rocks." Her marriage is what will be, "on the rocks," or in trouble. The next shot mirrors the previous tracking shot but to non-romantic effect. Coppola points the camera at the floor and tracks in a near identical movement. The camera follows Laura's bare feet. The floor is covered with children's clothes, toys, and food. She stoops to pick up the clothes and toys but leaves the food on the floor. In the next shot, she lies in bed, watching a comedy routine by comedian Chris Rock. "No one tells you that once you get married," Rock explains, "you will never fuck again. If you like fucking, marriage ain't for you." Laura laughs, likely at the accuracy with which it represents her life. The tracking shots and Rock's routine suggest the shape of Laura's experience. Cleaning up after her children has replaced her romantic and sexual connection with Dean. Within the context of that loss, the film will reveal that Laura's existence is, primarily, the labor of managing the emotions and lives of those within her household.

That same night, Dean creates emotional labor for Laura through his odd behavior. Dean returns home from a work trip to London, and he stumbles into their bedroom. As Laura will explain later, he took a sedative on the plane and is under its influence. Laura is asleep. He crawls into bed and on top of her. She wakes as Dean kisses her intensely. She is confused but gently pulls away from him and says, "Hi," as if, having not seen Dean for a while, she desires the intimacy of eye contact first. Dean opens his eyes and looks at her. He seems perplexed, rolls over, and passes out. A close-up shot on Laura registers her confusion at this odd behavior. This confusion is labor, because she does not feel she can be transparent with Dean about his behavior. The next morning, they do not speak about it; she behaves as if everything is normal.

Within this context, Dean harms Laura through his lack of appreciation for her emotional labor. The morning after Dean returns, Laura and the kids flutter about the house getting ready for school and eating breakfast. Everyone is running late. In this harried state, Laura performs emotional labor, first through her effort to create the conditions in which everyone can have a happy vacation. She reminds Dean about the deposit they need for the vacation house, saying, "I have to figure that out by tomorrow." Dean, trying to evade engaging in emotional labor, insists that he does not know anything about the matter. Laura widens her eyes in frustration at his dismissal. He responds, "I'll check." She also reminds him about a friend, Jimmy, who has recently opened a restaurant. She has to let Jimmy know which night to make a reservation. This emotional labor attempts to manage Jimmy's emotions. Making a reservation will likely evoke a positive response from him. Dean seems disinterested, shrugs, and says that Thursday works. As he leaves, he jokes sarcastically, "Any more questions?" Laura cocks her head sideways in kindhearted disapproval, but she expresses disapproval, nonetheless. Dean laughs. Laura smiles in annoyance, not only at his sarcasm but at the reality that he is making fun of the emotional labor she is performing for him and the family. Most of the scene plays out in a medium two shot of Dean and Laura. Unlike the intimacy of the single shot on Laura from the previous night, the tension in the scene is lighter, and the medium shot and the chaotic energy of the house reflects an almost comedic quality. Nevertheless, Dean fails to appreciate her emotional labor, and, like Hochschild's nurse, she experiences his lack of appreciation negatively.

A similar lack of appreciation occurs when Dean returns home after Laura's birthday. He takes her to a wine bar, where they each have a drink. However, the interaction is awkward for Laura, because he is preoccupied with work and is texting on his phone. After a moment of idle conversation, she invites Dean to labor emotionally with her. In a moment of vulnerability, she asks Dean what he thinks about sending Theo to preschool early. The question encourages Dean to share the emotional labor of managing Theo's future well-being, but Dean does not show any interest or appreciation. His response takes the form of a dismissal. "Whatever. I trust you." Because Laura wants to share the labor of managing Theo's future with Dean, his compliment, "I trust you," dismisses both her desire to collaborate and her anxiety about how best to care for their child. Like her previous response to his lack of appreciation, she performs emotional labor to cover her true feeling. Laura smiles, not in annoyance, but as a way to present a different emotion, contentment, with what she is feeling, sadness. Not unlike the surgeon and the nurse, Dean ignores and, hence, harms Laura.

The emotional labor she performs, including these negative interactions with Dean, occurs within the context of her daily routine, which moves at an unrelenting and monotonous pace. Coppola presents the monotony of daily life in two ways. First, Laura's daily routine includes the same events repeated with little or no variation. She prepares her children for their day, engages in activities like preparing food, dressing Theo, helping her brush her teeth, or fixing Maya's hair. With Theo in a stroller, Laura drops Maya off at school, walking her to her classroom. At school, she runs into Vanessa and listens to her talk incessantly about her personal life, with no regard for Laura. The latter politely excuses herself, returns home, and puts Theo to bed for a nap. While she sleeps, the protagonist tries and fails to write. In these sequences, Michael Nyman's minimalist composition "In Re Don Giovanni" captures the monotonous character of her experience. Composed in the late 1970s, Nyman's composition plays at *moderato*, or moderate tempo. Even though the tempo is not fast, the high strings play sixteenth notes throughout the entire piece, giving it a rushed feel. Additionally, they use a double stop technique, where the players strike two strings at a time with their bows. The double stops are played here with an almost aggressive, sawing motion with the bow. And the strings also play *forte*, or loudly, the entire piece, never varying their volume. These four elements—the continuous, double stopped sixteenth notes played loudly—gives the piece an unrelenting, monotonous, and emotionally monochromatic tenor. Like the unchanging nature of such instrumentation, Laura's daily routine impacts her with this same unrelenting monochromatic emotional impact. Her work, children, and husband provide no variation from her quotidian routine.

Where Laura tries to simply survive the emotional labor her day demands of her, Felix revels in his emotional labor, through which he aims to produce in others the feeling of recognition and affirmation. Three scenes illustrate this reality. The first occurs when Felix takes Laura out for lunch. Felix has three brief interactions in which he performs emotional labor. When Laura and Felix approach the restaurant, a stranger walks out, a pregnant woman. Felix affirms her in a way she likely does not usually experience, "Oh my gosh, do you look beautiful." The woman, slightly embarrassed, smiles and continues on her way. As they enter the building, Felix reminds Laura who the doorman is, an older gentleman named Cliff. When Cliff sees them, he smiles and shakes Felix's hand. The latter asks about Cliff's mother and her hip and Cliff says that she is well. As they end the exchange, Felix reminds Cliff that his mother has to perform her hip exercises or else she might "as well have kept the old one." This last statement implies that Cliff and Felix have likely had a series of personal conversations. One of the subjects of these talks has been Cliff's mother's health and physical therapy. Given their differing status and given Cliff's reaction, it is likely that the doorman experiences such acts of recognition as not only welcome but also as a form of respect. At their table, Felix takes note of their waitress' body and asks if she is a ballet dancer. She responds a bit sheepishly at first, perhaps because she is both surprised and is clearly not a working ballerina. But soon she speaks with a sense of pride and smiles. "Yes," she says with a Russian accent, "I studied at the Bolshoi." Once a private theater of Russian royalty, the Bolshoi Theater claims to be "one of the main symbols" of Russian culture.[11] She speaks as though she received an excellent education. Felix is delighted by the information. He raises his drink and, speaking Russian, toasts her. In each case, Felix's emotional labor provides a way for the person he is interacting with to be affirmed or recognized in some real and significant way. For women, being seen also includes discomfort, since his emotional labor revolves around their bodies.

Felix also performs emotional labor when the police detain him and Laura for speeding, trying to follow Dean and Fiona's cab. When police lights and a siren suddenly appear behind them, Felix says "Oops. We're gonna meet people. We're gonna make new friends, I'm afraid. Nothing to worry about." These lines reframe an encounter with law enforcement as a social opportunity, and they signal his intention to perform emotional labor. Once out of the car, Felix notices the officer's name badge and asks if he is the son of Tommy O'Callaghan. The officer, a bit stunned, responds that he is. Felix pulls out his phone to call Tommy, but the officer dissuades him. Felix then recounts another connection with the man's family. Having drank so heavily with the officer's grandfather at his retirement party, Felix is not sure how everyone made it home safely. And like his interaction with women, Felix presses into personal matters. He asks if the officer has children. The latter hesitates: "We're trying." Even though the response communicates a certain amount of pain around infertility, Felix transforms it into an affirmation and recognition, by way of a sex joke. "Attaboy!" says Felix. "It's the trying that's so much fun, isn't it?" The officer laughs enthusiastically in agreement. Felix brings the interaction to a conclusion as though they simply bumped into each other on the street. He tells the officer that it was good to see him, and, completely disarmed by the entire interaction, the officer decides to let them go without a ticket. Like his emotional labor in the restaurant, here Felix uses the existing knowledge he has curated over the years to recognize and affirm the officer, especially at what might be a painful place in his life—his difficulty having children.

The conclusion of the scene underscores a range of differences between Felix's emotional labor and others. Laura saying to Felix, "It must be very nice to be you," and Felix laughs in affirmation. As a woman, for example,

Laura's labor as a woman goes underappreciated and unnoticed. As a man, Felix's performs emotional labor to get what he wants, in this case, to break the law without consequence. But her statement implies a range of other hierarchical social arrangements, which Coppola and Rashida Jones make clear. In an interview with *The Hollywood Reporter*, journalist Mikey O'Connell asks about this scene, "Did you have any second thoughts about how it would fit in the film now that so many Americans have woken up to the relationship between police and people of color?"[12] Coppola acknowledges that mainstream understanding of interactions with the police for people of color have changed, "It's obviously so different now. I mean, it's always an issue—but it's been brought so to the forefront of our culture."[13] She concludes, saying, "Felix is the epitome of that kind of privilege, and he uses it."[14] While what Coppola means by "privilege" remains unclear, Jones clarifies. She says:

> It has always been happening. It's the history of this country . . . It is every level of privilege: older white man privilege, money privilege, charm privilege. All these things that are coming to this moment to conspire to really understand that character and also her relationship with that character. We talked about, like, "What does she say? She has to say something. You don't have a Black family at home and see that moment happen and think, "Oh that was fun." You think, "If my family was in this car, that would go down in a completely different way."[15]

What Jones' statement implies is that if Dean were in the car, the interaction would have certainly not resulted in the same outcome.

Despite the fact that Felix does not appreciate the nature of how his age, race, and class empower him over Laura and Dean, Felix also provides Laura recognition and affirmation, which is precisely what Dean fails to do. On Laura's birthday, Dean is out of town for work. However, he arranges for his daughters to give Laura a gift, instructing them via a video call. The present surprises Laura, and, at first, she becomes excited. However, it also disappoints her. Instead of a gift that recognizes her humanity outside of her unpaid, emotional labor, the present suggests that Dean sees her, primarily, through the labor she performs for the family. It also suggests his deep-seated assumption and expectation that Laura will continue to perform such labor. Dean gives her a Thermomix, a high-end, multi-use kitchen device that boasts, "24 different functions and techniques in one digitally powered countertop appliance,"[16] including but not limited to tasks like whisking, caramelizing, browning, chopping, steaming, blending, boiling, kneading, and emulsifying. Felix, on the other hand, provides her the recognition that Dean does not. Over dessert, Felix gives her a gift and a story. She opens a large jewelry box to find a man's watch and smiles. When Laura was a child, her father wore this watch, and she loved it. She puts it on. Felix then tells her the moment that he "recognized" her "as a person." Laura was less than a year old. They were in the country, presumably on vacation. She sat in mud and her diaper was soaking wet. When he picked her up, the two of them looked at one another "and just started laughing. And there you were. I saw who you were." Laura smiles. If Dean refuses or is unable to recognize her beyond her emotional labor, then, by contrast, Felix gives her what she longs for: to be seen for who she is outside of the monotonous, monochromatic emotional labor she performs.

## EXHAUSTION

Expanding on the insights of Hochschild's work, philosopher Shiloh Whitney theorizes the further impacts emotional labor has on workers. Whitney uses the term "byproductive" to describe the residue that emotional labor leaves in the worker's body, often toxic or harmful byproducts. What emotional labor (or as Whitney calls it, affective labor) produces differs from other forms of production. In an automotive factory, for example, the laborers leave the product, the car, at the factory. Emotional labor cannot be left at the place of work in the same way. Whitney submits that this expenditure sometimes has "unwanted . . . affective byproducts," that the laborer has to find a way to deal with, or "metabolize."[17] Metabolizing affective byproducts is, Whitney insists, part of the hidden, unseen, and unrecognized "after-hours cost" of emotional labor.[18] To illustrate what byproducts look like, Whitney refers to a passage early in Hochschild's book. A flight attendant has worked a day where she must act in a jovial and cheery manner. The flight attendant recounts, "Sometimes I come off a long trip in a state of utter exhaustion, but I find I can't relax. I giggle a lot, I chatter, I call friends. It's as if I can't release myself from an artificially created elation that kept me 'up' on the trip."[19] The impacts of exhaustion and the inability to rest are the kind of harmful bodily byproducts Whitney thinks individuals and corporations overlook.

Because workers cannot always metabolize emotional labor, byproducts can stay with the body, weakening or debilitating the laborer. In certain situations, byproducts can become unmanageable.[20] "Once produced," Whitney notes, "they do not take leave of her body, of her posture and disposition."[21] Byproducts can "amputate" or "dampen" laborers' ability to function, rendering them unable to perform well or unwilling to participate in further labors.[22] Recent popular reflection on emotional labor documents precisely this exhaustion. For example, journalist Jess Zimmerman describes the emotional labor she performs with a particular group of friends: "straight men with feelings."[23] After their romantic partners break up with them, Zimmerman's friends approach her for advice on how he might win the woman back. She wants to tell him, in a direct and transparent manner, that he cannot win the woman back, because she made a choice that he should respect. Unable to speak authentically, Zimmerman offers indirect ways of communicating, that usually "gets through."[24] Like the nurse, she does not seem to resent performing this labor. However, "the constant labor of placating men," she says, "and navigating patriarchal expectations is exhausting."[25] Journalist Gemma Hartley claims something similar. She recounts the emotional labor it takes to explain the existence of emotional labor to her husband, namely that her work around the house is both thankless and depleting. When her husband insists that he would be willing to do whatever she asks, she explains that such delegation is part of the unwelcome emotional labor she experiences. Delegating work, even to a willing partner, "is exhausting," because she does not want to give orders; she wants a partner.[26] In both cases, exhaustion is a common byproduct to their emotional labor.

Laura experiences exhaustion in response to the emotional labor of two relationships, the first of which is her family. Early in the film, Laura takes the children to visit her extended family: her mother Diane (Alva Chinn); her sister Amanda (Juliana Canfield); and her grandmother (Felix's mother), whom they call Gran (Barbara Bain). While the children play in the yard, the group discusses Felix and Dean. The women all agree that it is difficult to have a relationship with Felix. Gran notes that his priority is always to entertain or amuse himself, even as a child. Diane, Felix's ex-wife, comments that he always needed to be on the move and on to the next thing—a thinly veiled comment on Felix's sexual infidelity. Amanda turns to Laura and asks her how she can still be in a relationship with him, implying that, as his daughter, she no longer communicates with him. The string of statements functions to isolate Laura from her relationship with him, and she covers the negativity of her isolation with emotional labor: a smile and a shrug. Amanda then asks about Dean, if he is still travelling with his assistant, Fiona. When Laura responds affirmatively, Amanda's reaction suggests that she finds that behavior suspicious. Gran then asks a question that affirms Amanda's suspicion: "Is she very attractive?" It is this question that demands more emotional labor from Laura.

Gran's delivery of the question makes an implicit link between Felix and Dean. As the film will later reveal, Felix had an affair with his assistant, Holly. Since Dean's behavior appears consistent with Felix's, beneath her question is a deeper one: Is Dean doing to you what Felix did to your mother? Diane's eyes dart, communicating to Gran the inappropriateness of the question. Unwilling or unable to answer the question vulnerably, authentically, or transparently, Laura performs emotional labor to defend herself. She admits that, yes, Fiona is beautiful. Gran averts her eyes from Laura, perhaps ashamed or embarrassed for her. Laura's inflection changes. She protests but tries to do it calmly. In a place like New York City, she insists, beautiful people abound. Though she attempts to control her demeanor, her tone communicates that she wants to end the conversation. Amanda recoils from Laura, and the conversation ends. Coppola covers the majority of the conversation in individual close-up shots of each character. She ends the scene, however, pulling the camera back from group to a wide shot. There is silence and a bit of small talk that signals a shift to a different subject matter. The wide shot, the awkwardness of the pause, and the small talk all communicate how her relationship with both Felix and Dean has alienated Laura from the women in her family.

The emotional labor in this interaction exhausts Laura, and Coppola initially represents her disposition physically. When Laura returns home with her children, Coppola uses a single wide shot of her and her children coming through the door. A snippet of "In Re Don Giovanni" accompanies this shot. Her family participates in her monotonous routine. As Laura sets down her bag, she slumps slightly and lets her head fall back, as if she is tired. Once she leaves the frame, Coppola cuts to Laura's physical exhaustion. In a wide shot, she lies on top of her bed, which is completely made. She is so exhausted that she does not get under the sheets: her eyes are closed, and she does not move. Like Whitney notes, the byproducts stick to her body in her posture and disposition. She slumps when she comes home and is now rendered immobile. While nothing is amputated, Laura's capacity is clearly dampened, unable or unwilling to engage in further labor.

Coppola also registers her exhaustion symbolically. As Laura lies on the bed, a noise comes from the hallway, and the sound, a droning whir, motivates the camera's movement. The director pans from Laura to the door and tilts down to reveal a semi-autonomous robotic vacuum cleaner, a Roomba-style device. The latter enters the bedroom and runs into the wall; it hits the wall with enough velocity that the back end of the device lifts off the ground. The machine runs into the wall at the exact same spot three times before it decides to move to a different direction. The light violence and the number of times it takes the vacuum to change its behavior registers as comedic. It also reflects aspects of Laura's behavior and experience. The pace at which Laura moves through her days has reduced her to an object, mechanically running errands, caring for her children, and keeping the household on schedule. Like the monotonous sound of the robot, all the emotional labor it takes to manage her home, compounded with the devastating potential that Dean might be cheating on her, exhausts her. She not only has to defend herself from her extended family, but that defensiveness also alienates her from them. The harm here is one of isolation. She must nap in the middle of the day, leaving her children unattended, in order to recover. The interaction with her family is a unilateral interaction. It only demands her emotional labor, and her exhaustion is the cost.

In addition to her family, Vanessa is another such unilateral interaction that exhausts Laura. Vanessa, a fellow mother Laura sees at Maya's school, treats her like an object, foisting romantic troubles on her. In these interactions, Laura rarely speaks, except, when she is able, to end the conversation. When Laura drops Maya off at school for the first time, Vanessa speaks to her about a man with whom she has rekindled a romantic relationship. As is her pattern, Vanessa goes into excruciating detail on her self-destructive behavior. When Vanessa begins this self-disclosure, Laura slumps momentarily, not unlike she did when she returned home from her family. However, like a flight attendant might, Laura straightens her body and pretends to appear attentive. She hides how much this interaction demands of her. Laura lets Vanessa talk for a short period of time but, as soon as she can, politely excuses herself. During two subsequent encounters, Laura and Vanessa are in line, waiting for Maya's classroom to open. Because Laura is trapped, she cannot leave the conversation. Like the immobility she experiences on her bed, this situation restricts the protagonist's mobility. Laura leans against the wall and does not or cannot bring herself to make eye contact with Vanessa. When she does make eye contact, she is expressionless and only engages in minimal movement. In their final scene, Laura looks away from Vanessa, barely forces a smile, and mumbles. Vanessa is so self-involved she does not notice that Laura is exhausted. While not completely immobile, these interactions render her deadened or amputated in her ability to attend to the conversation.

Laura's interactions with Felix differ from all others, because he both exhausts and energizes her. On her birthday, Felix arrives, unannounced, at her apartment, just as Laura puts her children to bed. When he insists that she go out with him for her birthday, she sighs deeply and slumps her body. Unlike nearly every other interaction she has, she does not perform emotional labor here. She does not attempt to hide her exhaustion or anger. While her reaction is negative, this is one of the few moments of honesty and transparency that she has with another person. And Felix, unlike her sister Amanda, does not respond negatively to her anger. He does not experience her anger as a threat to their relationship. None of this, of course, diminishes the negativity of her response. Felix is exhausting in that he demands labor from her to keep him happy and content. However, Laura does not respond to Felix with amputated capacity, immobility, or an inability to metabolize the experience. Laura responds to Felix with an energy that is absent from her previous interactions. This emotional excitement is negative, but it is excitement, nonetheless.

Coppola also presents two moments when Felix unambiguously energizes Laura, providing her relief from her monotonous daily life. After Felix shows up unannounced, Laura finds a babysitter to watch the children. When the two of them leave their apartment building, the band who composed original music for the film, Phoenix, scores the moment with a handful of bright, shimmering chords on a synthesizer. Not only is this cue unique in the film, it differs sharply from "In Re Don Giovanni." If Nyman's composition expresses the unrelenting, monochromatic pace of Laura's routine, this moment presents her as emotionally differentiated from her daily life. With her father—unlike with her children, family, Dean, or Vanessa—Laura experiences herself as beautiful, lovely, and shimmering, which, as the music suggests, is unusual. In fact, Felix confirms what the music communicates by saying, "You look very lovely." Laura responds with a simple but relieved sense of appreciation at his recognition. "Thanks," she says. Once they sit at their table, Felix makes a pronouncement: he points to the table they are seated at and says that it is the table at which the Hollywood movie star Humphrey Bogart proposed marriage to Hollywood movie star Lauren Bacall. Unlike most of his pronouncements, Laura responds positively to this one. She acts surprised and is about to speak when Felix introduces another surprise: he slips his birthday gift on her table. The moment is a surprise within a surprise. If, as the Nyman cue indicated, Laura lives a monochromatic emotional life, and if interactions with her family and Vanessa exhaust her, then this moment serves as a profound but subtle contrast. With Felix, she feels things beyond monotony and exhaustion. Even though she is happy in this moment, throughout most of the film, she is quite unhappy.

## THE (UN)HAPPY HOUSEWIFE

Cultural studies scholar Sara Ahmed argues that the image of the so-called happy housewife did not begin in the mid-twentieth century; rather, it appeared as early as eighteen-century philosopher Jean-Jacques Rousseau's novel *Émile* (1762). While she examines his treatment of the protagonist, Émile, Ahmed focuses on his soon to be wife, Sophy. The novel explores Rousseau's claim that happiness emerges from a proper education. In describing Sophy, Ahmed writes that her education "is about what she must become in order to be a good wife for Émile." Rousseau thinks that women, like Sophy, need to be taught:

> to be pleasing in his sight, to win his respect and love, to train him in childhood, to tend him in manhood, to councel [counsel] and console, to make his life pleasant and happy, these are the duties of women for all time, and this is what she should be taught while she is young. [sic] The further we depart from this principle, the further we shall be from our goal, and all our precepts will fail to secure her happiness or our own.[27]

Ahmed's point is that for Sophy to be happy, she must be trained to make other people happy. She must align her happiness to that of others. This is not a form of mutuality and relationality; rather, it is a conditional happiness that instrumentalizes her existence and labor. She will only be happy if she is an instrument to make others so.

Rousseau justifies his claims about happiness from an appeal to nature, which is, in fact, only a self-affirming justification. The philosopher believed his perspective flowed, "naturally from how things are."[28] Happiness was simply what happens when someone follows the route nature lays out. Rousseau says, "I kept to the path of nature, until she should show me the path of happiness."[29] What he means is that if women were not wives, instrumentalizing their emotional labor to produce happiness in others, then they could not experience happiness themselves.[30] However, Ahmed notes that the philosopher simply used an appeal to nature to justify his own experience. "And lo!" says the philosopher, the paths of nature and happiness, "their paths were the same, and without knowing it this was the path I trod."[31] Nature is simply an appeal to the philosopher himself. In his rendition of happiness, unhappiness is what occurs when women refuse to align themselves to Rousseau's personal formation, which he passes off as nature. The tautology reveals how self-serving his portrait of Sophy is. Her so-called natural purpose, and by proxy all women, is simply to instrumentalize themselves and their emotional labor to make Rousseau, and men like him, happy.

Ahmed submits that this figure of the happy housewife, "is a fantasy figure,"[32] and in this context, a woman's unhappiness can critique the fantasy. Happiness hides the unequal distribution of power and labor, particularly within the heterosexual household: "How better to secure consent to unpaid or poorly paid labor," Ahmed opines, "than to describe such consent as the origin of good feeling?"[33] If the fantasy of the happy housewife and her good feelings can be a cover, then they can also be harmful to women. Therefore, the unhappy housewife can challenge "the assumption that happiness follows relative proximity to a social ideal."[34] In other words, an unhappy housewife shows the fantasy of happiness as what it is, a false reality.[35] While Ahmed does not define unhappiness, her writing suggests that it can consist of a wide range of negative feelings and emotions, including but not limited to sadness, invisibility, and distress. In Ahmed's experience, the unhappy woman is also often accused of being a "killjoy,"[36] because "their failure to be happy is read as sabotaging the happiness of others."[37] In an important sense, such women are "killjoys," because what counts as joy or happiness is harmful to women. If happiness can be a false reality, then embracing unhappiness and killing false joy can be a helpful form of critique.

Ahmed illustrates the power of unhappiness with the example of the fictional character Sissie, from Ama Ata Aidoo's poem "Our Sister Killjoy"

(1977). In the poem, Sissie, a Black woman, enters an airplane and takes her seat. A white flight attendant insists that she move from her seat to the back of the plane, where she can sit with two other Black individuals. The flight attendant affirms that these people are Sissie's friends, but Sissie has never seen them before. Sissie nearly protests, but she hesitates. If she expresses her unhappiness, then she would likely disrupt the happiness of others in the airplane. What sustains the happiness of the plane is nothing other than the imbalance of power. Sissy's hesitation reveals the racism at work when a flight attendant protects the happiness of some (white passengers) at the expense of others (Sissie).[38] Ahmed's account of unhappiness helps explain both Felix's misogyny and Laura's unhappiness.

Felix's misogyny takes the form of his desire for control linked with his denigration of marriage. The film opens with a short speech from Felix, who speaks to Laura when she was a child. Over a black screen and with no music playing, he says, "Don't give your heart to any boys. You're mine. Until you get married. Then you're still mine." While Felix, of course, thinks this form of control is love, his speech also denigrates her future marriage and her future autonomy to make decision about her own marriage. His statement implies that his control over Laura's emotional attachments extends beyond her choice, her own decision to love and marry someone. The darkness of the screen hints, perhaps, at the harm this control will have on Laura. Felix also denigrates marriage and monogamy elsewhere in the film. In the car on the way to lunch, he notices Laura's gold bracelet and compliments it. He then makes a pronouncement, "The bangle is a reminder that women were once men's property." Laura turns away from him in frustration. She reveals that Dean gave her the bracelet and insists that he did not intend to use it to make her his property. In denigrating marriage broadly, Felix denigrates his daughter in particular. Similarly, in the car on the way to Laura's birthday dessert, Felix and Laura discuss Dean's strange behavior. In response, Laura is exasperated and wonders out loud if any man can be monogamous. Felix makes another pronouncement, "Monogamy and marriage are based on the concept of property." Because Felix is a philanderer who left his wife and children, the contradiction between his desire to control Laura and his rejection of marriage (as a form of control over women) suggests that his rhetoric is merely self-serving.

Felix also makes self-serving, Rousseau-esque appeals to nature. When Laura and Felix have lunch, he takes long, lingering, and objectifying stares at the Russian waitress, especially as she walks away. Once she leaves, he makes a pronouncement, this time in a lengthy monologue. Using evolutionary terms, Felix describes a moment in evolutionary history before humans were bipedal: he claims that, at that time, the visual sight of women's "haunches" sexually aroused men. As humans evolved into bipeds, he claims, men's attraction to "haunches" evolved, too, now to women's "rounded breasts," because they bore a similar shape. He also claims that adolescent women "were easier to catch, therefore ultimately easier to mate." Hence, the contemporary qualities men desire, "small size, smooth skin, high voice, little or no beard," are derived from this evolutionary and natural development. Because Coppola links the monologue with his objectifying gaze on the waitress' body, Felix's appeals to nature ultimately serve to justify his own misogynistic way of moving through the world. Nature is what permits him to objectify women in the way that he does.

Later in that conversation, Felix and Laura discuss Dean's behavior. She insists that he is not like Felix, implying that Dean is not a philanderer who cheats on his wife and leaves his children, but he is a "good guy" and a "great dad." Felix disagrees and makes another appeal to nature: "He's a man. It's nature. Males are forced to fight to dominate and to impregnate all females." Like Rousseau, Felix's appeals to nature are self-serving excuses to justify his own behavior, such as what he does earlier in this scene—speaking in sexually suggestive ways to much younger women. Felix returns to this notion of domination when they follow Dean on his work dinner. As Felix and Laura watch from the car, Dean and Fiona get into a separate cab from their colleagues. Felix narrates his actions in the metaphor of an animal hunting prey, "He's cutting her out of the herd." Not only does his rhetoric demean women to the status of animals to be hunted and devoured, but also, in framing his own sexual behavior as instinctive and animalistic, it gives him permission to evade responsibility for his behavior. These self-serving appeals to nature produce in Felix what seems to be something like contentment or happiness, but Laura's primary posture is unhappiness. Early in the film, Coppola first presents her sadness in brief moments.

At first, because of the hurried pace of Laura's life, she only has space to experience tiny, passing, ephemeral flashes of unhappiness. Her routine inhibits the outward expression of her negative emotions, particularly as she cares for Theo. She must engage in emotional labor to conceal her unhappiness. When she finds opportunities to feel her unhappiness, they occur in passing moments. The first of such moments happens when she finds Fiona's bag in Dean's luggage. Laura ponders over the bag and the sensual implications of the body oil she finds in it. She crinkles her brow and sighs, but Theo is in the room and attracts her attention. She forces a smile for Theo but frowns before she puts the bag down. The next moment occurs when Laura takes Theo to a music class. While they are on the elevator, Theo counts the elevator buttons, and Laura smiles and praises her. In the moment between Laura's smile and when they step off the elevator, a brief flash of anxiety comes across the protagonist's face. She looks up at the ceiling as if she is contemplating Fiona's bag and Dean's odd behavior the previous night, but once the elevator door opens, she must manage her emotions to match the energy and fun of Theo's music class. After class, Laura makes Theo macaroni and cheese for lunch. She stirs the pasta but then pauses; she shifts her feet in such a way that her body lowers, almost like a slump. Her eyes shift slightly, again, as if she is worried about the bag and Dean's behavior. Such moments are fleeting but palpable embodiments of her unhappiness, particularly her anxiety.

However, with Felix present, Laura has the opportunity to explore the emotions surrounding her unhappiness. Nearly every time Laura greets him, she does so with a smile. Perhaps because he is a source of happiness for her, she is able to express and process her unhappiness with him. For example, after the police let Felix and Laura go, the two have drinks at a bar. Seeing Dean get into the cab with Fiona has almost certainly solidified for Laura that they are having an affair. In the bar, they sit in silence, staring into space. Laura frowns while Felix tries to lift her spirits, saying that they are making headway in the investigation. She declares, "This is pathetic," and then, like she has done previously, she blames herself for her unhappiness: "Maybe he's just not interested in me anymore." This internalization of her unhappiness is notable for what she does not say. She does not worry that her life, as she knows it, is over; she does not wonder how she is going to live or raise the children without Dean; she does not even imagine what her next steps might be. Instead, she blames herself and mourns the loss of her sexual desirability. Felix reassures her that that is not the case, and Laura offers a sincere "thanks." Then she shows her least attenuated expression of grief: she puts her elbow on the table, slouches, and rests her chin on her hand; she sighs, frowns, and stares into space. Felix reassures her that she is going to make it through this experience. Tears start to form in Laura's eyes, which she fights back. Coppola then cuts to a close-up of her martini glass. The image is almost abstract in its composition, mostly darkness and soft focus. The drink catches only slivers of light. Jazz musician Chet Baker's rendition of "I Get Along Without You Very Well" plays on the soundtrack. Like Baker, Laura does not think she will get along without Dean. In extreme slow motion, her single tear falls into the glass. While an admittedly sentimental image, this is Laura's most unhappy moment, which takes place in Felix's presence.

Laura not only expresses her unhappiness with Felix, but they also vulnerably explore the unhappiness his infidelity caused. In Mexico, Felix and Laura have dinner near the beach. In another gesture of self-justification, he offers a pronouncement. When a woman has an affair, people will often say positive things about her choice, "It's so wonderful she found someone." However, if a man has an affair, people demean the act, saying that he is simply "banging his secretary." Rightfully angered by his self-justification, Laura asks him a question she has likely never asked before: "Why did you do it?" Felix looks at Laura. A sadness comes over his face, as though he has been wanting to avoid this conversation. For a moment, Felix stops controlling Laura and does not engage in self-justifying rhetoric. He attempts authenticity and vulnerability, and explains that, when he and Laura's mother were first married, she "shone all her light" on him. Once they had children, Laura's mother shifted that attention away from him. The affair took place, Felix continues, when someone, in this case Holly, paid attention to him in the same way Laura's mother once did. Laura responds with disgust and characterizes his behavior as childish. In explaining his motive, Felix claims that everyone wants "love." Even more unhappy with him, she exclaims, "It's exhausting to try to love you enough!" Laura insists that his desire for love had profound and painful consequences for her. The conversation makes her unhappy, but they are able to explore unhappiness with one another. Then the conversation takes an unusual turn.

Felix shares with Laura his own sadness concerning Holly. He tells her that Holly died recently; he did not think that he would live longer than she would. The implication that, someday, Felix will die saddens Laura. He then shares positive memories about Holly: she was funny, intelligent, and a good artist. As Felix speaks, he holds back tears. Laura reacts as though she is conflicted during these moments, likely because she is experiencing empathy for the woman who, in part, broke her family apart and caused her so much unhappiness and pain. Laura eventually asks him the question that she has, perhaps, been waiting her whole life to ask him: "Was it worth it?" Felix offers an unsatisfying answer about how he caused everyone unhappiness: "It was heartbreaking for everyone." Felix holds back his tears, and Laura is shocked; her mouth is agape. The scene ends when they turn from each other and look out at the ocean.

While their vulnerability and the exploration of their unhappiness does not fit Hochschild's definition of emotional labor, Coppola's rendering of this moment suggests that what the characters are engaged in is, in some real way, labor of an emotional kind. Exploring unhappiness—pain, hurt, betrayal, and death—takes effort. This moment differs from others, perhaps, in that there is not any sense that either Felix or Laura is managing their own or each other's emotional experience. There is little sense that either of them desires to control the other. Rather, they share the labor being performed. Because Felix does not attempt to control the conversation or make proclamations, his transparency suggests that he is, indeed, capable of behaving in ways different from his normal misogynous ways of moving through the world. Furthermore, this sharing of emotional labor is precisely what Dean does not do (for example, with Theo's school). This emotional labor allows Felix and Laura to communicate with and recognize each other in ways they have not done before. Laura's unhappiness demonstrates to Felix that his fantasy of happy housewife was destructive and painful to her. When he describes the affair as "heartbreaking," he suggests that his behavior made him unhappy, which is, perhaps, what shocks Laura. While Felix's fantasy caused them both pain, the scene rightly suggests that the unhappiness was asymmetrical, harming Laura more than it did Felix. Like Felix's typical mode of emotional labor, this labor is fundamentally labor of recognition, not rooted in control but in vulnerability.

Ultimately, Laura expresses her unhappiness most directly to Felix in the form of anger. In Mexico after their dinner, the two characters discover that Fiona and Dean are not having an affair. In fact, Dean has left the trip early to return home to spend time with Laura and the children, and Fiona is romantically involved with a woman. Distraught, she returns to her hotel room and begins to pack. She wants to return home immediately. Felix follows into her room, and her anger erupts in a lengthy monologue. She is distressed because, in following her father to Mexico, she might have allowed Felix's meddling to ruin her marriage and accuses him with a question, "Can you let anyone be happy?" Her accusation implies that his behavior over Dean's possible infidelity has been the way he has behaved his entire life. Ultimately, he makes everyone unhappy. If Rousseau's version of happiness is, more or less, synonymous with Felix's, then Laura's accusation shows the outcomes of their misogynist vision of happiness. Misogyny, simply put, makes everyone unhappy, albeit in asymmetrical ways. She also explicitly critiques his misogynist appeals to nature by insisting that he is not an animal, and that he can control his sexual behavior and his objectification of women. Finally, she demeans him in, likely, the cruelest way she can imagine: "And can you be around a woman at all without hitting on her? Because it's starting to get pathetic." The insult is certainly in reference to his age; perhaps a younger man could constantly hit on women with rakish charm, but, she implies, women do not want to sleep with a man who is so old and past the peak of his sexual attractiveness and potency.

In response, Felix echoes what Ahmed observes about killjoys. Once Laura has completed her monologue, he says, "What happened to you? You used to be fun." This statement confirms what Gran said earlier in the film, that Felix always wants to amuse himself. The same applies here: Dean's potential infidelity is, for Felix, a situation in which he can have fun with Laura. Her unhappiness performs precisely what Ahmed claims: to a misogynist, like Felix, a woman's unhappiness is a killjoy. But, in killing the joy, Laura's unhappiness points out precisely how misogynistic his joy is. His fun and happiness are threats to her well-being. Up until this point, Laura has, as Ahmed says of Sophy, aligned her happiness to that of others, especially Felix. And, like Sissie, she has chosen not to let her unhappiness disrupt the joy of others. When she refuses to be Sophy and Sissie, Felix, in effect, calls her a killjoy. While their vulnerable conversation over dinner suggests that

Felix has the capacity to be a different kind of person, this scene confirms that his misogynist formation remains intact. One conversation cannot heal him from years of misogyny.

By way of conclusion, we offer a few implications our reading of emotional labor has for a critical and constructive account of love. When Felix claims that "Everyone wants to loved," Coppola offers an implicit critique of his (mis)perception of love. When he describes to Laura why he cheated on her mother, his use of the phrase "light shine on" is an equivalent to "love." Love is, in essence, a form of attention and recognition. His understanding of love reflects his typical emotional labor. Throughout the film, Felix constantly attempts to manage other people with whom he interacts, and he uses recognition and affirmation as his means of management. Love, for Felix, has become a mode of management or, as he implies at the beginning of the film, a form of control. Because, as Hochschild says, emotional labor can be sold, what Felix is doing, in essence, is selling love as a means of control or extraction, the clearest examples of which are the police officer and the Russian waitress. Here, as in our reading of *The Virgin Suicides*, Coppola demonstrates how love can be entangled with violence. Or, in a similar register, love is not some territory or virtue free from, as our reading *Lost in Translation* makes clear, colonial forms of oppression. Love can be entangled with capitalist forms of extraction. Emotional labor, as a means of love, can also be entangled in other hierarchical stratifications, which the scene with the police illustrates. After Felix performs emotional labor to escape his encounter with the police, Jones clarifies that Laura's statement, "It must be nice to be you," means that age, race, and class are at play in the scene (to which we would also add gender to the list). His emotional labor is profoundly different than Laura's or Dean's, although he refuses to acknowledge such realities. His lack of acknowledgement is also part his (mis)perception of love.

We agree with Black feminist scholar, bell hooks, that love can indeed be a "practice of freedom" and liberation.[39] What these films make clear is that love may never be an entirely safe space free from domination. This statement is analogous to Ahmed's observations about joy. Happiness or joy can, indeed, be sites of violence against women. *On the Rocks* serves as a warning on the ways misogyny, racism, and age can co-opt love to capitalist ends.

If Coppola's rendering of Felix points out how love can be co-opted, then her expansive account of emotional labor suggests a constructive account. As Hochschild argues, emotional labor is the regulation of one's emotions in order to manage the emotions of others. Both Laura and Felix perform these actions, not unlike flight attendants or nurses. However, as the dinner scene in Mexico illustrates, emotional labor can be something beyond this description. In the sequence, both Laura and Felix labor together in healthy and life-giving ways. If, as Ahmed claims, unhappiness is a form of critique, then transparency, vulnerability, and lack of control might be the conditions in which life, or even love, can thrive. This account of love names the dysfunctional ways Felix manipulates others. If love can, indeed, include ways of attending to others, like through recognition and affirmation, it would seem then that vulnerability and lack of control are additional conditions that keep love from becoming entwined with violence. Again, this expands bell hooks' account of love: "A love ethic emphasizes the importance of service to others" because, "[t]o serve another I cannot see them as an object, I must see their subjecthood."[40] Such service and seeing can be, as hooks explains, a means of healing. To hooks, we might add that seeing the subjecthood of another—that is, to recognize and affirm another in non-controlling ways—means, in part, that both subjects must be transparent and vulnerable to each other, perhaps particularly about the causes and realities of unhappiness, heartbreak, and mistakes. This might mean that love demands an honest account of violence, such that violence does not have the final word.

Like many of her other films, Coppola does not completely reform the men she portrays, but she hints at the possibility that a different future can exist. In their final scene, Felix meets Laura outside her apartment. He apologizes in the most vague and passive way about the trouble he caused her.[41] He then invites her on a cruise. As he is trying to convince her to go, she smiles and laughs, but she says that she cannot make it. He looks up at her apartment, where Dean and her family are and says, "You have your own adventure." She nods in agreement. Whatever he might or might not think about marriage, in this moment, he brings himself to recognize and affirm her marriage. The optimism here is perhaps too easy, but the hope remains. Felix might be able to relinquish his desire for control, then he might be able to embrace vulnerability along with his capacity for recognition and affirmation of others. Such a way of moving through the world would, as both hooks and Ahmed imply, redefine virtues like joy, love, and happiness to be lifegiving for all, not just some folks. We will expand more on the implications of these virtues in the final, concluding chapter.

## REFERENCES

Ahmed, Sara. *The Promise of Happiness*. Durham, NC: Duke UP, 2010.

Gleiberman, Owen. "'On the Rocks' Review: Bill Murray, His Scampishness Undimmed, Reunites with 'Lost in Translation' Director Sofia Coppola." *Variety*, September 22, 2020, variety.com/2020/film/reviews/on-the-rocks-bill-murray-rashida-jones-sofia-coppola-1234777605/.

Hartley, Gemma. "Women Aren't Nags—We're Just Fed Up: Emotional Labor Is the Unpaid Job Men Still Don't Understand." *Harper's Bazaar*, September

27, 2017, www.harpersbazaar.com/culture/features/a12063822/emotional-labor-gender-equality/.
Hochschild, Arlie Russell. *The Managed Heart: Commercialization of Human Feeling.* Oakland, CA: U of California P, 1979.
hooks, bell. *Outlaw Culture: Resisting Representation.* New York: Routledge, 2006.
"Mission." *The State Academic Bolshoi Theatre of Russia,* www.bolshoi.ru/en/about/hist/mission/.
Nolfi, Joey. "Meet Your Maker: How Drag, Dads, and NYC Icons Inspired Sofia Coppola." *Entertainment Weekly,* October 21, 2020, ew.com/movies/sofia-coppola-meet-your-maker/.
O'Connell, Mikey. "'On the Rocks': Sofia Coppola and Rashida Jones Talk About Their Long History and Bill Murray's Stunt Driving." *The Hollywood Reporter* (February 1, 2021), www.hollywoodreporter.com/movies/movie-news/on-the-rocks-sofia-coppola-and-rashida-jones-talk-about-their-long-history-and-bill-murrays-stunt-driving-4120731/.
Rousseau, Jean-Jacques. *Émile.* Translated by Barbara Foxley. London: Every Man, [1762] 1993.
"The All New Thermomix TM6." *Thermomix,* www.thermomix.com/tm6/.
Whitney, Shiloh. "Byproductive Labor: A Feminist Theory of Affective Labor beyond the Productive–Reproductive Distinction." *Philosophy and Social Criticism* 44, no. 6 (2018): 637–660.
Zimmerman, Jess. "'Where's My Cut?': On Unpaid Emotional Labor." *The Toast,* July 13, 2015, the-toast.net/2015/07/13/emotional-labor/.

## NOTES

1. Joey Nolfi, "Meet Your Maker: How Drag, Dads, and NYC Icons Inspired Sofia Coppola," *Entertainment Weekly,* October 21, 2020, ew.com/movies/sofia-coppola-meet-your-maker/.
2. Owen Gleiberman, "'On the Rocks' Review: Bill Murray, His Scampishness Undimmed, Reunites with 'Lost in Translation' Director Sofia Coppola," *Variety,* September 22, 2020, variety.com/2020/film/reviews/on-the-rocks-bill-murray-rashida-jones-sofia-coppola-1234777605/.
3. Ibid.
4. Arlie Russell Hochschild, *The Managed Heart: Commercialization of Human Feeling* (Oakland, CA: U of California P, 1979), xvii.
5. Ibid., xvii.
6. Ibid., 7.
7. Ibid., 167.
8. Ibid., 190.
9. Ibid., 200.
10. Ibid.
11. "Mission," *The State Academic Bolshoi Theatre of Russia,* www.bolshoi.ru/en/about/hist/mission/.

12. Mikey O'Connell, "'On the Rocks': Sofia Coppola and Rashida Jones Talk About Their Long History and Bill Murray's Stunt Driving," *The Hollywood Reporter* (February 1, 2021), www.hollywoodreporter.com/movies/movie-news/on-the-rocks-sofia-coppola-and-rashida-jones-talk-about-their-long-history-and-bill-murrays-stunt-driving-4120731/.
13. Ibid.
14. Ibid.
15. Ibid.
16. "The All New Thermomix TM6," *Thermomix*, www.thermomix.com/tm6/.
17. Shiloh Whitney, "Byproductive Labor: A Feminist Theory of Affective Labor beyond the Productive–Reproductive Distinction," *Philosophy and Social Criticism* 44, no. 6 (2018): 642.
18. Ibid.
19. Hothschild, *The Managed Heart*, 4. Quoted in Whitney, "Byproductive Labor," 645.
20. Ibid.
21. Ibid., 646.
22. Ibid., 657.
23. Jess Zimmerman, "'Where's My Cut?': On Unpaid Emotional Labor," *The Toast*, July 13, 2015, the-toast.net/2015/07/13/emotional-labor/.
24. Ibid.
25. Ibid.
26. Gemma Hartley, "Women Aren't Nags—We're Just Fed Up: Emotional Labor Is the Unpaid Job Men Still Don't Understand," *Harper's Bazaar*, September 27, 2017, accessed June 7, 2021, www.harpersbazaar.com/culture/features/a12063822/emotional-labor-gender-equality/.
27. Jean-Jacques Rousseau, *Émile*, trans. by Barbara Foxley (London: Every Man [1762] 1993), 393. Quoted in Sara Ahmed, *The Promise of Happiness* (Durham, NC: Duke UP, 2010), 55.
28. Ibid., 58.
29. Rousseau, *Émile*, 487. Quoted in Ahmed, *The Promise of Happiness*, 58.
30. Ibid.
31. Ibid.
32. Ibid., 50.
33. Ibid.
34. Ibid., 53.
35. Ibid.
36. Ibid., 65.
37. Ibid., 66.
38. Ibid., 69.
39. bell hooks, *Outlaw Culture: Resisting Representation* (New York: Routledge, 2006), 248.

40. Ibid., 249.

41. This apology echoes the way McBurney apologizes to the women and girls in *The Beguiled* (2017). While Felix's behavior is less violent that McBurney's, they both reflect men who are incapable of seeing or unwilling to see the true harm they caused.

# Conclusion

In order to bring the interdisciplinary approaches and four main themes of this book into sharper relief, this concluding chapter will perform two main tasks. First, we review the three main feminist options at play within Coppola studies. Scholars understand Coppola's work as either radically feminist, as being able to be put to feminist ends, or as compromised with postfeminist concerns. These three options are not exhaustive of scholarly approaches to Coppola's films and the scholars we review are also not exhaustive of the feminist options. Rather, we offer a representative outline of feminist reflection within Coppola studies. This outline not only helps situate our work within these options but also helps us identify that feminist reflection on Coppola's work is situated mainly within third wave feminism. A focus on the third wave opens up the possibility that Coppola studies can press more deeply into fourth-wave feminism, particularly with feminists of color. This possibility brings us to the second task of this chapter. In order to illustrate what a more robust conversation with fourth wave feminism might look like, we take the implications of each chapter of this book and put them to use to extend the insights of feminists of color, particularly bell hooks and Audre Lorde. And we do so around the four themes of this book: masculinity, sexual politics, bodies, and love. While this is only the beginning of a more robust engagement, we believe it illustrates the usefulness and relevance that Coppola studies can have to wider, fourth-wave feminist conversations. Part of what we learn in the process is how important vulnerability is to white-bodied individuals who desire to build a more just, equitable, and liberated world. But first, a brief outline of the main feminist options in Coppola studies.

## FEMINIST OPTIONS

Within the burgeoning area of Coppola studies, we find at least four feminist approaches to the director's body of work. These approaches do not exhaust the ways scholars read her films. In fact, several approaches are outside of the scope of our monograph, including fashion studies,[1] adaptation studies,[2] and philosophical reflection,[3] among others.[4] Amongst feminist reflection, some scholars tend to understand Coppola's work as radically feminist, while other critics put her films to feminist use, still others see her work as in some way supporting postfeminism, and at least one scholar puts Coppola's film to feminist use but sees them as complicit with whiteness. The scholars we discuss below are illustrative, not exhaustive, of these options.

Film studies scholars Anna Backman Rogers and Rosalind Galt are two authors who epitomize authors who view Coppola's work as radically feminist. Backman Rogers claims that the filmmaker's critiques of society are situated "almost entirely on the side of an outspoken and at times radical form of feminism"[5] with a clear "feminist agenda."[6] These radical, feminist critiques, however, do not reside on the surface of the films. Rather, they only become clear as Backman Rogers attends "to the form of her films."[7] In *Pretty: Film and the Decorative Image* (2011), Galt offers reflections on *Marie Antoinette* (2006). Rather than see Coppola's presentation of girliness as a frivolous act, she reads those passages as the precise "location of its political intervention. Its young Marie Antoinette is stripped of subjectivity and rendered as a (political) object."[8] Antoinette's physical body is first owned by the court in Versailles and then, by the end of the film, by the violence of the French populace.[9] But perhaps the most radical choice Coppola makes is to refuse "to blame the woman [Antoinette] for her out-of-control consumption."[10] Galt concludes, therefore, that the film explores the intersection of "rococo style, radical politics, and gender."[11] Despite these arguments, not all scholars feel comfortable situating Coppola as a radical feminist.

Charting a middle ground, other scholars claim that while Coppola's films may not be feminist per se, they can certainly be put to feminist use, the clearest example of which is literary scholar Todd Kennedy. He claims that the director displays an awareness of feminist film theory and openly disputes or rejects some its foundational sources. Referencing the groundbreaking essay, "Visual Pleasure and Narrative Cinema," Kennedy notes that film scholar Laura Mulvey argued that the "'magic of Hollywood style at its best arose . . . from its skilled and satisfying manipulation of visual pleasure'—a claim that originally led Mulvey to suggest film could not transform patriarchy without rejecting visual pleasure."[12] By embracing visual pleasure, *Marie Antoinette* rejects Mulvey's thesis in favor of feminist critic Claire Johnston. Johnston argued that women's cinema could offer an effective means of "interrogating . . . male bourgeois cinema" and do so within mainstream rather than the avant-garde modes of expression that Mulvey's work suggested.[13] In affirming Johnston's claim, Kennedy states that his reading of Coppola, attempts to develop a manner of looking at mainstream Hollywood production as (at least) a potential source for feminine, if not feminist, expression . . . I have sought to show that, contrary to the assumptions of many, mainstream American production can, and sometimes does, provide a space for radical filmmaking which, drawing on Johnston, may be the most effective means of uprooting patriarchal film form. Sofia Coppola provides an apt example of such expression. Her films repeatedly ask the audience to associate themselves with a feminine point of view as, in the absence of the ability to depict "real" women, Coppola asks her audience to become real women: to be gazed upon, objectified, and, even more importantly, aware of their complicit participation in this objectification.[14]

Coppola's films invite audience members to experience the violence, violation, and objectification of the male gaze, and, perhaps most importantly, the complicity with that gaze that many women experience in a patriarchal world. Within the complexity of the male gaze, Coppola's feminine point of view and viewer identification can, as Kennedy suggests, be put to feminist use. Many other scholars take up a similar structural approach to Coppola's film, expanding Kennedy's notion of "feminine point of view" into two categories—the point of view of Coppola's female characters and the point of view of Coppola's female authorship.

There are at least four scholars who use Coppola's characters to feminist ends. Writing about *Lost in Translation* (2003), film scholar Lucy Bolton argues that the director's "portrayal of Charlotte is subtly revolutionary."[15] Other directors might resolve Charlotte's problem by clearly attaching her to either her husband or Bob. Bolton thinks it "unlikely that Charlotte will continue to be her husband's travelling companion," and the film does not end with the protagonist "leaving one man for another."[16] Because the characters don't have clear attachments, Coppola provides the character far more possibilities and opportunities.[17] Because the film traced the protagonist's "individuality, desire, and intellect," the open ending suggests that she might have "a more honest and satisfying life" than the one she inhabits in the film. In their reading of *Marie Antoinette*, literary scholars Suzanne Ferris and Mallory Young explore Coppola's revisionist narrative as one that highlights "third wave feminist preoccupations."[18] Both Coppola and sympathetic audiences likely identify with Antoinette; like the queen, they are struggling through similar experiences of objectification in an age of rampant consumption. As a result, the "third-wave audience" of the film, like Coppola herself, does not "condemn her for having a great sense of style and the means to pull it off."[19] In her reading of *Spring Breakers* and *The Bling Ring*, film scholar Maryn Wilkinson, focuses on the figure of "the girl," who must move through and transgress "the consumer market" in order to assert her own agency.[20]

The defining feature of the girl is her "plasticity," or her ability to use fluidity as a performance.[21] The girl's plasticity transgresses and resists the capitalist forces that aim to restrain her.[22] She also engages in "collective female action."[23] While the characters in the film might not be able to overcome the marketplace, their use of plasticity and collectivity "may well be showing us the way" to assert feminist agency in a capitalist framework.[24]

Other scholars focus on Coppola's female authorship, or as it is sometimes called, her female auteurship, as having feminist possibilities. Communication scholar Amy Woodworth argues that while Coppola might not have an explicit political feminist agenda, she has resisted a form of auteurship that has preceded her, namely the male filmmaker as hero. Like the protagonist of many American films, the heroic male auteur overcomes incredible physical and psychological odds to present his artistic vision. In embracing a feminine auteurship, Woodward argues that Coppola's implicit rejection of the hero trope makes her "a feminist in spirit."[25] Literary scholar Katarzyna Paszkiewicz traces the commercialism at play in Coppola's auteurism. She claims that "even though *Marie Antoinette* is mainly concerned with surface and appearances, it is not superficial in its politics,"[26] and implies that there is a richness and depth to her femininity. Film studies scholar Sharon Lin Tay reads Coppola's work against the backdrop of the 1970's American New Wave. Cinema of this period presented characters, on one hand, who seemed helpless and unable to have agency in their world, while directors, on the other, engaged in imaginative formal innovations to American cinema.[27] Because this period was also profoundly masculine, Coppola auteurship intervenes with a "feminist politics," which enables Lin Tay to see more clearly the masculine "ideological framework" of the American New Wave.[28]

Some scholars understand Coppola's work not as resisting but, in some way, capitulating to or caught within postfeminism and capitalist culture. For example, film studies scholar Delphine Letort implies, particularly about the *The Bling Ring*, that Coppola's auteur brand has capitulated to both capitalism and postfeminism. She writes that the film "exploits celebrity culture through the incorporation of feminine celebrities as brands to be consumed, illustrating a capitalist mode of production that Sofia Coppola endorses by turning her feminine auteurist style into a brand."[29] Film scholar Belinda Smaill makes two separate arguments, one about Coppola's characters and the other about her auteurship. The scholar notes that critics sometimes reject the director's work as "girlish and insubstantial," mere "whimsical musings of an over-privileged female adolescent [Coppola]."[30] Such criticism has staying power, in part, because her films focus on the "inner life of women rather than their social position," producing an apolitical account of being a woman in patriarchal culture.[31] As a result, Coppola "responds to post-feminist sensibilities," but she does so in ambiguous and "unresolved ways."[32] Second, while the director's auteur image diverges from masculine auteurism, it is a "paradoxical mix of self-actualization and a lack of concern, a 'coolness,'" which "aligns more easily with the entrepreneurialism and consumerism of post-feminism."[33] For Smaill, these attachments to capitalism and post-feminism produce "an uneasy fit" between her avant-garde influences (like Chantal Ackerman and Michael Antonioni) and her themes.[34] Perhaps the clearest proponent of Coppola's inability to escape postfeminism is film scholar Fiona Handyside. She claims that the director's films are "unconsciously symptomatic of the problems and contradictions of postfeminism for girls and women."[35] No matter how deeply the films celebrate and make space for both femininity and female subjectivity, they "remain blind to the extent to which this is a restricted, privileged and elitist view. Coppola's girls and women may travel, but they remain safely within cosseted white worlds. They may use fashion as a means of expression, but this is elitist fashion that restricts and imprisons."[36] Handyside describes the director as a "postfeminist auteur," and her films as "products of a postfeminist moment."[37]

The final approach synthetizes two previous options, arguing that Coppola's films can be put to feminist use but are otherwise complicit with the processes of whiteness. In this regard, film studies scholar Kendra Marston offers one of the few explicit discussions of race, whiteness, and ambivalence within Coppola scholarship. Marston's broader project explores the melancholy (or melancholia) that white female characters experience in early twenty-first century films like *Blue Jasmine* (2013), *Gone Girl* (2014), *The Girl on the Train* (2016), *Black Swan* (2010), *The Virgin Suicides, Lost in Translation,* and *Marie Antoinette*. Whiteness is that unmarked or invisible standpoint that masks a host of "social, political and cultural advantages."[38] Her work, like whiteness studies more broadly, aims to "disrupt the invisibility of white, hegemonic power structures by exploring how these structures are . . . maintained through popular forms [and] powerful industry players."[39] She notes that white women have experienced ambivalence, living into many of the advantages whiteness offers while also experiencing the disadvantages of being marked as women. For example, during colonial expansion, white women "rarely made economic or military decisions relative to the expansion of empire, [but] they still held power over colonised members of both sexes."[40] Cinematic representations of white, female melancholia capture a particular form of ambivalence present for many in the early 21st century. Neoliberal postfeminism has, in many respects, failed white women as a group,[41] and these films present their "race privilege and affluence . . . as disabling sicknesses."[42] However much melancholia makes clear the problems and failures of capitalism, Marston notes how these women are unable to find "forms of empowerment that lie beyond the . . . same ideologies or the race and class hierarchies that they depend upon."[43] Like the white women of the colonial moment, contemporary white women face a similar ambivalence, experiencing both the advantages and harms that whiteness offers.

In Marston's analysis, Coppola's characters experience unhappiness with neoliberalism, are captured within apolitical whitneness, but Coppola, as a filmmaker, experiences the advantages of whiteness in building a career that romanticizes these experiences. Focusing on *The Virgin Suicides*, *Lost in Translation*, and *Marie Antoinette*, Marston notes how these films represent the alienation, aimlessness, and the utter "impossibility of living a fulfilling life under neoliberal capitalism."[44] The protagonists are also trapped within their upper-class whiteness, unable to search for meaningful alternatives outside their racialized and economic social location. And perhaps more importantly, exiting the racial and economic standpoint is never even "posed as a viable option" for her characters.[45] As a result, Coppola and her films remain perpetually apolitical, immersed within whiteness and privilege, "incapable of decentring" themselves nor able to "see, hear or otherwise relate to subjects racialised as non-white."[46] Coppola has, however, established herself as a commercially viable "high-profile and influential female auteur" primarily through representing feelings of alienation and apolitical entrapment through the romance of *ennui*, fashion, and ironic detachment.[47] Marston claims that any "examination of the heroine's role within her broader cultural context or a rupture of the melancholic state would jeopardize the commercial appeal of her [Coppola's] brand, which is built upon a fantasy aesthetic that idealises tragic, white femininity in all its ethereal glory."[48] Even though Coppola's films can be put to feminist ends, they and their director also benefit from the invisibility of their whiteness and are unable or unwilling to leave their privileged location.

These options provide a way to situate our own work, describe the third-wave feminist counters of Coppola studies, and provide a pathway to bring Coppola studies more deeply into conversation with fourth-wave feminist concerns. First, within Coppola studies, we draw on the radical feminist approach of Backman Rogers, the pragmatic approach Kennedy defines, and Marston's concerns with race. We are not completely convinced that Coppola's films are radically feminist, and, since Coppola remains consistently apolitical in her statements, we desire to remain agnostic as to whether or not Coppola herself holds to a radical feminist point of view. However, like Kennedy, we want to put her films to radical feminist uses. Like Backman Rogers, we agree that the deeper structures of her films, rather than the surface, are what provide the possibility of those radical readings. Whether or not feminists find our readings radical enough is an open question. Like Marston, we want to think more deeply about race and whiteness; precisely as cis-gendered, straight, white men, we want to center concerns of radical feminist of color as keenly as we are able.

These options also situate the majority of Coppola studies as foregrounding third wave feminist concerns. Suzanne Ferris and Mallory Young name this explicit concern. They describe Coppola not only as bringing with her an approach to *Marie Antoinette* that is characteristic of third-wave feminism, but they also present the film's audience as a third-wave audience. Likewise, Coppola studies suggest its affiliation with third-wave concerns by what it tends to deemphasize. As film scholar Hilary Neroni argues, "While intersectionality, critical race theory, queer theory, transgender theory, and more, came into being during third wave feminism they have had only a limited impact on the third wave."[49] The limited impact of feminists of color, for example, exists throughout Coppola studies. Perhaps because of Coppola's own centering of whiteness, scholars have tended to deemphasize detailed discussion of race and whiteness. While Handyside rightly names the whiteness and economic privilege of Coppola's characters, for example, she prioritizes other themes, including postfeminism, home, fashion, and authorship. With at least the exception of Marston, the same holds true throughout Coppola studies, where themes like whiteness, intersectionality, queer, and transgender identities are not explored in any substantial depth.

To the extent that Neroni's insight illustrates a shortcoming, it also suggests a possibility to bring Coppola studies more deeply into conversation with fourth-wave concerns. At a few points throughout this monograph, we have brough fourth-wave concerns to bear, namely by incorporating the reflections of feminists of color. For example, in our reading of *Lost in Translation*, we centered Chicana scholarship on decolonial love. The insights of Chicana scholar Gloria Anzaldúa allowed us to name a limited form of liberation present in reflections on *Marie Antoinette*. Like Marston, we named the unquestioned center of whiteness, or white professionalism, in *A Very Murray Christmas*. And in our chapter on *Somewhere*, we grounded our discussion of *habitus* in Saba Mahmood's account, rather than a more so-called classical choice like Aristotle. However, like much of Coppola studies, the potential for deeper engagement with feminists of color exists. Marston's work, for example, offers a much-needed, critical account of how whiteness functions. However, she leaves open the option to mobilize such critical insight into constructive conversations. In the remainder of this chapter, we offer a case study in what form a constructive conversation might take. We bring the insights from women of color—particularly bell hooks and Audre Lorde—into conversation with the implications of our chapters, and thereby suggest ways our readings can contribute to their agendas and insights. While these kinds of moves might provide possibilities for a productive future engagement, they also suggest that whiteness needs to be more deeply decentered from our own work. We admit that we, the authors of this book, have not listened to women of color deeply enough, and that failure should not keep us from taking time and space here to listen.

## FOURTH WAVE CONVERSATIONS

In the final section of this book, bring our work into conversation with fourth-wave feminist concerns. Moving through each section of the book, we review the implications of our readings of each film, point to the insights of a feminist of color, and put our readings to use to support and expand such insights. We begin with the theme of masculinity.

## MASCULINITY

Our analysis of *Somewhere* suggested four implications for the study of toxic masculinity. While toxic masculinity is composed of harmful behaviors, it is also a way of life, or a *habitus* of bodily practices, materials, and scripts. If toxicity is habitual, then it has the power to malform the interior lives of both men and women. The study of toxic masculinities should also attend to the patterns or cycles that structure toxicity. Such structures are precisely what Michelle Alexander suggests about the history of racism. While the content of racism in America changed—from slavery, to Jim Crow segregation, to mass incarceration—the structures of inequality remained in place. In *Somewhere*, Johnny does not exhibit overt acts of violence against women's bodies, but the structures of toxicity, namely the sexual objectification of women, remain in place. Also, without losing focus on the harm to women, *Somewhere* demonstrates that toxic masculinity produces asymmetrical suffering in the lives of men. Johnny's toxicity has made him a participant in the eradication of his own humanity, which he claims make him "nothing... not even a person." If toxic *habituses* of masculinity have the potential to eradicate one's humanity, then the language of *habitus* can provide a powerful way to imagine alternative ways of being men. Although the shape of that alternative masculinity remains an open question, *Somewhere* suggests that vulnerability, bodily presence, joy, play, and rest might lead to a recovery of men's humanity.

We also suggested three implications *The Virgin Suicides* has for the study of hegemonic masculinity. In order for men to live a life that continually refuses the death that hegemonic masculinity brings, men must be haunted by women's testimonies of suffering. Haunting, as Giorgio Agamben implies, takes place through the resonances between the site of trauma (like the soccer game at Auschwitz) and ordinary life (any other soccer match). Such change will occur only if men see figures like the Lisbon sisters in the lives of the women and girls they encounter. Additionally, in the same way that feminists have linked social and epistemic masculinity to violence, Coppola's film suggests love can also function as a domain of violence. When the boys say they loved the Lisbon sisters, their love facilitates their violence upon them. Last, unlike the boys in the film, who failed to live up to the standards of hegemonic masuclinity, men must also listen to the testimony of their own so-called failures, and through those failures, break of the frame of death that the standard holds on them. In such a moment, the failure to be masculine can become a threshold into a new form of masculinity.

If scholarly reflections on toxic and hegemonic masculinities offer critical accounts, bell hooks creates a pathway for our reflections to become constructive. "To offer men a different way of being," hooks argues, men must leave the hierarchical "dominator model" and embrace "interbeing and interdependency as the organic relationship of all living beings."[50] As part of the sense of interdependency and interbeing, what men need is "vulnerability" and "intimacy"; however, "many men seek to avoid," vulnerability and intimacy and may perhaps go their entire lives without such realities in their lives.[51] Our reflections on the *habitus* of masculinity, in a limited but practical way, respond to hooks' call for vulnerability, interdependence, and intimacy.

*Habitus* suggests that certain conditions must be present in the lives of men in order to support interdependence and vulnerability. Taking Saba Mahmood's account of *habitus* together with readings of *Somewhere* and *The Virgin Suicides*, we argue that the ability for men to leave behind the *habitus* of toxic, hegemonic, or dominator masculinities will not primarily occur through intellectual assent. Intellectual work is certainly a necessary part of the process, but it is a wholly insufficient part. Our work suggests that men should engage in an alternative way of life composed of bodily practices, materiality, and scripts that are alternatives to toxic, hegemonic, or dominating ways of life. In order to deconstruct patriarchal culture, men must practice vulnerability and interdependence before they become vulnerable and interdependent people. Practices, materiality, and scripts are, in a sense, the prerequisite realities that will create the conditions for the possibility of something like intimacy. *Somewhere* suggests that bodily presence, joy, play, and rest might be just some of the practices men need to become different people. It also suggests that materiality analogous to Johnny's car or his drug and alcohol use might also need to be abandoned in favor of other material more fitting for vulnerability. *Habitus* raises the stakes on mundane particularities of everyday life as of critical importance for men to change. Mundane realities like bodily presence, food, toys, games, play, time—all must be addressed in some way for change of *habitus* to take place.

*Habitus* also suggests that the negative example of the neighborhood boys in *The Virgin Suicides* can point to constructive possibilities. In the film, the neighborhood boys were unwilling or unable to hear the testimonies of women, to be haunted by them, and to use their so-called failures to live up to the standards of hegemonic masculinity as a resource to critique that system. In the early twenty-first century, it might seem common sense to claim that hearing the testimonies of women is essential. But such acts are so vital that, at this point in the history of feminism, they cannot be repeated enough. Men must hear, again and again, the ways toxicity and hegemony harm women. Furthermore, to bear witness to the testimony of women, men must let the stories of women haunt the particularities of their daily lives. Haunting, far from a passive practice, is an active, interpretive one. Men must rehearse women's stories to themselves and hear the echoes of women's voices as they participate in everyday bodily practices, inhabit everyday materiality, and engage in the scripts of daily life. Those haunting echoes should resonate long after women have stopped speaking. Men must also see their failures to live up to toxic and hegemonic standards as opportunities to inhabit new ways of being men. It never occurred to the neighborhood boys that their failure to "discover" why the Lisbon sisters took their own lives was a failure of their own masculinity. Many such failures—many such vulnerabilities, if you will—have the potential to open paths of connection with other women, men, and nonbinary peoples to discover together what it means to be who they are. Such connections demand trust. But shared vulnerability is, in fact, one of the paths to the trust necessary for men to leave behind domination and become the kind of people prepared for interdependence and intimacy.

## SEXUAL POLITICS

Bringing the music of *Marie Antoinette* and Chicana scholar Gloria Anzaldúa's insights into conversation with white feminist reflection, we suggest some limitations white scholars might consider, particularly the need to be increasingly critical of how resource dependent and individualistic white imaginations tend to be. If our imagining alternative worlds is, like it is for Marie Antoinette, both resource dependent and ultimately personal, then we may need to consider whom our liberation excludes. Anzaldúa's account of liberation encourages white scholars to keep liberation connected both to moving into the world with public action (against individualism) and to drawing on the resources and power of vulnerability (against resource dependency). Both in Antoinette's world and in our own, violent imperial powers continue to cause great and lasting harm. In such a setting, vulnerability functions as both a resource and a source of power, because it denies that violence will dictate what actions someone like Anzaldúa will perform with her own body. Vulnerability implies that a new world is possible, a world where both

Anzaldúa and Antoinette can have a future liberated from the internalized violence of racism and the external violence of the state, be it a reality like housing discrimination or the gift of Le Petit Trianon. Vulnerability, therefore, is both a resource and a source of power, because while Anzaldúa may have more ready access to it, it is not reserved only for women of color. White women and men can learn to become vulnerable. When we learn how to move out into the world with a posture of vulnerability, then perhaps we might be able to imagine a world liberated in the way Anzaldúa thinks it could be.

Through *The Beguiled*, we suggest important limitations to philosopher Jacques Derrida's notion of hospitality. Miss Martha wields *hospitium* based on the needs of her female-centered household. By contrast, Derrida's hospitality, which involves saying "yes" to every guest, is ultimately dangerous, because it, albeit unintentionally, centers masculine ways of meaning, what Derrida himself named phallogocentrism. For Derrida's hospitality to work, it should likely only be addressed to those in power, ideally to white men like the authors of this book. As the film shows, in wartime settings, men pose a threat to women's homes, bodies, and resources. Without Miss Martha's ability to control *hospitium* by subduing or preventing hostilities, inhabiting Derrida's hospitality would have been disastrous for the women and young girls at the seminary. Like Dido's acceptance of Aeneas, Miss Martha accepts McBurney to the seminary's (and more significantly, Edwina's) detriment. In this way, *The Beguiled* illustrates the limits within which women and minority groups must practice hospitality. The film also stands as a repudiation of androcentric storytelling. Unlike the phallogocentric stories of Dido, Dinah, and countless literary and cinematic examples of violence against women, Coppola's film repositions power according to Miss Martha's agency through her navigation of *hospitium*. Coppola reframes violence to incriminate and neutralize the masculine aggressor, and thereby represents the agency of women in a setting as precarious to women as war.

Concerning the violence men perform against women in *Marie Antoinette* and *The Beguiled*, then bell hooks centers the emotional impact of that violence, particularly the silence, fear, and anger that results. In the late 1970s, hooks claims to not have admitted to anyone her true feelings about men. "[N]ot only did I not understand men, I feared them."[52] But it was not only her. She noticed that women, as a group, seemed "afraid to speak openly about men . . . [about] what we have witnessed as daughters, sisters, grandmothers, mothers, aunts, lovers, occasional sex objects . . . our sense of fear and threat."[53] When women do speak about men, as early feminist reflection offered, women often register feelings of anger and hatred. While these feelings are important to express, they produced tacit permission for women to not only deny their more complicated feelings about men but also to wrongly assume that men were hopeless, incapable of change. By contrast, hooks desires a feminism that offers resolutions to rage and anger and acknowledges complex feelings. Resolutions and acknowledgments of this kind would, hooks suggests, create space for women to discusses what it means "to love men in patriarchal culture, to know how we could express that love without fear of exploitation and oppression," and ultimately "to imagine a culture of reconciliation where women and men might meet and find common ground."[54] To illustrate how our reading of *Marie Antoinette* and *The Beguiled* can contribute to hooks' agenda, we take a brief detour through Anna Backman Rogers's analysis of Kirsten Dunst's roles in Coppola films.

Backman Rogers argues that Coppola collaborations with Dunst present an intertextual character association, one that we claim also exists with Bill Murray. For Dunst's characters, the associations move from Lux Lisbon (*The Virgin Suicides*), to Marie Antoinette (*Marie Antoinette*), and eventually to Edwina Morrow (*The Beguiled*). The "intertextual reference," Rogers notes, "allows Dunst's incarnation of Lux Lisbon to be carried forward into her performance as the tragic, young queen of France to empathic effect."[55] The intertext echoes continues into *The Beguiled*. Edwina, like Lux, has her first sexual encounter where consent is questionable at best, but, unlike Lux, Edwina "comes to understand the nature of what she has given [her virginity] within the context of an imbalance of power."[56] Like Dunst, Murray has appeared in several Coppola films, and we focus here on *Lost in Translation* and *On the Rocks*. In *Lost in Translation*, Murray's Bob Harris is in relational and career crisis, alienated from his wife and trapped in unsatisfying work. Through his connection with Charlotte, and perhaps most notably through his vulnerability with her, Bob inhabits a love that defies exploitation. While Bob evokes jealousy from Charlotte (because he sleeps with the lounge singer), such jealousy does not define their relationship. Within Coppola's work, Bob is, in many ways, an idealized man—flawed and capable of profound vulnerability and connection. Rather than intensify, develop, or resolve the intertextual relationship between these roles, *On the Rocks* is a near polar inversion of *Lost in Translation*. As an overt misogynist, Felix Keane's offensiveness is rendered barely tolerable to his daughter, Laura, almost purely by the excitement he creates for her. One of Felix's key offenses is his denigration of marriage in general, and Laura's marriage in particular. Father and daughter eventually share moments of fleeting vulnerability, and Laura, in one scene, erupts in volatile anger and rage toward him. By the film's end, he undergoes a minimal change. He acknowledges her choice to be married as a legitimate one, as he calls it, her own "adventure."

Within wider American culture, *On the Rocks* exists in a moment, against bell hooks' assertion, in which there is significant evidence to support the claim that men are, indeed, hopeless. The United States of America installed an openly misogynist man, Donald Trump, to the office of president in 2016, a man who unrepentantly bragged about sexually assaulting women. Two years later, amidst allegation of rape, the Senate installed Brett Kavanaugh as associate Supreme Court justice. His appointment served as an echo of a similar allegation against the 1991 appointment of associate justice Clarence Thomas. The refusal of the Senate to believe Anita Hill in 1991 and later Christine Blasey Ford in 2016 illustrated that in 35 years, not much had changed for survivors of sexual assault. And while movements like #metoo have influenced the discourse of gender politics worldwide, they also show how, in the twenty-first century, violence against women seems still to be a matter of course. Against this backdrop, Felix is, perhaps, a representative of the kinds of misogynist men who litter the political landscape. But he and Laura illustrate precisely what hooks grapples with. Laura, like hooks, has complicated feelings, both love and hate toward the men in their lives. Such feelings must be expressed, explored, and resolved in some way. Furthermore, Laura's vulnerability and anger produces, in almost an idealized way, what hooks hopes it would—Felix changes. While his change might be microscopic and too easily won, it signals that he, and perhaps others like him, are not hopeless. If Felix is not hopeless, then perhaps Bob is not an unattainable dream. Perhaps he, foibles and all, is what hooks' sense of hope can deliver—a man who can not only love Charlotte but love her without the exploitation and abuse so many young women experience at the hands of older men. It is precisely this hope that can be used as a resource against the problems we raised in *Marie Antoinette* and *The Beguiled*.

While not diminishing the explicit problem of violent men, limited liberation and Derrida's hospitality suggest that the problematics of whiteness (and masculinity for that matter) run far deeper than its most visible incarnations. Because it is easy to imagine reconciliation with Bob Harris and perhaps to a lesser extent with Felix, it could be tempting to ask the question of reconciliation with Marie Antoinette's husband Louis, the French aristocracy, or Corporal McBurney. That question, while tempting, needs to be resisted, because it misses the deeper problem of whiteness. The deeper problem is similar to Martin Luther King Jr. classic formulation in "Letter from Birmingham Jail." The greatest problem for King was not the explicit racist but those termed as "the white moderate."[57] Such people, he claimed, possessed good will but shallow understanding, and "shallow understanding from people of good will is more frustrating than absolute misunderstanding from people of ill will."[58] Limited liberation and Derrida's hospitality are, we suggest, precisely the kinds of "shallow understanding from people of good will" that King identified decades ago. Which is to say, the explicit violence of misogynist men like McBurney are not the only kinds of violence women like bell hooks must navigate. What lies behind them is well-meaning whiteness. The question is not whether there is hope for people like Bob, Felix,

Louis, or McBurney. The question is will white people who support limited liberation or Derrida's hospitality be willing to embrace Anzaldúa's vulnerability and listen to hooks' rage, love, and hope? If we are able to move past our shallow (mis)understanding, then perhaps, like Felix, we can begin the process of change necessary for true liberation and hospitality.

## BODIES

*The Bling Ring* enabled us to suggest some religious implications for non-religious society, social media, bodily desire, and boredom. Even though the West is a secular and secularizing society, religious language still has the capacity to shed light on what might appear to be non-religious experiences, because portions of secular society retain remnants of a religious past. While the content of religious life may have vanished, structural aspects remain, like the embodied eroticism of relics. This same holds true of social media. If users of social media create online reliquaries, not unlike the way medieval Christians used their own, then perhaps, social media may simply reveal that certain aspects of bodily practice remain consistent over long periods of time. Christian reflections on *eros*, or bodily appetites, has the potential to contribute to scholarly reflections on embodiment more broadly, although the usefulness of such contribution is, by and large, yet to be made. And even though it seems too obvious to say that teenagers claim to be bored, the film turns the commonplace statement into a mediation on the religious implications of boredom. Perhaps boredom is an embodied, spiritual condition, one that the characters attempt to alleviate within the structure of religious experience. That release takes place at the site of the Bling Ring's bodies.

We concluded our chapter on *A Very Murray Christmas* with reflections on joy and equity. The film suggests that joy is only possible if the body and its lower, grotesque realities are affirmed and included. If *The Carpenters at Christmas* places the limiting conditions of perfection, professionalism, and disembodiment to joy, then Coppola's special suggests that joy needs imperfect, grotesque bodies. Furthermore, such an embodied joy can facilitate the inclusion of those with so-called incapacities. What communities perceive of (rightly or wrongly) as weaknesses, incapacities, or vulnerabilities may be more foundational to joy than any other criteria. Additionally, as Mikhail Bakhtin suggests, whatever is the center of a hierarchical society must be decentered for equity to exist. When Coppola presents "bad" or "good-bad" singers as sites of joy, she signals the possibility that a grotesque body can be a body that brings equality into being. However, she does not question the center of her film—whiteness. If white folks never question their own centrality, no subversion will ever produce anything like a true, fulsome, embodied joy or equity.

Like our engagement with hooks above, Audre Lorde's reflection on the erotic, joy, and belonging help explain how, even though these films take bodies seriously, they fail to overcome the exploitation and denial essential for whiteness to remain in place. In her essay "Uses of the Erotic: The Erotic as Power," Lorde identifies the function of the erotic for the self and others, and she describes how whiteness, or the Western tradition, undercuts the power of the erotic. The erotic serves two functions for Lorde, joy and belonging. The erotic enables individuals to experience the joy and satisfaction of completing bodily activity or work.[59] As examples, she cites the most mundane activities, like when she responds or dances to music. She also insists that a similar erotic sense of fulfillment can take place when someone builds a bookcase or writes a poem. But perhaps her most mundane erotic example is simply moving her body into the sunlight, next to her lover. If the erotic can provide the individual an internal sense of joy or fulfillment, the eroticism of joy can produce belonging between peoples.[60] Through deep bodily participation—like dancing, playing, and even fighting—erotic encounters can create the conditions in which people can begin the difficult work of creating new kinds of political arrangements that can serve as a foundation for creating understanding between peoples of profound difference. The erotic, therefore, can leap the gap between peoples whom the history of race and coloniality has divided. However, the European-American male tradition, or white masculinity, erodes or counteracts these erotic functions in two ways, first by exploiting erotic experiences rather than sharing in deep participation with others, and second by denying or looking away from injustices that exist.

What *The Bling Ring* and *A Very Murray Christmas* both make clear is precisely what eroticism, joy, and belonging look like without attending to the exploitation and denial Lorde names. But their negative examples also suggest constructive possibilities. Without naming it, *The Bling Ring* first highlights exploitation. While members of The Bling Ring clearly create erotic bridges from themselves to other members of the group, it is a belonging that enacts the exploitation of violence and does so at the site of their bodies. The film also erases or, as Lorde might say, looks away from the reality that people of color can capitulate to whiteness as well. In the real-life Bling Ring, Diana Tamayo, an undocumented immigrant from Mexico, participated in the same erotic acts of white masculinity as the other white members of the group. However, Coppola looked away or denied that she existed, erasing her from the film. While *A Very Murray Christmas* offered the shared joy of inclusion at the site of bodily vulnerability/weakness (i.e., singing "badly"), the film centered white professionalism by denying or minimizing bodies of color. What these shortcomings suggest is that it is precisely at the site of everyday bodily encounters that whiteness can be decentered. Not only does singing matter, but also the one with whom you sing matters. The one with whom you dance, play, and fight with matters. If erotic connections can bring into being alternative political conditions, then these mundane activities, if performed as part of a *habitus* or way of life, can decenter whiteness, but only if white folks refuse exploitation and denial. One of Lorde's fundamental insights on the erotic might be this: in order for white folks to change, we must collaborate on the conditions in which we can begin to sing, dance, play, and fight with those who are not like us. Without bodies and without *eros*, equitable belonging will remain an impossibility.

## LOVE

Based on our reading of *Lost in Translation*, we offer two implications. Malaise, in the way Charles Taylor describes it, is a necessary but insufficient way of understanding modernity. What Taylor misses, as Chela Sandoval and other Chicana scholars imply, are the colonial stratifications that mark the modern period. Also, this film presents a progression beyond what we covered in the "Masculinity" section. If *The Virgin Suicides* presents a world where love can be a domain in which violence takes place, *Somewhere* demonstrates that the work of untangling love from violence includes attending to *habitus*. In *Lost in Translation*, Bob and Charlotte experience a form of love approaching decolonial love, one which avoids many damaging Western binaries. When read in this order, *Lost in Translation* offers a massive, imaginative leap for the manner in which Coppola represents the possibilities of men (and women) to live outside of hegemonic and toxic masculinities. However, because Bob and Charlotte seem able to love only in the liminal space between Western and decolonial love, their love suggests problems that many white settlers have not fully confronted. Decolonial love demands of white settlers that they perform the challenging work of imagining and living a different form of life. What shape that form of life should take is an open question. But that is the question that white settlers need to engage, imagine, and live for not only to experience freedom but also for white settlers to experience it too.

For *On the Rocks*, we offer a critical and constructive account of love. Felix's way of loving others is a form of attention and recognition, consistent with the way he performs emotional labor. Because he attempts to manage other people, his love is nothing more than a form of control, violence, and oppression. While love can indeed be means of liberation, *On the Rocks* demonstrates how misogyny can co-opt love to capitalist ends. If Coppola's rendering of Felix points out how love can be co-opted, then her expansive account of emotional labor also suggests a constructive account of the emotional labor and love. As Arlie Hochschild argues, emotional labor is the regulation of one's emotions in order to manage the emotions of others. However, as the dinner scene in Mexico illustrates, emotional labor can be something beyond this description. In the scene, both Laura and Felix labor together in healthy and life-giving ways. If love can, indeed, include ways of attending to others, through recognition and affirmation, the scene suggests that vulnerability and lack of control are additional conditions that keep love from becoming entwined with violence. The emotional labor of love also demands an honest account of violence, such that violence does not have the final word. At the end of the film, Felix fully recognizes and affirms Laura's marriage, suggesting that he might, one day, be able to relinquish his desire for control and embrace vulnerability as a way of life. Such a way of moving through the world would redefine virtues like joy, love, and happiness to be lifegiving for everyone he encounters, not merely himself.

Taken together, our reflections on these films expand upon bell hooks' insights about the political power of love. Drawing on writers like James Baldwin, Martin Luther King, Jr., and Toni Morrison, hooks notes that part of what makes white supremacy culture so damaging is that it is a loveless way of moving through the world. However, an ethic of love, she argues, will create and sustain a just and equitable political reality.

> Love is profoundly political. Our deepest revolution will come when we understand this truth. Only love can give us the strength to go forward in the midst of heart break and misery. Only love can give us the power to reconcile, to redeem, the power to renew weary spirits and save lost souls. The transformative power of love is the foundation of all meaningful social change. Without love our lives are without meaning. Love is the heart of the matter. When all else has fallen away, love sustains.[61]

hooks also discusses the reality that oppressed peoples must learn to love those who oppress them. Such love does not permit oppressors to continue in their harmful activities, but it becomes a way of transforming and redeeming oppressors from their violent ways of life. Loving the oppressors is the only way to bring them into King's "beloved community."

Rooted in hooks' insights, our reading of *On the Rocks* and *Lost in Translation* points to the reality that white folks, as a group, will have to learn to be loved by those they have oppressed. If white people have created and perhaps unwittingly sustained a white supremacist culture, then part of what we are nurtured into is a loveless culture, a culture where we, like Felix, have perhaps mistaken control and violence for love. Part of what this means is that white people must not only unlearn what we assume to be love, but we must also learn to be loved by those who suffer under the weight of our violence. The claim that white people do not know what love is will strike some as a baseless claim. Certainly, white people love their partners and children, their families and friends. hooks' insights, rather, suggest that what counts as white love might be precisely its coloniality, its inability to join us to people who are not like us and do so in life-giving ways. To claim that white people do not truly understand love is to claim the reality that we need to be transformed and redeemed from white supremacy. That love will mean, like Laura does with Felix, that we will need to hear and internalize hard truths about ourselves, and that will require from us immense emotional labor and maturing. But if we have a chance of entering into the kind of decolonial love Sandoval discusses, we will have to overcome the error that Bob and Charlotte commit. We will have to first encounter those who live life "from below" and find ways to accept being loved by them. There are, of course, many things that must be in place for love to flourish. White people, for example, must demonstrate that they are trustworthy not to harm others. Love is not an excuse, as hooks insists, for oppressed people to endure more suffering.[62] White people might also need to engage in bodily practices like vulnerability, lack of control, laughing, dancing, and fighting, too. But perhaps the most foundational prerequisite is that white people must possess an erotic desire to be changed. "True love does have the power to redeem," says hooks, "but only if we are ready for redemption. Love saves us only if we want to be saved."[63] As white people, we should seek redemption before we can receive love and be changed by it.

If there is a single theme to which we have returned again and again in conversation with feminists of color like bell hooks and Audre Lorde, it is the theme of vulnerability. White people, more broadly, and white men, in particular, are perhaps the one people-group in the world who have the most trouble embracing vulnerability and are in the most need of it. If there is, indeed, a more just and equitable future, a true liberation for all peoples, then white vulnerability must be part of white ways of moving through the world. We would argue that in each of Coppola's films, one can find a blueprint for what vulnerability looks like and what we lose when we refuse to embrace it.

## REFERENCES

*A Very Murray Christmas*. Sofia Coppola, director. 2015; Netflix: Los Gatos, CA, 2015. Streaming. www.netflix.com/title/80042368.

Andersson, Therése. "Costume Cinema and Materiality: Telling the Story of Marie Antoinette through Dress." *Culture Unbound* 3 (2011): 101–112.

Arnold, Rebecca. "The New Rococo: Sofia Coppola and Fashions in Contemporary Femininity." In *Rococo Echo: Art, History and Historiography from Cochin to Coppola*, edited by Melissa Lee Hyde and Katie Scott, 295–312. Oxford: Voltaire Foundation, 2014.

Backman Rogers, Anna. "And That I See a Darkness: The Stardom of Kirsten Dunst in Collaboration with Sofia Coppola in Three Images." *Film-Philosophy* 23, no. 2 (2019): 114–136.

———. *Sofia Coppola: The Politics of Visual Pleasure*. New York: Berghahn, 2019.

Bolton, Lucy. *Film and Female Consciousness: Irigaray, Cinema and Thinking Women*. London: Palgrave Macmillan, 2011.

Brevik-Zender, Heidi. "Let Them Wear Manolos: Fashion, Walter Benjamin, and Sofia Coppola's *Marie Antoinette*," *Camera Obscura 78* 26 no. 3 (2011): 1–33.

Ferriess, Suzanne. *The Cinema of Sofia Coppola: Fashion, Culture, Celebrity*. London: Bloomsbury Academic, 2021.

Ferris, Suzanne and Mallory Young. "Marie Antoinette: Fashion, Third Wave Feminism, and Chick Culture." *Literature-Film Quarterly* 38, no. 2 (April 2010): 98–116.

Flores, Pamela. "Fashion and Otherness: The Passionate Journey of Coppola's *Marie Antoinette* from a Semiotic Perspective." *Fashion Theory* 17, no. 5 (2013): 605–622.

Galt, Rosalind. *Pretty: Film and the Decorative*. New York: Columbia University Press, 2011.

Handyside, Fiona. "Girlhood, Postfeminism and Contemporary Female Art-House Authorship: The 'Nameless Trilogies' of Sofia Coppola and Mia Hansen-Løve." *Alphaville: Journal of Film and Screen Media* 10 (Winter 2015): 1–18.

———. *Sofia Coppola: A Cinema of Girlhood*. London: L.B. Tauris, 2017.

hooks, bell. *All About Love: New Visions*. New York: William Morrow and Company, 2000.

———. *Salvation: Black People and Love*. New York: William Morrow and Company, 2001.

———. *The Will to Change: Men, Masculinity, and Love*. New York: Atria Books, 2004. iBooks.

Kennedy, Todd. "Off with Hollywood's Head: Sofia Coppola as Feminine Auteur." *Film Criticism* 35, no. 1 (2010): 37–59.

———. "On the Road to 'Some' Place: Sofia Coppola's Dissident Modernism Against a Postmodern Landscape." *Miscelánea* 52 (2015): 51–67.

King Jr., Martin Luther. "Letter from Birmingham Jail." *The Atlantic*, April 2018. www.theatlantic.com/magazine/archive/2018/02/letter-from-a-birmingham-jail/552461/.

Leadston, Mackenzie. "Letters from an Austrian Woman: Adapting Transhistoric Girlhood in Sofia Coppola's *Marie Antoinette* (2006)." *The Modern Language Review* 114, no. 4 (October 2019): 613–628.

Letort, Delphine. "The Cultural Capital of Sofia Coppola's *The Bling Ring* (2013): Branding Feminine Celebrity in Los Angeles." *Celebrity Studies* (2015): 1–14.

Lin Tay, Sharon. *Women on the Edge: Twelve Political Film Practices*. London: Palgrave Macmillan Limited, 2009.
Lorde, Audre. "Uses of the Erotic: The Erotic as Power," 54–59. In *Sister Outsider: Speeches and Essays by Audre Lorde*. New York: Crossway Press, 2007.
*Lost in Translation*. Sofia Coppola, director. 2003; Los Angeles, CA: Universal Pictures Home Entertainment, 2003. DVD.
*Marie Antoinette*. Sofia Coppola, director. 2006; San Francisco, CA: American Zoetrope, 2007. DVD.
Mida, Ingrid. "Fashion Exhibition as Cinematic Experience." *Film, Fashion & Consumption* 7 no. 1 (2018): 57–71.
Marston, Kendra. *Postfeminist Whiteness: Problematising Melancholic Burden in Contemporary Hollywood*. Edinburgh, UK: Edinburgh University Press.
Neroni, Hilary. *Feminist Film Theory and Cléo from 5 to 7*. New York: Bloomsbury, 2016.
*On the Rocks*. Sofia Coppola, director. 2020; New York City: A24, 2020. Streaming. tv.apple.com/us/movie/on-the-rocks/umc.cmc.1mydlea6wicrm013138speg6m.
Palmer, R. Barton. "Some Thoughts on New Hollywood Multiplicity: Sofia Coppola's Young Girls Trilogy." In *Film Trilogies: New Critical Approaches*, edited by Claire Perkins and Constantine Verevis, 35–54. London: Palgrave Macmillan Limited, 2012.
Paszkiewicz, Katarzyna. "'She Looks Like a Little Piece of Cake': Sofia Coppola and the Commerce of Auteurism." *Interférences Littéraires/Literaire Interferenties* 21 (December 2017): 107–128.
Pesce, Sara. "Ripping off Hollywood Celebrities: Sofia Coppola's *The Bling Ring*, Luxury Fashion, and Self-branding in California." *Film, Fashion & Consumption* 4, no. 1 (2015): 5–24.
———. "The Baroque Imagination: Film, Costume Design and Italian High Fashion." *Film, Fashion & Consumption* 5, no. 1 (2016): 7–28.
Smaill, Belinda. "Sofia Coppola." *Feminist Media Studies* 13, no. 1 (2013): 148–162.
*Somewhere*. Sofia Coppola, director. 2010; Universal City, CA: Focus Features, 2011. DVD.
*The Beguiled*. Sofia Coppola, director. 2017; Universal City, CA: Focus Features, 2017. DVD.
*The Bling Ring*. Sofia Coppola, director. 2013; New York City: A24, 2013. DVD.
*The Virgin Suicides*. Sofia Coppola, director. 1999; New York: The Criterion Collection, 2018. DVD.
Wilkinson, Maryn. "Leisure/Crime, Immaterial Labor, and the Performance of the Teenage Girl in Harmony Korine's *Spring Breakers* (2012) and Sofia Coppola's *The Bling Ring* (2013)." *Journal of Feminist Scholarship* 12, no. 12 (Spring/Fall 2017): 20–37.
Woodworth, Amy. "A Feminist Theorization of Sofia Coppola's Postfeminist Trilogy." In *Situating the Feminist Gaze and Spectatorship in Postwar Cinema*, edited by Marcelline Block, 138–167. Newcastle, UK: Cambridge Scholars Publisher, 2008.

## NOTES

1. For a book length treatment, see Suzanne Ferriess, *The Cinema of Sofia Coppola: Fashion, Culture, Celebrity* (London: Bloomsbury Academic, 2021). There are also many articles, including but not limited to: Sara Pesce, "Ripping off Hollywood Celebrities: Sofia Coppola's *The Bling Ring*, Luxury Fashion, and Self-branding in California," *Film, Fashion & Consumption* 4, no. 1 (2015): 5–24. Ingrid Mida, "Fashion Exhibition as Cinematic Experience," *Film, Fashion & Consumption* 7, no. 1 (2018): 57–71. Heidi Brevik-Zender, "Let Them Wear Manolos: Fashion, Walter Benjamin, and Sofia Coppola's *Marie Antoinette*," *Camera Obscura* 78 26, no. 3 (2011): 1–33. Therése Andersson, "Costume Cinema and Materiality: Telling the Story of Marie Antoinette through Dress," *Culture Unbound* 3 (2011): 101–112. Pamela Flores, "Fashion and Otherness: The Passionate Journey of Coppola's *Marie Antoinette* from a Semiotic Perspective," *Fashion Theory* 17, no. 5 (2013): 605–622. Rebecca Arnold, "The New Rococo: Sofia Coppola and Fashions in Contemporary Femininity," in *Rococo Echo: Art, History and Historiography from Cochin to Coppola*, eds. Melissa Lee Hyde and Katie Scott (Oxford: Voltaire Foundation, 2014), 295–312. Sare Pesce, "The Baroque Imagination: Film, Costume Design and Italian High Fashion," *Film, Fashion & Consumption* 5, no. 1 (2016): 7–28.

2. Mackenzie Leadston, "Letters from an Austrian Woman: Adapting Transhistoric Girlhood in Sofia Coppola's *Marie Antoinette* (2006)," *The Modern Language Review* 114, no. 4 (October 2019): 613–628.

3. Todd Kennedy, "On the Road to 'Some' Place: Sofia Coppola's Dissident Modernism Against a Postmodern Landscape," *Miscelánea* 52 (2015): 51–67.

4. One particular interesting area of reflection is on Coppola's first three films, sometimes understood to be a trilogy of girlhood. See for example, R. Barton Palmer, "Some Thoughts on New Hollywood Multiplicity: Sofia Coppola's Young Girls Trilogy," in *Film Trilogies: New Critical Approaches*, eds. Claire Perkins and Constantine Verevis (London: Palgrave Macmillan Limited, 2012), 35–54. Fiona Handyside, "Girlhood, Postfeminism and Contemporary Female Art-House Authorship: The 'Nameless Trilogies' of Sofia Coppola and Mia Hansen-Løve," *Alphaville: Journal of Film and Screen Media* 10 (Winter 2015): 1–18.

5. Anna Backman Rogers, *Sofia Coppola: The Politics of Visual Pleasure* (New York: Berghahn, 2019), 5.

6. Ibid.

7. Ibid.

8. Rosalind Galt, *Pretty: Film and the Decorative* (New York: Columbia University Press, 2011), 22.

9. Ibid.

10. Ibid.

11. Ibid.

12. Todd Kennedy, "Off with Hollywood's Head: Sofia Coppola as Feminine Auteur," *Film Criticism* 35, no. 1 (2010): 40.

13. Ibid.

14. Ibid., 56.

15. Lucy Bolton, *Film and Female Consciousness: Irigaray, Cinema and Thinking Women* (London: Palgrave Macmillan, 2011), 126.
16. Ibid.
17. Ibid.
18. Suzanne Ferris and Mallory Young, "Marie Antoinette: Fashion, Third Wave Feminism, and Chick Culture," *Literature-Film Quarterly* 38, no. 2 (April 2010): 99.
19. Ibid., 112.
20. Maryn Wilkinson, "Leisure/Crime, Immaterial Labor, and the Performance of the Teenage Girl in Harmony Korine's *Spring Breakers* (2012) and Sofia Coppola's *The Bling Ring* (2013)," *Journal of Feminist Scholarship* 12, no. 12 (Spring/Fall 2017): 35.
21. Ibid.
22. Ibid.
23. Ibid.
24. Ibid.
25. Amy Woodworth, "A Feminist Theorization of Sofia Coppola's Postfeminist Trilogy," in *Situating the Feminist Gaze and Spectatorship in Postwar Cinema*, ed. Marcelline Block (Newcastle, UK: Cambridge Scholars Publisher, 2008), 158.
26. Katarzyna Paszkiewicz, "'She Looks Like a Little Piece of Cake': Sofia Coppola and the Commerce of Auteurism," *Interférences Littéraires/Literaire Interferenties* 21 (December 2017): 126.
27. Sharon Lin Tay, *Women on the Edge: Twelve Political Film Practices* (London: Palgrave Macmillan Limited, 2009), 127.
28. Ibid.
29. Delphine Letort, "The Cultural Capital of Sofia Coppola's *The Bling Ring* (2013): Branding Feminine Celebrity in Los Angeles," *Celebrity Studies* (2015): 1.
30. Belinda Smaill, "Sofia Coppola," *Feminist Media Studies* 13 no. 1 (2013): 159.
31. Ibid.
32. Ibid.
33. Ibid.
34. Ibid.
35. Fiona Handyside, *Sofia Coppola: A Cinema of Girlhood* (London: L.B. Tauris, 2017), 35.
36. Ibid.
37. Ibid., 36.
38. Kendra Marston, *Postfeminist Whiteness: Problematising Melancholic Burden in Contemporary Hollywood* (Edinburgh, UK: Edinburgh University Press), 18.
39. Ibid., 17.
40. Ibid., 19.
41. Ibid., 3.
42. Ibid., 4.
43. Ibid, 25.
44. Ibid., 162.
45. Ibid., 163.
46. Ibid., 165, 164.

47. Ibid., 190.
48. Ibid.
49. Hilary Neroni, *Feminist Film Theory and Cléo from 5 to 7* (New York: Bloomsbury, 2016), 53.
50. bell hooks, *The Will to Change: Men, Masculinity, and Love* (New York: Atria Books, 2004), iBooks.
51. Ibid.
52. Ibid.
53. Ibid.
54. Ibid.
55. Anna Backman Rogers, "And That I See a Darkness: The Stardom of Kirsten Dunst in Collaboration with Sofia Coppola in Three Images," *Film-Philosophy* 23, no. 2 (2019): 122.
56. Ibid., 130.
57. Martin Luther King Jr., "Letter from Birmingham Jail," *The Atlantic*, April 2018, www.theatlantic.com/magazine/archive/2018/02/letter-from-a-birmingham-jail/552461/.
58. Ibid.
59. Audre Lorde, "Uses of the Erotic: The Erotic as Power," in *Sister Outsider: Speeches and Essays by Audre Lorde* (New York: Crossway Press, 2007), 54.
60. Ibid., 58–9.
61. bell hooks, *Salvation: Black People and Love* (New York: William Morrow and Company, 2001), 16–7.
62. bell hooks, *All About Love: New Visions* (New York: William Morrow and Company, 2000), 137.
63. Ibid., 167.

# Index

Academy Awards, 2, 4–5, 27
Aeneas, 16, 121–26, 138–39, 141nn7–8, 142n14, 145n61, 275
Aeneid, The (epic poem), 119, 121–22, 126–27, 141n8
Agamben, Giorgio, 70, 85–86, 89nn20–21, 272
agency, 14–17, 36–37, 47, 57, 70, 76, 84–85, 111, 134, 137–39, 143n34, 156, 267–68, 274–75
alcohol, 6, 8, 18, 41–46, 48, 50, 54, 57–58, 68, 80, 95, 107, 111, 130, 161–63, 179–80, 186–90, 212–17, 218–19, 245, 250–252, 263
alienation, 4, 18, 40, 108, 113, 209, 211–222, 228–230, 232, 235n11, 242, 250, 270, 276
allohistory, 138, 145n62
alternative masculinity, 14, 35–64, 272
ambivalence, 12, 65–76, 75–86, 162, 191–92, 194–197, 271
American Civil War, 8–10, 16, 119–146, 142n13, 143n27, 143nn31–34, 143n38, 143n42, 144n49
anachronism, 5–6, 15, 95–113
androcentrism, 135–139, 145n63, 275
Anzaldúa, Gloria, 16, 96, 110, 113–115, 118nn52–57

Bakhtin, Mikhail, 18, 178, 185–197, 201nn19–42, 204n59, 204n73
Barthes, Roland, 157
belonging, 13, 122, 136, 149, 240, 279–80
The Bible, 16, 87, 90, 119, 128, 135, 143–144n44

bodies, 13–18, 37, 42, 44–60, 66–67, 148–206
boredom, 17, 151, 167–69, 210, 278
Bow Wow Wow (band), 15, 95, 111–12
byproductive labor, 248–260, 262nn17–20

Cannes Film Festival, 1, 6, 8, 25nn1–2, 29n59, 138
capitalism, 108, 119, 129, 138, 149, 153, 155, 168, 174n60, 216, 230–34, 259–70, 280
Carnival, 185–186, 200n8
Carnivalesque, 18, 177–206, 202n42
castration, 9, 131, 134, 142n24
celebrity culture, 2, 6, 12–13, 17, 39–40, 57, 149–164, 172n5, 172nn9–12, 172n22, 173nn26–47, 268, 286n29; microcelebrity within, 17, 150, 152–62

# Index

Chicana studies, 13, 15, 18, 96, 113, 209, 216, 228, 231–32, 271, 274, 280
Christian monasticism, 187
Christianity, 17, 60, 124, 132–36, 144n51, 150–69, 174n52, 174n57, 180, 187, 278
classism, 10–13, 35–37, 133, 143n34, 186, 217, 230, 247, 259, 270
colonialism, 19, 27n37, 59–60, 75–76, 86, 122, 168, 208, 216–17, 223–34, 237n48, 259–60, 269–71, 277, 280–82
consumption, 5, 79, 90n31, 106–109, 113, 216, 266–69
control, 8, 19, 41–42, 73–74, 9, 123–33, 136–42, 166, 186, 203n51, 217–19, 226, 240, 254, 257–60, 275, 280–82
cycle (behavior), 14, 35–36, 40–51, 56–60, 233, 272

decolonial love, 18, 209–10, 215–17, 224, 228, 229–34, 238n18, 271, 280, 282
decolonialism, 16
Derrida, Jacques, 15–16, 119–26, 138, 141nn1–5, 275–77
Descartes, Rene, 73, 203
dichotomous love, 18, 120, 209, 216–17, 227–28, 230–31
Dido, 15–16, 121–26, 138–42, 201n17, 275
Dinah (Biblical Character), 16, 135–44, 275
disembodiment, 18, 168, 178, 184, 186–87, 190–92, 196, 203, 230, 278

Ecstasy of Saint Teresa (sculpture), 163
emotional labor, 19, 40, 239–59, 262nn23–26, 280–82
ennui, 2, 4–5, 105, 181, 210–11, 214–15
epistemology, 66–67, 73–80, 83–91
equity, 178, 196–97, 276
eros, 17, 163, 168
eroticism, 17, 43, 149–51, 166–68, 229–31, 278–79

exhaustion, 19, 239–40, 248–52

femininity, 1, 4–5, 13, 72–73, 100, 108–109, 113, 117n24, 121, 124, 268–70, 285n1
feminism, 1, 11–16, 30n99, 31n106, 66, 90n44, 95, 96, 108, 117n24, 141n4, 142n18, 203n51, 231, 265–66, 268–71, 274–75, 285n4, 286n18; fourth-wave, 13, 15, 19, 265, 270–72
feminist, 1, 12–19, 35–37, 49, 32nn3–17, 65–66, 73, 79, 90nn42–44, 91n59, 96, 106, 108–109, 113, 115, 117n14, 126, 141n2, 142n25, 143n34, 158, 172n3, 203n51, 216, 230, 259, 262n17, 266–75, 281, 286n25
film music, 97–101, 110, 115, 117nn4–5; diegetic, 198, 102–108; non-diegetic, 98, 102–104

gender politics, 9, 12–15, 36, 119, 138, 266, 277
Golden Globe Awards, 7, 28n45
Gregory of Nyssa, 164
Grosz, Elizabeth, 16, 30n99
grotesque, 17–18, 177–78, 186, 190–97, 277

habitus, 35–38, 42, 47–60
Haraway, Donna, 73, 77, 86–87, 90n44
hegemonic masculinity, 74
hegemony, 14, 59–60, 66–67, 71–90, 126–27, 131, 135–39, 233, 269, 281–84, 280
hierarchy, 41, 72–74, 143n44, 150, 153–55, 185–87, 196–97, 210, 230, 269, 273, 278
hooks, bell, 13, 18, 30n87, 31nn108–10, 216, 259–62, 265, 271–82, 289n50, 289nn 61–62
hospes (Latin), 120–25, 141n1, 141n8
hospitium, 122–39, 275
hostpitality, 15–16, 119–25, 136–41, 275, 277, 278

hybridization, 18, 178, 191–95

Instagram, 109, 152–53, 172nn15–21
interdependence, 273
intimacy, 7, 19, 69, 154, 157–61,
  163, 167, 209, 220, 223, 225–29,
  243–44, 273–74
Irigaray, Luce, 16, 30n100, 107–108,
  113, 117n25

joy, 14, 18, 36, 52, 55–60, 106,
  177–97, 204nn75–76, 253, 258–59,
  272–73, 278–81

Kierkegaard, Søren, 18, 55, 64n47

labor, 18–19, 40–41, 239–40, 242–
  59, 262nn17–26
Lacan, Jacques, 16, 75, 99, 142n22
liberation, 14–17, 36–37, 95–115, 259,
  271, 274–82
liminality, 12, 18, 81, 209–10,
  230–33, 280
Lorde, Audre, 175n60, 216, 265, 271,
  280–81, 287n59

malaise, 209–215, 221, 225, 233, 280
male gaze, 100, 255, 267
martyrdom, 163–64
masculinity, 13–14, 19–20,
  35–43, 56–61
masculinity studies, 59
masquerade, 96, 106–15
materiality, 6, 35–38, 43, 53, 57–58,
  161, 192, 233, 273–74, 285n1
media ecology, 174
Merleau-Ponty, Maurice, 16
mimicry, 14–15, 65–67, 75–80,
  85–86, 90n46, 91n51, 96, 106–10,
  113–14, 117n29
minimalism, 2, 4, 6, 8, 11, 49, 245
misogyny, 16, 19, 65, 119, 126, 168,
  187, 240, 254–55, 257–59, 276–80
Moraga, Cherríe, 118nn52–57, 216
musicology, 13, 105, 117n18, 127, 196

objectification, 14, 67, 76–79, 86,
  203n51, 213, 258, 267, 272
Ovid, 122

parareligion, 149, 157, 159, 173n27,
  173n33, 173nn42–44
patriarchy, 16–17, 36, 59–60, 85,
  108–10, 114, 119, 123, 126, 131,
  133, 135, 138–39, 203n48, 249,
  266–68, 276
perfection, 194–96, 278
postcolonialism, 66, 75, 231
postfeminism, 1, 12–13, 59, 62nn17–19,
  106–109, 143n34, 265–71

racism, 9–11, 29nn71–72, 59, 115, 178,
  235n12, 253, 259, 272, 274, 277
rape. See sexual assault
relic, 17, 150–51, 161–67, 278
religion, 13, 17, 37, 96, 102, 119, 132–
  39, 149–51, 157–59, 163, 166–81,
  200n9, 213–214, 232, 278
romanticism, 112, 187, 192
Rousseau, Jean-Jacques, 19, 240, 252–
  58, 260nn27–38
rupture, 99, 110–11, 217–21, 228, 270

Sandoval, Chela, 18, 209, 216–25, 228–
  35, 236nn15–25, 236nn27–33
secular society, 17, 150–51, 167, 278
sex, 18, 42–43, 46–48, 50, 57, 68, 78,
  96–97, 112, 120, 129, 131, 142n23,
  144n51, 158, 163, 165, 178, 186–90,
  202n42, 203nn48–51, 217, 275
sexual assault, 59, 68, 86, 126,
  128, 132–36, 144n46, 187,
  201n15, 276–77
sexual politics, 13–19, 138–44,
  265, 274–75
sexual surface, 46–48
Shamanism, 158, 161–63
social media, 9, 17, 150–54,
  159–62, 167–69
social transformation, 18–19, 209–
  12, 217, 231

suture, 95–111, 131

Taylor, Charles, 73, 90n40, 209–10, 235nn1–9, 280
testimony, 65–71, 80, 85–89, 273–74
toxic masculinity, 13–14, 35–43, 51–60, 233, 272–74, 280
trauma, 14, 60, 65, 68–71, 80, 89n6, 272

veil, 35, 37–38, 43, 56–58, 243, 249; hijab as, 39; Ferrari as, 42–44, 54, 56
violence, 8, 14, 31n103, 40–42, 58, 67, 72–80, 85–87, 115, 122–29, 131, 138–40, 143n32, 164–68, 190, 203, 209m, 216, 233, 250, 259–60, 263n41, 266–67, 272–81

Virgil, 15, 119, 121, 123–126, 141nn7–8
virginity, 119, 133, 135–37
vulnerability, 16–17, 19, 35–36, 43–60, 113–15, 123, 132, 134, 186, 210, 215, 223, 225–27, 229, 233, 240, 242, 244, 249, 256, 257, 260, 265, 272–82

White Feminism, 11, 15, 231
white privilege, 9–11, 15, 247, 249–71
white supremacy, 9, 281–82
whiteness, 8–11, 18, 143n34, 266, 269–71, 277–80
wholeness, 18–19, 100, 144n51, 192, 209–10, 217, 227–29

# About the Authors

**Naaman K. Wood** (PhD, Regent University) is Instructor of Speech Communication at Saint Paul College and has taught media and communication courses at Tidewater Community College, Spring Arbor University, Northwest University, and Redeemer University. His work has been published in the journals *Symbolic Interaction, Jazz Perspectives*, and the books *Critical Companion to James Cameron, Critical Companion to Steven Spielberg, Critical Companion to Terrence Malick, Prophetic Critique and Popular Media: Theoretical Foundations and Practical Applications* and *More than "Precious Memories": Critical Essays on the Rhetoric of Southern Gospel*. He has co-edited *Words and Witnesses: Communication Studies in Christian Thought from Athanasius to Desmond Tutu* and the forthcoming *Humility and Hospitality: Changing the Conversation on Civility*.
**Christopher (Topher) Booth** (PhD, Catholic University) studied Music Theory at SUNY Potsdam and Musicology at The Catholic University of America in Washington, D. C., focusing most of his research on the hermeneutics of film music. His work has been published in the books *Classical Music and the Jewish Experience, Music, Narrative, and the Moving Image: Varieties in Plurimedial Interrelations*, and *The Women of Woody Allen* (forthcoming). He currently teaches music history courses at Old Dominion University in Norfolk, Virginia.

www.ingramcontent.com/pod-product-compliance
Lightning Source LLC
Chambersburg PA
CBHW021347300426
44114CB00012B/1118